Media Law for Producers

Media Law for Producers
Fourth Edition

Philip H. Miller

AMSTERDAM • BOSTON • HEIDELBERG
LONDON • NEW YORK • OXFORD • PARIS
SAN DIEGO • SAN FRANCISCO
SINGAPORE • SYDNEY • TOKYO

Focal Press is an imprint of Elsevier

Focal Press is an imprint of Elsevier.

Copyright © 2003 Philip H. Miller

Permissions may be sought directly from Elsevier's Science and Technology Rights Department in Oxford, UK. Phone: (44) 1865 843830, Fax: (44) 1865 853333, e-mail: permissions@elsevier.co.uk. You may also complete your request on-line via the Elsevier homepage: http://www.elsevier.com by selecting "Customer Support" and then "Obtaining Permissions".

Library of Congress Cataloging-in-Publication Data

Miller, Philip, 1954–
    Media law for producers / Philip Miller.—4th ed.
        p. cm.
    Includes bibliographical references and index.
    ISBN 0-240-80478-3
    1. Motion pictures—Law and legislation—United States. 2. Video recordings—Law and legislation—United States. 3. Copyright—United States. I. Title.
KF4298.M55 2002
343.7309′9—dc21   2003054711

British Library Cataloguing-in-Publication Data
A catalogue record for this book is available from the British Library.

The publisher offers special discounts on bulk orders of this book. For information, please contact:

> Manager of Special Sales
> Focal Press
> 200 Wheeler Road, Sixth Floor
> Burlington, MA 01803
> Tel: 781-313-4700

For information on all Focal Press publications available, visit our website: http://www.focalpress.com

10 9 8 7 6 5 4 3 2

Printed in the United States of America

To AMS, co-adventurer

Contents

1

Media Law: An Overview   1

2

Managing Relationships: Contracts and the Media Production Process   29

3
_____

**Getting It in Writing: Sample Media Production
Contracts   51**

4
_____

**Getting Permission: Copyright Concerns During Media
Production   101**

5
_____

**Playing It Safe: Permits, Releases, Libel, and Production
Insurance   147**

List of Illustrations

List of Cases

This list includes all cases cited in this book. Page numbers or note numbers follow each entry.

ACLU v. *Reno*, 929 F. Supp. 824 (E.D. Pa. 1996), Ch. 8, n.5, Ch. 8, n.11.

Action for Children's Television v. *FCC*, 932 F.2d 1504 (D.C. Cir.1991), cert. denied, 112 S. Ct. 1281 (1992), Ch. 9, n.21.

Allen v. *Men's World Outlet, Inc.*, 679 F. Supp. 360 (S.D.N.Y. 1988), Ch. 5, n.12.

Allen v. *National Video, Inc.*, 610 F. Supp. 612 (S.D.N.Y. 1985), Ch. 5, n.12.

Amsinck v. *Columbia Pictures Industries*, 862 F. Supp. 1044 (S.D.N.Y. 1994), Ch. 4, n.4.

Anderson v. *Liberty Lobby, Inc.*, 477 U.S. 242 (1986), Ch. 5, n.21.

Berlin v. *E. C. Publications, Inc.*, 329 F.2d 57 (2d Cir. 1964), Ch. 6. n.7.

Bindrim v. *Mitchell*, 92 Cal. App. 2d 61, 155 Cal. Rptr. 29 (1979), Ch. 5, n.15.

Bose Corp. v. *Consumers Union*, 466 U.S. 485 (1984), Ch. 5, n.28.

Campbell v. *Acuff-Rose*, 114 S.Ct. 1164 (1994), Ch. 6, n.7.

Cardservice International, Inc. v. *McGee*, 950 F. Supp. 737 (E.D. Va. 1997), Ch. 8, n.21.

Commerce Union Bank v. *Coors*, 7 Med.L.Rptr. 2593 (Tenn. Chanc. Ct. 1982), Ch. 5, n.7.

Community for Creative Non-Violence v. *Reid*, 490 U.S. 730 (1989), Ch. 3, n.1.

Comp Examiner Agency, Inc. v. *Juris, Inc.*, 1996 U.S. Dist. Lexis 20259 (C.D. Cal. 1996), Ch. 8, n.21.

Digital Equip. Corp. v. *Alta Vista Tech., Inc.*, 960 F. Supp. 456 (D. Mass. 1997), Ch. 8, n.21.

Edwards v. *National Audubon Society*, 556 F.2d 113 (2d Cir. 1977), cert. denied, 434 U.S. 1002 (1977), Ch. 5, n.25.

Elsmere Music, Inc. v. *National Broadcasting Co.*, 62 F.2d 252 (2d Cir. 1980), Ch.6, n.7.

Foreword

As media productions have become more sophisticated, so have the legal issues that can affect their development and distribution. From performer contracts to copyright registration, producers need to be able to recognize the legal questions that can come up during production projects and to be ready with the appropriate responses. This is true not only for producers of major film and television projects but also for independent and corporate producers involved with industrial and other nonbroadcast programs.

Media Law for Producers helps producers and other production professionals meet this need. The book can work in two ways: as a general overview of media law that helps you anticipate and head off legal problems, and as a handy reference that you can pull off the shelf when questions and problems do arise. This mix of background material and practical information also makes *Media Law for Producers* appropriate as a text for courses on media production and law.

Before readers proceed any further, a word of caution is in order. Although *Media Law for Producers* provides important information, it is not intended as a substitute for professional legal counsel. Turn to this book for a general understanding of the basic principles underlying media law, descriptions and examples of the various legal questions that can come up during production, and sample forms and agreements that can help you anticipate and avoid legal snags. Turn to an attorney for answers to legal questions not covered in this text, for information about laws and regulations that are specific to individual states and municipalities, and for detailed advice on contracts and other legal matters that do arise during production.

Media Law for Producers begins with an introduction to the sources and basic principles of media law. This is followed by chapters that address key areas of concern for media production professionals: establishing contracts and production agreements; using public domain and copyrighted materials; securing appropriate releases and permissions; avoiding libel and right of privacy challenges; licensing music; working with unions; registering copyright and trademarks; understanding the laws affecting programs that will be broadcast; and negotiating licensing and distribution agreements. The book ends with a glossary that defines important legal terms, a bibliography that lists useful references, and appendixes that provide the names and addresses of important organizations.

Most of the chapters begin by reviewing the basic concepts that form the foundation for a specific aspect of media law. This background information is followed by examples that show how this area of media law applies to various production situations and contexts, precautions that producers can take to avoid legal entanglements, and suggestions for dealing with problems when they do appear. Wherever possible, the chapters provide sample forms and agreements that producers can use to set the framework for documents tailored to their particular needs.

Readers should also be aware of what *Media Law for Producers* does not cover. Because the book focuses on legal aspects of the production process, it does not deal with many of the policy and technical issues that are generally considered part of communications law. For example, *Media Law for Producers* does not discuss the public policy issues raised by the manner in which the Federal Communications Commission assigns broadcast licenses, the technical standards that are imposed on broadcasters, or the ongoing debate over concentration of ownership in the communications industry. While these are all important issues, they are not among the day-to-day concerns of most media production professionals.

Media Law for Producers also does not examine, in depth, many of the more intricate financial and ethical aspects of negotiating deals and doing business as a media producer. Because media production and distribution deals are often very complex business transactions, and because what is "standard practice" in the industry can vary from year to year, many producers choose to have an experienced attorney, agent, or other knowledgeable and trusted adviser review all of their deals before they commit to a binding agreement.

As readers will discover, many of the examples used in *Media Law for Producers* refer to video productions developed for nonbroadcast distribution. However, most of the legal principles covered in the chapters apply with equal validity to a wide range of production situations—from the preparation of multimedia presentations that will be shown to a small group of corporate clients to the development of a television series scheduled for broadcast on a major network.

Earlier in this foreword, I was careful to point out that *Media Law for Producers* is not intended as a substitute for professional legal counsel. However, after reading the chapters that follow, media producers should be familiar with enough of the legal landscape to make their way around and through many of the minor legal entanglements that can slow the production process. Just as important, readers should end up knowing enough law to know when they need to call a lawyer and what questions they need to ask.

Barbara J. Shulman, Esq.
New York, New York

Preface

This fourth edition of *Media Law for Producers* provides a general update to the prior editions. This edition also adds several new sample agreements and forms. The most significant change in the law since the publication of the third edition was the passage, in 1998, of the Sonny Bono Copyright Term Extension Act, which extended the basic copyright term 20 years. The implications of this change are addressed in Chapter 4. On the technology front, the most significant development continues to be the increasing importance of the Internet as a development, distribution, and marketing medium. Various legal issues related to use of the Internet by media producers are addressed in Chapter 8. My hope is that, with these updates and changes, *Media Law for Producers* will continue to serve as a practical guide for producers and other professionals involved in the day-to-day details of media production.

In preparing this edition of *Media Law for Producers*, I am grateful for the support and guidance of my colleagues at Irell & Manella, LLP, particularly Juliette Youngblood, Clark Siegel, and the other attorneys in the Entertainment Law Group. I am also thankful for the support of our former colleague and continuing friend Lois Scali. Their high standards are a reminder that attorneys cannot care too much about their clients and the quality of their work. Thank you, also, to my secretary, Diane Larsen, for her invaluable assistance and to Paula Allen for her word processing help.

I am, as always, deeply indebted to my amazing wife, Anne, and my equally amazing children, Christopher and Rosemary, for their understanding as I spent evening and weekend hours working on this manuscript. Anne remains living proof that the best chance at success and happiness is to marry well.

I remain grateful to those who helped me with prior editions of *Media Law for Producers*. Barbara Shulman reviewed each section of the first edition and provided very patient and valuable counsel. Without her expertise and guidance, *Media Law for Producers* never would have made the transition from rough drafts to finished work. Any errors or omissions that remain in the book are my responsibility, not hers. I am also grateful to Amy Jollymore, Jessica Carlisle, Theron Shreve, Mamata Reddy, and others at Focal Press who guided this edition through the publishing process.

I owe additional thanks to Kit Laybourne. As I began my work on the first edition, Kit provided sample contracts and materials that helped focus my research. Thanks also to John LeBaron, my original mentor in the book-writing business.

Important Notice

This book provides general information, not legal advice, on a wide range of issues related to the production of media programs. To the author's best knowledge, the information was accurate at the time of printing. Laws and regulations change, however, and the manner in which particular laws and policies are interpreted and enforced can vary from time to time and case to case. In addition, no single volume can ever cover all of the laws, regulations, and policies that might be applied to a specific production situation. As a result, readers should not rely on this book as their sole source of legal information or as a substitute for professional legal counsel. Neither the author nor the publisher can offer any guarantees as to the information contained here or the manner in which it is interpreted and applied.

Media Law: An Overview

Media law is a very broad body of law that incorporates elements of copyright and trademark law, contract law, labor law, defamation and privacy law, telecommunications law and policy, and the many legal issues that arise from the First Amendment's guarantees of free speech and freedom of the press.

To protect themselves from lawsuits and other legal entanglements, media producers need to be familiar with these key areas of law. Just as important, media professionals must be able to recognize the various guises under which legal issues can appear during the production process. Consider this fictional account of the legal roadblocks that confronted one unwary producer:

> *Richard Newman is the director of production in the corporate media department of a large financial firm. At the request of the firm's training division, Newman produced a 45-minute program on management communication skills titled* Listen While You Work. *Newman assumed that, like all of the other programs he had produced for the firm,* Listen While You Work *would be limited to distribution within the company.*
>
> *In producing the program, Newman faced a familiar battle. He wanted to create an engaging, effective training program, but he was constrained by a limited production budget and tight schedule. As a result, Newman found himself borrowing material from a variety of sources. To illustrate the effects of poor communication, for example, he used footage from a vintage theatrical film he had rented from his neighborhood video store. To add some punch to the audio track, he inserted clips from several popular rock-and-roll recordings.*
>
> *Newman shot most of the original video material in the company's headquarters, using employees as his "talent." Newman also wrote the script, with some help from a friend who is a professional writer. The script included dialogue adapted from several case studies published in a popular management text, plus*

material taken from videotaped interviews with management consultants. Portions of the script were performed by an announcer Newman hired on a flat-fee basis.

With deadlines pressing, and assuming that Listen While You Work *would be limited to internal use at his company, Newman did not bother to negotiate formal contracts with the scriptwriter or announcer. He also did not bother to ask for signed releases from the employees who appeared in the program or the management consultants who had participated in the videotaped interviews.*

Newman put a great deal of his own time into the production, completing the final edits himself on the weekend before the program was scheduled to premiere at the company's annual management training conference. His hard work paid off. The program played to a packed house and received rave reviews from company management.

The production also received something that Newman had not expected— an offer to distribute the program outside the company. The offer came from the company's marketing department, which was looking into new ways to generate revenues from the firm's internal resources.

Although Newman was flattered by the offer, he realized that his haste in producing the program might have left some legal strings untied. A call to the corporate legal office confirmed that many questions needed to be resolved before the production could be cleared for external distribution. Faced with the prospect of having to wait for answers to those questions, the marketing department withdrew its offer to distribute the program.

Newman was wise to contact his corporate legal department, but it does not take a trained legal mind to recognize many of the matters that were cause for concern. A partial list follows:

- Use of copyrighted footage from a motion picture without seeking permission from the individual, group, or organization that owns or controls the film's copyright
- Use of copyrighted music recordings on the soundtrack without obtaining clearances from the songwriters or music publishers and record companies
- Use of copyrighted excerpts from a book without obtaining permission from the book's author or publisher
- Failure to secure releases from employees featured in the production. Because of this oversight, employees who may feel that the program depicts them in an unfavorable light might be able to sue Newman or the company for which Newman

works for invasion of privacy or defamation. Employees featured in the production also could sue to collect a portion of the revenues that the program generates through outside distribution.

- Failure to secure written contracts or release forms from the scriptwriter and announcer who worked on the program. Although the scriptwriter and announcer apparently agreed to participate on a flat-fee basis that would not provide them with any ownership or residual interest in the program, they might change their minds now that the program has the potential to generate revenues through outside sales. With no written releases or contracts, Newman would have no tangible evidence to support his contention that the pair agreed to provide their services on a flat-fee basis and that they assigned all rights in their work to his company.
- Violation of guild agreements. If the scriptwriter and announcer were members of a union or guild, Newman and his company also might find themselves in trouble for not complying with the terms of guild agreements. As discussed in Chapter 7, however, this would not be the case if Newman's company was not a signatory to the relevant guild agreements. In that case, the writer and announcer themselves could face sanctions from their own guilds.

Newman's case also raises another key issue. Who would actually own *Listen While You Work*, Newman or his company? Under U.S. copyright law, the company would have the most legitimate claim to ownership of the finished production, unless Newman's employment contract stated otherwise. This would be the case because Newman produced the program within the normal scope of his employment—even though he spent some of his own time on the project. To avoid disputes over the ownership of materials produced on the job, many companies require employees to sign release forms as part of their employment agreement.

One final issue is worth addressing. Would Newman have been free of these legal concerns if, as he had originally assumed, *Listen While You Work* had been limited to internal distribution? As discussed in subsequent chapters, the answer to that question is no, even though limiting distribution of the program certainly would have reduced his exposure and the risk of litigation.

How Much Law Do You Need to Know?

Although the *Listen While You Work* scenario was stretched to make a point, it does raise some of the very real legal troubles and concerns that can afflict unwary producers. This is not to suggest, though, that producers should become paranoid, paralyzed by fears that any action they take will leave them open to lawsuits or other litigation. Instead, producers should seek the creative freedom that comes from understanding when it is necessary to take specific steps and precautions to protect their work. Leave the heavy worrying and the paranoia to the lawyers.

Above all, as a media professional, a producer does not need to be a lawyer. A producer does not need to know, for example, how to draft legal documents, how to conduct and analyze a copyright or trademark search, or how to defend a case in court. As the individual with primary responsibility for a media production, however, a producer should know the following:

- When it would be prudent for the parties in a production deal to sign legally binding agreements
- What permissions, permits, and releases are required during the course of a production
- When it is permissible to incorporate copyrighted materials in a production without the copyright owner's authorization
- What special steps are necessary to add music to a production
- What legal issues are involved in working with, and working without, guild and union members
- What statements or portrayals in a video production may constitute libel, an invasion of privacy, or a violation of the right-of-publicity
- What special precautions are recommended in connection with productions that will be used to advertise a product or service or programs that will be broadcast, cablecast, or transmitted over the Internet
- How copyright and trademark registration can help protect finished productions

This book examines how these and other legal issues can arise during media production and how producers can take steps to address these issues in a manner that protects both them and their media properties.

First, though, it helps to understand just who creates, interprets, and enforces media law.

Who Creates Media Law?

According to most high school social studies texts, laws are created in a fairly straightforward manner. At the federal level, the Congress, responding to a public need, drafts and then passes a piece of legislation or *bill*. Congress next sends the bill to the president, who either signs or vetoes it. Once the president signs the legislation, or once Congress overrides a veto by the president, responsibility for interpreting and applying the newly enacted law falls to the federal courts. If the law is challenged on constitutional grounds, the federal courts also are responsible for determining whether the new law conflicts with the U.S. Constitution, the venerable document that establishes the scope and structure of the federal government and that defines and delineates federal lawmaking powers.

The textbooks provide a parallel model for lawmaking at the state level. According to this model, state laws are created when state legislatures draft and pass legislation and the governor signs or vetoes the bill. Once the governor signs the legislation or once the state legislature overrides a veto by the governor, the courts in that state are responsible for interpreting and applying the law.

Although these textbook models are essentially accurate, they do not tell the whole story. In drafting legislation, for example, Congress and individual state legislatures often are responding as much to private and political pressure as to public need. Private lobbying groups, including many groups representing media interests, work overtime to promote or prevent the passage of legislation that affects their industries. Similarly, various public interest groups may lobby for or against particular legislation based on its potential impact on the interests and positions that these groups represent. In addition, before most bills are voted on by the full Senate and House of Representatives or by the comparable state legislative bodies, the bills must make their way through a gauntlet of committee meetings and hearings.

Figure 1.1 illustrates, in a very general way, the process through which a bill becomes law at the federal level. Although this process may help ensure that all evidence for and against a bill is heard, it also opens almost limitless opportunities for backstage deals and political

Figure 1.1 An overview of how federal laws are made.

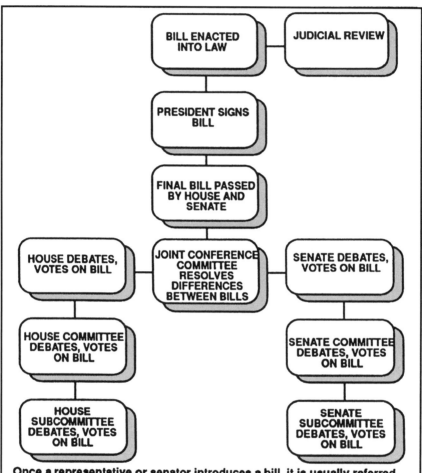

Once a representative or senator introduces a bill, it is usually referred to the appropriate standing committee for action. Most bills are then passed down to one or more subcommittees. If the subcommittee reports favorably on the bill, it moves to the full committee. If the full committee votes favorably on the bill, it is brought before the House or Senate, where it is debated and then voted on or referred back to committee. If the House and Senate vote favorably, the bill's next stop may be a joint conference committee, where any differences between the House and Senate versions of the bill are resolved. Assuming that the House and Senate approve identical versions of the bill, it is sent to the president. Once the president signs the bill, or once a two-thirds vote of Congress overrides the president's veto, the bill is enacted into law. The new law is then subject to judicial review by the federal courts.

trade-offs. The result is often a piece of legislation that resembles a patchwork quilt of conflicting aims and interests rather than a clear, coherent law.

The Role of the Courts

Civics texts and conventional wisdom also tend to simplify the role of the courts in the lawmaking process. Most texts describe a primarily reactive, interpretive role for the judiciary in the lawmaking and governing process. In truth, however, the federal and state courts often play an active role in shaping both the scope and impact of statutes enacted by the lawmaking branches of government. This is especially true for the U.S. Supreme Court and the federal appeals courts, whose rulings serve as legal precedents that lower federal courts (and, in matters involving constitutional questions, state courts) are obliged to follow. In fact, these higher court rulings often have the effect of law, particularly in areas where legislative statutes are vague or incomplete. This "judge-made" law is discussed more fully in the section on types and categories of law that follows.

The Role of Regulatory and Administrative Agencies

Another fact that many texts tend to downplay is the power that regulatory and administrative agencies exercise in creating and applying laws. Acting under legislative authority, government agencies and commissions create regulations and rules that, in most respects, have the same force and effect as formally enacted laws. This would come as quite a surprise to the framers of the U.S. Constitution, who never defined a formal role for federal bureaucracies in the system of checks and balances that is supposed to govern lawmaking.

State and Local Governments

As suggested previously, state and local governments add more layers of complexity to the lawmaking process. Every state has its own executive, legislative, and judicial branches of government—and its own administrative bureaucracy. Although the U.S. Constitution dictates that no state law can contradict federal law in areas where the federal government has exclusive jurisdiction, the states are free to extend and enhance federal statutes and to establish laws in areas where federal legislation or jurisdiction is limited. County and city governments also get into the lawmaking act, passing laws and ordinances designed to protect the safety and well-being of their residents.

Types and Categories of Media Law

As the preceding sections show, laws and regulations come from a variety of sources and in assorted types, shapes, and sizes. This section describes in more detail several major categories of law: constitutional law, statutory law, case law, and regulatory law.

Constitutional Law

Federal Constitutional Law

Federal constitutional law is based on the articles and amendments that form the U.S. Constitution. Because the Constitution is the supreme law of the United States, any statute or regulation that contradicts the Constitution is invalid. As mentioned earlier, the federal courts, particularly the Supreme Court and the federal appeals courts, are responsible for determining whether a federal, state, or local law is constitutional. For that reason, constitutional law includes both the articles and amendments of the Constitution (the letter of the Constitution) and the key federal court decisions and opinions that determine how the Constitution is applied in specific circumstances.

Because it incorporates opinions and precedents issued by the courts, and because the Constitution is subject to amendment, constitutional law is continually growing and changing. Constitutional law shares this characteristic with all categories of law.

State Constitutional Law

Like the federal government, each state government has a constitution that serves as the supreme law of that state. The court system in each state interprets and applies the constitution of that state. In some cases, this involves determining whether a law passed by the state legislature or a county or city government is valid under the provisions of the state constitution. Many counties and cities also have constitutions or charters that define their governing and lawmaking powers. Keep in mind, though, that no provision of a state, county, or city constitution can contradict the U.S. Constitution.

Constitutional Law and the Media

Constitutional law is an important component of media law. For example, the right of media professionals to ply their craft free from government censorship is guaranteed by the First Amendment to the U.S. Constitution, which declares that Congress shall make no law "abridging the freedom of speech or of the press." Numerous court decisions have confirmed that protection of the First Amendment extends not just to journalists and news reporters but also to individuals and companies involved in commercial media production. In addition, the copyright laws that protect producers' rights to profit from sale of their media properties are based on Article 1, Section 8 of the U.S. Constitution, which states that Congress is empowered to establish laws that give "authors and inventors the exclusive right to their respective writings and discoveries."

Statutory Law

Statutory law consists of legislative acts (or statutes) passed by Congress, state legislatures, and local governments. Much statutory law is organized into codes, which are indexed compilations of laws arranged around specific subjects (e.g., the penal code, the motor vehicle code). One widely distributed code is the U.S. Code, which includes most federal statutes organized into various areas of law. The Communications Act of 1934 and the Copyright Act of 1976 are examples of federal statutes relevant to media professionals that are published in the U.S. Code.[1]

Federal Statutes Governing Media Law

The Communications Act of 1934 and the Copyright Act of 1976 are fundamental federal statutes that govern two key areas of media law. The Communications Act of 1934 lays the ground rules for broadcast, telephone, and cable communications in the United States. In particular, the act determines who controls the broadcast airwaves by defining procedures for allocating television and radio frequency assignments in the United States. The act also created the Federal Communications Commission (FCC) to administer and enforce those procedures.

In contrast to the Communications Act of 1934, which determines who controls broadcast channels, the Copyright Act sets out the rules governing who owns and controls the programs that are transmitted on those channels. The Copyright Act also defines who owns industrial training programs, educational video productions, and other forms of nonbroadcast programming. In fact, the Copyright Act establishes rights of ownership in all forms of intellectual property, including books, feature films, and audio recordings. Because of its importance to all media producers, the Copyright Act is discussed in detail in Chapter 4.

Statutory Law and the Courts

As already mentioned, the responsibility for interpreting and applying statutes falls to the courts. Generally, the federal courts interpret federal statutes and the state courts interpret state statutes. In interpreting statutes, the courts establish precedents that influence how the law will be applied in the future. That is why many statutory codes are published in annotated versions that set forth how various courts have interpreted statutes in specific cases.

In more than a few cases, courts have declared that a specific federal, state, or local statute is invalid. This generally happens only when a law is found to be in conflict with a preexisting statute or when the law appears to contradict one or more provisions of the U.S. Constitution. A state court also may declare a state statute invalid if it is found to be in conflict with the state's constitution.

Case Law

Sometimes known as *common law* or *judge-made law*, case law is based on judicial precedent. When judges issue decisions and opinions that establish legal precedents or distinctions, they are contributing to the body of case law.[2]

Case law tends to be most important and influential at the state level. Each state has its own court system and its own body of case law. As a result, case law in important areas such as contracts and torts (two areas of law with a rich common law heritage) often varies from state to state; however, no state case law (or statute) can contradict federal constitutional law, federal statutes, or rulings of federal courts in areas over which the federal government has exclusive jurisdiction.

Case law can serve an important function in the American legal system. When statutory law lags behind social changes or important social needs, case law can help fill in the gaps. In matters in which a clear injustice has occurred, or matters that involve new technological or scientific issues, the courts will first look to existing statutes for a remedy. If the present body of statutory law offers no obvious remedy, a judge might extend or reinterpret the existing laws to cover the current case. In some cases, judges actually will establish new legal rights in this manner.

Privacy and copyright are two areas of media law in which courts frequently have had to interpret and extend existing statutes to accommodate new technological developments. In *Sony Corp. of America v. Universal City Studios*,[3] for example, the U.S. Supreme Court was called on in 1984 to decide if manufacturers of home video recorders could be held liable for contributory copyright infringement because their machines facilitate the off-air taping and duplication of copyrighted television programs. Reading the Copyright Act of 1976 broadly, the court concluded that there was no contributory infringement because home video recording of television programs was, for the most part, a noninfringing "fair use" under the copyright law. Similarly, in the area of privacy law, courts have had to determine whether existing statutes and regulations can be expanded to cover the threats to personal privacy created by new surveillance and information technologies.

The Interaction of Judge-Made and Statutory Law

Some who study the lawmaking process argue that the courts have been much too willing to reinterpret and modify statutory law. According to these observers, Congress and state legislatures should be making laws, not federal and state judges. Defenders of judicial activism point out that judge-made law often is just a temporary fix until Congress or state legislatures are able to address the question at issue. If precedent-setting court decisions raise important public policy issues, Congress and state legislatures can and often do pass laws that either incorporate or correct elements of judge-made law. This was true for copyright law, when decades of judicial interpretations applied to the Copyright Act of 1909 finally were pulled together, revised, and refined in the Copyright Act of 1976. As discussed in Chapter 4, the Copyright Law of 1976 has been amended many times and now is the subject of much judicial review and interpretation, particularly in the areas of works-made-for-hire and new reproduction and distribution technologies. So the process of judicial review and interpretation of statutory law continues.

Distinguishing Cases

Although case law is based on judicial precedents, judges do not always strictly abide by those precedents. Faced with changing social circumstances, or with a legal proceeding that presents new conditions or issues, a judge may decide to "distinguish" the case at hand by showing that an old, seemingly controlling precedent is not determinative in this instance. When judges distinguish cases in this manner, they establish new precedents that, when applied by other judges to analogous sets of facts, become part of the body of case law.

Regulatory Law

Regulatory or administrative law is bureaucratic law, the vast inventory of rules, regulations, and procedures promulgated by agencies at all levels of government. These regulatory agencies often are empowered to both write and enforce laws. For example, an agency responsible for worker safety might write codes that apply to specific industries, seek out employers who violate those codes, hold hearings to evaluate the evidence, and penalize "convicted" violators.

Legislative Oversight of Government Agencies

With all of this authority, many government agencies wield considerable power. There are some substantial checks on this power, however. First, most government agencies are created through legislation and are subject to continual legislative scrutiny. In fact, the same statute that creates an agency often places strict limits on its jurisdiction. In addition, because the legislature gives power to an agency, it can also take it away—either through additional legislation or reductions in an agency's funding.

Judicial Supervision of Regulatory Agencies

Regulatory agencies also are subject to judicial supervision through the appeals process. Most regulatory decisions can be appealed either to special administrative courts or to the state or federal courts, depending on whether the agency involved is a state or federal agency. One example of this appeals process relevant to the media is the case known as *Midwest Video II*, a 1978 appeal to the U.S. Court of Appeals for the Eighth Circuit. In this case, the FCC had issued a regulation that required local cable television systems to set aside part of their channel capacity as "public access" channels. The FCC based this public access rule in part on constitutional grounds, citing its belief that publicly programmed cable channels would facilitate the free exchange of ideas that is both promoted and protected by the First Amendment.

Although the Court of Appeals acknowledged the noble objectives of the public access requirements, it found that the FCC had exceeded its regulatory authority by requiring cable television systems to offer these channels. Specifically, the Court of Appeals found that the FCC's public access requirements exceeded its mandate under the Communications Act of 1934, the federal statute that created the FCC and under which the FCC derives its regulatory authority. In the court's words:

> We deal here with the Federal Communications Commission, not the Federal First Amendment Commission. We are aware of nothing in the Act . . . which places with the Commission an affirmative duty or power to advance First Amendment goals by its own tour de force, through getting everyone on cable television or otherwise. Rhetoric in praise of objectives cannot confer jurisdiction.[4]

In other words, the Court of Appeals was reminding the FCC that the federal courts, not federal regulatory agencies, ultimately are responsible for interpreting the Constitution.

Other Regulatory Agencies That Affect Media Law

In addition to the FCC, several other government agencies and offices create regulations, policies, and procedures that are of interest to media producers. Those entities include the following:

- The Federal Trade Commission (FTC), which regulates advertising practices
- The U.S. Copyright Office, which establishes procedures for copyright registration

  • The Patent and Trademark Office, an agency of the U.S. Department of Commerce, which establishes procedures for patent and trademark registration

The rules promulgated by these and other federal regulatory agencies are published in the Code of Federal Regulations (CFR).[5]

Media professionals should also be aware of the various state, county, and municipal agencies that issue regulations related to media production. For example, many states have offices that help producers find shooting locations for film and television programs and that also may check to make sure that production companies conduct their businesses safely and with the proper permits and insurance.

Criminal Cases versus Civil Cases

Federal and state courts hear two types of cases: criminal cases and civil cases. The distinctions between these two types of cases are described in this section.

Criminal Cases

Criminal cases are those involving charges of burglary, robbery, murder, manslaughter, and other acts that violate penal statutes and threaten the safety or well-being of society as a whole. These cases are prosecuted by the state, with taxpayers picking up the bill for the cost of the prosecution. When defendants are convicted in criminal cases, they can face punishments that range from fines and probation to jail sentences and the death penalty. Because the penalties in criminal cases can involve loss of the defendant's liberty (or, in capital cases, the loss of the defendant's life), the prosecution must prove a criminal defendant's guilt "beyond a reasonable doubt."

Media producers rarely find themselves caught up in criminal cases resulting from their professional activities. This did happen, however, to film producer John Landis, who was accused of involuntary manslaughter in the July 1982 deaths of actor Vic Morrow and two children during filming of *The Twilight Zone*. Although Landis was acquitted of this criminal charge in 1987, he and his production company still faced the possibility of civil litigation brought by the families of the victims.

Civil Cases

Because the sanctions in civil cases are limited to awards of monetary damages, civil cases usually are considered less severe than criminal cases, and the standard of proof is less stringent. In civil cases, one party (an individual, group, or corporation or other entity) claims that another party has caused it physical, emotional, or financial injury. The result is a dispute between the two parties, rather than between an accused criminal and the state, with the courts serving as arbitrator. If the "preponderance of evidence" establishes that the party who brought the lawsuit (the plaintiff) was injured by the defendant, then the court may award the plaintiff damages in the form of money or some other appropriate compensation. In some cases, the court also may award punitive damages as a way of punishing the guilty party. Unlike in criminal cases, however, the defendant in a civil case cannot be sentenced to jail.

The key distinctions between civil and criminal cases were driven home to many members of the general public through the massive publicity surrounding the O.J. Simpson trials. In 1996, the jury in the criminal case acquitted Simpson, concluding that the prosecution had not proven Simpson's guilt in the murders of his former wife, Nicole Brown Simpson, and Ronald Goldman beyond a reasonable doubt. Had he been convicted in the criminal trial, Simpson could have been sentenced to life in prison. In 1997, the jury in the civil case reached a different result, concluding that the lawyers for the Brown and Goldman families had proven by a preponderance of the evidence that Simpson in fact was liable for the deaths. The jury then awarded the families $8.3 million in actual damages and $25 million in punitive damages. Under the "double jeopardy" doctrine, however, because he had been acquitted in the 1996 criminal trial, Simpson no longer faced the possibility of being retried in criminal court in connection with the murders.

Media Producers and Civil Litigation

When media producers find themselves involved in litigation, it most probably is a civil case. For example, a television producer might sue a production company for failing to deliver promised services, a motion picture producer might sue a film distribution company for not living up to the terms of a distribution contract, or a video producer might sue another video producer over the rights to market a program that they co-produced. These kinds of civil cases are very common in the world of media production, where the many deals that make up any major project can sometimes turn sour. Many civil cases of this type are settled out of court, with lawyers or other negotiators for the parties working out a compromise.

Most civil litigation involving media production is based on one of two types of wrongs: a breach of a contract or a tort. A breach of contract is a wrong that occurs when one or more parties to a contract fail to perform an act that was required by the contract or otherwise violate a provision of the contract. A tort is almost any wrong other than a breach of contract in which a party claims injury by another party. When a producer sues a subcontractor for failing to deliver an agreed-on service, the suit is a breach of contract action. When a performer sues a producer over an injury that occurred on the production set, the suit is a tort action. One important difference between contract and tort cases is that punitive damages generally are not available in contract cases. That is, although plaintiffs in tort actions often can sue for punitive damages in excess of the actual damages they have suffered, plaintiffs in contract actions usually are limited to the actual monetary losses resulting from the breach that they can establish to a reasonable certainty.

The Court System

No general overview of media law would be complete without at least a quick description of the court system. In the United States, there are actually two court systems: the federal courts and the state courts. Within both the federal and state systems, there also are several types and levels of courts. Figure 1.2 shows the types of courts and where they fit within the federal and state systems. The figure also shows the path that a case follows through the trial and appeals process. When the case is an appeal from a federal regulatory agency decision, it is brought before a U.S. Court of Appeals.

Federal Jurisdiction versus State Jurisdiction

What determines whether a case falls under the jurisdiction of the state courts or the federal courts? For the most part, the state courts retain

Figure 1.2 The federal and state judicial systems and the appeals process.

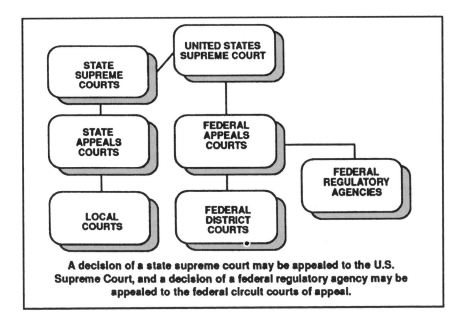

A decision of a state supreme court may be appealed to the U.S.
Supreme Court, and a decision of a federal regulatory agency may be
appealed to the federal circuit courts of appeal.

jurisdiction unless the case involves matters of federal law. The framers
of the Constitution were very careful to grant the federal judiciary
jurisdiction over specific legal matters, with the remaining powers left
to the states.

Federal Jurisdiction: Copyright and Interstate Commerce

One of the powers that the Constitution gives to the federal government is the authority to pass laws in the areas of copyright and interstate commerce. That is why most cases that involve copyright and
broadcasting, which is considered a form of interstate commerce, fall
under federal jurisdiction. The federal courts also have primary jurisdiction over all other cases that hinge on constitutional questions,
including those cases that raise free speech and free press issues. In
some instances, a federal court may even intervene to overturn a ruling
of a state court on appeal because, in the opinion of the federal
court, the state court has failed to interpret a constitutional question
correctly.

Diversity of Citizenship

Federal courts also may assume jurisdiction from state courts in cases that involve "diversity of citizenship." This situation occurs when a citizen of one state initiates legal action in that state against a citizen of another state. Because the court in either state might be prejudiced in favor of its own citizen, a federal court must hear the case if requested to do so, as long as the two parties are truly diverse and the amount of potential damages in controversy exceeds an established threshold (currently $75,000). By serving in this capacity, the federal court helps prevent either party in the case from gaining a home court advantage. Many legal disputes that grow out of media productions can end up as diversity cases because productions often involve several companies and parties from different states or location work performed in one state by a production company based in another state.

Shared Jurisdiction

In many areas of law, the federal government shares subject matter jurisdiction with state governments. This is true in the area of trademark law, for example, where there are both state and federal trademark statutes, so that certain types of trademark-related proceedings can be brought in either state or federal court. In areas such as this, the federal and state courts are said to have concurrent jurisdiction. In addition, in lawsuits filed in state courts that involve plaintiffs and defendants from different states, a party can move to have the case heard in federal court under the diversity jurisdiction described earlier. Also, in cases involving both federal and state law issues (e.g., a suit that raises claims under both the federal copyright law and state-law right of publicity issues), the federal court can hear the state claims under the concept of pendant jurisdiction, the doctrine under which a federal court can hear and determine both federal and state claims that are based on the same or a closely related set of facts.

The Federal Court System

Cases that fall under federal jurisdiction enter the federal court system. As Figure 1.3 shows, the federal court system is divided into 13 circuits. The term *circuit* is a throwback to the frontier era, when judges would "make their rounds" by traveling from town to town on

Figure 1.3 The federal judicial circuits.

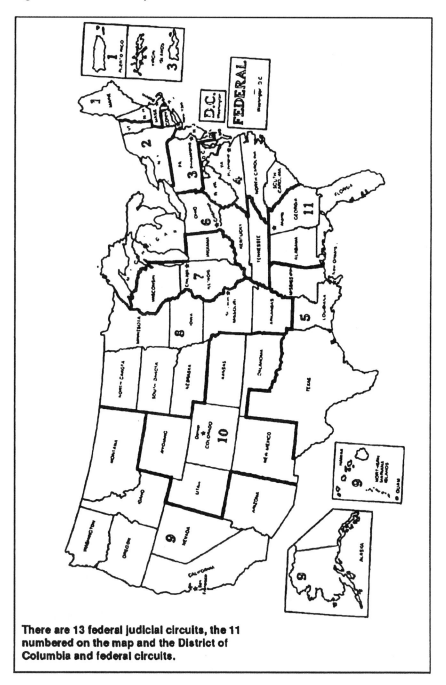

There are 13 federal judicial circuits, the 11 numbered on the map and the District of Columbia and federal circuits.

horseback. Today, each circuit includes one court of appeals (also called *circuit courts*) and several district courts.

The U.S. District Courts

The first stop for a case coming into the federal court system usually is one of the U.S. district courts. These are trial courts that handle both civil and criminal cases. There are more than 90 U.S. district courts, with at least one in each state.

The U.S. Courts of Appeals

If you lose your case in the district court, you can appeal to the circuit court for your region. Formally called the U.S. Courts of Appeals, the circuit courts are responsible for determining whether the case under appeal was handled and determined properly at the U.S. district court level. In hearing an appeal, the circuit court judges generally focus on matters of law and interpretation, not directly on matters of guilt or innocence.

Most federal appeals are heard by a panel of three circuit court judges. The appeal is decided when at least two of the three judges form a majority. Usually, the judges who form the majority will issue an opinion in which they explain the legal logic that led to their decision. These opinions are important because they are published in case-books, called *reporters*, and often carry considerable weight as legal precedents.

Along with hearing appeals that come up from district courts, the circuit courts handle the appeals of decisions made by federal regulatory agencies (e.g., the FCC, FTC). For this reason, the District of Columbia Circuit Court of Appeals and the Federal Circuit Court of Appeals are among the busiest of the circuit courts.

The U.S. Supreme Court

If you lose your appeal at the circuit court level, the next stop is the U.S. Supreme Court—but only if the Supreme Court agrees to hear your case. Out of the thousands of petitions that are submitted to it each year, the Supreme Court typically agrees to hear, or to "grant certiori" in, only a few dozen of those cases. Generally, the Supreme Court gives preference to those cases that involve important or far-reaching legal issues or cases in which two or more lower courts have interpreted a legal issue in conflicting ways.

At least four of the nine Supreme Court justices must vote in favor of hearing a case for it to be placed on the court's calendar. If a petition does not receive the necessary votes, the decision of the lower court is allowed to stand. This means that the justices have decided that the case does not warrant a full hearing before the nation's highest court. It does not necessarily mean that they agree with the original decision.

Although this petitioning process is the most common way for cases from the circuit courts to reach the Supreme Court, it is not the only way for a case to be scheduled on the court's calendar. The Supreme Court will hear cases that involve disputes between two states, and it is the court of first appeal for cases that come out of certain special courts, including the U.S. Court of Claims. In addition, the U.S. Supreme Court sometimes will accept appeals of cases that state supreme courts have either ruled on or refused to hear, particularly when those cases have important constitutional implications. Also, Congress sometimes inserts into federal legislation a requirement that the Supreme Court must hear an appeal of any lower court decision holding that the legislation is unconstitutional. This provision was included in the Communications Decency Act of 1996, the federal statute intended to restrict obscene and indecent communications on the Internet.[6]

The Supreme Court truly is the "supreme" court of the United States. The opinions issued by the justices often capture headlines nationwide, and the Supreme Court's decisions are binding on all lower courts. As mentioned earlier, the Supreme Court also is responsible for determining whether federal laws and regulations are constitutional, a responsibility that often casts the justices as key players in the lawmaking process.

State Courts

Like the federal court system, the 50 state court systems are divided into tiers: lower courts and upper courts. The lower courts are trial courts that hear cases involving violations of state laws. The upper courts are appellate bodies that hear appeals from the lower courts.

In large states, the appellate courts are divided into two tiers: state courts of appeals and the state supreme court. Cases from the lower courts are appealed first to the state appeals court and then to the state supreme court. States that feature this two-tier appeals system include (among many others) California, Illinois, Michigan, New York, Ohio, and Pennsylvania. In New York, though, the highest court is called the Court of Appeals, and lower-level courts with the power to hear some kinds of appeals are called supreme courts.

In some smaller states, there are no intermediate appeals courts. Instead, cases from the trial courts are appealed directly to the state supreme court. In recent years, however, the crush of litigation and appeals has moved many of these states to introduce intermediate appellate courts.

The trial courts that make up the lower court system sometimes are divided into civil courts, which hear civil cases, and criminal courts, which hear criminal cases. Along with these trial courts, the lower court systems in many states include various special jurisdiction courts: probate courts, family courts, juvenile courts, and so on.

Local and Municipal Courts

The lowest of the lower courts are the local and municipal courts that rule on matters involving county, city, town, and village laws and ordinances. Included in this category are traffic courts, police courts, small claims courts, and justices of the peace. Generally, state statutes limit these local courts to ruling on civil cases involving relatively small sums and criminal cases involving only minor offenses. Because the cases tried in these courts are so minor, they are rarely appealed, even though most states do make provisions for such appeals through their appellate court systems.

Alternative Dispute Resolution

Media professionals should also be aware of arbitration and mediation, two methods of alternative dispute resolution that can eliminate the need for conventional courtroom litigation in specific cases.

Arbitration

In arbitration, a dispute between parties is brought before one or more independent arbitrators, rather than before a judge and jury. Arbitration has become an attractive way of resolving disputes in certain civil cases, particularly as the number of lawsuits has grown and the cost of trial lawyers has reached several hundred dollars per hour plus expenses.

Along with saving money and reducing the need for a lawyer, arbitration can save a great deal of time. Conventional litigation can drag on for years, but cases placed in arbitration often are resolved in a matter of weeks. To media professionals, the time saved can be critical, particularly when a contract dispute threatens to tie up the completion or distribution of a production.

Of course, arbitration has some limitations. First, the type of arbitration described here works only in civil cases and usually only in cases involving claims that grow out of contract or other commercial disputes. Second, for the process to work at all, both parties must agree to submit the matter to arbitration. Usually, this means that an arbitration clause must be part of the original contract between the parties. Here is a simple version of such a provision:

> The parties hereby agree that any dispute, claim, or controversy arising out of this agreement or any breach thereof shall be submitted to binding arbitration in [name of city] under the Commercial Arbitration Rules of the American Arbitration Association. Judgment upon any final award of the arbitrators may be entered in any court of competent jurisdiction. The prevailing party shall be entitled to its costs and expenses (including reasonable attorney fees) in connection with the arbitration and entry of judgment.

In the United States, many arbitration cases are conducted under the auspices of the American Arbitration Association (AAA). The AAA typically will furnish forms for the parties to complete, arrange for a place to hold the arbitration sessions, and propose a list of arbitrators who have expertise in the disputed matter. Once both parties have had the option of reviewing the list and striking off names, the AAA chooses the arbitrators from the names that remain—unless the parties have agreed to an alternate method for selecting an arbitrator.

In some respects, the typical arbitration is similar to trying a case before a judge. Each party has the opportunity to state its case, to present evidence and witnesses, and to respond to the accusations and claims made by the other party. The rules that govern arbitration sessions are relatively relaxed compared to courtroom proceedings, however. This often makes it easier for parties to present evidence, to cross-examine witnesses, and to present affidavits that contain the sworn testimony of witnesses who cannot appear in person. It also makes it easier for individuals to serve as their own lawyers, although many parties still prefer to use a lawyer. Note that the sample provision states that the prevailing party will be entitled to its costs and expenses (including reasonable attorney fees, which are usually the most substantial expense) in connection with the arbitration. In contrast to the "costs and expenses to be shared equally" language that appears in some arbitration clauses, this "loser pays" provision raises the stakes for the party that initiates arbitration. For this reason, some producers see this provision as a deterrent to a party that might be inclined to demand arbitration of relatively small or frivolous claims.

Once the arbitration hearing is completed, the AAA general guidelines allow the arbitrators up to six months to announce their decision, although the decision usually comes sooner (and may come much sooner if the arbitration was conducted on an expedited basis). Assuming that all parties involved have agreed to binding arbitration (including the award of damages, if any), the final decision of the arbitrators has the same impact and authority as a judgment of the courts. The decision becomes a true judgment once it is filed in a court of competent jurisdiction. Appeals are possible but usually succeed only if one of the parties can convince the appellate court that the arbitration was conducted improperly.[7]

Mediation

Mediation is another form of alternative dispute resolution. Although similar to arbitration in many respects, mediation usually is less formal and often involves a single mediator, rather than the multiple-member panel that is often used in commercial arbitration. In addition, mediation often results in the mediator issuing a set of conclusions or findings, rather than the binding decision (and, in some cases, an award of damages) that is the standard outcome of arbitration proceedings. For this reason, parties to a contract sometimes agree to mediation as an intermediary requirement before proceeding to binding arbitration or a trial.

As an intermediary step, mediation gives the parties a chance to have their legal and factual arguments evaluated in a neutral forum, so each party can assess its likelihood of prevailing in binding arbitration or litigation. Once the parties are able to make this assessment, they are in a better position to evaluate the cost and benefits of settling the dispute against the cost and likely benefits of proceeding to arbitration or trial.

Unlike arbitration, mediation does not have a dominant organization such as the AAA with standardized rules and procedures that have been accepted and adopted in most U.S. jurisdictions. Instead, mediation rules and procedures will vary among jurisdictions and individual mediators.[8] Attorneys who handle civil disputes are usually familiar with the mediation process and individuals and groups that provide mediation services in their jurisdictions. In many instances, the mediator selected and the procedures followed in a particular case are the result of negotiation between attorneys for the parties after a dispute arises. As with arbitration, however, it is also possible to require the parties to mediate disputes, and to lay out some mediation ground rules in advance, by including appropriate language in the contract between the parties. Here is a sample contract provision that requires the parties to mediate before arbitrating or litigating a dispute:

> The parties hereby agree that any dispute, claim, or controversy arising out of this agreement or any breach thereof shall be submitted for mediation to [name of mediation entity] in [name of city] prior to such matter being submitted to binding arbitration in accordance with the terms of this agreement. Either party may commence mediation by submitting to [name of mediation entity] and to the other party a written request for mediation setting forth the subject matter of the dispute and the relief requested. The parties agree (i) to cooperate with [name of mediation entity] and one another in scheduling the mediation and selecting a mediator, who must be mutually approved by the parties; (ii) to participate in the mediation in good faith; and (iii) to share all mediation costs equally. The parties further agree that the foregoing mediation requirement may be enforced by any court of competent jurisdiction, with the party against which enforcement is ordered obligated to pay all costs and expenses, including reasonable attorney's fees, incurred by the party that sought enforcement.

The final sentence of this sample mediation provision anticipates that one party may need to enlist the assistance of a court to force the other party to adhere to the mediation requirement. In such an instance, the recalcitrant party will be obligated to pay the costs and legal fees of the party that is seeking enforcement of the requirement. This sample provision also states that the parties will share all other costs of the mediation equally—a covenant that contrasts with the "loser pays" language included in many arbitration provisions. In fact, this distinction highlights an important difference between mediation, which typically results in a nonbinding set of findings from which it is not possible to deduce a clear winner or loser, and arbitration, which typically results in a final, binding disposition that either grants or denies the relief sought by one or both parties. Moreover, if the "loser pays" requirement applies, the arbitrator's decision will usually stipulate which party "won" the right to recover its attorney fees and expenses.

Summary

- *What is media law?* Media law is a very broad body of law that incorporates elements from a variety of legal disciplines. Those disciplines include copyright and trademark law, contract law, labor law, the laws and regulations concerned with privacy and defamation, telecommunications law and policy, and the many legal issues and interpretations that arise from the First Amendment's guarantees of free speech and freedom of the press.
- *How much law must media producers know?* Producers and other media professionals do not need to be lawyers; however, producers should be able to anticipate and identify the many legal issues that can come up during production and recognize when it is necessary to call in a lawyer. Producers also should know when it is necessary to secure licenses, releases, permits, and permissions for a particular production.
- *Who makes media law?* Media law is created by Congress and state legislatures; federal and state courts; and federal, state, and municipal regulatory agencies. The courts create law by establishing legal precedents (case law) that determine how laws and regulations are interpreted and enforced. Federal offices and regulatory agencies involved in media law include the Federal Communications Commission (FCC), the Federal Trade Commission (FTC), and the U.S. Copyright Office.
- *What are the major types and categories of law?* In the United States, there are four major categories of law: constitutional law (law based directly on the U.S. Constitution), statutory law (laws passed by Congress and state and local legislatures), common law or case law (law established by the courts through judicial

decisions that become precedents), and regulatory or administrative law (rules and regulations promulgated by regulatory agencies).

- *What is the difference between civil cases and criminal cases?* Criminal cases involve crimes such as burglary and murder that threaten the safety and well-being of society as a whole and that are prosecuted by the state. Civil cases typically are private lawsuits in which one party (the plaintiff) claims that another party (the defendant) has broken a contract or caused the plaintiff physical, emotional, or financial harm. In criminal cases, the prosecution must prove its case "beyond a reasonable doubt," and a defendant who is found guilty can be sentenced to prison or, in the most extreme cases, death. In civil cases, the plaintiff generally must prove its case by a "preponderance of the evidence," and the losing party risks the loss of only monetary damages. Most cases that grow out of media production are civil cases.

- *What is the court system?* In the United States, there are two court systems: the federal system and the state system. The federal system includes U.S. District Courts, the U.S. Courts of Appeals, and the U.S. Supreme Court. The state systems include the municipal and county courts, trial courts, appeals courts, and a supreme court located in each state.

- *Must all legal disputes be settled in court?* Arbitration and mediation are two ways in which the parties in a civil suit can avoid the cost of going to court. If the parties want either of these methods of alternative dispute resolution to serve as an option, a clause to that effect should be written into the contract between them. Many cases also are settled out of court by mutual agreement of the parties involved.

Notes

1. The Communications Act of 1934, as amended, is published in Title 47 of the U.S. Code. The Copyright Act of 1976, as amended, is published in Title 17 of the U.S. Code.

2. Like many areas of U.S. law, our common law is based in part on the English legal system. When state and federal courts first began

in the new nation, they adopted many of the English judicial traditions that had been the basis for common law in the American colonies.

3. *Sony Corp. of America v. Universal City Studios, Inc.,* 464 U.S. 417 (1984).

4. *Midwest Video Corp. v. FCC,* 571 F.2d 1025, 1042 (8th Cir. 1978).

5. Title (volume) 37 of the CFR includes regulations related to copyright; Title 47 contains regulations related to telecommunications, including television and radio broadcasting.

6. The Communications Decency Act of 1996 is Title V of the Telecommunications Act of 1996, Pub. L. No. 104–104, 110 Stat. 85 (1996).

7. For more information about arbitration, contact the American Arbitration Association at 140 West 51st Street, New York, NY 10020; (212) 484–4000. On the West Coast, the AAA can be reached at 3055 Wilshire Boulevard, 7th Floor, Los Angeles, CA 90010; (213) 383–6516.

8. Although there are no dominant mediation organizations, the AAA has adopted mediation procedure rules that, while not as widely used as its arbitration rules, are being adopted in full or in part in many mediations. Media producers may find the AAA mediation rules specified as the required or preferred rules in contracts that include a mediation provision, particularly when the contract requires that any disputes not resolved through mediation will then be submitted to arbitration under the AAA rules.

2

Managing Relationships: Contracts and the Media Production Process

Like any business, the business of media production involves managing many working relationships. In a typical video production, for example, a producer must manage relationships with the talent, the writer, the production crew, postproduction personnel, and the client who has commissioned the project, as well as with any subcontractors or suppliers providing music, stock footage, title sequences, and other production materials. In addition, once the project is finished, some producers are responsible for negotiating relationships with program distributors. The success of any production project depends, to a significant degree, on the producer's success in managing and coordinating these relationships.

In an ideal world, all production relationships could be based solely on trust. The producer could explain what he or she expected of an actor or editor, for example, and what the actor or editor could expect in return. Then the producer could sit back and relax, confident that the agreed-on services would be delivered on time and in an acceptable form. The actor and editor also could relax, assured by the knowledge that they would receive the agreed-on compensation for their work.

Unfortunately, the world of media production rarely is ideal. As a result, producers rarely can afford to rely solely on the good faith of performers, crew members, suppliers, and subcontractors to guarantee that the services needed to complete a project will be delivered. Instead, experienced producers usually will seek more formal, contractual assurance that the promised goods and services will show up on time and in suitable shape.

Production Contracts

Production contracts provide a formal legal foundation on which to build production relationships. Although they cannot guarantee the success of those relationships, production contracts can do the following:

- Specify the responsibilities of the various individuals and groups involved in the production.
- Designate delivery dates for the goods and services that these parties will provide.
- Describe the required quality and condition of the designated goods and services.
- Delineate the compensation that parties will receive in return for delivering the designated goods and services.
- Provide for what happens if any of the parties breach the terms of an agreement.

Above all, contracts can help with managing production projects because they require the parties to a production relationship to agree on the terms of their relationship up front, before deadlines are pressing and tempers are short. Just as important, because they require the parties to put terms in writing, contracts can help deter disagreements during a production—and the lawsuits that sometimes can follow.

What Is a Contract?

When most people hear the word *contract*, they think of a thick document printed in tiny type and filled with incomprehensible legal jargon. As Figure 2.1 shows, however, contracts actually can be fairly brief documents written in the form of business letters. Many business contracts are written in relatively plain English. As a matter of fact, as discussed later in this chapter, contracts do not necessarily have to be written at all, although all media production contracts should be.

Figure 2.1 Letter agreement.

Corporate Video Center
Advanced Technologies, Inc.
4400 Industrial Drive
Houston, Texas 77061

February 19, 2002

Mr. Jason McDonald
737 Stadium Street
Houston, Texas 77056

Dear Jason,

This letter, when signed by you below, will form a binding agreement between you and Advanced Technologies, Inc. (the "Company").

The Company offers to hire you as the voiceover narrator for a training videotape currently titled "Better Systems, Better Management" (the "Project") that is under production in our Corporate Video Center. The voiceover recording session will take place on March 14, 2002, at Soundsgood Studios located in Houston at 47 Halford Highway. We will need you for the complete session, which will run from 9 a.m. to approximately 5 p.m. We will send you the script at least one week before the session.

As full and complete consideration for your services, the Company will pay you a one-time fee of $1,500. Should we require your services on the Project beyond the March 14 recording session, the Company will pay you $200 for each additional hour of your time. The Company's payment terms are net thirty (30) days from the completion of your services on the Project. This offer will remain valid for five (5) calendar days from the date of this letter. Should you not indicate your acceptance by that date, the offer will expire.

You acknowledge and agree that the Company will own all results and proceeds of your services in connection with the Project. You further acknowledge and agree that those results and proceeds will be a "work-made-for-hire" under all relevant copyright laws. If for any reason it is ever deemed that you do have a copyright or other ownership interest in the results and proceeds of your services, you hereby irrevocably assign to the Company all of your right, title, and interest thereto. You agree to execute

Figure 2.1 Letter agreement. (continued)

any documents that the Company may require to register, perfect, assign, or license its ownership rights in the Project and to further the purposes of this Agreement.

You acknowledge that you are an independent contractor and that you will be solely responsible for all taxes, fees, and assessments due with respect to your compensation hereunder. As an independent contractor, you also agree not to make any claims against the Company for insurance, workers' compensation, or any other benefits offered by the Company to its employees.

This agreement constitutes the entire understanding of the parties and supersedes all prior or contemporaneous agreements, communications, and representations, oral or written, between you and the Company concerning the subject matter hereof. This agreement may only be modified or amended by a written instrument signed by both parties.

If you agree to the terms set forth above, please sign both copies in the space provided below and return one signed copy to me.

Sincerely,

Robert S. Hansen
Advanced Technologies, Inc.

AGREED AND ACCEPTED

_____   _____
Jason McDonald   Date:

In its most basic form, a contract is simply a binding agreement between two or more parties. A lawyer might prefer a more formal definition, such as that provided by *Black's Law Dictionary*: "An agreement between two or more persons which creates an obligation to do or not to do a particular thing [and] the writing which contains the agreement of parties, with the terms and conditions, and which serves as proof of the obligation."[1]

As this definition indicates, a contract is an agreement that creates obligations between two or more parties. In addition, once the contract is placed in writing and signed by the parties, the signed document serves as documentary proof of those obligations. That is why, even though oral contracts are considered valid under many circumstances, all media production contracts should be placed in writing. In the event that a dispute occurs among the parties, the written contract provides immediate proof of the terms and conditions to which they agreed.

The "terms and conditions" written into a contract are important because these provisions often place qualifications on the parties' primary rights and responsibilities under the agreement. For example, a video producer in a corporate communications department and an outside production facility might execute a contract that obligates the outside facility to deliver an opening title and graphics sequence. In return for this work, the corporate video producer would agree to pay the facility the fee designated in the contract, subject to the following terms and conditions:

- The title and graphics sequence must be delivered by a designated date.
- The sequence must run for the exact time specified.
- The sequence must meet defined technical standards.

Depending on the situation, the video producer and outside facility also might want to specify a number of other terms and conditions affecting the parties' performance obligations. For example, the video producer might decide to designate several checkpoint dates for reviewing preliminary versions of the title sequence. The outside facility might decide to specify, in turn, that the video producer must deliver an approval within 24 hours of receiving the preview versions of the agreement. In fact, in many media production contracts, the list of terms and conditions included in the contract runs much longer than the core agreement itself.

Some media producers prefer not to bother with formal contracts for many production transactions. This is particularly true in the world of corporate communications and nonbroadcast video, where business often is based on promises made during last-minute phone calls to talent, production crews, and subcontractors. Producers should understand that, under the law, a simple, unilateral promise is not the same as a contract, even when the promise is made in writing. As the section that follows explains, an agreement must contain at least three basic components to form a binding contract.

The Components of a Contract

A contract must contain three components: the offer, the consideration, and the acceptance. A contract missing any of these elements may not be enforceable under the law. Of course, a contract can contain other components as well, including the conditions and provisions mentioned earlier. Often, though, these additional elements are contained as part of the offer, the consideration, or the acceptance. Figure 2.1 shows a simple contract that contains these three key components plus several additional provisions. (For greater detail, see the media production contract checklist and sample contracts in Chapter 3.)

Offer

The offer is the fundamental proposal that initiates the contract formation process. In its most basic form, the offer that initiates a typical video production transaction says, "We want you to do this for us." In a contract between a video production company (the "offeror") and a songwriter (the "offeree"), for example, the basic offer might be, "We want you to write and produce a theme song for our current production." Usually, the offer will also indicate how much the company is willing to pay the songwriter, although technically, this is part of the consideration.

In actual practice, most offers are made subject to several terms and conditions. Here are some sample conditions that might be attached to the theme song offer described in the preceding paragraph:

- The offer must be accepted within a specified time period.
- The songwriter must agree to relinquish all claim of ownership in the song, so the video production company becomes the sole owner of both the lyrics and the music.
- The songwriter must deliver the lyrics and music for preliminary approval by a specified date.
- The songwriter must deliver the completed song by a specified date.

- The songwriter must deliver the song in a specified form.
- The completed song must meet specified time requirements (e.g., 1 minute, 45 seconds).
- The completed song must meet certain technical specifications.

What this full offer really says, then, is: "If you meet all of these requirements, we agree to live up to our end of the deal." Of course, before deciding whether to accept the offer, the songwriter should take a close look at the part of the contract that describes what he or she will get in return for performing the work. This "what's in it for me" part of a contract is called the consideration.

Consideration

Consideration is the component of a contract that describes in detail what the accepting party will receive in return for accepting and satisfying the terms of the offer. In most contracts, the consideration is entirely or mostly money. Consideration in media contracts can also involve other sorts of compensation, however, including the following:

- Credits at the beginning or end of the program for the songwriter, scriptwriter, performer, production crew member, or subcontractor
- A provision to provide performers or writers residual (royalty) payments from revenue generated through certain types of distribution
- The "right of first refusal" to perform similar work for sequels and other subsequent projects
- The right to receive copies of the completed production

Some producers also include bartered services as part of the consideration. For example, a contract between a video production company and a songwriter might call for the production company to provide the songwriter with access to its recording and mixing facilities as full or partial consideration for the songwriter's work on a video soundtrack.

Under contract law, consideration actually cuts both ways. For the party that has made the offer, the consideration is the goods or services that it will receive from the party that accepts the offer. For the accepting party, the consideration is the payment that it will receive for delivering those goods and services.

Consideration is a critical component of any contract. By specifying what each party will receive in return for fulfilling its end of the contract, consideration establishes a "mutuality of obligation" between the parties. This mutuality of obligation distinguishes a contract from a unilateral promise or nonbinding agreement.[2]

Needless to say, both the offer and consideration portions of a contract are often subject to lengthy negotiation. For example, a songwriter might prefer to retain certain rights in the song, to be paid more for the song than the production company has offered, or to take longer to complete the project than the offer specifies. Because making changes to drafts of contracts can be time consuming, many of these issues are often worked out in communications between the parties before preparing a full written draft. That way, once the written contract is sent to the offeree, acceptance of the full agreement is more likely to follow without undue delay.

Acceptance

Acceptance occurs when the parties agree to be bound by the contract's terms. Although the exact manner of accepting (or "executing") a contract can vary from one agreement to the next, almost all written contracts call for the parties to indicate acceptance by signing in the space or spaces provided in the contract. For agreements in which one or both parties are groups or corporations, an authorized representative will sign the contract on behalf of each group or corporation. It also is possible to indicate acceptance orally or by a specified action (such as accepting delivery of a product), although this rarely is the case with written media production contracts.

Increasingly, parties are executing agreements by having each party sign a copy of the agreement sent by facsimile and then faxing the signature page to the other party. This "execution by facsimile" process eliminates the need for the parties to meet physically to sign the agreement and reduces or eliminates the delay in execution that results from one party signing the agreement and then sending signed originals to the other party or parties for execution. Although this process generally is a valid way to execute agreements, if you expect that you may want to execute an agreement by fax, it is advisable to include a provision in the agreement authorizing execution "by facsimile signature." Several of the sample contracts in Chapter 3 contain this provision. In addition, many parties that use this option to expedite the execution process follow up by circulating original, confirming copies for execution. This ensures that at least one clean, fully executed original copy contains all of the required signatures in the event that a party challenges the validity of the facsimile version.

Always keep in mind that, by signing a contract, you are accepting all of the terms of the contract. As a result, you should make sure that all of the terms are acceptable before signing. With deadlines pressing, some parties to media production contracts make the mistake of signing a contract containing vague or questionable provisions and simply assuming that "things will work out." Unfortunately, those items that are left unresolved often do not work out.

It also is a mistake to assume that you can simply mark a few changes in the margins of a contract and then accept it. Under contract law, making even small modifications to an offer can be interpreted as constituting a rejection of the offer. To arrive at a final contract, you will need to renegotiate with the party that made the offer, receive a new written offer that includes the renegotiated terms, and then accept that new offer.

One way to get around rewriting the entire contract when there are disputed issues is to reach agreement on those issues and to attach a list of amendments to the agreement. Another, even simpler method is to mark changes on the agreement and to have all parties initial the changes. These options work well when the matters under dispute are relatively minor or when one or both of the parties wishes to clarify a provision of the offer. If the disputed items include basic terms of the offer, however, renegotiating and rewriting the contract is the recommended alternative.

Sunset Provisions

You should always take the time to review all of the terms and conditions of an offer before accepting it; however, some offers contain a "sunset provision" that requires you to respond to an offer by a specified date. If you do not respond in time, the offer is automatically withdrawn. For example, the contract in Figure 2.1 states that the offer will remain open for only five days, at which point it will expire if not accepted. If the offer calls for you to respond through the mail, your acceptance usually will become effective on the day that you mailed it, provided that the contract does not say that the acceptance actually must reach the party that has made the offer by a specified time.

Offer versus Contract

Keep in mind that an offer and a contract are not the same thing. Often, a media producer may make an informal offer to a performer or writer, for example, with the understanding that a written contract will follow if the performer or writer is interested in considering the offer. The written contract is what contains the complete terms of the offer and consideration and what the performer or writer must sign to signal acceptance. Also, as discussed previously, an offer in fact must be accepted to form a binding contract. As a result, no binding contract exists between a producer and a writer, when, for example, the producer offers to hire the writer on a project and the writer says, "I'll get back to you." Instead, the contract is formed when the writer in fact gets back to the producer and accepts the offer. In addition, most written contracts, including the sample contract in Figure 2.1, include an "integration clause" stating that the written contract as executed by the parties supersedes all prior agreements or communication between the parties concerning the subject matter of the agreement. This clause makes clear that the written contract—not any prior discussions or communication between the parties—expresses the final word on their agreement.

Other Issues and Concerns

As a media professional, you should be aware of several other issues related to the creation of enforceable contracts.

Mental Competence

The law assumes that all of the parties to a contract were mentally competent and sober at the time of acceptance and that none of the parties was accepting the contract under physical or psychological duress. For most contracts, the law also assumes that the parties are adults, although the exact age at which a person reaches legal majority can differ from one state to the next. If a media producer wishes to place a child performer under contract, a parent or legal guardian must sign for the child. As shown in Chapter 5, this includes releases in which minors are agreeing to appear in a production for little or no monetary compensation.

Illegal Acts

It is not legal to enter into a contract that requires someone to perform an illegal act. For example, a contract that calls for a stunt person to drive a car down a busy city street at 100 miles per hour would not be legal because it requires the stunt person to break the law. Contracts also can be declared invalid if they require a party to perform actions that run counter to public moral standards, although those standards often are difficult to define.

Fraud and Mistake

A contract can be declared void or rescinded if one of the parties is proven to have committed fraud in forming the contract or if a party can prove in court that the contract is based on a fundamental misunderstanding or "mutual mistake." Because it is difficult to prove that the parties entered into an agreement based on a fraudulent misrepresentation, misunderstanding, or mutual mistake, however, few contracts actually are invalidated on these grounds.

Sources of Contract Law

Unlike copyright law, which is governed almost exclusively by the Copyright Act of 1976 as amended, contract law is not governed by a single, overriding federal statute. Instead, most contract law is based on common law and on statutes enacted by individual states. To provide some consistency across state boundaries, all states except Louisiana have adopted the Uniform Commercial Code (UCC), a standardized body of laws governing the sale of goods and certain other commercial transactions. Most states also have adopted some form of the Statute of Frauds, a body of rules that determines whether a particular type of contract must be placed in writing. In all states, the law gives individuals the right to enter into legally binding contracts, to go to court when necessary to have those contracts enforced, and to receive some form of compensation or redress when a contract is breached.

Categories of Contracts

There are many different types and categories of contracts, including some that are specific to certain types of businesses and transactions. For media producers, the distinctions between express and implied contracts and between oral and written contracts are especially important.

Express Contracts versus Implied Contracts

An express contract is a written or oral agreement that is expressly declared at the time that it is made. In other words, an express contract is one in which the terms are made explicit and in which all parties are aware that they are agreeing to those terms and entering into a binding agreement. All of the sample media production contracts provided in Chapter 3 are express contracts.

In contrast, an implied contract is an agreement that is not expressly stated but instead is implicit in a transaction or relationship between parties. Like all contracts, an implied contract obligates the parties to perform certain responsibilities. In an implied contract, however, those obligations are not made explicit through a formal agreement. For example, when you order a pizza by telephone, you are entering into an implied contract that obligates you to pay for the pizza once it arrives, even though you did not expressly state, "I will pay for the pizza once it arrives," when you placed the order. The pizza vendor is obligated, in turn, to deliver the pizza that you ordered within a reasonable amount of time. If the wrong pizza arrives six hours later, the vendor has breached the terms of the implied contract, and you are not obligated to pay. On the other hand, if the pizza vendor fulfills its obligations but you refuse to pay, the vendor could initiate legal action against you for breaching the implied contract.

Of course, neither you nor the pizza vendor is likely to initiate formal legal action over the price of one pizza. As a matter of justice, however, the law does allow individuals and corporations to seek redress against parties that violate implied contracts. This doctrine evolved as a way to establish equitable rights and responsibilities in the innumerable business and personal transactions that occur every day but that are not covered by express contracts. If an implied contract dispute reaches the litigation stage, the court must determine what rights and responsibilities were implied and understood through the transaction in question.

As the examples provided in Chapter 3 show, each significant business transaction that grows out of a media production project should be covered by some form of express contract. You should be aware that, even when no express written contract exists, a typical media production transaction still creates rights and responsibilities under the doctrine of implied contracts. For example, when you license video footage to a producer with knowledge that it will be used in an upcoming production, you imply that you have the necessary rights to license the footage. If the buyer discovers that this was not the case, you could find yourself sued for breach of contract, even though you never entered into a written contract with the buyer. In this instance, the best protection for all parties would have been to enter into an express contract that defined what rights you had to the video footage and what rights you were transferring to the other party. In fact, one of the best reasons for drawing up an express contract is to anticipate and avoid the conflict and confusion that can arise from production disputes. For this reason alone, all of the relationships in media productions should be covered by express written contracts.

Oral versus Written Contracts

Many media professionals are surprised to learn that a contract does not always have to be placed in writing to be enforceable. For many types of transactions, oral agreements can constitute a legally binding contract, as long as the three key components of a contract (i.e., offer, consideration, and acceptance) are present. State statutes and the UCC do, however, require certain types of contracts to be placed in writing. In most states, this includes contracts that cover the following:

- Transactions for the sale of goods that exceed a certain price ($500 under the UCC)
- Agreements that cannot be completed within one year (or within some other period defined by state statute). Under this provision, a multiyear production contract would not be legal unless it were placed in writing.
- Transactions that involve the sale of real estate or the lease of property for more than one year (three years in some states).

Under this rule, a four-year lease agreement for video production facilities must be placed in writing.

- Agreements in which you assume another person's obligations (e.g., an agreement in which you agree to take over a production contract that another party could not complete or the debts of another company as part of acquiring the company)

Many state statutes regarding written and oral contracts are based on the Statute of Frauds, a British law enacted in 1677 that was eventually adopted, in whole or part, by most of the United States. Where the UCC covers only transactions involving the sale of goods, the Statute of Frauds applies to contracts for both goods and services.

Because the laws and regulations governing contracts can vary from state to state, it is important to check with a lawyer to determine what contracts are required to be in writing under the laws of your state. The safest and recommended route is to place all media production contracts in writing, even if the written contract is a brief document that only confirms an oral agreement. This is particularly important in media production agreements that involve work-made-for-hire arrangements, which are discussed in more detail in Chapter 3.

As mentioned earlier in this chapter, a properly drafted contract can help deter disputes and disagreements during the production process because it provides tangible proof of the terms that the parties are obligated to honor. If a transaction involves both a written and an oral contract and the two contracts contain conflicting terms, a court usually will give precedence to the written version.

When Do You Need a Lawyer?

With lawyers' fees reaching several hundred dollars per hour, many media producers have begun looking for ways to limit the number of occasions for which they seek an attorney's help on contract matters. Unfortunately, no simple set of guidelines can tell you when a call to your lawyer is in order. As a general rule, however, you should always seek a lawyer's advice under the following circumstances:

- When you are drafting a standard contract that you will use as a model for the individual contracts offered to talent, writers, crew members, subcontractors, and so on

- When you are being asked to sign a contract that contains terms you do not fully understand
- When you are being asked to sign a contract that commits you or your company to a long-term obligation
- When you are negotiating a contract for a deal that is vital to the success or survival of your company
- Whenever you feel uneasy or unsure about a contract matter

Many media producers work with their lawyers to prepare standard form contracts that cover a variety of production relationships (e.g., hiring performers, writers, and crew members; subcontracting production services; renting production facilities and equipment). The producers then tailor the contracts to particular productions by filling in the blanks with the appropriate names, dates, and amounts. After their initial involvement, the lawyers are called in only when circumstances require a producer to make major modifications to a standard contract. Even then, it usually takes much less time for a lawyer to review changes to a standard contract than it does to draft individual contracts to cover each new production relationship.

Many producers prepare and store their standard form contracts on their computers. This makes it easy for them to call up the standard form; add names, dates, and amounts; make minor modifications; and print a legible and professional-looking copy.

As a safety measure, some production companies bring a lawyer back into the process whenever the amount of money involved in a pending contract exceeds a predetermined threshold. The exact figure used for this threshold varies from company to company, depending on how much risk the organization is willing to take with a contract to save on upfront legal fees. Of course, having a lawyer review a contract does not provide any guarantee that the agreement is risk free, but an experienced attorney can point out areas of the contract that appear to contain risks and that may result in considerable legal expense down the road.

If you work in a corporate setting, you should also be aware of your company's policy on preparing and entering into contracts. In many companies, all contracts must subscribe to a specific format and pass through the corporate legal office. In fact, in some organizations, only one or two officers of the corporation are permitted to sign contracts that will bind the company. Even in companies with the strictest contract policies, however, the legal department may be willing to work with you to create standard agreements that cover many production situations. No corporation wants to see its high-powered legal staff drown in the stream of small contracts that can flow from a corporate media production facility.

Broken Contracts

As mentioned earlier, contracts establish a "mutuality of obligation" between parties. In fact, one of the main benefits of a carefully written contract is that it defines each party's obligations in specific detail. Once all involved parties accept the terms of a legally binding contract, they can be required to fulfill their obligations.

What happens, however, when one party fails to live up to its end of the deal? For example, what happens if a computer graphics facility that you hired to create an opening for a video production fails to deliver the finished materials by the date specified in the contract? Or what happens when a performer who signed a contract to appear in a television program never bothers to show up for the production?

In both of these examples, one party to a contract has breached a material term of the agreement. Once that happens, the other party is no longer obligated to honor its end of the contract. For example, if the contract called for you to pay the animation facility $10,000 if it delivered the opening sequence by a specified date, you are no longer obligated to pay the $10,000 if the material is not delivered by that date. Similarly, you would not be required to pay the performer who failed to show up for work.

Seeking Compensation

Unfortunately, the fact that you are not obligated to pay for an undelivered product or service may be little consolation if an important project is delayed by an unfulfilled contract, particularly when the main purpose for entering into the contract was to ensure that the product or service would be delivered on time and in acceptable condition. If you find yourself in this situation, you may want to seek compensation from the offending party. How you go about doing this depends on what kind of compensation you are after and, in some instances, what sorts of potential remedies were written into the original contract.

When a key production contract is broken, the immediate goal of most media producers is to find a way to keep the project moving. With this in mind, they often will look for a way to "work something out" with the offending party by modifying the original contractual arrangement. For example, in the case of the missing animation sequence described earlier, you or your lawyer might contact the animation facility to work out a revised deal for delivering the sequence. The new deal might call for the facility to deliver the finished footage at a later date for reduced compensation. For instance, if the original contract specified that the animation facility would receive $10,000 for delivering the sequence by May 15, a revised arrangement might call for you to pay $9,000 if the facility delivers the finished goods by May 22. To obtain leverage as the new deal is negotiated, you or your lawyer also might drop some hints about taking the animation facility to court for breach of contract if the company fails to meet the revised delivery date. Finally, if the company still fails to deliver, you may ask your lawyer to initiate a lawsuit (or, if the contract requires, arbitration) against the company.

Of course, the last thing that most media professionals really want is to get caught up in an extended court battle over an unfulfilled contract. That is why many media production contracts contain a schedule of payments that calls for subcontractors to be paid in stages as they deliver sections or preliminary versions of a product or service. The partial-payment dates then serve as checkpoints that let the producer know how the subcontractor is progressing. Just as important, these intermediate dates also provide incentives to keep a subcontractor's attention focused on a particular project.

Remedies, Litigation, and Damages

Many media production contracts also include clauses that specify what forms of remedies and damages are available if a party defaults on its obligations. For example, if the contract calls for a film production company to receive a down payment on signing a contract, it might also require the company to return the payment and all interim payments if it fails to deliver the final product specified in the contract. Another remedy might give the producer the option to fix the final product at the subcontractor's expense when the product arrives if it does not meet the specifications detailed in the contract. In this case, the repair costs probably would be deducted from the payments due to the subcontractor.

If your efforts to settle a contract dispute out of court fail and the remedy language written into the contract does not provide for an adequate resolution, the next step may be to initiate formal proceedings against the offending party. As mentioned in Chapter 1, contracts can include a provision that requires disputes to be settled through arbitration. Unless the contract in question contains this provision, however, or unless both parties agree to arbitration, the only alternative may be litigation. In all but the smallest matters, this usually means having a lawyer conduct the case.

At this point, you should stop to ask yourself if litigation really is worth it. Is the amount of money that you potentially stand to recover worth all of the time, effort, and lawyers' fees that a lawsuit can involve? Or, are you acting out of a desire to "get back" at the other party? When "getting back" or "getting even" is your primary motivation, litigation is never really worth the time and money involved.

Keep in mind that, if you do decide to proceed with litigation, you will be the plaintiff in a civil action. As a result, the burden of proof will be on you and your lawyer. You must prove by a preponderance of the evidence that the defending party violated the terms of a legally binding contract, and you must show that you incurred losses as a result. You also must present evidence to refute any claims or counter-allegations that the defending party offers as a defense. For example, the defendant could claim that, for one or more of the reasons discussed earlier in this chapter, the contract in question was not a legally binding agreement. Or the defendant could show that its failure to fulfill its obligations was the result of an "act of God" or some other reason beyond its control.

Despite all of these considerations, breach of contract actions can be worth pursuing. In fact, if the contract was carefully drafted and the evidence is strong enough to convince a jury, the payoff can be substantial. At a minimum, the jury or judge (if the case was not tried by a jury) usually will award actual damages—compensation for losses that you can document. Typically, this means that you will receive any money that you paid to the party under the unfulfilled contract—minus, in some instances, the value of any products or services that were delivered in partial fulfillment of the contract. You might also recover consequential or special damages. These are damages that, although not directly tied to specific out-of-pocket expenses, were reasonably foreseeable when the parties entered into the contract. In addition, if you can prove that the breach of contract caused additional expenses on a production project, you could be awarded actual or incidental damages to cover those costs.

In evaluating whether to pursue a breach of contract action, it is important to consider what you are not likely to recover if you emerge as the prevailing party. First, in the United States, the prevailing party in contract cases generally is not entitled to recover its attorney fees. Second, unlike the plaintiffs in many tort actions, plaintiffs in contract cases may not as a rule seek punitive or "exemplary" damages, a money award that is intended to punish defendants whose conduct has been willful and malicious. Finally, courts generally are reluctant to order the specific performance of a contract. That is, in cases where damages will be sufficient to compensate a plaintiff for its losses, courts will not order a defendant to "perform" the contract by actually delivering the promised goods or services. A court may be willing to order specific performance, however, where the goods or services to be provided under the contract are unique or where the nonbreaching party will suffer irreparable harm if the goods and services are not delivered in accordance with the terms of the agreement.

Summary

- *What is a contract?* A contract is a binding agreement that establishes mutual obligations between two or more parties.
- *What are the key components of a contract?* The key components of a contract are the offer, the consideration, and the acceptance. If a contract is missing any of these elements, it may not be enforceable under the law.
- *What are the sources of contract law?* Contract law is not governed by a single, overriding federal statute. Instead, much contract law is based on common law and statutes enacted by individual states. All states except Louisiana have also adopted the Uniform Commercial Code (UCC), a standardized body of laws governing the sale of goods and various other commercial transactions.
- *What is the difference between an express contract and an implied contract?* An express contract is an agreement in which the terms are made explicit and clear at the time that the contract

is made and in which all parties are clearly aware that they are agreeing to those terms. An implied contract is a binding agreement that is not expressly stated but that is implied in the transaction between parties.

- *Must all contracts be placed in writing?* Contracts do not necessarily have to be placed in writing to be binding, although all media production contracts should be. Written contracts can help deter and resolve disputes because they provide tangible proof of the conditions and terms that the parties are obligated to honor. Under the UCC and statutes in many states, certain contracts must be placed in writing, including contracts for the sale of goods worth $500 or more.

- *When should a lawyer review contract matters?* No simple set of guidelines can determine when a lawyer's help is required to review or resolve contract matters. As a general rule, you should always seek a lawyer's advice (1) when you are drafting a standard contract that will be used as a model for various business contracts, (2) when you are being asked to sign a contract that contains terms that you do not fully understand or that commits you to a long-term obligation, or (3) whenever you feel uneasy or unsure about a contract matter. If you are working in a corporate setting, you should also inquire about your company's contract review policy.

- *What happens when a contract is broken?* Many contracts include remedies or damages clauses that describe the compensation due to the parties if one or more of the parties fails to live up to its obligations. In most cases, the parties will try to reach a quick settlement or compromise. If this fails, a breach-of-contract dispute may go to the courts.

Notes

1. Henry Campbell Black, *Black's Law Dictionary*, 5th ed. (St. Paul, MN: West Publishing Co., 1979), p. 291.

2. Despite this general rule, courts sometimes will conclude that a unilateral promise in fact is a binding obligation under the doctrine of "promissory estoppel." Under this doctrine, "a promise which the promisor should reasonably expect [would] induce action or

forbearance on the part of the promisee or a third person and which does induce such action or forbearance is binding if injustice can be avoided only by enforcement of the promise." Restatement (Second) of Contracts, Section 90. Applying this doctrine, a court could find, for example, that a producer's promise to give a particular post-production facility all of the producer's projects for six months is a binding obligation if the facility, in reasonable reliance on the producer's promise, foregoes the opportunity to take on other work during that period but the producer then decides to use some other facility. In this case, the postproduction facility could attempt to recover from the producer the profits that it lost in foregoing other work in reliance on the producer's promise or, alternatively, the profits that it would have made if the producer had kept his or her promise and given the work to the facility.

Getting It in Writing: Sample Media Production Contracts

Chapter 2 described the basic components of contracts, the fundamental principles of contract law, and several ways that you can use contracts to manage production relationships. In this chapter, you will see the general guidelines and principles introduced in Chapter 2 put to use in sample contracts that define five production relationships. The sample agreements are as follows:

- A crew contract that describes the role and responsibilities of a freelance camera operator hired for a production
- A writer's contract that defines the relationship between a production company and a freelance researcher and writer
- A facilities contract that establishes the terms of a rental agreement between a producer and a studio facility
- A project contract or "production agreement" that details an agreement between a production company and a client that has commissioned the company to produce a program
- An option/purchase agreement that secures a producer's right to pursue development of a media production based on an existing literary work

Of course, the samples do not cover all of the contracts that you might initiate or be asked to sign during the course of a production. Several other types of media production contracts—including guild and union agreements, music contracts, and distribution agreements—are discussed in Chapters 6, 7, and 8.

The sample contracts included here are intended to serve as examples that suggest the structure and scope of a typical production agreement. Because each media production is unique, you should not assume that the sample agreements can serve without considerable modification as the basis for your own production contracts. You also should not assume that you can simply pick and mix clauses from the sample agreements to create a contract that covers all of the requirements of a particular production. If you are not sure which terms and provisions apply to a particular production situation, be sure to consult an attorney.

Contracting for the Right Rights: Works-Made-for-Hire

When subcontractors supply materials and services for productions, producers must make sure that they receive all of the rights necessary to use those materials and services. For example, if you are a staff producer who has hired a freelance writer to prepare a script for a production that will be part of your company's sales training effort, you must make sure that your company will have the right to distribute the program based on the script within the company. You also may want to obtain the right to distribute the program based on the writer's script to other companies, to the general public, and perhaps even via cable television or some other distribution channel.

The place to guarantee these rights is in your contract with the individual or company that is supplying the goods or services. In most cases, the contract should include language stipulating that the subcontractor is transferring ownership of the materials to the producer or production company and foregoing the right to have any financial participation in future uses of the materials. This frees you from having to go back to the subcontractor and renegotiate for the right to reuse the materials or to distribute a production that incorporates the materials in a manner that you may not have anticipated originally. As discussed in Chapter 7, however, such a total buyout is not always possible when you are dealing with writers, performers, or technicians who are guild or union members. At a minimum, however, the contract must guarantee you the right to use the materials in the manner that you intend on this particular production.

In the past, some producers assumed that they automatically obtained full ownership and control of such materials because arrangements with subcontractors were considered work-made-for-hire relationships. But this assumption has been called into question by a 1989 U.S. Supreme Court ruling that took a close look at the work-made-for-hire provisions of the U.S. Copyright Act.[1] Briefly, Section 101 of the Copyright Act states that an employer or person who commissions a work that is subject to copyright protection is the copyright holder when the work is "prepared by an employee within the scope of his or her employment" or when the work is "specially ordered or commissioned for use as a contribution to a collective work (or) as part of a motion picture or other audiovisual work . . . if the parties expressly agree in a signed writing that the work is to be considered a work-made-for-hire."[2] In other words, you own the copyright on materials that are prepared by your employees as part of their jobs. You also own the copyright on materials developed by independent subcontractors for inclusion in an audiovisual production—as long as your written agreements with the subcontractors expressly state that they are producing the materials as works-made-for-hire.

The 1989 Supreme Court ruling concerned a case in which the group that was paying for the work—an advocacy group for the homeless that had commissioned a sculptor to create a depiction of a homeless family—did not have a contract that clearly defined who would own the completed work. The Supreme Court ruled that, in the absence of such an express agreement, the sculptor retained the copyright to the work.

For media producers, the implication is clear. All contracts with parties who will be providing materials for a production should state that those materials will be works-made-for-hire under all applicable copyright laws. In addition, as the sample contracts in this chapter show, it is advisable to go further and specify that, in the event that the materials are ever deemed not to be works-made-for-hire, the agreement constitutes an assignment of all ownership rights in the materials.

Media Production Contract Checklist

The media production contract checklist (Figure 3.1) can be used as a quick reference when you are reviewing or participating in drafting

Figure 3.1 Media production contract checklist.

Use the following checklist as a general guide when preparing or reviewing a media production contract. If you are not sure whether a provision listed in the checklist should be part of the agreement, consult an attorney. An attorney can also determine if your contract should contain other terms and conditions that are not included here.

1. *Does the contract include a clear and definite offer?* Does the contract describe, in detail, the goods or services that will be delivered under the agreement? Does the contract state when and where these materials must be delivered? Is it clear to whom the offer is being made? Is the offer transferable or assignable to another party?

2. *Does the contract specify, in detail, the consideration that the party or parties will receive for delivering the goods or services?* Exactly how and how much will the party or parties be paid for fulfilling the terms of the contract? Are the contracted services being performed for a flat fee, or will the consideration include royalty or residual payments? Will one component of the consideration be a credit for the contracting party in the final production credits?

3. *Does the contract specify how the parties will indicate their acceptance of the terms of the agreement?* Will the parties indicate their acceptance by signing the contract (the usual manner in which parties indicate their assent to the terms of a written agreement)? If so, who will sign? Must the parties accept the agreement by a specified date? Does the contract provide for execution by facsimile and in counterparts?

4. *Does the contract include delivery and payment schedules?* Will the products or services be delivered in stages? If so, when are the partial products (e.g., treatments, storyboards, rough cuts) due? Are payments tied to these delivery dates (usually a good idea), or will the contractor be paid in a single lump sum?

5. *Does the contract establish guidelines for reviewing and approving deliverables?* Who has the right to approve or reject the deliverables? Is this approval right absolute, or is it subject to a reasonableness requirement? Does the delivery schedule provide for approvals of partial products? Must the approvals be in writing? If the final product is rejected, who is responsible for fixing it? Who pays for fixing it?

6. *Does the contract indicate who will own the goods and services delivered under the agreement?* Is the contract being performed on a work-made-for-hire basis? Will the party that produces the deliverables retain some right of ownership in the finished productions? Who will retain the

Figure 3.1 Media production contract checklist. (continued)

right to use the deliverables in subsequent productions? Does the contract provide for reuse fees if the materials are used in a subsequent production?

7. *Does the contract include appropriate representation/warranty and indemnification provisions?* In media production agreements, representation/warranty clauses typically specify that the party who has agreed to deliver goods under the contract has all necessary rights to those materials, that those goods will not infringe on the rights of any third parties, and that no other contract or obligation would prevent the party from entering into and performing the agreement. Indemnification clauses stipulate that the party who has made these "reps and warranties" will be held responsible for any damages and legal fees resulting from lawsuits by third parties alleging facts that would constitute a breach of the reps and warranties. For example, a third party might sue a production company claiming that one of the company's productions contains special effects sequences that were developed and owned by that third party, rather than by the contractor who provided the sequences to the production company. If the production company's contract with the special effects contractor contains the reps and warranties and indemnification provisions indicated, the subcontractor ultimately would be held responsible for any damages and legal fees resulting from a lawsuit brought by the third party.

8. *Does the contract define the working relationships between the parties?* Will the work be performed on a guild or union basis? (See Chapter 7.) If the contracting party is performing the work as an independent contractor, does it agree to waive all rights to claims against the company for insurance, workers' compensation, and other benefits of employment?

9. *Does the contract offer the right of first refusal to perform similar work on related projects?* Will the party who is performing services under the contract be given the right of first refusal to perform similar work on related or derivative projects? If so, what are the terms and limitations of that right?

10. *Does the contract stipulate the circumstances under which the agreement can be terminated?* Under what conditions and circumstances can the contract be terminated? What violations or breaches of the agreement will give the nonbreaching party the right to terminate the agreement? How and when must the parties receive notification of the breach and/or termination? Must the breaching party be given the opportunity to correct or cure the breach before termination?

11. *Does the contract specify remedies if either or both parties breach terms of the agreement?* If the contract is terminated, or if terms of the agreement are breached, what remedies will be available to the parties?

Figure 3.1 Media production contract checklist. (continued)

Will the parties be required to return any payments that they have already received? Who will own the work that has already been completed? Will the parties receive partial compensation for this work? Can the production company repair materials that arrive in unacceptable condition and deduct the repair costs from any payments due to the contractor? Do the parties agree to submit all disputes to binding arbitration?

12. *Does the contract include appropriate boilerplate provisions?* Most contracts include (and usually conclude with) several standard or boilerplate provisions. For example, most media production agreements should include an "integration" clause stating that the agreement constitutes the entire understanding of the parties, a "jurisdiction/choice of law" clause stating which state's laws will apply to the agreement and where lawsuits based on the agreement can be brought (or an "arbitration" clause requiring that any disputes be submitted to binding arbitration), and an "assignment" clause specifying the conditions under which the parties can assign their rights under the agreement. These and other boilerplate provisions are included in the sample production agreements reviewed in this chapter.

a media production contract. As the checklist shows, you should always begin by making sure that the agreement includes a clear and definite offer, a thorough description of the consideration, and a way for the parties to indicate their acceptance. The checklist also lists various terms and provisions that should be part of most media production contracts, including provisions that define who will own the products or services delivered under the terms of the agreement. To see these terms and provisions at work in actual contracts, examine the sample agreements shown in Figures 3.2 through 3.6 in this chapter.

Of course, not every item on the checklist will be appropriate for all types of production contracts. When any of the criteria from the checklist is missing from a contract, however, you should always pause and ask why. If the answer is not clear, consult a lawyer.

Finally, be careful not to rely on this checklist as your sole means of evaluating a contract. Even when a contract meets all of the criteria specified in the checklist, it still may not be in your best business interest to offer or accept it. Be sure to read all of the terms of a contract carefully, and seek a lawyer's advice if something seems to be missing or out of place.

Sample Crew Contract

Figure 3.2 is a sample contract that defines the relationship between a production company and a camera operator. Although the contract is relatively brief, it does contain the three key components of a legally binding agreement discussed previously: offer, consideration, and acceptance.

The offer is presented in paragraph 1. That paragraph describes what the contractor's responsibilities will be, when and where she will discharge those responsibilities, and how long her services will be required.

Paragraph 2 defines the consideration that the contractor will receive. For fulfilling the terms of the offer, the contractor will be paid a flat fee of $1,200. The contractor is responsible for submitting an invoice for her work, and the company is obligated to pay her within 30 days of receiving the invoice. As paragraph 3 points out, however, the production company does retain the right to dismiss the contractor if her work proves unsatisfactory. If the production company exercises this right, it must pay only for the work that the contractor has performed up to the point of dismissal. Paragraph 4 also provides that the contractor will deliver her services on a nonunion basis and that, as an independent contractor, she will not be considered an employee of the producer for any purposes (e.g., taxes, benefits, workers' compensation).

Paragraphs 5 through 7 detail other conditions placed on the basic agreement defined in paragraphs 1 and 2. One particularly important condition appears in paragraph 5, where the contract establishes that all results of the camera operator's work and services on the project will be considered a "work-made-for-hire"—as that term is defined in the U.S. Copyright Act of 1976—and, should that ever be determined not to be the case, the camera operator assigns all ownership rights in her work on the project to the production company. Although a camera operator typically does not obtain a copyright interest in a production, including this clause in the contract precludes the camera operator from claiming that, through her work on the project, she has any copyright claim or any other right of ownership in the finished program.

Another condition appears in paragraph 7, where the contract states that the "agreement will be governed by the laws of the State of California" and that any disputes concerning the contract will be subject to the jurisdiction of courts in Los Angeles County, the "home

Figure 3.2 Sample crew contract.

November 7, 2002

The following, when signed by the parties below, will constitute a binding agreement between RoBo Productions, Inc., a California corporation (hereafter "RP"), and Catherine Mairead, a freelance video camera operator (hereafter "Contractor").

1. RP offers Contractor, and Contractor hereby accepts, a position as a video camera operator on "Infrequent Flier," a television commercial production. The Contractor's services will be required for three shooting days scheduled for November 20, 21, and 22. The Contractor will report to the RP offices at 167 Leland Avenue, Los Angeles, CA, at 8:30 a.m. on each of these days. Each shooting day will run from 8:30 a.m. to 5:30 p.m., with one hour off for lunch. Should the Contractor's services be required beyond 5:30 p.m., RP agrees to pay the Contractor $75 for each hour or part-hour of additional time.

2. As full and complete consideration for the work performed under this agreement, RP will pay the Contractor $1,200. Payment will be mailed to the Contractor within 30 days upon receipt of an invoice.

3. If RP determines that the Contractor's work is unsatisfactory, RP can terminate the contract and pay the contractor for work completed to that point, with payment calculated on a pro rota basis.

4. The Contractor acknowledges that this is a nonunion production. The Contractor represents and agrees that the Contractor's work on the production will not be subject to the terms of any guild or union agreement. The Contractor further acknowledges that, as an independent contractor, she will not be considered an employee of RP for any purpose (e.g., taxes, benefits, workers' compensation).

5. RP will own all right, title, and interest in and to the results and proceeds of the Contractor's services under this agreement. All such results and proceeds will be considered a "work-made-for-hire" as defined in the U.S. Copyright Act. If that is ever determined not to be the case, the Contractor hereby assigns all rights in such results and proceeds to RP.

6. This offer must be accepted by 5 p.m. on November 15, 2002. Should the Contractor not accept by that date, the offer will be withdrawn.

7. This agreement will be governed by the laws of the State of California, and disputes hereunder will be subject to the jurisdiction of courts

Figure 3.2 Sample crew contract. (continued)

located in the County of Los Angeles within that state. The parties hereby agree to submit to the jurisdiction of such courts.

To indicate acceptance of these terms and conditions, the Contractor should sign in the space indicated below. The Contractor should sign and return both copies to RP.

Very truly yours,

Robert Hanczor

President

ROBO PRODUCTIONS INC.

AGREED AND ACCEPTED:

_____

Catherine Mairead

_____

Dated

_____

Federal Tax Identification or Social Security Number

turf" of the production company. This choice of law and jurisdiction provision is especially significant when the parties to a contract reside in different states or countries, as the laws governing contracts can vary from one jurisdiction to the next, and it can be difficult and expensive to litigate in a distant jurisdiction. When you are entering into an agreement with a party from another state or country, it almost always is in your best interest to have the agreement governed by the laws and courts of your state. That way, if a contract dispute results, you will not be forced to travel to another state for any legal proceedings (including a possible trial) and to find a lawyer who is licensed to practice in that state.[3]

The contract ends by describing how the parties will indicate their acceptance of the agreement. In this case, as in most written contracts, the parties will accept the terms and conditions of the agreement by signing in the space provided at the end of the contract. As discussed in Chapter 2, parties increasingly are executing agreements by facsimile signature, although that option is not expressly provided for in this sample agreement.

Significantly, this crew contract is being offered to a nonunion camera operator for work on a nonunion production. If the work were to be performed on a union or guild basis, certain aspects of the basic relationship between the camera operator and the production company would be governed, instead, by the current union or guild agreement. These agreements are discussed in Chapter 7.

Sample Writer's Contract

Figure 3.3 is a contract in the form of a business letter that defines the relationship between a company that is producing a corporate video program and a freelance writer/researcher. In contrast to the camera operator hired under the previous contract, who was retained to deliver a relatively narrow service over a relatively short period, the writer/researcher in this contract is responsible for performing and producing a much wider range of services and materials over a longer period. That is the main reason why the writer's contract in Figure 3.3 is much more detailed than the camera operator's contract presented in Figure 3.2.

The offer is set forth in paragraphs 1 through 5 of Figure 3.3. Corporate Media Corporation, the hiring company, begins by dividing the writer's job into a series of tasks and responsibilities, each of which is listed in paragraph 1. In paragraphs 2 through 5, the company goes on to indicate who will evaluate and approve the materials that the writer submits, what those materials are and when they are due, and what responsibility the writer will have for revising the materials and meeting with the production staff.

In return for all of this work, the writer will receive the consideration described in paragraphs 6 through 9. The writer's total compensation will be $19,000. That fee will be paid in three installments, each of which is tied to the delivery of one of the materials that the writer is responsible for providing. As mentioned earlier in the chapter,

Figure 3.3 Sample writer's contract.

September 6, 2002

Ms. Maria Cortes
47 Palmetto St.
Atlanta, GA 30301

Dear Maria:

This letter, when signed by you in the space provided below, will constitute a binding agreement (the "Agreement") between you and Corporate Media Corporation (the "Company"), a corporation organized under the laws of the State of Georgia. The Company hereby engages your services as a writer on "Future Flight," a 30-minute video production (the "Production"), in accordance with the following terms and conditions:

1. You will be responsible for performing and/or delivering the following:

   (a) interviews and site visits
   (b) background research and preparation of a 20-page minimum, typed, double-spaced background report
   (c) attending research and script meetings
   (d) writing a detailed treatment based on your research materials
   (e) writing a script based on the treatment

The background report, treatment, and script are the "Materials" that you will be required to deliver under this Agreement.

2. You will coordinate your work with Ms. Karyn Mariano (the "Producer"). The Producer must evaluate and approve, in Producer's sole discretion, each of the Materials listed in paragraph 1.

3. The Term of this Agreement will commence on October 1, 2002, and continue until the later of January 31, 2003, or the date on which the last service or Materials required hereunder are performed and/or accepted.

4. The schedule for delivering the Materials is as follows:

MATERIALS	DUE TO PRODUCER
Background Report	November 4, 2002
Detailed Treatment	December 6, 2002
Finished Script	January 17, 2003

The last two weeks of the Term (January 14–31, 2003) will be reserved for making final changes and adjustments to the script. During this time, you

Figure 3.3 Sample writer's contract. (continued)

may also be asked to meet with the Producer and others to discuss production of the script.

5. Upon receiving each of the Materials listed in paragraphs 1 and 4, the Producer will have five working days to evaluate each item and to return it to you with comments. If the Producer requests revisions to any of the Materials, you will have five working days to make the changes and to return a revised copy.

6. As full and complete compensation for your services and for all the rights therein granted by you to the Company under this Agreement, the Company will pay you the total sum of $19,000. The total sum will be paid in three installments tied to the delivery and acceptance of the Materials as follows:

Delivery and Acceptance of Research Report:	$3,000
Delivery and Acceptance of Detailed Treatment:	$6,000
Delivery and Acceptance of Finished Script:	$10,000

Following delivery and acceptance, these payments will be made upon the Producer's receipt of an invoice for each payment.

7. If at any time the Company determines that your performance is unsatisfactory, the Company may terminate this Agreement and pay you only for work completed and expenses incurred at the time, plus a $1,000 termination fee. All Materials prepared by you as of the point of termination will be owned by the Company, as provided in paragraph 10.

8. The Company agrees to reimburse you for all reasonable expenses you incur during your work on the Production, provided that all expenses over $50 are approved, in advance, by the Producer. All expenses must be submitted to the Company with appropriate documentation, including receipts for and written descriptions of each expense. Expense reports and requests for reimbursing expenses to date should be submitted at each of the deliverable dates described in paragraph 4.

9. Provided that all of the Materials are accepted by the Company, you will receive screen credit as Researcher and Writer. The size and placement of this credit will be determined by the Company at its sole discretion. If the Company rejects any or all of the Materials, the Company will be under no obligation to provide you with screen credit, although it may do so at its own discretion. You also have the right to remove your name from the credits, provided that a written request to that effect is received by the Company on or before February 21, 2003.

Figure 3.3 Sample writer's contract. (continued)

10. You acknowledge and agree that the Materials and all other results and proceeds of your work and services hereunder have been specially ordered and commissioned by the Company as contributions to an audiovisual work and will be considered "works-made-for-hire" under all applicable copyright laws. In the event that the Materials and said results and proceeds or any portion thereof are ever determined not to be works-made-for-hire, you hereby irrevocably assign and convey to the Company all rights of ownership and intellectual property rights therein, including all so-called moral rights. You agree not to challenge the validity of the Company's ownership of the Materials and said results and proceeds.

11. The Company will have complete creative control of the Materials and the Production. The Company may, at any time and at its sole discretion, revise or rewrite any part or parts of the Materials.

12. You warrant and represent to the Company as follows:
    (a) The Materials (except for any portions thereof provided by the Company) are original with you and are not subject to any claim of authorship or ownership by any other party.
    (b) You have not made, authorized, or consented to and will not make, authorize, or consent to any commitment, agreement, obligation, grant, assignment, encumbrance, or other disposition of any rights in the Materials or otherwise perform any act that would conflict with any rights granted to the Company hereunder.
    (c) As of the date hereof, there are no adverse claims of which you are aware, and you know of no possible claims relating to the Materials.
    (d) You have the right and authority to enter into this Agreement and to assign the rights granted herein, and you have not authorized the exploitation of any rights in the Materials other than as set forth herein.
    (e) The exercise of the rights granted herein will not infringe on any rights of any third party, including but not limited to copyright, trademark, unfair competition, defamation, privacy, and publicity rights.
    (f) The Materials and your work under the Agreement will not be subject to the terms and conditions of any guild or union contract.

13. You agree to indemnify to the Company at all times and hold it harmless from and against any and all claims, damages, liabilities, costs, and expenses, including but not limited to legal expenses and reasonable counsel fees, arising out of (i) the use by the Company of the Materials and all results and proceeds of your services under this Agreement, or (ii) any

Figure 3.3 Sample writer's contract. (continued)

third-party claim or allegation that, if proved, would constitute a breach of any representation, warranty, or covenant made by you in this Agreement. In the event that the Company receives notice of any claim involving the foregoing indemnification, the Company shall promptly notify you thereof. You will promptly adjust, settle, defend, or otherwise dispose of such claim at your sole cost. If you have been so notified and you do not diligently pursue such matter, the Company may take such action on its own behalf to adjust, settle, defend, or otherwise dispose of such claim. In this event, you shall, upon being billed therefor, reimburse the Company in the amount thereof.

14. You will regard all the ideas, concepts, information, and market data divulged to you by the Company or its clients to be strictly confidential during the term of this Agreement and thereafter. You shall not reveal to any third party or use any such ideas, concepts, information, and data without the Company's express written permission.

15. The Company may use and authorize others to use your name, likeness, and biographical information to publicize the production; however, no direct endorsement by you of any product or service shall be made or implied without your written consent.

16. You are being engaged as an independent contractor. As such, you shall make no claims against the Company for insurance, workers' compensation, or any other employee benefits offered by the Company. You also acknowledge that you will be solely responsible for all taxes, fees, and assessments due with respect to your compensation hereunder.

17. This document contains the entire understanding between you and the Company and supersedes all prior or contemporaneous agreements and understandings, written or oral, concerning the subject matter hereof. No amendment, waiver, consent, variation, or modification shall be made to this Agreement unless it is set forth in a document signed by the Company and you.

18. The provisions set forth in the following paragraphs will survive any termination of this Agreement: 10, 11, 12, 13, 14, 18, 19, and 20.

19. Should any dispute arise between you and the Company, you and the Company agree that, at either's request, the dispute will be submitted to binding arbitration in Atlanta, Georgia, under the commercial arbitration rules of the American Arbitration Association.

20. This Agreement shall be governed by the laws of the State of Georgia as applied to contracts executed and intended to be fully performed within that state. Any dispute hereunder that is not submitted to binding

Figure 3.3 Sample writer's contract. (continued)

arbitration shall be subject to the sole jurisdiction of courts of competent jurisdiction in Atlanta, Georgia.

21. This Agreement is freely assignable by the Company, but may not be assigned by you without the express written consent of the Company, which consent may be withheld by Company in its sole discretion. This Agreement may be executed by facsimile signature and in counterparts.

If you agree with the foregoing terms and conditions, please indicate your acceptance by signing in the space below and returning the signed Agreement to the Company by September 23, 2002. If you do not return the signed Agreement by that date, this offer will be deemed withdrawn.

Very truly yours,

_____

By _____
For Corporate Media
Corporation, Inc.

AGREED AND ACCEPTED:

By _____
Maria Cortes

_____

Date

_____

Federal Tax Identification or Social Security Number

this sort of installment plan generally is recommended in contracts of this type because it provides the hiring party with a series of checkpoints that can be used to assess the contractor's progress and performance.

Paragraph 7 establishes a way for the hiring company to terminate the contract if the writer's work proves inadequate. If the company does cancel the contract, it must pay the writer for all work performed and expenses incurred up to that time, plus a termination fee of $1,000. This paragraph also states that any materials completed at the point of the termination will be owned by the production company.

As part of the consideration, the writer will also receive the screen credit described in paragraph 9, provided that her work on the project proves satisfactory. Screen credits can be a very important consideration, particularly for young writers or performers who are trying to establish a reputation and build a portfolio of their work. As shown here, however, it usually is in the production company's best interest to state that the size and placement of the credit will be determined by the company in its sole discretion. As discussed in Chapter 7, if the writer is a guild member and the program is being produced on a guild basis, certain aspects of the phrasing and placement of the writer's credits (as well as the minimum compensation payable to the writer) would be governed by the terms of the guild agreement.

Paragraphs 10[4] through 14 place several conditions on the writer's work. First, paragraph 10 states that, by accepting the terms of the agreement, the writer will be agreeing to provide her services on a work-made-for-hire basis. This means that Corporate Media Corporation, the hiring company, will own the copyright to the materials that the writer will deliver under the contract and that it will be considered the "author" of those materials under U.S. copyright law. As a safety measure, paragraph 10 also provides that, if it is ever determined that the materials are not a work-made-for-hire, the agreement constitutes an assignment of the writer's ownership rights in the materials to the company. In addition, paragraph 11 states that the company will retain complete creative control over the materials and may revise or edit them in any way.

Most contracts that involve the delivery of creative materials require contractors to warrant that they actually own the materials that they are being paid to deliver. As paragraphs 12 and 13 show, this sample writer's contract is no exception. Along with guaranteeing that the work is entirely her own in paragraph 12, the writer accepts full responsibility for—or indemnifies the hiring company against—any legal action or judgment that may result from disputes over ownership of the materials. The writer also represents and warrants that she has the authority to enter into the agreement and that neither the materials that she provides nor her work under the agreement will be subject to the provisions of any guild agreement.

Note that the representation and warranty provisions in paragraph 12 and the related indemnification provisions are being made unilaterally on the writer's part. That is, no comparable provisions are being made by the production company. This is not unusual in a contract of this type, given that the writer will be delivering goods and services under the agreement and that most of this language pertains to ownership and other rights in those goods and services. Depending on the situation, however, some production agreements may contain parallel representation, warranty, and indemnification provisions made on behalf of all contracting parties. This is the case, for example, in the sample production agreement included later as Figure 3.5.

In paragraph 14, the writer is agreeing not to disclose any confidential information and market data that she receives through her work under the contract. This sort of confidentiality clause is common in contracts that cover corporate media projects because such projects often result in the disclosure of sensitive information about new products, services, and technology to those involved in production of the project.

Paragraph 19 stipulates that any disputes arising out of the agreement will be submitted to binding arbitration at the request of either the writer or the company. As mentioned in Chapter 1, with the costs of courtroom litigation continuing to rise, arbitration has become an increasingly attractive alternative for resolving contract disputes.

Paragraph 21 provides that the agreement may be freely assigned by the production company, but that any assignment by the writer must be approved in writing by the company. Although such an unbalanced assignment provision might seem unfair on its face, it actually is fairly typical in production agreements. For its part, the production company is entering into a contract with this particular writer based on her experience and skills, and the company needs to be assured that she will not simply assign her rights and responsibilities under the agreement to a person with lesser skills or experience. The production company also needs the right to assign the agreement in the event that the company or the company's rights in the production are sold or transferred.

For her part, the writer is probably not overly concerned about the production company assigning the contract to another party, as long as that party agrees to honor the company's obligations under the agreement (particularly the obligation to pay her the amounts specified in the agreement). To this end, some assignment provisions (including the assignment provision in Figure 3.5) condition any right to assign the agreement on the potential assignee agreeing to accept fully the assigning party's obligations under the agreement.

The contract closes by describing how the parties will indicate their acceptance of the agreement. As in the sample crew contract in Figure 3.2, this contract requires the writer to return the signed agreement by the date specified or the offer will be withdrawn. In addition, this agreement expressly provides for execution by facsimile signature and in counterparts, an increasingly popular provision that was discussed in Chapter 2.

Sample Facilities Rental Contract

Figure 3.4 is a facilities rental contract between Mag Media Corporation, a video production company, and Lakeshore Studios, a television production facility. Like most well-constructed and balanced agreements, this contract benefits both parties. For Mag Media, the agreement guarantees that the equipment, crew, and studio space it needs will be available at the designated time and for the specified price. For Lakeshore Studios, the agreement provides written proof of the crew, facilities, and services that the production company has hired and the price that it has agreed to pay.

Sample Project Contract

Figure 3.5 is a project contract or "production agreement" between Bayside Distributors, a video distribution company that has commissioned a 30-minute exercise program, and Meyer Video, the production company that has agreed to produce the program.

In this type of agreement, it is especially important to spell out who will own the completed program and whether the production company will retain a royalty or other "contingent compensation" interest in the project. The sample contract indicates that the idea for this particular project originated with Bayside Distributors and that Bayside is paying Meyer Video to produce the program on a work-made-for-hire basis. Under this arrangement, Bayside will keep all rights of ownership to the program, including the right to register copyright in the production under its name. As part of the deal, however, Bayside has agreed in paragraph 4.3 to pay Meyer royalties on a

Figure 3.4 Sample facilities rental contract.

January 11, 2003

The terms described below will define the binding agreement (the "Agreement") between Mag Media Corporation (the "Company"), an Illinois corporation, and Lakeshore Studios, Inc. ("Lakeshore"), an Illinois corporation. The Company and Lakeshore agree as follows:

1. The Company hereby hires Lakeshore's Studio 2 for three working days commencing February 10, 2003, and ending February 12, 2003.

2. Included in this Agreement are Studio 2 and its facilities and the following additional equipment: 4 lavalier microphones, 1 video recorder and monitor, and supplemental studio lights as required.

3. Also included in this Agreement are the following crew to be provided by Lakeshore: lighting director, 2 camera operators, video engineer, tape operator, audio engineer, gaffer/grip, and studio manager. All payment obligations to these crew members will be the responsibility of Lakeshore.

4. The length of each shooting day will be 9 hours (1 hour setup, 1 hour lunch, and 7 hours shooting). The first half of the day on February 10 will be devoted to assembling the set and setting up and testing lighting, sound, and video. Principal photography will begin after lunch on February 10 and continue through February 12. The last two hours of the shooting day on February 12 will be devoted to striking the set.

5. As total compensation for the facilities, services, and crew described above, the Company agrees to pay Lakeshore $12,575.

6. February 13 will be reserved as a bumper day. If the Company requires the studio on February 13, an extra charge of $4,250 will apply.

7. The Company will supply its own videotape stock. The Company understands that, should bulbs burn out in the studio lights during the shooting days, it will be assessed the replacement fee listed on Lakeshore's standard rate card.

8. This Agreement can be terminated by the Company without penalty through written notice received by Lakeshore on or before 5 p.m. on January 24, 2003. If termination occurs after that date, Lakeshore reserves the right to assess the Company a single cancellation fee of $4,250.

9. At all times, Lakeshore will be responsible for providing reasonable security and reasonable care for the studio, storage areas, and any other areas where the Company's personnel or property may at any or all times be located.

Figure 3.4 Sample facilities rental contract. (continued)

10. Lakeshore will maintain workers' compensation, fire, theft, and comprehensive general personal and property liability insurance (under which the Company is named as an additional insured) in a form and in reasonable amounts satisfactory to the Company. Such insurance will cover the personnel and property of the Company on Lakeshore's premises as well as all personnel provided by Lakeshore.

11. In the event that the equipment provided by Lakeshore fails to operate properly and that this equipment failure causes a delay in production, or delays in production occur due to the actions or inactions of Lakeshore personnel, then the Company may at its option: (a) extend the term of this Agreement by the amount of time equal to the time lost due to the delays at no additional cost to the Company or (b) continue production activities into overtime, provided that the amount of overtime shall not exceed the amount of time lost due to the delays, and provided that such overtime will be at no additional cost to the Company for services provided by Lakeshore.

12. The terms and conditions set forth above comprise the entire agreement between the Company and Lakeshore. No amendment, waiver, variation, or modification may be made to this Agreement unless set forth in a written document signed by both the Company and Lakeshore.

13. This Agreement will be subject to the jurisdiction of the courts and governed by the laws of the State of Illinois as applied to contracts executed and intended to be fully performed within that state. The parties hereby agree to submit any dispute arising under this Agreement to the exclusive jurisdiction of courts located in Chicago, Illinois.

If you are in accordance with the foregoing, please indicate your acceptance by signing in the space indicated below and returning the signed Agreement to the Company.

AGREED AND ACCEPTED:

_____   _____
For Mag Media Corporation: For Lakeshore Studios:

_____   _____
Name   Name

_____   _____
Title   Title

Figure 3.5 Sample production agreement.

Agreement made this 16th day of June, 2003, by and between BAYSIDE DISTRIBUTORS CORP., a Massachusetts corporation with its principal offices located at 343 Hastings Street, Boston, Massachusetts 02140 (hereafter "Bayside"), and MEYER VIDEO PRODUCTIONS, INC., a Massachusetts corporation with its principal offices located at 1186 Newton Boulevard, Boston, Massachusetts 02151 (hereafter "Meyer").

WHEREAS Bayside has a concept and treatment for the production of one thirty (30)-minute video program tentatively titled "The Executive Exercise Workout" (the "Project"); and

WHEREAS Bayside desires to engage Meyer to produce and deliver the Project, pursuant to the terms and conditions set forth herein; and

WHEREAS Meyer is in the business of producing video programs and desires to be engaged by Bayside to produce the Project.

NOW, THEREFORE, the parties agree as follows:

1. *Description of the Project:* Meyer will produce the Project on Bayside's behalf. The Project will be marketed as a videocassette and DVD through video retailers and direct-mail solicitations. The Project will be based on a treatment supplied by Bayside. Bayside will also provide the on-camera talent for the Project and an opening logo. All other personnel, planning, and production materials (including scripts, storyboards, and music) will be created or supplied by Meyer. The materials to be created and supplied by Meyer, including the deliverables set forth in paragraph 2 (other than any components of those deliverables provided by Bayside), are hereinafter referred to as the "Project Materials."

The Project will be suitable for broadcast use and for reproduction and distribution on videocassettes and DVDs.

The Project will feature opening and background music created or acquired and supplied by Meyer.

2. *Project Schedule and Delivery Dates:*
PHASE 1 Deliverable(s): Rough storyboards and rough script based on the treatment supplied by Bayside. Delivery Date: August 18, 2003.

PHASE 2 Deliverable(s): Final storyboards and shooting script. Delivery Date: September 15, 2003.

PHASE 3 Deliverable(s): Offline edited workprint of the Project, including music. Delivery Date: October 20, 2003.

Figure 3.5 Sample production agreement. (continued)

PHASE 4 Deliverable(s): Final edited program, including all music, titles, and credits. Delivery date: November 21, 2003. Once Meyer receives Bayside's written approval of the final edited program delivered in Phase 4, Meyer will have two days from that date to deliver to Bayside's offices three (3) copies of the finished master tape and three (3) copies of the master tape.

Meyer acknowledges that time is of the essence in the performance of its duties under this Agreement. Meyer will use its best efforts to conform to this schedule and any revisions to the schedule, as approved in writing by Bayside.

3. *Approvals:* Once Bayside receives the Project Materials described in paragraph 2, Bayside will use reasonable efforts to review the Project Materials promptly and either:

3.1. Approve the Project Materials, thereby enabling Meyer to proceed to the next scheduled phase.

3.2. Request in writing specific changes and corrections that will permit the Project to proceed to the next scheduled phase once Meyer has made the requested changes and corrections.

3.3. Reject the Project Materials and terminate this Agreement.

All approvals related to the Project Materials delivered in the various phases will be made in a writing addressed to the Project producer to be designated by Meyer at Meyer's offices.

If Meyer does not receive a response from Bayside within 10 working days of Bayside's receipt of the Project Materials, the Project Materials will be deemed approved.

Bayside shall be the sole judge as to whether the Project Materials are satisfactory, and Bayside shall have the sole and exclusive right to reject the Project Materials and terminate this Agreement; however, if Bayside exercises the option described in this paragraph 3.3 and terminates the Project, or if Bayside terminates the Project for any reason other than material breach of contract, Meyer is entitled to a $20,000 fee plus reimbursement of all expenses related to the Project that have been incurred or committed at the date of termination.

If Bayside wishes to make changes to the Project Materials completed in a particular phase after Bayside has approved the Project Materials, such changes will be made at Bayside's sole expense. Meyer will provide cost projections for such changes.

Figure 3.5 Sample production agreement. (continued)

4. Consideration:

4.1. For producing the Project and delivering the Project Materials described in paragraphs 1 and 2 of this Agreement, Bayside will pay Meyer the total sum of $73,000. The payment schedule is as follows:

DATE OR ACTION	PAYMENT
Signing of this Agreement	$13,000
Delivery and approval of Phase 2 Project Materials	$15,000
Delivery and approval of Phase 3 Project Materials	$20,000
Delivery and approval of Phase 4 Project Materials	$25,000

Meyer will submit an invoice to Bayside for each payment, and Bayside will issue payment within ten (10) working days of its receipt of each invoice. None of these payments is refundable in whole or in part.

4.2. Any payments for additional work performed on the Project at the request of Bayside will be paid in a single, lump sum due upon the completion and delivery of such work.

4.3. Meyer will be entitled to contingent compensation for the Project based on the following schedule:

First 1,000 units	0% of Gross Receipts
Second 1,000 units	5% of Gross Receipts
All sales after 2,000 units	8% of Gross Receipts

"Gross Receipts" is defined as all revenue actually received by Bayside from distribution and exhibition of the Project, less returns and other adjustments as provided below.

Bayside will provide Meyer with quarterly statements showing, in summary form, the appropriate calculations under this Agreement. These statements and royalty payments due, if any, will be issued on April 30, July 31, October 31, and January 31 for each preceding calendar quarter. The statements rendered by Bayside may be changed from time to time to reflect year-end adjustments made by Bayside's accounting department, returned merchandise, or corrections to errors. If Bayside shall extend credit to any party with respect to distribution of the Project, and if such credit has been included in the Gross Receipts, and if, in the opinion of Bayside, any such indebtedness shall be uncollectible, the uncollected amount may be deducted in any subsequent earnings statement. If Bayside makes any overpayment to Meyer for any reason, Bayside shall have the right to deduct and to retain for its own account an amount equal to such

Figure 3.5 Sample production agreement. (continued)

overpayment from any sums that may thereafter become due or payable to Meyer, or Bayside may demand repayment from Meyer, in which event Meyer shall repay the same when such demand is made.

All amounts payable to Meyer hereunder shall be subject to all laws and regulations now or hereafter in existence requiring deductions or withholdings for income or other taxes payable by or assessable against Meyer. Bayside shall have the right to make such deductions and withholdings and the payment thereof to the appropriate government agency in accordance with its interpretation in good faith of such laws and regulations; however, Bayside shall not be liable to Meyer for making such deductions or withholdings or the payment thereof to the appropriate government agency.

Bayside shall keep books of account relating to the distribution of the Project, together with vouchers, exhibition contracts, and similar records supporting the same (all of which are hereinafter referred to as "records"). To verify earning statements rendered hereunder, Meyer may, at its own expense, audit the applicable records at the place where Bayside maintains the records. Any such audit shall be conducted only by a public accountant during reasonable business hours and in such a manner as not to interfere with Meyer's normal business activities. In no event shall an audit with respect to any earnings statement commence later than 24 months from the rendition of the earnings statement involved; nor shall any audit continue for longer than 30 consecutive business days; nor shall such audits be made more frequently than once annually; nor shall the records supporting any earnings statement be audited more than once. All earnings statements rendered hereunder shall be binding upon Meyer and not subject to objection for any reason unless such objection is made in writing, stating the basis thereof and delivered to Bayside within 24 months from the rendition of the earnings statement, or if an audit is commenced prior thereto, within 30 days of completion of the audit. Meyer's right to examine Bayside's records is limited to the Project, and Meyer shall have no right to examine records related to Bayside's business generally or with respect to any other project for purposes of comparison or otherwise.

4.4. If at any time, for any reason, Bayside decides to discontinue promoting or distributing the Project, Bayside shall be responsible only for that compensation earned to date based on the above payment and royalty schedules. Meyer is not entitled to any of the anticipated royalty or licensing revenue had the Project been promoted further.

5. *Ownership of Project Materials and Copyright:* Bayside will be the sole owner of the Project Materials and all other results and proceeds of Meyer's

Figure 3.5 Sample production agreement. (continued)

work and services under this Agreement (the Project Materials and said results and proceeds are hereinafter referred to as "the Work"). Meyer acknowledges and agrees that the Work is being specially ordered by Bayside for inclusion in an audiovisual work and shall constitute a "work made for hire" for Bayside under all relevant copyright laws. If, for any reason, the Work or any element thereof shall be deemed not to be a work made for hire for Bayside, Meyer hereby agrees that this Agreement shall constitute an irrevocable, perpetual assignment to Bayside and its successors and assigns of any and all of Meyer's right, title, and interest in and to the Work, including but not limited to any and all worldwide copyrights and renewals, extensions, and restorations thereof. In addition to its rights under all relevant copyright laws, Meyer hereby transfers, conveys, and assigns to Bayside and its successors and assigns all other intellectual property rights in and to all elements of the Work throughout the world and in any language, including but not limited to all trademark rights. Meyer hereby waives any so-called droit moral rights, moral rights of authors, and all other similar rights in connection with the Work however denominated throughout the world. Meyer will, upon Bayside's request, execute, acknowledge, deliver, and/or record such additional documents as Bayside may deem necessary to evidence and effectuate Bayside's rights hereunder. Meyer hereby grants Bayside the right, as Meyer's attorney-in-fact, to execute, acknowledge, deliver, and record in the U.S. Copyright Office or elsewhere any and all such documents that Meyer fails to execute, acknowledge, deliver, and record.

Without limiting the foregoing, Meyer acknowledges and agrees that, as between Meyer and Bayside, Bayside will be the sole and exclusive owner of all copyright, title, and interest in the Project and all components thereof and that Bayside will have the right to secure and renew copyright in its name for the Project, for any related versions and/or sequels, and for all components thereof.

Meyer agrees that it shall not engage the services of any third party to provide services or materials in connection with the Project unless, before commencing or providing such services or materials, such third party executes a "work-made-for-hire" agreement substantially in the form of Exhibit A attached hereto.

6. *Meyer's Representations and Warranties:* Meyer represents and warrants that the Project Materials will not violate any law or infringe on or violate the intellectual property, privacy, publicity, or other rights of any person or entity.

Figure 3.5 Sample production agreement. (continued)

In the event that Meyer incorporates into the Project Materials any materials that are protected by copyright, Meyer will notify Bayside of such materials, and will present for approval to Bayside and its counsel releases, permissions, or other evidence of right to use the protected materials.

Meyer further represents, warrants, and covenants that it has all necessary rights and power to enter into and fully perform this Agreement and that the Project Materials will be free of any liens, claims, or encumbrances whatsoever in favor of any other party, and that the Project Materials, and all elements thereof, will be Meyer's own and original creation, except for matter in the public domain, copyrighted matter identified to Bayside as provided above, or matter provided to Meyer by Bayside.

Meyer also warrants that it will comply with all laws, rules, and regulations applicable to the production of the Project Materials and the Project and the employment of individuals therefor, including, but not limited to, employment and immigration laws.

7. *Indemnification:* Meyer agrees to indemnify Bayside at all times and hold it harmless from and against any and all claims, damages, liabilities, judgments, costs, and expenses, including legal expenses and reasonable counsel fees arising out of (i) the use by Bayside of any material produced by Meyer under this Agreement or (ii) any breach by Meyer of any representation, warranty, or covenant made by Meyer in this Agreement. In the event that Bayside receives notice of any claim or service of process involving the foregoing indemnification, Bayside shall promptly notify Meyer thereof. Meyer will promptly adjust, settle, defend or otherwise dispose of such claim at Meyer's sole cost. If Meyer has been so notified and in Bayside's reasonable judgment does not diligently pursue such matter, Bayside may take such action on its own behalf to adjust, settle, defend, or otherwise dispose of such claim. In this event, Meyer shall, upon being billed therefor, reimburse Bayside in the amount thereof.

Bayside agrees to indemnify Meyer at all times and hold it harmless from and against any and all claims, damages, liabilities, judgments, costs, and expenses, including legal expenses and reasonable counsel fees arising out of the use by Meyer of any materials provided to Meyer by Bayside. In the event that Meyer receives notice of any claim or service of process involving the foregoing indemnification, Meyer shall promptly notify Bayside thereof. Bayside will promptly adjust, settle, defend, or otherwise dispose of such claim at Bayside's sole cost. If Bayside has been so notified and does not diligently pursue such matter, Meyer may take such action on its own behalf to adjust, settle, defend, or otherwise dispose of such claim. In this

Figure 3.5 Sample production agreement. (continued)

event, Bayside shall, upon being billed therefor, reimburse Meyer in the amount thereof.

8. *Credits:* Provided that Meyer performs its obligations under and is not in material breach of this Agreement, Bayside agrees that the published work shall, in an appropriate place and in a separate frame, display the words:

> Produced by Meyer Video Productions
> Boston, Massachusetts

Bayside further agrees that these words will also be displayed in all print and television advertising, if any, for the Project in which Bayside is credited; however, Bayside's inadvertent failure to include Meyer's credit in advertising shall not constitute a material breach of this Agreement.

Bayside also agrees that, upon receipt of a written request from Meyer, it will use diligent efforts to remove Meyer's credit from all newly manufactured copies of the published work and all new advertising for the work.

9. *No Obligation to Distribute:* Nothing in this Agreement shall be deemed to obligate Bayside to publish, distribute, or exhibit the Project. The decision to publish, distribute, or exhibit the Project shall be in the sole discretion of Bayside.

10. *Independent Contractor Status:* Meyer shall provide all work and services hereunder as an independent contractor. Meyer shall have the entire responsibility as an independent contractor to discharge all of its obligations under any federal, state, or local laws, regulations, or orders now or hereafter in force, including, without limitation, those relating to taxes, unemployment compensation or insurance, social security, workers' compensation, disability benefits, tax withholding, and employment of minors, and including the filing of all returns and reports required of independent contractors, and the payment of all taxes, assessments, contributions, and other sums required of them.

Nothing in this Agreement shall be construed as making Bayside and Meyer partners, principal and agent, or joint venturers, or making either entity an employee of the other.

11. *Right of First Negotiation and Last Refusal:* Provided that Meyer performs its obligations under and is not in material breach of this Agreement, Meyer will retain a Right of First Negotiation and Last Refusal to serve as producer of any sequel to the Project. Bayside and Meyer will first negotiate in good faith with respect to such sequel. If the parties are

Figure 3.5 Sample production agreement. (continued)

unable to reach an agreement within fifteen (15) business days, Bayside will be free to negotiate with a third party with respect thereto; provided, however, that before entering into any such third-party agreement, Bayside will notify Meyer in writing of the terms of any such agreement. Meyer will have ten (10) business days from receipt of such notice to accept the engagement on the terms set forth in said agreement. If Meyer fails to so accept such engagement, Bayside will be free to enter into the third-party agreement free of any lien or claim by Meyer, but only on the terms as set forth in the notice to Meyer.

12. *Insurance:* Upon execution of this Agreement, Meyer shall promptly secure a policy of the type generally called "producer's errors and omissions insurance" applicable to the production of the Project. Such policy shall have a limit of at least $1 million per occurrence with respect to each loss or claim involving the same act or failure to act. Such policy shall (i) be secured at Meyer's own expense, (ii) name Bayside as an additional insured, (iii) include a provision requiring the insurance company to notify Bayside of any material diminution or cancellation thereof, and (iv) be deemed primary insurance covering any claims arising at any time (whether prior to or after the delivery of the final Project Materials) in connection with the production of the Project. Before proceeding with production, Meyer shall promptly furnish to Bayside a certificate attesting to such insurance and describing its terms and limits.

13. *Force Majeure:* If Meyer or Bayside fails to perform any obligation hereunder because of unavailability of services or materials, labor disputes, governmental restrictions, or any other circumstances beyond their control, such failure shall not be deemed a breach of this Agreement, and if any time period for performance is specified, such period shall be deemed extended accordingly.

14. *Termination:* This Agreement may be terminated by Bayside as expressly provided in paragraph 3 and by either party in the event of a material breach by the other, provided that such breach has not been cured within thirty (30) days of written notice thereof to the breaching party. The Ownership, Insurance, Representation and Warranty, and Indemnification provisions of this Agreement will survive termination.

15. *Miscellaneous Provisions:*
15.1. *Applicable Law:* This Agreement will be subject to and construed in accordance with the laws of the Commonwealth of Massachusetts applicable to agreements made and to be entirely performed therein without regard to that jurisdiction's choice of law provisions. The parties hereby agree that any claim or dispute arising from this Agreement shall

Figure 3.5 Sample production agreement. (continued)

be subject and submitted to the exclusive jurisdiction of courts of competent jurisdiction located in Boston, Massachusetts.

15.2. *Modification, Amendments, or Waiver:* No modifications or amendments to this Agreement shall be made, or no waiver of the terms and conditions of this Agreement shall be effected, except as may be mutually agreed upon in writing by both Meyer and Bayside.

15.3. *Successors and Assigns:* Meyer may not assign this Agreement or its rights hereunder, or delegate its obligations hereunder, in whole or in part, without the advanced written consent of Bayside. Bayside may assign this Agreement or any or all of its rights hereunder to any person or entity and will be relieved of all its obligations to Meyer hereunder to the extent that such obligations are assumed in writing by any such assignee.

15.4. *No Injunctive Relief:* In the event of a breach of this Agreement, the nonbreaching party's remedy shall be limited to an action at law for damages, if any. Under no circumstances will any party be entitled to injunctive or other equitable relief to enjoin or otherwise restrict production or distribution of the Project.

15.5. *Entire Understanding:* This Agreement, together with all exhibits attached hereto, is intended by the parties to be the final, complete, and exclusive expression of their agreement and understanding and supersedes all prior and contemporaneous contracts, representations, and understandings (written or oral) between the parties concerning the subject matter hereof.

15.6. *Severability:* In the event that any provision of this Agreement shall be deemed invalid, unreasonable, or unenforceable by any court of competent jurisdiction, such provision shall be stricken from the Agreement or modified to render it reasonable, and the remaining provisions of this Agreement or the modified provision as provided above, shall continue in full force and effect and be binding on the parties so long as such remaining or modified provisions reflect the intent of the parties at the date of this Agreement.

15.7. *Notices:* Any and all notices and written approvals required to be given under this Agreement shall be deemed to be made if they are mailed postage prepaid by certified mail, return receipt requested, to the party at the respective address set forth above, or at such address as may from time to time be designated by the party as a change of address. Any notice period shall begin running as of the date provided on the return receipt.

Figure 3.5 Sample production agreement. (continued)

15.8. *Paragraph Headings:* The paragraph headings used in this Agreement are for convenience only and shall not be deemed to be a binding portion of the Agreement.

15.9. *Facsimile Signatures, Counterparts:* This Agreement may be executed by original or facsimile signature and in counterparts, each of which when so executed shall be deemed an original, and all of which taken together shall constitute one and the same document.

IN WITNESS WHEREOF, the parties hereto have executed this Agreement as of the day and year first above written.

BAYSIDE DISTRIBUTORS CORP.

_____

Donald E. Sweeney
Its President

MEYER VIDEO PRODUCTIONS, INC.

_____

Cheryl S. Meyer
Its President

Figure 3.5 Sample production agreement. (continued)

EXHIBIT A
WORK-MADE-FOR-HIRE AGREEMENT

This Agreement ("Agreement") is made and entered into as of _____,
20 ___, by and between [NAME OF THIRD PARTY CONTRACTOR]
("you") and Bayside Distributors Corp. ("Bayside") with respect to your
engagement by and under the supervision of Meyer Video Productions, Inc.
("Meyer") to render services in connection with a video production
tentatively titled "The Executive Exercise Workout" and any projects related
thereto and/or derivative thereof (collectively, the "Project"). In
consideration of the terms and conditions set forth below, Bayside and you
agree as follows:

1. You will provide the following services and/or products in connection
with the Project:

[DESCRIBE SERVICES AND PRODUCTS.]

Any and all results, products, and proceeds of your services in connection
with the Project, including but not limited to any and all of the foregoing,
are hereinafter referred to as "the Work." The Work shall be provided by
you in accordance with the instructions of Bayside, shall be subject to the
approval of Meyer and Bayside exercisable in their sole discretion, and
shall not contain any obscene or inappropriate materials.

2. As full compensation for your services, the Work, and any and all rights
granted or assigned to Bayside by you under this Agreement, Bayside, or
Meyer on Bayside's behalf will pay you [AMOUNT TO BE PAID] as follows:
[SCHEDULE OF PAYMENTS]

You acknowledge that payment to you by Bayside or by Meyer on
Bayside's behalf pursuant to this paragraph 2 will constitute full and
complete satisfaction of any and all payment obligations under this
Agreement.

3. You acknowledge and agree that the Work is being specially ordered by
Bayside as a contribution to an audiovisual work and shall constitute a
"work-made-for-hire" for Bayside under all relevant copyright laws. If, for
any reason, the Work or any element thereof shall be deemed not to be a
work-made-for-hire for Bayside, you agree that this Agreement shall
constitute an irrevocable, perpetual assignment to Bayside and its
successors and assigns of any and all of your right, title, and interest in
and to the Work, including but not limited to any and all worldwide
copyrights and renewals, extensions, and restorations thereof. In addition to
your rights under all relevant copyright laws, you hereby transfer, convey,

Figure 3.5 Sample production agreement. (continued)

and assign to Bayside and its successors and assigns all other intellectual property rights in and to all elements of the Work throughout the world and in any language, including but not limited to any and all trademark rights. You hereby waive any so-called droit moral rights, moral rights of authors, and all other similar rights however denominated throughout the world. You will, upon Bayside's request, execute, acknowledge, deliver, and/or record such additional documents as Bayside may deem necessary to evidence and effectuate Bayside's rights hereunder. You hereby grant Bayside the right, as your attorney-in-fact, to execute, acknowledge, deliver, and record in the U.S. Copyright Office or elsewhere any and all such documents that you fail to execute, acknowledge, deliver, and record. Bayside will have the right to use, at its option and in its sole discretion, your name, likeness, and biographical information to promote and advertise the Project or any other use of the Work. You acknowledge that Bayside will not be obligated to exercise any of the rights granted to Bayside herein or make any use of the Work.

4. You represent and warrant that (a) you have the full power and authority to enter into and to fulfill the terms of this Agreement and to grant the rights described herein; (b) you have not entered and will not enter into any agreements or activities that will or might interfere or conflict with the terms hereof; (c) the Work is and will be wholly original with you and not copied in whole or in part from any other work except materials in the public domain or supplied to you by Bayside; and (d) to the best of your knowledge, neither the Work nor the use thereof infringes on or violates any right of privacy or publicity of, or constitutes a libel, slander, or any unfair competition against, or infringes on or violates the copyright, trademark rights, or other intellectual property rights of any person or entity.

5. In the event of an actual or alleged breach of this Agreement, or under any other circumstances whatsoever, any rights and remedies you may have against Bayside or its successors, licensees, or assigns will be limited to the right to recover damages, if any, in an action at law. You hereby waive any right or remedy in equity, including but not limited to any right to rescind or terminate Bayside's rights hereunder or to seek injunctive relief of any kind against Bayside or its successor licensees or assigns.

6. You may not assign this Agreement or your rights hereunder, or delegate your obligations hereunder in whole or in part. Bayside may assign this Agreement or any or all of its rights hereunder to any person or entity and will be relieved of all its obligations to you hereunder to the extent that such obligations are assumed by any such assignee.

Figure 3.5 Sample production agreement. (continued)

7. Each party hereto is an independent contractor, and this Agreement will not be construed as creating a joint venture, partnership, or agency relationship between the parties hereto, nor will either party have the right, power, or authority to create any obligation or duty, express or implied, on behalf of the other.

8. This Agreement will be subject to and construed in accordance with the laws of the Commonwealth of Massachusetts applicable to agreements made and to be entirely performed therein without regard to that jurisdiction's choice of law provisions. The parties hereby agree to submit any dispute arising under this Agreement to the exclusive jurisdiction of courts located in Boston, Massachusetts. This Agreement is intended by the parties to be the final, complete, and exclusive expression of their agreement and understanding and supersedes all prior and contemporaneous contracts, representations, and understandings (written or oral) between the parties concerning the subject matter hereof. This Agreement may not be changed or modified except by a writing signed by both parties.

Please indicate your acceptance of and agreement to the foregoing terms and conditions by signing in the space provided below.

AGREED AND ACCEPTED:

_____

[CONTRACTOR'S SIGNATURE]

Name: _____

Date: _____

BAYSIDE DISTRIBUTORS CORP.

By: _____

Its: _____

Date: _____

MEYER VIDEO PRODUCTIONS, INC.

By: _____

Its: _____

Date: _____

percentage of gross revenues after the first 1,000 copies of the program are sold.[5] Including this type of "contingent compensation" provision can complicate an agreement because it necessitates adding the accounting, payment, and audit provisions that complete paragraph 4.3.

In addition to stating that the production will be considered a work-made-for-hire for Bayside, paragraph 5 requires Meyer to have any third parties that it hires for the production (e.g., writers, artists, or editors who are not employees of Meyer) to sign the work-made-for-hire agreement attached as Exhibit A to the agreement. This helps ensure that these third parties will not claim that, by virtue of their work on the production, they have any proprietary interest in the finished program.

Many of the other provisions of the production agreement should be familiar from the sample contracts presented earlier, particularly the writer's contract shown in Figure 3.3. Like that contract, the production agreement in Figure 3.5 begins by describing the materials that the contractor will be responsible for delivering, defining a delivery schedule for the materials, and delineating an approval process that will be followed once Bayside receives the materials. As in the writer's contract, the consideration will be paid in installments tied to the delivery schedule, and the contractor will receive a termination fee if the hiring company elects to cancel the project.

Paragraph 6 of the contract contains a warranty clause similar to the warranty provisions included in the writer's contract. The warranty provisions are coupled with an express indemnification clause (paragraph 7), in which Meyer agrees to protect Bayside from any liability resulting from Meyer's breach of its warranties. This clause would protect Bayside if, for example, the materials that Meyer delivers contain segments stolen from another copyrighted production and the owner of that production brings an infringement action against Bayside.

Paragraph 7 also includes a cross-indemnification running from Bayside to Meyer. Bayside's indemnification is limited, however, to any liabilities arising from the production's use of materials to be provided by Bayside (see paragraph 1). If Bayside was not providing any materials for inclusion in the production, this indemnification would be unnecessary. In fact, in many production agreements, no indemnification is made by the party commissioning the production. Instead, the representations and warranties and related indemnification are entirely unilateral on the part of the producing company.

The project contract in Figure 3.5 also includes several other clauses and provisions worth studying, including the following:

- A "no obligation to distribute" clause (paragraph 9) that frees Bayside from any obligation to publish or distribute the finished production. This sort of clause is particularly significant in contracts that provide for royalty or other payments contingent on the project generating revenue because withdrawing a project from distribution would cut off the flow of royalty payments to the production company. This provision would prevent Meyer from prevailing on a claim that it has suffered financial injury resulting from Bayside's failure to distribute the production and generate royalty revenue for Meyer.
- An "independent contractor clause" (paragraph 10) that reminds Meyer of its obligations as an independent contractor and reminds the world that the agreement between Meyer and Bayside does not place the two companies in a partnership, joint venture, or employer-employee relationship.
- A "right of first negotiation" clause (paragraph 11) that requires Bayside to offer Meyer the chance to produce any sequels to or spin-offs from the project. This provision works to Meyer's benefit and, although not rare in a contract of this type, certainly is not required.
- An "insurance" clause (paragraph 12) that requires Meyer to secure an "errors and omissions" type insurance policy applicable to the production that names Bayside as an additional insured. Such a policy provides an extra layer of protection for Bayside beyond Meyer's indemnification contained in paragraph 7. Although this type of insurance requirement is common in contracts covering larger-scale production projects, it is somewhat unusual in a contract like this one for a non-broadcast video production with a relatively modest production budget. A distributor such as Bayside typically would require a production company to carry errors and omissions insurance where it was uncertain whether the production company had the financial wherewithal to back up its indemnification.
- A "force majeure" clause (see paragraph 13) that protects the parties if they fail to deliver on their contractual obligations because of circumstances beyond their control.

The project contract ends with a list of miscellaneous provisions that further define the scope and limits of the agreement. Included in those provisions are clauses that define what state's law will apply to the contract and the manner in which the agreement may be amended and modified (here, as almost always should be the case, only in a writing agreed to by both parties).

In addition, one of the miscellaneous provisions is a "successors and assigns" clause (paragraph 15.3) that defines the circumstances under which either party may assign the agreement. As that clause indicates, Bayside will have the right to assign the agreement without Meyer's permission, provided that the assignee assumes all of Bayside's obligations, but Meyer may not assign the agreement unless it receives the advanced written permission of Bayside. As discussed earlier in this chapter in connection with the sample writer's agreement, although this language may seem unfairly tilted in Bayside's favor, it actually is common for the entity that is contracting with a production company to place substantial constraints on the production company's right to assign the contract because companies such as Bayside contract with companies such as Meyer based on the company's experience and reputation (and, often, the experience and reputation of specific individuals who own or work for such companies). Here, Bayside wants to be able to prevent Meyer from simply turning around and assigning (or "flipping") the agreement to a company that may have less experience and a lesser reputation. Conversely, Meyer probably is not too concerned about Bayside assigning the contract (as long as the assignee assumes all of Bayside's payment obligations), and Bayside will want the freedom to assign its rights under the contract if Bayside is ever sold or merged with another company or if it decides to sell its rights in the program to another company.

Finally, like the other sample contracts, this project contract is a nonguild and nonunion production. For information about guilds and unions, see Chapter 7.

Sample Option/Purchase Agreement

Many media productions are based on or derived from existing works such as novels (e.g., the classic film *Gone with the Wind*, based on the novel by Margaret Mitchell), nonfiction books (e.g., the television miniseries "Band of Brothers," derived from the book by Stephen Ambrose), and original scripts (e.g., the feature film *Shakespeare in Love*, developed from the script by Marc Norman and Tom Stoppard). In recent years, major media productions have also been developed from a variety of other existing properties, including comic books (e.g., "Spider-Man") and video games (e.g., "Tomb Raider").

Figure 3.6 is a sample option/purchase agreement. This type of agreement allows a producer to "lock up" the production rights in an existing property for a defined period while the producer attempts to secure financing and other commitments necessary to proceed with production. In this sample agreement, the existing work is a nonfiction work titled *Zen There, Done That*, which the producer plans to develop as a video production.

In paragraph 1 of the sample agreement, the author of *Zen There, Done That* grants the producer, WorkForce Productions, a six-month option to purchase the rights to the book that are specified in paragraph 5. This initial option will cost the producer $500. Paragraph 2 gives the producer the right to extend the initial option for one or two renewal periods of six months each. The renewal periods will cost the producer $1,000 each. If the producer exercises the option, the initial option payment of $500 will be applicable against (deducted from) the purchase price. In contrast, the renewal payments, if any, will not be applicable against the purchase price. Although this arrangement is fairly standard, it is preferable from the producer's perspective to have all option payments applicable against the purchase price.

Paragraph 3 provides that the producer may exercise the option by (1) giving written notice to the author at any time during the initial option term or any renewal term and (2) paying the author the purchase price. That price is defined in paragraph 4 as $5,000 (less any applicable option payments).

Paragraph 5.a begins by specifying that, during the option period and any renewal period, the producer will have the exclusive right to negotiate with third parties concerning projects based on the work and to engage in development, preproduction, and production activities. This provision is important because a producer will typically want to engage in these types of activities to determine whether a project based on the work is viable before exercising the option and paying the purchase price.

Upon exercising the option, the producer will own the rights defined in the second part of paragraph 5.a. It is usually to the

Figure 3.6 Sample option/purchase agreement.

OPTION/PURCHASE AGREEMENT

Agreement ("Agreement") dated as of March 4, 2002, by and between WorkForce Productions, Inc. ("Producer") and Gary Lyndon ("Author") with respect to that certain published nonfiction book written by Author entitled ZEN THERE, DONE THAT, including without limitation all elements thereof and copyrights therein (collectively, the "Work"). In consideration of the representations, warranties, and agreements made herein, the parties agree as follows:

1. *Initial Option.* In consideration of Producer's efforts to obtain a commitment to finance and produce a Production (as defined below) based on the Work and the payment of $500, Author hereby grants Producer an irrevocable option to acquire the Rights (as defined below) for a period of six months commencing on the date first written above (the "Initial Option Period"). The payment for the Initial Option will be applicable against the Purchase Price payable to Author if the option is exercised.

2. *Renewal Right.* Producer shall have the right to renew the option for two additional terms of six months each (the "Renewal Periods") by (i) notifying Author in writing of its intent to renew the option before the expiration of the then-current option period, (ii) paying Author $1,000 in consideration of the first such renewal exercised, and (iii) paying Author $1,000 in consideration of the second such renewal exercised. The total amount paid to Author by Producer to renew the option (the "Renewal Fee") shall not be applicable against the Purchase Price payable to Author if the option is exercised.

3. *Exercise of Option.* At any time during the Initial Option Period or any Renewal Period(s) (if exercised), Producer may exercise the option by giving written notice to Author and paying Author the "Purchase Price" described in Paragraph 4.

4. *Purchase Price.* If Producer exercises the option, Producer will make a one-time payment to Author (the "Purchase Price") of $5,000.

5. *Producer's Rights.*

    a. During the Initial Option Period and the Renewal Period(s) (if exercised), Producer will have the exclusive worldwide right to approach, negotiate with, and enter into agreements with third parties with respect to projects based on the Work and to undertake (at Producer's own expense)

Figure 3.6 Sample option/purchase agreement. (continued)

development, preproduction, and production activities in connection with such projects. Subject only to Producer's exercise of the option and payment of the Purchase Price, Author hereby grants to Producer the following exclusive, perpetual, worldwide rights ("Rights"): (i) all right, title, and interest in and to the Work (excepting solely the "Reserved Rights" set forth in subparagraph [b] below), including but not limited to all rights to develop, produce, and exploit, in any and all media and devices, whether now known or hereafter developed, one or more audiovisual projects ("Production[s]") based on the Work, and to distribute such Productions by means of theatrical distribution, nontheatrical distribution, Internet distribution, television (including, without limitation, free, pay, cable, and satellite transmission), videocassette and DVD, and any and all media and technologies now known or hereafter developed and ownership of all copyrights therein and any and all renewals and extensions thereof, and all allied, subsidiary, and ancillary rights therein, including but not limited to merchandising, commercial tie-in, soundtracks, music publishing, arcade games, video games, CD-ROM, Internet, computer software, and theme park rights and (ii) all rights to use Author's name, likeness, voice, and biography in connection with the Productions and any other projects and materials based on the Work, and in the advertising, publicity, and promotion thereof. Producer will have the unlimited right to modify, edit, cut, rearrange, or change the Work in its sole discretion in the exercise of its rights hereunder. To the maximum extent allowed, Author hereby expressly waives, in perpetuity, without limitation, any and all rights in law, equity or otherwise, that Author may have or claim to have with respect to the Work under any law relating to the "moral rights of authors" or any similar law throughout the universe.

b. Author reserves the following rights in the Work: (i) book publication rights (including "books on tape" and electronic or electromechanical reproductions of the text of the Work); (ii) radio reading; and (ii) legitimate stage (including the right to broadcast such types of productions on television) (collectively, "Reserved Rights"). Notwithstanding the Reserved Rights, Producer shall have the right, for the purpose of exploiting the rights granted Producer in subparagraph (a) above, to produce and publish, stories, synopses, and excerpts of the Work, not to exceed 5,000 words; provided, however, that the foregoing will not be deemed to limit Producer's rights to produce, distribute, exploit, advertise, and promote the Production and the other productions referred to in paragraph 5.a above in any and all manners and media, whether now known or hereafter devised.

Figure 3.6 Sample option/purchase agreement. (continued)

6. *Contingent Compensation and Supplemental Payments.* In addition to the Purchase Price, Author shall be entitled to the following contingent and supplemental payments based on Producer's exploitation of the Work, provided that Author is not in material breach or default of this Agreement:

a. *Net Proceeds.* Author shall be entitled to receive five percent (5%) of one hundred percent (100%) share of the "net proceeds," if any, actually received by Producer from the distributor of the Production(s) and from any other exploitation of the Work pursuant to the Rights. Author's "net proceeds" will be defined, computed, and paid in the same manner as Producer's share of net proceeds is defined, computed, and paid.

b. *Supplemental Payments.* Author shall receive one half of the Purchase Price for each subsequent Production beyond the initial Production, payable upon the commencement of principal photography of each such subsequent Production.

7. *Failure to Exercise Option.* If Producer does not exercise the option during the Initial Option Period or Renewal Period, the option will terminate and Author will have the right to approach, negotiate with, and enter into agreements with third parties with respect to projects based on the Work; provided, however, that if within six months after the end of the option, Author enters into an agreement with any individual or entity approached by Producer during the Initial Option Period or Renewal Period(s), said agreement between Author and such third party must provide that Producer will be attached as Producer of the project at Producer's then-current producing fee.

8. *Cooperation and Access to Materials.* Author agrees to use best efforts to assist Producer in the development and production of projects based on the Work. Such cooperation will include, but not be limited to, using best efforts to procure for Producer at no additional cost those releases Producer deems necessary, from individuals or entities who are described, mentioned, or depicted in the Work, and providing access to Author's notes, interviews, and other written and recorded materials relevant to the Work, all of which materials will be deemed included within the definition of "Work" as used in this Agreement. Author agrees to permit the inclusion of said materials in any project produced by Producer.

Figure 3.6 Sample option/purchase agreement. (continued)

9. *Representations and Warranties.* Author represents, warrants, and agrees that Author has the full right, authority, and legal capacity to grant to Producer the rights granted herein; that Author has not previously granted and will not grant to any third party and that no third party possesses or controls any right to use or exploit any of the rights granted to Producer herein; that Author has not entered into and will not enter into any agreements or activities that might interfere or conflict with the rights granted to Producer herein; that the Work is free from any liens or encumbrances; and that the Work is wholly original with Author and will not violate the rights of any third party, including but not limited to by means of copyright infringement, defamation, libel, slander, or violation of any right of privacy or publicity. Author will defend, indemnify, and hold Producer and its employees, agents, representatives, successors, assigns, and licensees harmless from and against any and all claims, damages, liabilities, losses, costs, and expenses (including reasonable attorneys' fees and costs) arising out of or in connection with any breach by Author of any of the representations, warranties, and agreements contained in this Agreement.

10. *Credit.* Subject to any restrictions and/or requirements of applicable guild agreements and approval of the principal domestic distributor or other financier (or network/broadcaster), Author will be accorded credit on the Production as author of the Work in the form "Based on the Book by Gary Lyndon" (or, if a different title is used, "Based on the Book "Zen There, Done That" by Gary Lyndon") on screen, on a separate card, in the main titles (if the screenwriter's credit is accorded in the main titles), in the same size of type as the screenwriter's credit, and in all paid ads in which the screenwriter receives credit, other than congratulatory, award, or nomination ads.

11. *Remedies.* Author acknowledges and agrees that if Producer fails to make any of the payments to Author provided for herein, or if Producer breaches any other covenant or condition hereof, Author's sole remedy will be an action at law to recover such payment and/or monetary damages. In no event will any of the rights granted to Producer hereunder be affected or impaired, nor will Author have a right of rescission or right to injunctive or other equitable relief. It is mutually understood and agreed that the rights granted herein are special, unique, unusual, extraordinary, and of an intellectual character, giving them a peculiar value, the loss of which cannot

Figure 3.6 Sample option/purchase agreement. (continued)

be reasonably or adequately compensated in damages in an action at law, and that in the event of any breach by Author, Producer will be entitled to equitable relief by way of injunction or otherwise.

12. *Force Majeure*. If any development, preproduction, or production activities in connection with any project based in whole or in part on the Work, including but not limited to the writing of any treatments or screenplays, are prevented or interrupted because of an act of God, fire, strike, labor dispute, governmental order, court order, war, riot, civil commotion, or any other event beyond Producer's control, or if there are any claims concerning the Work inconsistent with any of Author's representations, warranties, or agreements hereunder, the option term (including any Renewal Term[s]) will be extended for the number of days such force majeure event or such claim existed and a reasonable time thereafter.

13. *Reversion*. If Producer has exercised the option but has not commenced principal photography of a Production within five (5) years after the date of the exercise of the option, the Rights will revert to Author subject to a lien in favor of Producer for repayment to Producer of all sums paid or payable to third parties in connection with the Work and the Production, including without limitation, to Author, and all sums paid or payable by Producer in connection with the development of the Production, plus interest at a rate of prime from time to time in effect. Such amounts will be payable to Producer upon the earlier of commencement of principal photography of a subsequent production based on the Work or Author's receipt of first proceeds from a third party from a sale of such rights, as and when received.

14. *No Obligation to Exploit*. Nothing contained in this Agreement will obligate Producer to exercise the option granted herein, to produce a project based on the Work, or to otherwise exploit any of the rights granted to Producer herein.

15. *Right to Use Material in the Public Domain*. Under no circumstances will Producer, or Producer's successors, assigns, or licensees, be in a less favorable position with respect to the right to use material in the public domain (including, without limitation, that public domain material contained in the Work) than they would have been if Producer had not optioned the Work from Author.

Figure 3.6 Sample option/purchase agreement. (continued)

16. *Assignment.* Author agrees that Producer may freely assign this Agreement and grant its rights hereunder, in whole or in part, to any person, firm, or corporation, and Producer will be relieved of its obligations to Author hereunder upon such assignment.

17. *Additional Documents.* Author agrees to execute, acknowledge, and deliver, or cause to be executed, acknowledged, and delivered, to Producer the following documents as provided by Producer: (a) Publisher's Release, (b) Short Form Option, (c) Short Form Assignment, and (d) any and all further instruments as Producer may from time to time deem reasonably necessary or desirable to evidence, effectuate, or protect Producer's rights hereunder (the Short Form Assignment to be held by Producer and deemed executed and delivered by Author on such date, if ever, as Producer exercises the Option). Author hereby irrevocably appoints Producer as the true and lawful attorney-in-fact of Author, which power is coupled with an interest, for the purpose of executing, acknowledging, and delivering any such instrument that Author fails, refuses, or neglects promptly to execute, acknowledge, and deliver.

18. *Notices.* All notices shall be in writing sent by fax, air courier, personal delivery, or certified mail. Unless otherwise specified in writing, all notices shall be addressed as follows:

To Producer: To Author:
WorkForce Productions, Inc.   Mr. Gary Lyndon
865 Delvaney Ave.   64 West 72nd Street
Los Angeles, CA 90024   New York, NY 10019

19. *Choice of Law; Jurisdiction.* The validity, construction, interpretation, and effect of this Agreement shall be governed by the laws of the State of California applicable to agreements made in and entirely performed in that State, and without regard to that State's choice of law rules. The parties hereby agree to submit any dispute arising under this Agreement to the exclusive jurisdiction of courts located in Los Angeles, California.

20. *Entire Agreement; Modification.* This Agreement constitutes the entire agreement between the parties with respect to the subject matter hereof and supersedes all prior and contemporaneous agreements, understandings, and negotiations by or between the parties, whether written or oral,

Figure 3.6 Sample option/purchase agreement. (continued)

---

express or implied, and cannot be modified except by a written instrument signed by each of the parties.

IN WITNESS WHEREOF, the parties hereto have executed this Agreement as of the date first written above.

PRODUCER   AUTHOR

_____   _____

Workforce Productions, Inc.   Gary Lyndon

---

producer's benefit to define the rights being acquired as broadly as possible. Here, the acquired rights are defined as all rights to the book except only the reserved rights specified in paragraph 5.b. Those reserved rights are limited to book publishing rights, radio reading, and legitimate stage rights. That is, the author will continue to own the exclusive right to publish the book in print and electronic form, to read or have the book read on the radio, and to produce a legitimate stage version of the book. All other rights in the book, including audiovisual and ancillary (e.g., merchandising, commercial tie-in) rights, will be owned by the producer.

Paragraph 6 describes the contingent compensation and supplemental payments that will be payable to the author based on the exploitation of the book by the producer (or the producer's licensees or assignees). Under paragraph 6.a, the author will be paid 5 percent of the net proceeds received by the producer from projects and products based on the book. Option/purchase agreements that include this type of provision also often include lengthy and painfully detailed definitions of net proceeds (or *net profits*, if that term is used). Here, the producer has avoided adding (and negotiating) such a provision by stating that the definition of *net proceeds* applied to the author will be the same as that applied to the producer. This approach will often work, particularly if the assumption is that exploitation of the work will occur through third parties (e.g., financiers, studios, distributors, networks) that will pay the producer a portion of their net proceeds.

Some parties will insist that the producer include a fully developed net proceeds definition, however, either in the body of the option/purchase agreement or as an exhibit.

In addition to this net proceeds participation, the author's contingent compensation will include supplemental payments (sometimes called *royalties*) if the producer exploits the work in subsequent productions beyond the initial production. These supplemental payments are set in paragraph 6.b as a fixed amount of "one half of the Purchase Price" for each subsequent production. Rather than using this type of fixed fee that applies to every supplemental production, some option agreements specify supplemental payments that vary depending on the type of production involved (e.g., feature film, television movie of the week, television series). In the case of television series, the supplemental payment can be a fee for each completed episode of the series.

Paragraph 7 makes it clear that, if the producer fails to exercise the option during any of the option periods, the option will terminate, and the author will be free to license the optioned rights to the work to any other party. The only restriction is that if, during the six-month period following termination of the option, the author enters into an agreement for a production involving the work with any party that the producer had approached during the option period, the producer must be attached to the project at its then-current producer fee. Provisions similar to this are found in many option/purchase agreements. They are intended to deter less-than-scrupulous third parties who negotiate at length with a producer for an optioned property but then, rather than conclude a deal, simply wait for the option to expire in the hope that they can cut a better deal directly with the author or other rights holder.

This sample option/purchase agreement also includes a reversion provision in paragraph 13 specifying that, upon exercise of the option, the producer has five years to commence principal photography on a production based on the work. If the producer fails to do so, all rights in the work revert to the author, and the author is free to assign or license those rights to any party. As is often the case, however, this reversion of rights is subject to a lien on the work in the amount of all sums paid to the author under the agreement and all sums paid to third parties to develop materials (plus applicable interest), with those amount to be repaid and the lien released if and when the production is set up elsewhere. Although this lien is meant to protect and reimburse a producer's investment in a property, this type of reversion or turnaround provision actually works to protect authors or other rights holders from producers who obtain the rights to works after paying a relatively modest purchase price and then simply sit on those rights.

The sample option/purchase agreement shown in Figure 3.6 includes various other clauses and provisions. Most of these clauses are fairly standard (e.g., representation and warranties, credits, restrictions on remedies, force majeure, no obligation to exploit, assignment, jurisdiction), the purpose and significance of which should be familiar from the same or similar provisions included in one or more of the other sample agreements discussed in this chapter. Paragraph 15, which may not be familiar, simply states that the producer will have the same rights as the general public with respect to any material that is in the public domain, including public domain material that is included in the work being optioned. This provision is intended to protect the producer, who may be involved in developing many different media projects at any one time, from a claim that one or more of those projects that may share similar general themes or ideas with the author's work actually involves the author's work (so that this option/purchase agreement would apply to those similar works). As discussed in Chapter 4, under copyright law, general literary themes and ideas may not be owned by any individual or entity. Consequently, any author (or producer) is free to develop a work that includes the same general themes and ideas addressed by another author (or producer) in an existing work, as long as they do not copy the original manner in which those themes and ideas are expressed in the existing work. Similarly, anyone is free to republish or develop a media production based on a literary work that may have once been subject to copyright protection but that has since fallen into the public domain (e.g., *Huckleberry Finn*, *Oliver Twist*). Paragraph 15 simply affirms that, if the work being optioned contains such public domain material, the producer has the same rights to exploit that material as any member of the general public, with no obligation of any kind to the author.

Summary

- *What is the first step in drafting a media production contract?* You should always begin by making sure that the contract includes a clear and definite offer, a thorough description of the consideration, and a way for the parties to indicate their acceptance. Once you have built this basic framework, you should add the other terms and provisions that will further define the production relationship covered by the contract.

- *What are some of the other terms and provisions that should be included in most media production contracts?* Most media production contracts should include schedules that indicate when and how the contractor will deliver the goods and services covered by the agreement. Production contracts should also establish guidelines for approving the deliverables and procedures for paying the contractor. In addition, the contracts should define the working relationships between the production parties. Will the contract work be performed on a guild or union basis? Also, if the party that is performing the work is acting as an independent contractor, does it agree to waive all rights to claims against the company for insurance, workers' compensation, and other benefits of employment? As discussed next, media production contracts also should define clearly who will own the results and proceeds of the contractor's work and services under the agreement.

- *How should issues of ownership be addressed in media production contracts?* All production contracts should include language that clearly defines who will own the materials that will be delivered under the agreement and who will own the finished program. In most cases, the contract should state that all results and proceeds of the contractor's services under the agreement will be a "work-made-for-hire" for the producer, so that the producer owns the copyright in those results and proceeds. As an extra precaution, the contract should stipulate that, in the event that it is ever determined that the results and proceeds of the contractor's services are not a work-made-for-hire, the agreement constitutes an assignment of all of the contractor's rights of ownership to the producer. The contract should also state that the producer will retain complete ownership of the finished production.

- *What role should warranty and indemnification clauses play in production contracts?* Warranty clauses in media production contracts typically specify that the party that has agreed to deliver goods under the contract has full rights to the material and that there is no other contract or condition that prevents the party from entering into and performing its obligations under the agreement. Indemnification clauses stipulate which party will be held responsible for any liabilities, judgment, and/or legal fees if a dispute over ownership of the materials arises or if a party should otherwise breach any of its warranties.

- *What is a jurisdiction clause?* Through a jurisdiction clause, the parties to a contract agree that the contract will be governed by the laws of a specific state or, in the case of an international production, by the laws of a specific nation. This provision is especially significant when the parties to the contract reside in different states or countries because the laws governing contracts can vary from one jurisdiction to the next. As the producer, it is almost always in your best interest to have the agreement governed by the laws of your home state and require that any disputes concerning the contract be submitted to the jurisdiction of courts in your home state, county, or city. As discussed in Chapter 1, many media production contracts now include arbitration provisions requiring that any disputes under the agreement be submitted to binding arbitration. In contracts containing this sort of provision, the arbitrator has primary jurisdiction over any such disputes, and the arbitrator's decision may be submitted to a court of competent jurisdiction for the entry of a final judgment or enforcement of the decision.

- *What is a termination clause?* Termination clauses define the conditions under which the parties' rights and obligations and the respective responsibilities of the parties under the agreement may be ended. Generally, the right to terminate is tied to the failure of one or more parties to live up to its material obligations under the agreement.

Notes

1. *Community for Creative Non-Violence v. Reid*, 490 U.S. 730 (1989).
2. Copyright Revision Act of 1976 (P.L. 94–553), (90 Stat. 2541), Sec. 101.

3. Although jurisdiction provisions such as the one discussed here generally are enforceable, their enforceability may be challenged in some jurisdictions. As a result, such provisions do not always guarantee that the laws of the specified state will apply and that all litigation will take place in the specified locality.

4. Paragraph 10 states that the writer assigns her moral rights in the materials to the company. Moral rights, which are discussed in Chapter 4, essentially are the author's rights to control the subsequent alteration of his or her work.

5. This agreement calculates royalties as a percentage of gross revenues. Royalties are often calculated instead as a percentage of net revenues or net receipts. If that had been the case here, the agreement would need to define net revenues or net receipts (e.g., "Net Revenues is defined as amounts received from the sale or distribution of the project, exclusive of shipping charges and sales and other taxes, less (i) the amount of any credits or refunds for returns and (ii) any commissions paid in connection with such sales or distribution."). Generally, computing royalties as a percentage of net, rather than gross, revenues favors the company that will be paying out the royalties because it allows the company to deduct specified costs and expenses before calculating the royalty. Conversely, calculating royalties as a percentage of gross receipts generally favors the company or individual that will be receiving the royalty payments.

4

Getting Permission: Copyright Concerns During Media Production

Most media productions actually are a mix of materials that a producer has pulled together from a variety of sources. In developing a video documentary, for example, a producer might commission a freelance writer to write the script, an animation house to prepare a title sequence, and an outside video facility to produce special effects segments. The producer might also buy or borrow existing materials to enhance the production: stock footage, still photographs, music, excerpts from other video or television programs, and so on.

Chapters 2 and 3 examined how contracts can help define the relationships between a producer and the various performers, writers, and crew members commissioned to provide services or original materials for a production project. In contrast, this chapter focuses on the many legal issues involved in incorporating existing materials, such as video clips and photographs, into a production. These materials already exist in one form or another and were not created as contract items for the production in question.

Some producers make the mistake of assuming that it is permissible to incorporate existing materials into a production as long as they use only a brief excerpt or as long as they acknowledge the source of the materials in the production credits. The following discussion will show that this assumption is dangerous to make. To understand why, it helps to begin with an introduction to the fundamental concepts underlying copyright law.

An Introduction to Copyright Law

For media producers, copyright cuts two ways. On the one hand, copyright protects a producer's right to control and profit from the reproduction, distribution, and sale of his or her work. On the other hand, copyright prevents producers from using the work of others without their permission. This chapter discusses the preventive role that copyright plays during the media production process. For information about the ways that copyright can protect a producer's right to control and profit from a completed work, see Chapter 9.

What Is Copyright?

Copyright is a group of rights granted to the creators of literary, artistic, musical, dramatic, and audiovisual works. Under U.S. law, copyright gives the creators of these intellectual properties the exclusive right:

- To reproduce and distribute copies of the copyrighted works (in other words, the "right to copy")
- To create derivative works based on the copyrighted work
- In the case of certain works, to perform and display the copyrighted work publicly

Above all, copyright gives authors, artists, musicians, and media producers the right to own and control their completed works. Significantly, as part of that control, the owners of copyrighted materials can authorize others to copy, distribute, and adapt their work. This happens all the time in the world of media production, where video and film producers regularly license publishers and distributors the right to reproduce and distribute copies of their work in return for royalty payments or other compensation. It also happens when the owners of video, film, photographic, and music materials authorize their work to be used in media productions and when authors allow their works to be adapted for the stage, cinema, or television.

Although copyright gives authors, artists, and media producers the power to control their creative properties, federal copyright law does place some restrictions on that power. First, copyright is limited to a defined period—currently the author's life plus 70 years for most works. In addition, as discussed in Chapter 6, under the compulsory licensing provisions of U.S. copyright law, the creators of published musical compositions cannot prevent certain uses of their compositions by others. Under some circumstances, U.S. copyright law also allows media producers and others to use and adapt copyrighted materials without securing permission from the copyright owner. This "fair use" provision is discussed in detail later in this chapter.

Sources of Copyright Law

Like much U.S. law, federal copyright law is rooted in English common and statutory law. In England, copyright first emerged as a legal concept with the development of movable type and related printing technologies in the 15th and 16th centuries. In 1709, after more than a century of government attempts to license printing and publishing rights, the English Parliament passed the first comprehensive copyright law. Known as the Statute of Anne, the 1709 law gave authors the exclusive right to own and profit from their works for a period of 14 years.

The notion that individual authors—not guilds or printers—should retain control of their creative works eventually made its way into Article I, Section 8 of the U.S. Constitution, known as the "copyright and patent" clause:

> *The Congress shall have [the] power . . . to promote the progress of science and useful arts, by securing for limited times to authors and inventors the exclusive right to their respective writings and discoveries.*

As this language suggests, the framers of the Constitution, several of whom were authors, believed that copyright involved both individual rights and a national need. By granting Congress the power to pass copyright legislation, they hoped to protect the rights of individual authors to control and to profit from their creative works. In doing so, they also anticipated that copyright legislation would help promote "the progress of science and useful arts" in the new nation.

In 1790, drawing on its powers under Article I, Section 8 of the U.S. Constitution, Congress enacted the Copyright Act of 1790. This first federal copyright statute covered books, maps, and charts. Like the Statute of Anne, the Copyright Act of 1790 granted authors the exclusive right to publish and profit from their work for 14 years.

Under the 1790 act, however, this initial grant of copyright could be renewed for an additional 14 years.

Federal copyright law has been revised many times since 1790, usually in response to the emergence of new recording, image reproduction, and transmission technologies (e.g., photography, phonograph records, motion pictures, photocopying, radio and television, videotaping). Comprehensive revisions occurred in 1831, 1870, 1909, and 1976. Copyright also has been the subject of much federal case law, particularly when new technologies have raised issues that were not yet addressed in federal copyright statutes.

It is important to note that, unlike many areas of media production law, copyright law is governed by a single, preemptive federal statute. This means that the individual states are restricted to playing only a minor, secondary role in regulating copyright. It also means that case law in the area of copyright is almost exclusively federal case law—case law that is based on judgments rendered in federal courts. In the United States, copyright registration procedures are administered by the U.S. Copyright Office, an office of the Library of Congress.

The federal statute that currently dominates the U.S. copyright landscape is the Copyright Act of 1976. Passed after more than two decades of research and debate, the Copyright Act of 1976 became fully effective on January 1, 1978. The 1976 act supersedes the Copyright Act of 1909, a statute that was the subject of many amendments and much federal case law over the years. The 1976 act has also been the subject of several significant amendments, most recently in 1998 with the passage of the Sonny Bono Copyright Term Extension Act. This amendment is discussed later in this chapter in the "Duration of Copyright" section.

The Copyright Act of 1976 set down new rules governing what can and cannot be copyrighted, the scope and duration of copyright, and the steps involved in establishing copyright. The 1976 act also was the first federal copyright statute to include provisions for the fair use of copyright materials, a doctrine that was an established concept under common law but that had never been formally recognized in federal statutory law. As discussed later in this chapter, fair use is of particular interest to media producers.

What Can Be Copyrighted?

Under the Copyright Act of 1976, almost any creative work can be protected by copyright. A partial list includes the following:

- Books of fiction, nonfiction, and poetry
- Films, radio programs, television programs, and other audiovisual works
- Scripts for films, radio programs, television programs, and other audiovisual works
- Photographs
- Paintings, illustrations, sculptures, and other works of art
- Dramatic works
- Music and sound recordings
- Choreographic works and pantomimes
- Computer software

As this list suggests, most media properties can be copyrighted, as long as those properties are fixed in tangible form.

Although copyright law is quite broad, it does not cover all types and categories of materials. For example, an idea or concept for a television program is not eligible for copyright, even when the idea is expressed in tangible form. A treatment or script developed from the idea could be copyrighted, however, as could the television show that is based on one or more of those materials. In other words, the particular form in which an idea is expressed is eligible for copyright protection, not the idea itself. Not surprisingly, however, the exact boundary between "idea" and "expression" has been the subject of considerable copyright litigation over the years.

In addition to ideas, other items and materials that cannot be copyrighted include the following:

- Information and materials produced by federal government employees as part of their jobs
- Scientific, historical, and other factual information, including the news (although a specific selection and arrangement of factual information can be copyrighted)
- Inventions and industrial processes
- Titles of products or services

Although these items cannot be copyrighted, they may be eligible for other forms of protection. For example, inventions and certain industrial processes can be protected by patents, and titles can be protected by trademarks. Patents and trademarks are discussed in Chapter 9.

How Is Copyright Established?

Under the Copyright Act of 1976, copyright is established as soon as you create, in fixed form, a work that is eligible for copyright protection. To help preserve your copyright, you should also add a copyright notice to the work. If you have created a television program or slide tape show, for example, you would display a notice that looks like this:

Copyright 2003 by Magic Media, Inc.

Unlike the Copyright Act of 1909, the 1976 law is fairly flexible in its rules regarding the form and placement of the copyright notice. Section 401 of the 1976 law does, however, stipulate that the copyright notice on "visually perceptible works" should include the following:

1. The symbol © (the letter C in a circle) or p (for sound recordings), the word "Copyright" or the abbreviation "Copr."
2. The first year of publication of the work.
3. The name of the owner of the copyright in the work, or an abbreviation by which the name can be recognized, or a generally known alternative designation of the owner.[1]

Section 401 of the Copyright Act also requires that the notice "shall be affixed to the copies in such a manner and location as to give reasonable notice of the claim of copyright." In other words, the notice should be displayed in a prominent position, rather than buried deep inside the work. In most films and television programs, the copyright notice appears as part of the opening titles or closing credits. On videocassettes and DVDs, a copyright notice usually appears on both the program material and the cassette or DVD label and packaging materials.

Significantly, as part of the change made to the 1976 law in advance of the United States joining the Berne Convention in 1989, a copyright notice is no longer required as a condition of copyright protection, although it is still strongly recommended. For more information, see the section on the Berne Convention later in this chapter.

Who Owns the Copyright in a Copyrightable Work?

As just discussed, under the current copyright law, copyright vests in a work as soon as the work is created and fixed in a tangible form. But who owns the copyright? The general rule is that the copyright in a work that qualifies for copyright protection is owned by the individual (or, in the case of jointly authored works, the individuals) who created the work. As discussed in Chapter 3, the major exception to this rule is when the work is created as a "work-made-for-hire." Under U.S. copyright law, this means that the work was either (1) created by an employee within the scope of his or her employment (in which case the copyright is owned by the employee's employer) or (2) specially ordered or commissioned for use as part of a motion picture or other audiovisual work or for inclusion in one of the other categories of eligible works listed under the "work-made-for-hire" definition in Section 101 of the Copyright Act, provided that "the parties expressly agree in a signed writing that the work is to be considered a work-made-for-hire" (in which case the copyright is owned by the contracting party who commissioned the work). For more information, see the section of Chapter 3 titled "Contracting for the Right Rights: Works-Made-for-Hire."

Registering with the U.S. Copyright Office

Displaying the proper copyright notice on fixed copies of a creative work is the first recommended step in protecting copyright in a work. The second step is registering the work in the U.S. Copyright Office. This involves filling out the appropriate application and returning the completed forms, together with a small fee and copies of the completed work, to the Copyright Office. The copyright registration process is discussed in more detail in Chapter 9.

Under the current law, registering a work with the Copyright Office is not required as a condition of continuing copyright protection. In other words, if you fail to register a work that you created, you will still retain the copyright for that work. There are, however, several significant advantages to registering with the Copyright Office, particularly if your work becomes the subject of a copyright dispute. First, registration establishes a public record for a copyrighted work, a record that can come in handy in the event of legal proceedings concerning the work. In addition, if someone has violated your copyright, you must register the work before you can bring a suit for copyright infringement before a court of law. Although it is possible to register the work after the infringement has occurred, this will limit you to suing for monetary losses that you can actually prove. If you had taken the time to register before the infringement occurred or within the first three months after the work was published, you would be eligible to sue for attorney's fees and statutory damages—damages awarded by the court when the actual monetary loss is either difficult to prove or relatively small. Because the actual monetary loss from copyright infringement is often difficult to prove, being able to sue for statutory damages is a definite advantage.

Special Cautions for Incorporating Existing Works into Media Productions

Media professionals who are planning to incorporate existing works into a production should also be aware that, as discussed already, copyright is established under U.S. law as soon as a work that qualifies for copyright protection is created in a fixed form. In other words, the act of creating such a work establishes copyright, not the act of displaying a copyright notice or registering the work with the Copyright Office. As a result, media producers who assume that a work is in the public domain simply because it does not include a copyright notice may discover that the work is protected by copyright after all. Unfortunately, if they have used the work in a production without the proper permissions, they may also discover that they are the subject of an infringement action brought by the copyright owner. In this case, the producers probably would not be held liable for extensive damages, as long as they could show that they were innocent infringers who were misled by the absence of the copyright notice. The court could, however, require the producers to remove the copyrighted material from the production or to pay reasonable licensing fees for continuing to use the material. For more information about securing copyright protection for completed media productions, see Chapter 9.

Duration of Copyright

Under the Copyright Act of 1909, an author's copyright began the day that a work was published and extended for 28 years. At the end of this initial period, the author could renew the copyright for an additional 28 years. If the author failed to renew the copyright, the work fell into the public domain.

This changed on January 1, 1978, when the Copyright Act of 1976 went into effect. The 1976 act changed the term of copyright to the life of the author plus 50 years. For works with joint authors, the term of copyright became the life of the last surviving author plus 50 years. For anonymous or pseudonymous works, the term was extended to 75 years from the date of publication (the day when the work was first distributed to the public) or 100 years from the date that the work was created, whichever expires first. If the author is listed as a group or organization, as is often the case with media productions, the 75-year term from date of creation applied. This was also the case for works-made-for-hire.

This all changed again in 1998, however, when Congress passed the Sonny Bono Copyright Term Extension Act.[2] The Bono Act amended the Copyright Act of 1976 to extend the term of copyright by 20 years. Accordingly, the copyright term for works by individual authors is now the life of the author plus 70 years. For jointly authored works, the term now extends for the life of the last surviving author plus 70 years. For anonymous or pseudonymous works, the term is now 95 years from the date of first publication or 120 years from the date that the work was created, whichever expires first. For works-made-for-hire and works for which the author is a group or organization, the copyright term is now 95 years from the date of creation.

These latest extensions work to delay the date on which the copyright in eligible works expires—the date on which the work falls into the public domain. Significantly, however, neither this nor prior extensions of the copyright term restore copyright on works that were already in the public domain at the time the extensions became effective. The factors that determine whether a work is in fact in the public domain are discussed in more detail later in this chapter.

Copyright Infringement

Copyright infringement occurs when someone uses a copyrighted work in a manner that violates the copyright owner's exclusive rights to the work. As described earlier in this chapter, those exclusive rights include the right to reproduce and distribute copies of the work, to create derivative works, and (for certain works) to perform and display the work publicly. When someone exercises one or more of these rights without the express permission of the copyright owner, he or she is committing copyright infringement.

Significantly, one of the rights reserved for copyright owners is the right to determine whether all or parts of their works are used in another work. For media producers, this means that it is illegal to duplicate a copyrighted work in its entirety or to incorporate a copyrighted work as part of a production without securing the copyright owner's permission; however, there are two important exceptions to this rule: fair use and compulsory music licensing. Fair use is described later in this chapter. Compulsory music licensing is discussed in Chapter 6.

Infringement Suits

Producers who use copyrighted works illegally may find themselves the defendants in copyright infringement suits. Because copyright infringement violates federal law, infringement suits are almost always filed in federal district courts.[3] A copyright owner who has brought an infringement suit can seek one or more of the following remedies:

- An injunction or restraining order to stop further infringements
- A court order to impound the materials that are the subject of the suit
- If the suit is successful, a court order to destroy the infringing materials
- A court order requiring the infringer to turn over all profits from the infringement
- Compensation for "actual damages," monetary losses resulting from the infringement that the copyright owner can actually prove
- Compensation in the form of "statutory damages," a sum that is set by the court when actual damages are small or difficult to prove
- Reimbursement of court costs and attorney fees

As mentioned earlier in this chapter, the last two remedies in this list, statutory damages and reimbursement of legal costs, are available only if the work in question was registered with the U.S. Copyright Office at the time the alleged infringement occurred.

To prove that an infringement occurred, the copyright owner must establish that the alleged infringer had access to the work in question and used a substantial portion of the work without permission.

Significantly, to establish liability, the copyright owner does not have to prove that the infringement was conscious, deliberate, or malicious. Instead, the copyright owner is required to prove only that the infringement occurred.

Actual and Statutory Damages

The amount of actual damages awarded in infringement suits varies, depending on how much monetary damage the infringer actually inflicted on the copyright owner. Although actual damage awards can be substantial, the burden to prove the extent of the actual monetary loss rests with the copyright owner who has filed the suit.

The copyright owner typically begins by providing evidence of the infringer's gross revenues from use of the disputed material for the period in question. In determining the actual award, the court first allows the infringer to prove that part of that gross revenue was derived from sources other than the copyrighted work in question. The court then deducts these "other" revenues plus any documented expenses from the infringer's total revenues to derive a final profits figure that becomes the basis for an actual damages award.

Because actual damages are often difficult to prove, many copyright owners opt to sue for statutory damages. With statutory damages, the amount of the award is set by the court. Section 504 of the Copyright Act of 1976 does require, however, that the awards fall within some fairly specific boundaries. Section 504 currently stipulates that in most individual infringement cases, the court may award statutory damages of "not less than $750 or more than $30,000." In cases where the infringement was deliberate and willful, however, the court can award up to $150,000. If the infringer is able to show that this was a case of "innocent infringement" (i.e., that "the infringer was not aware and had no reason to believe that his or her acts constituted an infringement"), Section 504 permits the court to reduce the award of statutory damages to $200.

Under certain circumstances, infringers may be subject to criminal penalties as well. Those circumstances include cases in which:

- The infringer knowingly places a fraudulent copyright notice on a work.
- The infringer knowingly removes a copyright notice from a work for fraudulent purposes.

- The infringer willfully violates a copyright for purposes of commercial advantage or private financial gain.

Depending on the circumstances, criminal infringement can result in any or all of the following penalties: fines, imprisonment, and forfeiture and destruction of the infringing goods and the equipment used to manufacture the goods.

Fair Use of Copyrighted Works

Is it ever permissible for producers to use copyrighted works without securing permission from, or making payment to, the copyright owners? Surprisingly, the answer to this question is yes, but only when the producer's actions fall within the fair use guidelines set down in Section 107 of the Copyright Act of 1976. Four factors determine whether an unauthorized use is a fair use:

1. The purpose and character of the use, including whether such use is of a commercial nature or is for nonprofit educational purposes
2. The nature of the copyrighted work
3. The amount and substantiality of the portion used in relation to the copyrighted work as a whole
4. The effect of the use on the potential market for or value of the copyrighted work

Because these criteria leave much room for interpretation, there is no way to be certain in advance that a specific use of a copyrighted work constitutes a fair use. An unauthorized use stands the best chance of securing fair use protection, however, if it is educational or informational in nature, if the work being copied is a reference or other nonfiction work, if the use involves copying a relatively small portion of the work, and if the use has little or no effect on the potential market for the copyrighted work.

Unfortunately, very few cases are this clear-cut. As a result, the courts often must mix and match the Section 107 criteria and other considerations to come up with fair use determinations. For example, a court might decide that, although an unauthorized use was commercial rather than educational in nature, the material used was small enough in relation to the entire copyrighted work to constitute fair use. Conversely, a court might rule that a purely educational use of copyrighted material fails the fair use test because it involves enough of the entire work to diminish the potential market for the work.

If this seems confusing, the copyright statute is partly to blame. In addressing the fair use question, Congress deliberately drafted guidelines that require the courts to review each case on its own merits. Even so, the situation is less confusing now than it was before the Copyright Act of 1976, when fair use existed only as a common law concept. The 1976 law at least defines a single set of statutory guidelines that must be applied in all fair use determinations.

Incidental Background Use of Copyrighted Materials in Productions

It is not always easy to spot potential copyright violations in a production. For example, imagine that you have included within a production a humorous scene that flashes back to the psychedelic days of the late 1960s. Sparing almost no expense, you have costumed your actors in genuine tie-dyed hippie garb and decorated the set with furniture and wall posters from the era. You have also gone to the expense of licensing several acid rock songs from the period to establish the proper mood for the scene. With properly executed music licenses (see Chapter 6) and work-made-for-hire agreements (see Chapter 3) in hand, you feel certain that you have all of your copyright bases covered.

A careful review of the scene, however, reveals at least one potentially uncovered base. One of the wall posters displayed in the background is a reproduction of a famous photograph of Janis Joplin, the legendary rock performer. That photograph is a distinct, copyrighted work. To the surprise of many television and video producers, the display of such a copyrighted photograph or work of art within a production can, in the opinion of some courts, constitute an infringement of the copyright owner's exclusive rights to the work, even when the work is displayed only in the background of a scene.

In some cases, courts have concluded that such a background use of a copyrighted work qualifies as a fair use of the work. This was the court's conclusion in *Amsinck v. Columbia Pictures Industries*,[4] a case in which the plaintiff accused Columbia of infringing his copyright to several teddy bear images by including those images in a "Baby Bears

Musical Mobile" used in the film *Immediate Family*. The court rejected the plaintiff's infringement claim on fair use grounds, finding that the display of the images (which appeared for less than two minutes) was fleeting and that their use in the film would probably have little effect on the market for the plaintiff's work.

In other instances, however, courts have not been so willing to dismiss comparable claims on fair use grounds. For example, in *Woods v. Universal City Studios*,[5] the court refused to dismiss the plaintiff's allegation that Universal and director Terry Gilliam infringed a copyrighted drawing titled "Neomechanical Tower (Upper) Chamber" by incorporating many elements of the drawing into the design of the opening scenes of the film *12 Monkeys*. The court concluded that the prominent use of the design in the film's opening scene and its use for five of the film's 130 total minutes tilted the balance against a finding of fair use.

Although these and other cases have reached conflicting results, they do suggest several factors that courts will weigh in determining whether a background or incidental use of a copyrighted work constitutes a fair use of the work. A key consideration is whether the work is displayed briefly and fleetingly, rather than repeatedly or in a manner that deliberately draws attention to the work (as when the work is shown in close-up or is handled, manipulated, pointed out, or discussed by an actor or actors). The more brief or incidental the use, the more likely is a finding of fair use. The court also will consider the other Section 107 criteria discussed previously, including the potential impact of the unauthorized use on the market for the infringed work. Of course, the only way to cover this copyright base with any certainty is to secure written permission to use the work from the copyright owner.

The Fair Use Checklist

How can you determine whether a particular use of copyrighted material falls within the federal fair use guidelines? Although no sure-fire formula will apply to all situations, the checklist shown in Figure 4.1 can help. The checklist includes a list of questions that will help you evaluate the risks involved in using copyrighted material without the copyright owner's permission. Keep in mind, though, that a court will weigh and balance these and all other relevant factors to come up with a fair use determination. As a result, you should evaluate all of the

Figure 4.1 Fair use checklist for media producers.

1. *Is your production a noncommercial (nonprofit) production?* An unauthorized use is more likely to be considered a fair use if the copyrighted material is being added to a noncommercial, educational production. Conversely, adding the copyrighted materials to a commercial production—a category that includes corporate video programs intended for internal distribution—is less likely to pass the fair use test.

2. *Is your production informational in nature?* The courts tend to be more generous in conceding fair use when the copyrighted material is used in a production that serves some informational or educational purpose. Productions that fit this criterion include commercial or nonprofit documentaries and public affairs and instructional programs.

3. *If the material is being added to an informational production, will it serve informational goals?* When you are adding copyrighted material to an informational production, make sure that you are adding the material for informational rather than artistic or entertainment purposes. For example, using a brief clip from the movie *The Godfather* in a documentary on the public's perception of organized crime could potentially constitute fair use, as long as you could show that the clip is directly tied to the informational content of the production. Using the clip simply for artistic purposes—as the background for a credits sequence, for example—probably would not constitute fair use.

4. *Is the copyrighted material taken from a factual or reference work?* Generally, the courts are more likely to let you borrow material from an encyclopedia or almanac than from a short story, novel, or other work of fiction. The assumption here is that, as reference works, encyclopedias and other compilations of factual information are intended to be used as resources in the creation of other works. Even so, the courts will look closely at the amount and nature of the material taken from a factual work.[6]

5. *Are you using a small enough excerpt of a copyrighted work to have little or no effect on the market value of the whole work?* Under the federal fair use guidelines, the courts must consider "the effect of the use upon the potential market for or value of the copyrighted work." To determine this effect, a court usually will begin by looking at how much of the work you used. A production that incorporates a 30-second segment from a two-hour film would probably pass this part of the fair use test because the court would probably find that the use is small enough to leave the market for the work unaffected. Taking 30 seconds of material from a five-minute film would be a different matter, however, because the excerpt is a large

Figure 4.1 Fair use checklist for media producers. (continued)

enough portion of the entire work to undermine the potential market for the work.

6. *Will the copyrighted material constitute only a small portion of your production?* The courts tend to frown on productions that use too much copyrighted material without authorization. Although the definition of "too much" can vary, the use would probably not be considered fair use of unauthorized copyrighted material if it constitutes more than a small part of the total production.

7. *If the unauthorized use in question involves displaying a copyrighted photograph or work of art within a scene, is the work displayed briefly and inconspicuously?* The incidental or background use of a copyrighted work in a production (e.g., hanging a copyrighted poster or painting on a wall within a scene), in the opinion of some courts, can constitute an infringement of the copyright owner's exclusive rights to the work. If challenged by the copyright owner, such a use will be more likely to qualify as fair use if the work is displayed briefly or fleetingly in a manner that does not draw viewers' attention to the work.

8. *Is the production intended for limited distribution?* If your production is intended for limited distribution to selected audiences, you stand a better chance of securing a finding of fair use than would the producer of a program that is scheduled for repeated showings to more general audiences.

9. *Is this unauthorized use of copyrighted material a single, spontaneous occurrence?* A single, spontaneous use of copyrighted material is more likely to be considered fair use than an instance that is part of an ongoing pattern of copyright abuse.

10. *Will you credit the copyright owner?* When you use a copyrighted work without authorization, you should always credit the copyright owner in the production. Although this will not guarantee a favorable fair use ruling, crediting the copyright owner will at least show that you are acting in good faith. Without this show of good faith, some courts are reluctant to grant a fair use waiver.

circumstances surrounding your production and your use of the copyrighted materials before assuming that your actions will constitute fair use. When in doubt, contact a lawyer who has expertise in copyright law.

The items in the fair use checklist are presented in question form. Before going ahead with an unauthorized use of copyrighted materials, review the checklist and answer yes or no to each question. If all of the responses are yes, the unauthorized use probably constitutes fair use. One or more no responses indicate that the use is problematic, and a call to an attorney is in order. The more no responses, the less likely it is that the use would pass the fair use test in a court of law.

As the checklist shows, fair use almost always is problematic for media professionals who produce programs for profit. Significantly, this group includes video producers working in corporate settings, even when the programs they create are limited to internal distribution. Although most corporate video programs are not sold for profit, lawyers for copyright owners can claim that the productions generate profits for companies by enhancing the performance of employees or sales of the company's products. Otherwise, why would companies put up the money to make them?

Public Domain

When the copyright on a work expires, the work falls into the public domain. Once a work is in the public domain, you are free to use it without the copyright owner's permission. You can make and sell copies of public domain materials, and you can incorporate the materials into other works. But you cannot copyright public domain materials yourself, even when those materials are being used as part of another production. In that case, you could copyright the part of the production that you created, but your copyright would not give you any right to control the distribution or use of the public domain portion.

What Materials Are in the Public Domain?

Public domain works include materials that were never subject to copyright protection (although, as discussed earlier, works that are eligible for copyright protection become protected as soon as they are fixed in a tangible form), materials that cannot be copyrighted under

U.S. law (a category that includes U.S. government publications), and copyrighted materials for which the copyright has expired (e.g., some of the early silent films). Because copyright is granted for only a limited period, all copyrighted materials eventually fall into the public domain, but it is not always easy to determine whether and when that fall from copyright protection occurred. You can start by checking the copyright notice on the work. If the original copyright notice is dated before January 1, 1923, the work is probably in the public domain under current U.S. law. If there is more than one copyright notice on the work, as there might be on updated versions of an older work, the most recent notice must be dated before January 1, 1923.

What about works that do not carry a notice of copyright? In some cases, the fact that a work does not carry a copyright notice may signal that the work is in the public domain. To make sure, ask yourself the following questions:

- *Is the work truly a published work?* Prerelease or prepublication versions of a work are not required to carry a copyright notice; most eventually carry a copyright notice upon publication.
- *If the work is a published work, when was it published?* Works published before January 1, 1978, with the copyright owner's consent but without a copyright notice, may be in the public domain. If the work was published after January 1, 1978, but before March 1, 1989, however, the copyright owner has five years to correct the error before the work falls forever into the public domain. Works published after the United States joined the Berne Convention on March 1, 1989, are even more problematic because the Berne Treaty does not require the display of a proper notice to ensure continued copyright protection.
- *Is this work based on another work?* Although the work in question may not include a copyright notice, it may be based on or developed from a work that does.
- *Is the copyright notice absent or just missing?* In some cases, the copyright notice may have appeared on the original work, but it has since been accidentally or intentionally removed. When this happens, the work is still protected by copyright.

With very limited exceptions, once a work falls into the public domain, the author cannot reclaim it and reinstate copyright. It remains in the public domain forever.[7]

As mentioned earlier, works created by U.S. government employees as part of their official duties cannot be copyrighted under U.S. law. This means that most print and media materials published by the federal government are in the public domain, and you are not required to seek permission to use them. You may be required to identify the U.S. government as the source, however, particularly if your work contains a high percentage of U.S. government material.[8]

Determining Whether a Work Is in the Public Domain

To determine whether a work is in the public domain, you should first examine the work for a copyright notice. Once you find the notice, check the date of copyright. If the date indicates that the work became subject to copyright protection:

- Prior to January 1, 1923, the work is in the public domain—unless the work was modified and published with an updated copyright notice.
- After January 1, 1923, but before January 1, 1950, the work is probably not in the public domain—unless the initial copyright term expired before 1978 and the copyright was not renewed.
- On or after January 1, 1950, the work is almost definitely not in the public domain—unless the last copyright owner took the unusual step of abandoning the copyright.

In the last two cases, the way to determine with the highest degree of certainty if the work is in the public domain is to run a formal copyright search. Copyright searches and investigations are discussed in detail later in this chapter.

If there is no copyright notice on the work, the public domain status is even more difficult to determine. For reasons described earlier, the absence of a copyright notice does not necessarily mean that the work is in the public domain. To make sure, you must determine whether the work is a published or prepublication version, whether the copyright notice truly was left off the published work or simply is missing from your copy, whether the notice was initially left off the work but later restored under applicable provisions of U.S. copyright law, and whether the work might include other copyrighted material. You must also determine when the work was published. Once you

have all of this information, check to see which of the following guidelines applies:

- If the copyright notice is truly absent from a work that was published before 1978, it is probably in the public domain.
- If the copyright notice is truly absent from a work that was published after 1978, it may or may not be in the public domain
because changes in U.S. and international copyright law have
lessened the significance of copyright notices as signals of a
work's copyright status.

If you plan to use materials that fall into the last category, most copyright lawyers would recommend conducting a formal inquiry into the
copyright status of the work. This is particularly true now that the
United States adheres to relevant provisions of the Berne Copyright
Convention, which is discussed later in this chapter, because the Berne
Convention does not require the display of a copyright notice as a condition of copyright protection.

International Issues

The public domain question becomes even more complex when materials cross international boundaries. Here is how the U.S. Copyright
Office has described the problem:

> *Even if you conclude that a work is in the public domain in the United States,
> this does not necessarily mean that you are free to use it in other countries. Every
> nation has its own laws governing the length and scope of copyright protection,
> and these are applicable to uses of the work within that nation's borders. Thus,
> the expiration or loss of copyright protection in the United States may still leave
> the work fully protected against unauthorized use in other countries.*[9]

As this statement warns, the laws governing the status and use of
public domain materials often differ from one nation to the next. In
fact, under recent international agreements to which the United States
is a party, some foreign works that had fallen into the public domain
may have their copyright status reinstated under U.S. law in certain
limited circumstances. As a result, if you are planning to incorporate
public domain materials in a production that will be sold or distributed internationally, or if you are considering including foreign public

domain materials in a production, be sure to consult a lawyer who is familiar with international copyright law. More information on international copyright issues appears later in this chapter.

Purchasing Rights-Free Materials

Rather than spending time searching for public domain or other rights-free materials, many producers prefer to purchase needed items from services that specialize in rights-free works. There are two primary advantages to this approach. First, because most services stockpile and catalogue large libraries of materials, they usually can help you find appropriate items relatively quickly and efficiently. Second, because many agencies will warrant that the materials indeed are free from third-party copyright claims, there is much less reason to worry about infringement suits initiated by irate copyright owners. Considering how difficult it can be to determine whether a work is truly in the public domain, this last advantage is especially significant.

If you do plan to purchase rights-free materials, make sure that your arrangement with the supplier is covered by a written agreement like the one shown in Figure 4.2. Your agreement should specify the items that you are purchasing, the rights that you have to use and modify those items, and how long you will retain the rights to the items. Just as important, your contract should contain warranty and indemnity clauses that protect you from any legal action arising from copyright claims.

The sample contract in Figure 4.2 is a blanket agreement that defines the relationship between a cable television network and a supplier of film and video footage. In this case, the cable network is producing a program about animals, and the supplier will provide footage from its inventory to use in the program. The contract stipulates that the network, The Nature Channel, can license footage from the supplier's inventory at a flat rate of $500 per minute for material actually used in the production. The contract also stipulates that the rights granted to the network are nonexclusive (meaning that the supplier is free to sell the same footage to someone else), that the rights to the footage are limited to the program specified (meaning that the network is not free to use the materials in other programs), and that the network is allowed to edit or modify the footage in any way that it sees fit.

Figure 4.2 Contract covering the licensing of rights-free film or video material.

Agreement dated November 4, 2002, by and between The Nature Channel, Inc., 1108 Broadway, New York, NY 10017 ("TNC") and Sweeney Film Library, 217 West 62nd Street, New York, NY 10019 ("Grantor").

TNC and Grantor (the "Parties") hereby agree as follows:

1. **Definitions.** The following terms when used herein shall have the meanings set forth below:

1.1. "Picture(s)" means any film or video material selected from the Grantor's library by TNC.

1.2. "Cable Television" means the medium in which audiovisual works are delivered or transmitted by any technological means, now or hereafter known, through affiliates (such as affiliated systems or stations), to customers ("Subscribers") who are not all assembled in a single location and who are obligated to pay for the privilege of receiving such exhibitions on particular channels or stations, it being understood that the license to the subscribers shall not entitle them to receive possession of physical materials embodying such audiovisual works and that TNC will not authorize subscribers to charge an admission fee for the privilege of watching any such audiovisual work.

1.3. "Exhibition Day" means any 24-hour period beginning at such time as TNC shall determine in each instance, which may vary from day to day and from time zone to time zone. Under the terms of this Agreement, the number of Exhibition Days in the License Period will be unlimited.

1.4. "License Period" means the period from January 1, 2003, through December 31, 2008.

1.5. "Territory" means the United States, its territories and possessions (including Puerto Rico), and Canada.

2. **Grant of Rights.** For each Picture, Grantor hereby grants to TNC the nonexclusive right and license to exhibit, distribute, transmit, and perform each Picture or part thereof on Cable Television as part of the TNC program "Nature's Way" in the Territory an unlimited number of times on each Exhibition Day during the License Period, and in connection therewith to use and perform any and all music, lyrics, and musical compositions contained in each Picture.

3. **Incidental Rights.** TNC shall have editing rights with respect to each of the Pictures, including the right to cut and dub each Picture, to excerpt

Figure 4.2 Contract covering the licensing of rights-free film or video material. (continued)

portions of each Picture, to combine the excerpts with material from other pictures and programs, and to replace or superimpose matter over the music and soundtracks of each Picture.

4. **Reserved Rights.** All rights not specifically granted herein are reserved to Grantor.

5. **Delivery of Materials.** Copies of materials selected from the Grantor's library shall be delivered on a videotape format to be mutually agreed upon by TNC and Grantor within five (5) working days of the Grantor's receipt of a written request for the materials from TNC. At the end of the License Period, TNC will return all materials received under this Agreement to TNC.

Upon Grantor's request, TNC shall deliver individual copies of programs in which Grantor's materials have been used to Grantor, and Grantor shall store the copies throughout the License Period at Grantor's sole cost and expense. At the end of the License Period, Grantor shall return all such copies to TNC.

6. **Consideration and Payment Terms.** In full consideration of all rights granted herein and all services performed hereunder, TNC shall pay Grantor a License Fee of $500.00 per minute of Pictures used in the TNC program "Nature's Way." The License Fee for fractions of minutes used by TNC will be prorated accordingly.

During the License Period, TNC will provide Grantor with an accounting of, and Grantor will invoice TNC for, Pictures used in "Nature's Way" on a monthly basis. Payment will be due within thirty (30) days following the receipt of each such invoice by TNC. Late payments will be assessed interest at the rate of 1.5% per month.

7. **Grantor's Representations and Warranties.** Grantor hereby represents and warrants that it is free to enter into and fully perform this Agreement. Grantor further represents that each Picture is either in the public domain or that Grantor owns and/or has the right to grant all rights granted herein with respect to the Pictures. Without limiting the foregoing, Grantor represents and warrants that TNC's exercise of the rights in the Pictures granted herein will not violate any copyright, trademark right, right of publicity, or other personal or property right of any individual or entity.

8. **Indemnity.** Grantor shall at all times indemnify and hold harmless TNC, its licensees, assignees, and affiliated companies, and the officers,

Figure 4.2 Contract covering the licensing of rights-free film or video material. (continued)

directors, employees, and agents of TNC against and from any and all claims, damages, liabilities, costs, and expenses, including reasonable counsel fees, herein collectively called "claims," arising out of any breach by Grantor of any representation, warranty, or other provision hereof. In the event of any claim or service of process upon TNC involving the indemnification set forth in this section of this Agreement, TNC shall notify Grantor of the claim. Grantor will promptly adjust, settle, defend, or otherwise dispose of such claim at its sole cost. If Grantor has been so notified and is not diligently and continuously pursuing such matter, TNC may take such action on behalf of itself and/or as attorney-in-fact for Grantor, to adjust, settle, defend, or otherwise dispose of such claim, in which case Grantor shall, upon being billed therefor, promptly reimburse TNC in the amount thereof.

TNC shall at all times indemnify and hold harmless Grantor, its licensees, assignees, and affiliated companies, and the officers, directors, employees, and agents of Grantor against and from any and all claims, damages, liabilities, costs, and expenses, including reasonable counsel fees, herein collectively called "claims," arising out of TNC's use and exploitation of the Picture, except to the extent that any such claim results from a breach by Grantor of its representations and warranties contained herein. In the event of any claim or service of process upon Grantor involving the indemnification set forth in this section of this Agreement, Grantor shall notify TNC of the claim. TNC shall promptly adjust, settle, defend, or otherwise dispose of such claim at its sole cost. If TNC has been so notified and is not diligently and continuously pursuing such matter, Grantor may take such action on behalf of itself and/or as attorney-in-fact for TNC, to adjust, settle, defend, or otherwise dispose of such claim, in which case TNC shall, upon being billed therefor, promptly reimburse Grantor in the amount thereof.

9. **Miscellaneous.** This Agreement contains the entire understanding and supersedes all prior understandings between the parties relating to the subject matter herein. This Agreement cannot be modified, or amended, except in a writing signed by both parties. This Agreement shall be governed by the laws of the State of New York as applied to agreements intended to be performed entirely within that state. The parties hereby agree to submit any dispute hereunder to the exclusive jurisdiction of courts located in New York, New York. This Agreement may be freely assigned by either party to any competent assignee that is capable of fulfilling the terms herein, provided that any such assignee agrees in writing to assume all of the assigning party's obligations under this Agreement. This Agreement

Figure 4.2 Contract covering the licensing of rights-free film or video material. (continued)

may be executed by original or facsimile signature and in two or more counterparts, each of which will be deemed an original, but all of which together will comprise a single instrument.

IN WITNESS WHEREOF, the parties hereto execute this Agreement as of the date first specified above.

SWEENEY FILM LIBRARY   THE NATURE CHANNEL, INC. ("TNC")

By: _____   By: _____

Its: _____   Its: _____

The license period for the footage runs from January 1, 2003, to December 31, 2008. If The Nature Channel plans to exhibit the programs containing the footage after that date, it must negotiate a new agreement with the supplier. Other clauses in the contract define the territory where the programs containing the footage can be transmitted, how many times the programs can be transmitted, and how and when the supplier will be paid for the footage.

Although the contract shown in Figure 4.2 was written to cover the purchase of copyright-free material, a similar sort of agreement should be drawn up when you are negotiating for the right to use copyrighted materials. For more information, see the section on negotiating with copyright owners that appears later in this chapter.

Conducting a Copyright Investigation

If you are unable to determine whether a work is copyrighted or you require more information about the current copyright status of a work, a copyright investigation may be in order. Although this may sound like something that only a lawyer could conduct, the process is quite simple. All it requires is a little time, a little information, and a little money. Because a copyright investigation involves the services of a government agency, it also requires a little paperwork.

Initiating a Copyright Investigation

Most copyright investigations follow a straightforward, two-step process. You first examine the work in question for a copyright notice and any other information that may help identify the author, publisher, and place and date of publication. Then you complete the search request form shown in Figure 4.3 and submit the form to the Copyright Office. For a fee of $75 per hour or each fraction of an hour, the Copyright Office will review its records and issue a search report. The form shown in Figure 4.3 and the rules and guidelines governing copyright searches are also available online at www.copyright.gov. It is also possible to conduct a limited search of copyright records at this site.

The more information you are able to supply with your request, the more successful the search is likely to be. The Copyright Office asks that you provide as much of the following information as possible:

- The type of work involved (e.g., book, play, musical composition, sound recording, photograph)
- The title of the work, with any possible variants
- The name of the authors or creators, including possible pseudonyms
- The approximate year when the work was created, published, or registered with the Copyright Office
- The name of the probable copyright owners, which may be the publisher or, in the case of audiovisual works, the producer

Many films, video productions, and audiovisual works are based on copyrighted books, short stories, or magazine articles. Many also may include music or video footage that exists under a separate copyright. If you want the Copyright Office to search for information about these underlying materials, you must indicate this in your search request. You also must provide as many details as possible about the underlying materials. This information is often available as part of the copyright notice or production credits on the work in question.

Once the Copyright Office receives your information, it will send you an estimate of how much your copyright search is likely to cost. If you prefer, the Copyright Office will convey the estimate and the results of the search by telephone. To receive the information by phone, you simply check the appropriate box on the search request form and

Figure 4.3 Copyright search request form.

search request form

Library of Congress
Copyright Office
101 Independence Ave., S.E.
Washington, D.C.
20559-6000

Reference & Bibliography Section
(202) 707-6850
8:30 a.m. to 5 p.m. eastern time
Monday through Friday,
Fax: (202) 252-3485

Type of work:

☐ Book ☐ Music ☐ Motion Picture ☐ Drama ☐ Sound Recording ☐ Computer Program
☐ Photograph/Artwork ☐ Map ☐ Periodical ☐ Contribution ☐ Architectural Work ☐ Mask Work

Search information you require:

☐ Registration ☐ Renewal ☐ Assignment ☐ Address

Specifics of work to be searched:

TITLE: _____

AUTHOR: _____

COPYRIGHT CLAIMANT: _____
(name in © notice)

APPROXIMATE YEAR DATE OF PUBLICATION/CREATION: _____

REGISTRATION NUMBER (if known): _____

OTHER IDENTIFYING INFORMATION: _____

If you need more space please attach additional pages.

Estimates are based on the Copyright Office fee of $75 an **hour or fraction of an hour** consumed. The more information you furnish as a basis for the search, the better service we can provide. The time between the date of receipt of your fee for the search and your receiving a report will vary from 8 to 12 weeks depending on workload.*

Names, titles, and short phrases are not copyrightable.

Please read Circular 22 for more information on copyright searches.

YOUR NAME: _____ DATE: _____

ADDRESS: _____

DAYTIME TELEPHONE NO. (_____) _____

Convey results of estimate/search by telephone
☐ yes ☐ no

Fee enclosed? ☐ yes Amount $ _____
☐ no

Copyright Office fees are subject to change. For current fees, check the Copyright Office website at *www.copyright.gov,* write the Copyright Office, or call (202) 707-3000.

provide your daytime phone number. Otherwise, the estimate and search report will be sent by mail.

The $75-per-hour charge covers the cost of the Copyright Office employee who will perform your search. If you would rather not pay this fee or if you require the information immediately, you can conduct your own copyright search. Most records of the Copyright Office are open to public inspection weekdays from 8:30 a.m. to 5 p.m. Of course, unless you live in the Washington, D.C., area or near one of the libraries in the United States that maintains a copy of the Copyright Office's Catalog of Copyright Entries, a do-it-yourself search will cost you traveling expenses. It also will necessitate time away from the office, studio, or editing room for you or a designated employee. For these reasons, most media producers let the Copyright Office do the searching for them. If you work in a corporate setting, your company's legal office may be willing to handle the search for you. You can also hire a professional service to conduct a search and generate a copyright report. The cost for such services runs several hundred dollars and up, depending on how quickly you require results and the complexity of the search.

Limitations of Copyright Investigations

Although a copyright investigation can uncover key information about a work, the results of a copyright search are not always conclusive. Notably, you should not assume that a work is in the public domain simply because a search fails to turn up a record of the work. The reason for this is simple: The Copyright Office files contain records on all works registered through the office, but a work does not have to be registered to be copyrighted.

For reasons explained elsewhere in this chapter, the following types of materials probably are protected by copyright even though they are not currently registered with the U.S. Copyright Office:

- Any work published after 1978 (although there are several advantages to registering)
- Works published before 1978 but after December 31, 1922, provided that the copyright owner has complied with applicable copyright renewal and notice requirements
- Unpublished works created before 1978 that are entitled to copyright protection under provisions contained in common law

- Works that were originally published or registered in a foreign country that subscribes to one or more international copyright agreements to which the United States also is a party

A copyright search may be inconclusive for any of these reasons:

- The work may have been registered recently, and the information has not yet been cataloged.
- The information in the search request may not have been complete or specific enough to identify the work.
- The work may have been registered under a different title or as part of a larger work.

For all of these reasons, search reports are most useful for documenting the status of copyrighted works that are registered with the Copyright Office. They are much less useful for fully verifying that a work is free from copyright protection.

Obtaining the Right to Use Copyrighted Materials

As the preceding sections have shown, media producers who use or borrow other people's material must consider the implications of their actions. Producers who simply shrug off these concerns place themselves, their productions, and their companies at considerable risk. This does not mean that producers should avoid using copyrighted material in their programs—only that they should follow proper permissions procedures.

When you are thinking of adding someone else's material to a production, follow these steps:

1. *Determine whether the material is protected by copyright or in the public domain.* To make this determination, use the guidelines provided earlier in this chapter on the use of public domain materials. If you determine that the work is in the public domain, you are free to use it without seeking permissions or clearances. If the work is not in the public domain, proceed to step 2.
2. *Determine whether your use of the copyrighted material will qualify as fair use under the Copyright Act of 1976.* To make this

determination, review the fair use checklist and guidelines on fair use from this chapter (see Figure 4.1). If your use clearly qualifies as fair use, you are free to use the materials without seeking permissions or clearances. If the use fails the fair use test, proceed to step 3.

3. *If the materials fail the public domain or fair use test, you must contact the copyright owner and request permission to use the work.*[10]

To receive permission to use a copyrighted work, you must first find the copyright owner. Then, once the copyright owner indicates a willingness to grant permission, you must negotiate the specific rights that you will have to the work. In most cases, you will also need to negotiate a fee for using the work.

Rather than complete this process on their own, some producers prefer to hire rights and permissions services that specialize in securing licenses to use copyrighted materials. Appendix B provides contact information for several such services. In addition, Chapter 6 includes suggestions for working with rights and permissions services. Although those suggestions are offered in the context of obtaining music clearances, they are also generally applicable when using services to obtain rights in film and video footage, literary works, and other copyrighted materials.

Contacting the Copyright Owner

Reaching the current copyright owner is not always as simple as it sounds. Often, the original copyright owner listed on the work is not the current copyright owner. And even when the copyright notice does list the correct individual as the copyright owner, sometimes the work offers no clues to the individual's current whereabouts.

When information about the current owner is hard to come by, media producers must become copyright detectives. Start by searching the work for any clues that might help you locate the owner. For example, even though the copyright notice may not reveal the copyright owner's address, the address of the publisher or distributor is probably provided somewhere on or in the work. In many cases, the copyright owner has given the publishing or distribution company the rights to license the work. When this is the case, a call to the company's rights and permissions department may be all that is needed to get the permissions process started. If the copyright owner has retained these sublicensing rights, the publisher or distributor can usually provide the address or phone number of the current copyright owner.

Here are some suggested steps for producers who find themselves thrust into the role of copyright detectives:

1. *Examine the work for a copyright notice.* The notice will list the name of the company or individual who owned the work when this version was published. Search the copyright notice and the area surrounding the notice, the title page (in the case of printed material), and the credits and outside packaging (in the case of videotapes, DVDs, and other audiovisual materials) for clues to where the copyright owner can be reached. If this search uncovers sufficient information, try to contact the copyright owner directly.

2. *If you are unable to reach the copyright owner, search the work for information about the publisher or distributor.* If this search is successful, contact the publisher or distributor and determine if the company has the rights to negotiate permissions for the copyright owner. If the company has these rights, begin the negotiations. If the company does not have the rights, have it put you in touch with the copyright owner.

3. *If you are unable to determine the copyright owner or publisher, you may need to conduct a copyright investigation.* As explained earlier in this chapter, a properly conducted copyright investigation will uncover any information about the work that is stored in the files of the Copyright Office. Assuming that the work was registered with the Copyright Office, the files will contain information about the original copyright owner and any transfers of ownership that have been registered with the office.

Needless to say, this detective work can consume considerable time and effort. Before beginning the process, determine how much you want the work in question and exactly how much time you are willing to devote to securing the proper permissions. You should also have some alternative materials in mind. As you approach your time limit, evaluate the situation. Are you close to reaching a deal with the copyright owner? If you are not close, how much additional time and effort are the materials worth? Will alternative materials suffice?

When the permissions process drags on, producers sometimes are tempted to abandon the copyright quest and use the materials without permission. If this temptation strikes, resist it. If you do decide to give up the copyright quest, be sure that you also decide, at the same time, to abandon any thought of using the materials.

Negotiating with Copyright Owners

Once you contact the copyright owner, the negotiations for the right to use the materials can begin. During the discussions, keep one key consideration in mind: Copyright is a property right. This means that copyright owners truly do own and control their creative works, much in the way that you might own and control the use of a home, automobile, or some other piece of personal property. In other words, if a copyright owner does not want to let you use his or her creative property, he or she does not have to.

In actual practice, however, most copyright owners will be willing to grant the permission that you are after—provided that they have something to gain. Usually, this something is cash payment, promotional considerations, or both. For example, most movie studios willingly supply film clips to television reviewers as part of their effort to promote their new films. For the same reason, many record companies have been willing to supply music videos to MTV and other music-oriented television services. As production costs have risen, however, some record companies have determined that the promotional value provided by the music television programs is not sufficient consideration. As a result, many companies now require music television programs to pay for the videos they air.

Before you enter into serious negotiations with a copyright owner, take time to assess your bargaining position. In many cases, you may discover that you have the advantage in the negotiations, not the copyright owner. After all, you will be offering many copyright owners what amounts to an unexpected gift, the chance to collect a bit of revenue from a property that might otherwise simply sit on a shelf collecting dust. Of course, this is more likely to be the case if you are asking for permission to use clips from a documentary production or corporate video program, rather than material from a hit television show or feature film.

If possible, begin your negotiations with a phone call to the copyright owner. Explain what materials you would like to use, how you plan to use them, and what you are willing to offer as consideration. Then, assuming you are able to agree on these fundamental terms, follow up with a written agreement that specifies the following:

- The material you are licensing. Include the running time of the segments, plus a brief description that identifies the material (e.g., "the 5-minute, 45-second interview with Charlie Elliot, legendary jazz guitarist, from your film *The Guitar Slingers*")
- How you will use the material (e.g., "for use in a video documentary on the history of jazz music in the United States")
- How your production will be distributed (e.g., "for sale on videocassette and DVD to schools and libraries")
- How long you will have the rights to use the material (e.g., "for the 10-year period beginning January 1, 2003, and ending December 31, 2012")
- What rights you will have to modify and edit the material
- What consideration you will provide to the copyright owner for the right to use the material

Like the agreement shown in Figure 4.2, your contract should include a clause in which the copyright owner warrants that he or she truly does have the right to license the materials.

During your negotiations with copyright owners, much of the bargaining will focus on the consideration, or payment, that you are offering in return for the rights to use the material. As you negotiate the consideration, remember the guidelines offered earlier. Above all, know how badly you need the materials and exactly how much you are willing to pay. Do not expect the copyright owner to give materials away, but do not allow yourself to be held hostage to unreasonable demands. Instead, have some alternative materials in mind, and make it known that you are willing to use the alternatives if the price is not right.

Another potential snag in negotiations with copyright owners is the issue of artistic control. As the person who is paying for rights, you want complete control over how material will be used in your production. In particular, you want the right to edit and modify the materials so they fit with the purpose and look of your production.

That may be what you want, but that may not be what the copyright owner is willing to provide. As part of licensing agreements, some copyright owners insist on retaining some measure of control over how their materials are used. This is particularly true when the materials have historic or artistic significance. For example, the family of a deceased actor may be unwilling to license clips from the actor's classic films unless you certify that the clips will be used to portray the actor in a positive light. As discussed in Chapter 7, if an actor featured in a clip from a film or television production is a member of SAG or AFTRA, the permission of the actor (or the family, if the actor is deceased) may be required in addition to the permission of the party that owns the copyright in the clip. Also, as discussed in the section on "The Right of Publicity" in Chapter 5, permission from the actor is generally required if you will use the clip in a commercial or other context in which the actor may appear to endorse a product or service.

As a rule, avoid agreements that restrict the manner in which you can use the licensed materials. Even though these restrictions may seem innocent, they leave your production decisions open to interpretation and, ultimately, legal action. If you must sign a licensing agreement that restricts your ability to edit or modify the materials, make sure that the restrictions are spelled out in detail. In particular, the agreement should specify how and when the copyright owner will be allowed to review the production, as well as how any dispute over the use of the materials will be resolved.

Finally, many copyright owners will ask that you acknowledge the source of the materials in credits within the program and, in some cases, on packaging and promotional material for the program. Most producers are willing to agree to reasonable credit requirements, particularly because such requirements do not require out-of-pocket payments by the producer. Be careful, however, to specify in agreements that contain such credit requirements that the producer's inadvertent failure to abide by the requirements will not be deemed a material breach of the agreement, provided that the producer agrees to correct such failures prospectively (i.e., on future releases of the production or promotional materials).

Moral Rights

Media producers should also be aware of the growing movement to grant artists the right to control how their work is modified even after they have sold the copyright. Proponents of "moral rights" or "droit moral" hold that artists in the United States should have the legal right to prevent the distortion or mutilation of their work. This right is well established in many European countries, particularly those countries that subscribe to the Berne Copyright Convention and its provision that authors should have the right to object to the distribution or modification of their works even after the works have been sold.

In the United States, federal law does not grant most creators of copyrighted works this type of protection. Several states have enacted legislation in this area, however, and a 1990 amendment to the Copyright Act of 1976 did grant the creators of certain visual works (but not audiovisual productions) limited rights to protect the integrity of their works after sale.[11]

What does all of this mean for media producers? First, producers in New York, California, Massachusetts, and other states that have passed moral rights legislation should be aware of what restrictions, if any, these state laws place on their right to edit and modify licensed materials without the original copyright owner's consent.[12] In these states, it is particularly important that your contract with the copyright owner spells out these rights in detail. Second, producers who are licensing the rights to use works created in countries other than the United States should make sure that their use of the materials is governed by U.S. law rather than by the laws of the nation in which the works were originally copyrighted. In most cases, this is simply a matter of making sure that the licensing agreement includes a clause to this effect. Finally, as a general rule and as shown in several of the sample agreements in Chapter 2, the "ownership" or "assignment of rights" provisions in all production agreements that cover the creation of copyrightable works such as scripts or video footage should provide that the contractor expressly waives all "so-called moral rights of authors and all other similar rights however denominated throughout the world" to the maximum extent permitted by applicable laws.

Finally, producers should continue to monitor efforts at state and federal levels to broaden artists' moral rights to works that they have sold or licensed. This will be especially important if, as has been proposed, Congress further amends the Copyright Act of 1976 to incorporate more of the moral rights granted under the Berne Convention and other international copyright agreements.

Errors and Omissions Insurance

Many licensing agreements include a clause that requires the licensor (the individual or company that is selling the materials) to certify that the transaction is covered by errors and omissions (E&O) insurance.

E&O insurance protects both parties if the licensor's right to license the materials is ever called into question. A typical E&O clause might include the following legal language:

> *Upon execution of this agreement, and prior to the payment of any portion of the license fee described hereunder, the licensor shall secure a policy of Errors and Omissions liability insurance applicable to the program material described hereunder. Such policy shall name the licensee as additional insured and shall have limits of at least $1 million per occurrence with respect to each loss or claim involving the same offending act, failure to act, or matter whether made by one or more persons and regardless of frequency of repetition. Such policy shall be secured at the licensor's own cost and shall be maintained by the licensor until thirty (30) days after the expiration of the license period described hereunder. Promptly after execution, Licensor shall provide Licensee with a certificate of insurance outlining the foregoing terms and provisions.*

In simple terms, this language requires the licensor to certify that the materials are covered by an E&O policy, that the licensee (the group that is purchasing the materials) is listed as an additional insured on the policy, and that the policy provides for adequate levels of protection if disputes over ownership of the licensed materials result in judgments against the parties.

E&O clauses are most common in contracts that cover the licensing of entire films or videos from distributors and production companies. Because the distributor or production company often is not the original or sole copyright owner, the group that is licensing the work usually will seek some extra protection against the possibility of copyright suits over licensing rights. E&O insurance provides this protection. (For more information about production insurance, see Chapter 5.)

Additional Concerns for Licensing Certain Materials

The guidelines offered so far should cover most situations in which a producer is licensing the rights to use copyrighted materials. Certain situations and materials warrant special caution, however. Here is a selected list:

- *The use of copyrighted photographs in media productions.* As intellectual properties go, an 8-by-10-inch photograph may seem too small to create much of a copyright fuss. As creative properties, however, photographs can be, and generally are, protected by copyright. As a result, you must secure permission from the copyright owner before using a photograph in a production. Significantly, because you usually will display the entire photograph, the use of a copyrighted photograph rarely qualifies as fair use.

- *The use of works created as works-made-for-hire.* In these cases, the copyright owner is not the creator of the work, but rather the company or entity for which the creator worked. Make sure that you are negotiating with the correct party.
- *The licensing of scripts.* When you are licensing a finished script, take special care to define the rights that the writer will retain to the work. Is the deal a buyout, or will the writer receive royalties from the revenues generated by the finished production? Is the writer a member of the Writer's Guild of America (WGA), so that the residual, reuse, and ownership provisions of the WGA agreement will apply? (See Chapter 7.)
- *The licensing of film or video rights to a literary work.* Is the deal a buyout, or will the author of the work receive royalties? Also, is the literary work based on underlying works that may raise additional copyright questions?

In the last two cases, the licensing agreement should take the form of a full-fledged contract that is prepared, or at least reviewed, by an attorney who is experienced with such agreements. For more information about contracts, see Chapters 2 and 3.

International Copyright

As previously discussed, works created by U.S. citizens are protected by the Copyright Act of 1976 as amended. But what about works created in foreign countries, or works created in the United States by foreign citizens? These materials are also protected by the Copyright Act of 1976, provided they meet one or more of the following qualifications from Section 104 of the act:

- They are unpublished works, which the act protects "without regard to the nationality or domicile of the author."

- They are published works created by an author who, on the date of first publication, is a domiciliary of the United States or a "national, domiciliary, or sovereign authority of a foreign nation that is a party of a copyright treaty to which the United States is also a party."
- They are published works created by an author who, on the date of first publication, is a "stateless person, wherever that person may be domiciled."
- The work was first published in the United States or a foreign country that, on the date of first publication, was a party to the Universal Copyright Convention.
- The work was first published by the United Nations or the Organization of American States.
- The work comes within the scope of copyright protection extended under a presidential decree issued when the president determines that a foreign nation is providing copyright protection to U.S. authors "on substantially the same basis" as that provided to its own citizens.
- The work is a Berne Convention work. (See the following discussion of the Berne Convention.)

As Figure 4.4 shows, more than 150 nations are signatories to one or more international copyright treaties to which the U.S. subscribes. In most cases, this means that foreign authors from a signatory nation must receive the same copyright protection within the boundaries of another signatory nation as that nation extends to its own citizens.

Figure 4.4 lists countries that had established formal copyright relations with the United States as of May 1999. You should not assume, however, that a foreign work is free from copyright protection simply because it was created in a country that is absent from the list. The country in question may be a recent signatory to a copyright treaty, it may have only recently clarified its copyright position, or it may be covered by copyright protection extended under a presidential decree. To determine a country's current copyright status, contact the U.S. Copyright Office or an attorney who is knowledgeable in this area.

For media producers, the message is clear: Approach all works created by foreign citizens with the same care and caution that you direct toward works by Americans. In fact, foreign materials often require extra caution and care. The exact copyright status of these works can be difficult to determine, and the copyright owners often

Figure 4.4 Countries that have established formal copyright relations with the United States as of May 1999.

The following lists countries that have established some level of formal copyright relations with the United States. In most cases, this means that the country is a signatory to at least one international treaty or agreement to which the United States is also a signatory.

Albania	Cuba
Algeria	Cyprus
Andorra	Czech Republic
Antigua and Barbuda	Czechoslovakia
Argentina	Denmark
Armenia	Djibouti
Australia	Dominica
Austria	Dominican Republic
Azerbaijan	Ecuador
Bahamas, The	Egypt
Bahrain	El Salvador
Bangladesh	Equatorial
Barbados	Guinea
Belarus	Estonia
Belgium	Faso
Belize	Fiji
Benin	Finland
Bolivia	France
Bosnia and Herzegovina	Gabon
Botswana	Gambia, The
Brazil	Georgia
Brunei	Germany
Bulgaria	Ghana
Burkina	Greece
Burundi	Grenada
Cambodia	Guatemala
Cameroon	Guinea
Canada	Guinea-Bissau
Cape Verde	Guyana
Central African Republic	Haiti
Chad	Honduras
Chile	Hong Kong
China	Hungary
Colombia	Iceland
Congo	India
Costa Rica	Indonesia
Cote d'Ivoire (Ivory Coast)	Ireland
Croatia	Israel

Figure 4.4 Countries that have established formal copyright relations with the United States as of May 1999. (continued)

Italy	Paraguay
Jamaica	Peru
Japan	Philippines
Kazakhstan	Poland
Kenya	Portugal
Korea	Qatar
Kuwait	Romania
Krgyz Republic	Russian Federation
Laos	Rwanda
Latvia	St. Christopher (St. Kitts) and Nevis
Lebanon	Saint Lucia
Lesotho	Saint Vincent and the Grenadines
Liberia	Saudi Arabia
Libya	Senegal
Liechtenstein	Sierra Leone
Lithuania	Singapore
Luxembourg	Slovakia
Macau	Slovenia
Macedonia	Solomon Islands
Madagascar	South Africa
Malawi	Spain
Malaysia	Sri Lanka
Maldives	Suriname
Mali	Swaziland
Malta	Sweden
Mauritania	Switzerland
Mauritius	Tajikistan
Mexico	Tanzania
Moldova	Thailand
Monaco	Togo
Mongolia	Trinidad and Tobago
Morocco	Tunisia
Mozambique	Turkey
Myanmar (formerly Burma)	Uganda
Namibia	Ukraine
Netherlands	United Arab Emirates
New Zealand	United Kingdom
Nicaragua	Uruguay
Niger	Vatican City
Nigeria	Venezuela
Norway	Vietnam
Pakistan	Yugoslavia
Panama	Zaire
Papau New Guinea	Zambia
	Zimbabwe

can be difficult to contact. With this in mind, you may want to work with a lawyer who is familiar with international copyright law.

The Berne Convention

International trade in intellectual properties such as theatrical films, books, television programs, videocassettes, and computer software has increased dramatically in recent years. Today, major motion pictures released by Hollywood studios often generate more revenue internationally than domestically, television shows such as "Baywatch" and "Friends" are viewed worldwide, and software companies such as Microsoft are among the leading U.S. exporters. Along with this increasing internationalization of the entertainment and information marketplace has come the increased internationalization of copyright law.

The United States, a longtime holdout on the international copyright front, recently has taken substantial steps to bring U.S. copyright law more in line with international practice. A major step occurred on March 1, 1989, when the United States officially entered into the Berne Union for the Protection of Literary and Artistic Property, the entity more commonly known as the Berne Convention.[13] As mentioned earlier in this chapter in the section on Moral Rights, one implication of the United States joining the Berne Convention is that authors eventually may be given new rights to control the modification of their work. Another implication is that the display of a proper copyright notice no longer is required to ensure continued copyright protection. This last change was made when Congress passed the Berne Convention Implementation Act of 1988, a bill that made several, mostly small, changes to the Copyright Act of 1976 to bring it more in line with the Berne treaty. In addition, the United States recently has subscribed to several other international pacts with important copyright implications, including the Uruguay Round Agreements of 1994[14] and the World Intellectual Property Organization (WIPO) Copyright Treaty of 1996.[15]

To media producers, one clear benefit of the United States joining the Berne Convention and other international copyright agreements is broader international protection of their finished productions. All members of the Berne Convention must provide at least the minimum level of copyright protection specified in the treaty. In addition, members must agree to offer citizens of foreign countries the same level of copyright protection that they offer to their own citizens.

Summary

- *What is copyright?* Copyright is a group of property rights granted to the creators of literary, artistic, musical, dramatic, and audiovisual works. Copyright gives the creators of these works the exclusive right to reproduce and distribute copies of their works, to create derivative works, and to perform and display the works publicly. Copyright also gives creators and authors the right to determine whether their work will be used as part of another work, including films, video programs, and other audiovisual productions.

- *What are the sources of copyright law?* In the United States, the primary source of copyright law is the Copyright Act of 1976. This comprehensive federal legislation effectively supersedes all state copyright law and all previous federal copyright laws.

- *What can be copyrighted?* Almost any creative work that appears in a fixed form can be copyrighted. Works that can be copyrighted include books and plays; films, television programs, and other audiovisual works; scripts for audiovisual works; photographs and paintings; musical compositions and sound recordings; and computer software.

- *What cannot be copyrighted?* Items that cannot be copyrighted include ideas, materials produced by federal government employees as part of their jobs, scientific and factual information, inventions and industrial processes, and titles of products or services. Several of these items may be eligible for other types of protection, however, including patents and trademarks.

- *How is copyright established?* Under current U.S. copyright law, copyright is established automatically as soon as a work eligible for copyright protection is created in fixed form. To ensure maximum protection, the work should include a copyright notice and be registered with the U.S. Copyright Office.

- *How long does copyright last?* Works created after January 1, 1978, are protected for the life of the author plus 70 years. If the author is listed as a group or organization, as is often the case with media productions, the term of a copyright is 95 years from the date of publication. The term for works created before 1978 varies. The maximum term for these works is 95 years from the date that the copyright first became effective.

- *What is copyright infringement?* Copyright infringement occurs when someone uses a work in a manner that violates the copyright owner's exclusive rights to the work. The most common violations include duplicating copies of the work or creating derivative works without the copyright owner's express permission. Copyright infringement is a violation of federal law.
- *What is fair use?* Section 107 of the Copyright Act of 1976 defines several conditions under which it is legal to use a copyrighted work without the copyright owner's permission. When a use satisfies Section 107's criteria, it qualifies as a fair use. An unauthorized use is most likely to qualify as a fair use if it is educational or informational in nature, if the work being copied is a reference or other nonfiction work, and if the use has little or no impact on the potential market for the work.
- *What are public domain materials?* Public domain materials are works that are free from copyright protection. This category includes works that were never copyrighted, works that cannot be copyrighted, works for which the copyright has expired, and works for which the copyright has been abandoned. When a work is in the public domain, you are free to use it without seeking permission from the original creator or copyright owner.
- *How do you obtain the rights to use copyrighted materials?* To obtain the rights to use copyrighted materials, you must first contact the individual, group, or company that controls the copyright. Then you must negotiate a licensing agreement that specifies the materials that are covered by the agreement, the rights that you will have to use and modify the materials, the duration of those rights, and the consideration that you will offer the copyright owner.

Notes

1. Copyright Act of 1976, 17 U.S.C. § 401(b).
2. Pub. L. 105–298, 112 Stat. 2827 (October 27, 1998).
3. One exception to the general rule that copyright infringement actions are filed in federal court is when the copyright infringe-

ment claim is one component in a larger case involving breach of contract, business tort, or other state law claims. In such a case, the plaintiff may elect to file the case in state court, although the defendant can seek to "remove" the case to federal court based on the presence of the federal copyright claim. Typically, however, plaintiffs prefer to litigate in federal courts if possible, since (among other reasons) federal court dockets often are less crowded than state court dockets.

4. *Amsinck v. Columbia Pictures Industries*, 862 F. Supp. 1044 (S.D.N.Y 1994).

5. *Woods v. Universal City Studios*, 920 F. Supp. 62 (S.D.N.Y. 1996).

6. The U.S. Supreme Court has made clear that facts are not subject to copyright protection, so that "second comers" may use the facts contained in existing works in creating their own works. The "original selection and arrangement" of facts within an existing work is copyrightable, however, as is the particular textual or visual context (such as an encyclopedia entry) in which the facts are presented. *Feist Publications Inc. v. Rural Telephone Service Co.*, 449 U.S. 340 (1991).

7. The primary exception to this general rule is that, under Section 104A of the Copyright Act as amended, copyright may be restored for certain eligible foreign works that fell into the public domain under U.S. law while still protected in their countries of origin.

8. These provisions apply only to U.S. government materials. Materials published by state and local governments may be copyrighted.

9. *How to Investigate the Copyright Status of a Work*, Circular R22. Washington, DC: Copyright Office, Library of Congress.

10. As mentioned earlier, the permissions process for music differs from the process described here. For more information about licensing music, see Chapter 6.

11. The Visual Rights Act of 1990, Pub. L. 101–650, 104 Stat. 5128 (December 1, 1990) added Section 106A to the U.S. Copyright Act. Section 106A gives the authors of "works of visual art" certain "rights of attribution and integrity" to their works comparable to the moral rights protected under the Berne Convention, including the right to be correctly identified with their works and to prevent mutilation of their works in ways that would adversely affect their professional reputations.

12. The California statute, the California Art Preservation Act, is CALIFORNIA CIVIL CODE §§ 987–989. The Massachusetts statute is MASSACHUSETTS GENERAL LAWS, ch. 231, §§ 85S. The New York

statute, the New York Artists' Authorship Rights Act, is NEW YORK ARTS AND CULTURAL AFFAIRS LAW §§ 6 11.01–16.01. Other states with "artist rights" statutes include Connecticut (CONN. GEN. STAT. § 42–116t), Louisiana (LA. REV. STAT. § 2152–2156), Maine (ME. REV. STAT. §§ 303), and New Jersey (N.J. STAT. ANN. §§ 2A:24A1–2A:24A8).

13. In addition to the Berne Convention, the other major international copyright agreement to which the United States is a party is the Universal Copyright Convention (UCC).

14. Congress implemented certain aspects of the Uruguay Round Agreements by passing the Uruguay Round Agreements Act of 1994, Pub. L. 103–465, 108 Stat. 4809 (December 8, 1994), which amended Section 104A of the U.S. Copyright Act to provide for restoration of copyright in certain foreign works that had fallen into the public domain under prior U.S. law but that remained protected by copyright or comparable rights in their country of origin.

15. Addressing a concern raised by the rapidly increasing use of the Internet, the WIPO Copyright Treaty confirmed that the digital transmission and distribution of literary and artistic works is one of the exclusive rights reserved to copyright owners of such works under the Berne Convention.

5

Playing It Safe: Permits, Releases, Libel, and Production Insurance

As the preceding chapters have shown, part of a producer's job is to think defensively. Producers must anticipate the many legal matters that can come up during production, and they must work to protect their projects against the possibility of lawsuits and other legal challenges. Chapters 2 and 3 discussed ways that carefully written contracts can protect all parties in a media production, and Chapter 4 described steps that producers can take to prevent problems concerning the use of copyrighted materials. This chapter introduces three more weapons that should be part of every producer's defensive arsenal: shooting permits, talent and location releases, and production insurance. You also will learn about privacy and libel law, two areas of media law that are of increasing concern for media producers.

Shooting or Location Permits

Many states and municipalities require producers to obtain permits for location work, particularly when that work will be performed on public thoroughfares or government property. In some localities, these shooting or location permits are issued by state, county, or city offices that serve as liaisons between producers and the police department, fire department, and other public agencies that will provide services or supervision during the course of the shoot. Many of these film and television offices now make their permit applications available online.

For the names and addresses of selected film and television offices, see Appendix A.

Types of Permits

The term *shooting permit* actually is misleading because keeping a location shoot legal can involve obtaining an entire series of permits and licenses. If you were planning a location shoot in Los Angeles, for example, some of the required federal, state, county, and local forms might include the following:

- If you will be shooting on property owned or controlled by the U.S. government, you may need to obtain a permit from the federal agency that administers the property.
- If you will be shooting on any state-owned or -operated property, you will need to complete the State of California photography/motion picture permit (see Figure 5.1).
- If you will be employing actors who are minors, you will need an entertainment work permit from the California Division of Labor Standards Enforcement.
- Because the shoot will take place in Los Angeles, you will have to complete the Los Angeles filming permit (see Figure 5.2).
- If your shoot will include any special effects that involve explosions, smoke, open flames, or other pyrotechnics, you will need to obtain a special effects permit from the Los Angeles Fire Department.
- If you will be working with animals, you will need a motion picture, television, and theatrical permit from the Los Angeles Department of Animal Regulation.

How can you determine which types of forms and permits apply to your production? Begin by contacting the film and television office operated by the state or municipality where you will be conducting your location work. The agency will be able to tell you what state permits you must complete and what, if any, county or local film bureau serves the area where you will conduct your location work.[1]

In your dealings with government film agencies, remember that most serve a dual role. Their first duty is to attract your media production business and the jobs and tax revenue that your business generates to the state or community that they serve. Then, once they have

Figure 5.1 Sample photography/motion picture permit.

Application

Today's Date:_____

State of California
Photography/Motion Picture Permit
California Film Commission
7080 Hollywood Boulevard, Suite 900
Hollywood, California 90028

Permit Category:
(Please check one)
☐ **Caltrans**
☐ **Parks**
☐ **Buildings/Facilities**

Phone: 323.860.2960
Toll free: 1.800.858.4749
Caltrans Fax: 323.860.2976
Parks Fax: 323.817.4126
State Bldgs./Facilities Fax: 323.860.2972

Revision(s) # _____

Company:

Name:_____

Address:_____

City: State: Zip: Country:

Telephone #'s:

Main #:_____

Fax #:_____

Loc. Dept #:

Project:

Title:_____

Type:_____

Cell:_____ Pager:_____

Permit Service:

Personnel:

Producer:_____

Director:_____

UPM:_____

Loc.Mgr/Asst:

Locations: Including city and county. Caltrans applications include directions i.e. North, South, East, West and parameters.

Activities/Action: Including camera and equipment placement, request for traffic control or closures, etc.

Shoot Dates: Including prep and strike.

Call-Wrap Times: Military time e.g. 06:00 – 22:00

# of Vehicles:

Trucks:_____   Motorhomes: _____

Autos: _____   Picture Cars: _____

Vans: _____   Camera Cars: _____

Cater: _____   Generator: _____

Trailer: _____

Other:

Total # of

Days:

_____

Total # of

Personnel:

_____

Pyrotechnics:

Description:_____

Technician:_____

License #:_____

Phone #:_____

F/X Permit #:_____

CFC 10/12/01

Figure 5.1 Sample photography/motion picture permit. (Continued)

State of California
Photography/Motion Picture Permit Application
California Film Commission
Terms and Conditions

Indemnification: Permittee waives all claims against the State, its officers, agents and employees, for loss or damages caused by, arising out of, or in any way connected with the exercise of this permit.

Permittee agrees to indemnify, defend and save harmless the State, its officers, agents and employees, from any and all claims and losses accruing or resulting to any and all contractors, subcontractors, suppliers, laborers, and any other person, firm or corporation furnishing or supplying work services, materials, or supplies in connection with the exercise of this permit, and from any and all claims and losses accruing or resulting to any person, firm or corporation who may be injured or damaged by Permittee in the exercise of this permit.

The State shall have the privilege of inspecting the premises covered by this permit at any or all times. This permit shall not be assigned.

The State may terminate this permit at any time if Permittee fails to perform any covenant herein contained at the time and in the manner herein provided. The State agrees it will not unreasonably exercise this right of termination.

The parties hereto agree that the Permittee, its officers, agents and employees in the performance of this permit, shall act in an independent capacity and not as officers, employees or agents of the State.

No alteration or variation of the terms of this permit shall be valid unless made in writing and signed by the parties hereto.

Permittee agrees to maintain all State required insurance, as set forth in the California Film Commission's Insurance requirements.

Permittee will not discriminate against an employee or applicant for employment because of race, color, religion, ancestry, sex, age, national origin, or physical handicap.

Permittee agrees to comply with the terms and conditions contained in the attached exhibit(s), which terms and conditions are by this reference made a part thereof.

Permittee hereby agrees to comply with all the rules and regulations of the facility or institution subject to this permit. A copy of this permit is to be maintained at the location at all times during filming activities.

Representative signs upon issuance of permit.

_____

Company representative signature

_____

Print name of representative

_____

Date

_____

Title of project

CFC 10/12/01

Figure 5.2 Sample filming permit request.

COUNTY & CITY OF LOS ANGELES
FILMING PERMIT REQUEST

PAGE_1_ OF____ PAGES

DATE:_____

E.I.D.C. - LOS ANGELES FILM OFFICE
7083 Hollywood Blvd., Suite 500, Los Angeles, CA 90028

FAX THIS REQUEST TO: (323) 962-4966
If you have trouble with transmission, phone: (323) 957-1000

PLEASE NOTE THE FOLLOWING:
1) YOUR LA CITY, LA COUNTY AND/OR E.I.D.C. INSURANCE ENDORSEMENT MUST BE CURRENT AND ON FILE.
2) THIS REQUEST FORM DOES NOT CONSTITUTE A PERMIT.
3) TYPE OR PRINT CLEARLY.
4) NAME OF APPLICANT MUST BE THE SAME AS APPEARS ON YOUR INSURANCE FORM(S).
5) YOU MUST ENTER YOUR FAX NUMBER IN SPACE PROVIDED.
6) LOCATIONS AT CITY OR COUNTY FACILITIES MUST INCLUDE PREP AND STRIKE DATES & TIMES.
7) THIS FORM CANNOT BE USED FOR STREET/LANE CLOSURES. PLEASE REFER TO INSTRUCTIONS.

Applicant (Company Name): _____ Agency _____

Representative: _____ Phone:( )_____

Fax:( )_____ Pager:( )_____ Mobile: ( )_____

Prod. Title: _____

Type of Prod.: FEATURE( ) TV SERIES( ) TV MOVIE( )
COMMERCIAL( ) MUSIC VIDEO( ) STILL PHOTO( ) OTHER _____

Producer: _____ Director: _____

Prod. Mgr.: _____ 1st A.D.: _____

Lg. Trucks: _____ Other Trucks: _____ Vans: _____ Mtr. Hms./Dr Rms.: _____ Generator: ____

Camera Cars:_____ Pic. Vehicles:____ Cast/Crew Cars:____ Crew:____ Cast:_____ Extras:_____

LOC#: _____ **Type of structure** _____ **Open to public** _____ **Closed to public** _____

Address [Include Street type (St. Ave. etc.) & Thomas Bros map book Pg. & Grid]:

Date(s):_____ To _____ Time: _____ To_____ **Note: Please indicate arrival and departure times. Time should be military time (ie: 0700-1700).**

Summary of Scenes: _____

ITC: _____ ANIMALS - TYPE(S): _____ NUMBER: _____

Gunfire: YES( ) NO( ) HRS. REQUESTED _____ TO _____ AUTOMATIC:( ) SINGLE SHOT:( )
LOAD: FULL( ) ½( ) ¼( )

Special Effects: YES( ) NO( ) FX#: _____ SQUIBS/BULLET HITS:( )EXPLOSION:( )

FIRE EFFECTS:( ) SPARK EFFECTS:( ) OTHER: _____

Streets to be Posted (Include Thomas Bros. map book Pg. & grid): _____

attracted your business, the agencies are responsible for making sure that you conduct your productions safely and with the proper permits. If you supply the agency staff with information about your production, they should be very willing to work with you to obtain and complete the necessary forms and permits. Some state film bureaus also provide one or more of the following services:

- Listings and photographs of potential shooting locations
- Information about production insurance
- Assistance with highway and street closings
- Help in resolving disputes with county and local agencies

For a list of the government agencies that serve as liaisons with media producers, see Appendix A.

Typical Requirements

The sample permit forms shown in Figures 5.1 and 5.2 suggest the range of information and assurances that media producers must supply to secure location permits from the relevant government agencies. Although the exact requirements will vary from one jurisdiction to the next, most applications for shooting permits ask producers to supply the following:

- The names and addresses of the production company and the principal contacts for the shoot
- Dates of the shoot and approximate times
- A list of the locations and vehicles that will be used in the shoot
- Information about the nature of the production (e.g., television movie or series, feature film, television commercial)
- Brief summaries of the scenes to be shot
- A list of traffic and crowd control requirements
- Evidence of liability insurance

Most applications also require producers to indemnify the issuing government authority against any claims for personal injuries or property damage that may arise from the production. In addition, the producer must assure the issuing authority that the production will comply with all local laws and regulations and that all locations and public facilities used in the shoot will be left in their original condition. To help ensure that production crews comply with this last requirement, state and local governments sometimes ask production companies to post "faithful performance" bonds—deposits that are forfeited to the state or local government if the production company skips town without repairing any damage done to the location. For more information, contact the appropriate agency listed in Appendix A.

Fees and Penalties

The fees charged for location work will vary, depending on where you will be shooting and your need to involve the police department, fire department, or other service agencies. You may be required to pay some or all of the following:

- An application fee for the shooting permit
- Application fees for any additional permits that you may need to obtain from the police department, fire department, or other government agencies
- Fees to cover police, fire, and custodial services required for the shoot or a blanket payment that covers all government services provided during the course of the production
- Any special rental fees required by the agency or authority that administers the shoot site

If you are caught shooting without the proper permits, the penalties can be severe. At a minimum, you will be forced to suspend production until you obtain the necessary clearances, a delay that can prove extremely costly as talent, crew members, and rented equipment stand idle. You also may be subjected to substantial fines. For some severe violations, particularly unauthorized use of pyrotechnics, the sanctions can include criminal penalties.

Privacy and Releases

In the United States, privacy laws protect individuals from intrusion into their personal lives and from the unauthorized use of their names or likenesses for commercial purposes. For media producers, this means that it is necessary to secure a written release from each person who appears in a production. In addition, if the production will include location footage shot on private property, it is necessary to obtain a written release from the property owner. Failure to do so can leave a production open to lawsuits for invasion of privacy or other claims.

Overview of Privacy Law

As legal concepts go, privacy is a relatively recent development. Most scholars trace the origins of privacy law in the United States to 1890, the year in which Samuel D. Warren and future U.S. Supreme Court Justice Louis D. Brandeis wrote an article that argued for statutory or common law recognition of an individual's right to lead a private life.[2] Samuel Warren's interest in privacy was apparently partially a personal matter. His wife was a prominent and very proper Bostonian, and Warren was searching for some legal means to protect his family from becoming unwilling stars of newspaper society and gossip pages.

Although the Warren and Brandeis article attracted attention to the issue of privacy, the statutory or common law recognition that the article recommended was slow in coming. After the turn of the 20th century, however, a series of state and federal court decisions gradually began to shape a common law concept of the right to privacy, and some state legislatures passed statutes designed to protect individuals from certain types of intrusions. Unfortunately, these state statutes and common law precedents often conflicted, and the privacy protection that emerged varied greatly from one state to the next.

Privacy law continues to be a confusing mix of common law, state statutes directed at specific kinds of privacy violations, and a growing number of federal statutes aimed at preventing the misuse of government records and electronic surveillance. Through all of the confusion and conflicts, however, four fairly clear categories of privacy protection have emerged:

- *Appropriation.* Individuals have a right to protection against the unauthorized use of their names or likenesses for commercial purposes (a right that is often referred to as the "right of publicity" and that is discussed in more detail later in this chapter).
- *Intrusion.* Individuals have a right to protection against unwarranted intrusion on their solitude and private affairs.

- *False light.* Individuals have a right to protection against disclosures of private facts that place them in a false light before the public.[3]
- *Public disclosure.* Individuals have a right to protection against the public disclosure of embarrassing facts about their private lives (although, as discussed later in this chapter, the law provides less protection for public officials than private citizens).

Together, these four areas of privacy protection constitute the individual's "right to be left alone." Significantly, the right to be left alone includes the right to be left out of media productions. When individuals consent to waive this right, the waiver should take the form of a written, signed release that is retained by the producer.

Performer Releases

As the preceding paragraphs have suggested, releases play an important role in protecting productions from the possibility of invasion-of-privacy lawsuits. As a rule, producers should secure written releases from all performers who appear in a production. The only exceptions would be those individuals who show up as faceless forms in crowd scenes or remote shots. Just make sure that these individuals truly do appear in a form that would not be recognizable to family, friends, or a judge and jury.

For performers who are professional actors, the release language is usually included in a complete contract that covers all aspects of their appearance in the production (see Chapter 3). For other performers, including employees depicted in corporate video productions, a release agreement similar to the model shown in Figure 5.3 should suffice. Although the exact wording will differ, all releases should share the following characteristics:

- *Releases should be written, even though oral releases are valid in some states.* By putting the release in writing, you create a record that documents the exact terms under which the performer has agreed to appear in the production.
- *Releases should define the duration and extent of the producer's right to use the performer's name, likeness, and performance.* Exactly what rights will the performer be waiving? How and where will the

production in which the performer appears be distributed? How long will the producer retain the right to use the performer's appearance? Ideally, producers should obtain the right to use the performer's appearance within the production in perpetuity and in any manner or medium.

- *Releases should require the performer to warrant that he or she is free to appear in the production and to sign the release.* Is the performer under any other contract that would prevent his or her appearance in the production? Is the performer old enough to sign the release, or will a parent be required to sign? If the performer is a minor, a parent or guardian must sign the release.
- *Releases should describe the consideration (compensation) that the performer will receive for appearing in the production.* As discussed in Chapter 2, consideration is a critical component of all legally binding contracts. Because releases are a type of contract, they should spell out the consideration—even if the performer will receive only a nominal fee or is appearing for promotional consideration. At a minimum, the performer should acknowledge that he or she is executing the release in return for "good and valuable consideration, receipt of which is hereby acknowledged." To avoid potential disputes over whether promotional consideration constitutes sufficient consideration for entering into a release, some producers make a practice of paying performers at least a nominal sum.

Some companies require employees to sign a blanket release as a part of their employment contract. If you are shooting in a corporate setting and using employees as talent, check with the company's legal department or personnel office to see if this is the case. Even when it is the case, however, the blanket release may be valid only as long as the employee continues to work for the company. As a result, it is still a good idea to obtain a written release from each employee depicted in a production.

Make sure that performers understand the terms of the release before they sign it. If a performer prefers not to sign or demands extensive changes to the release before signing, find someone else to fill that role. Once all of the performer releases for a production are signed, store them in a secure, preferably fireproof, location. You should also keep additional copies of the releases in a separate secure location.

Figure 5.3 Sample performer release.

I_____ ("Performer") hereby irrevocably assign to _____ ("Producer") the right to record my voice and likeness for use in a media production (the "Production") that is tentatively titled _____.

In assigning these rights, Performer grants to Producer and its successors, assigns, and licensees the full and irrevocable right to produce, copy, distribute, exhibit, and transmit Performer's voice and likeness in connection with the Production by means of broadcast or cablecast, videotape, DVD, film, print, Internet, or any other electronic or mechanical method or medium now known or hereinafter invented.

Performer acknowledges and agrees that any picture or recording taken of Performer under the terms of this license will become the sole and exclusive property of Producer in perpetuity. Performer and Performer's heirs and assigns shall have no right to bring legal action against Producer for any use of the pictures or recordings, regardless of whether such use is claimed to be defamatory or censorable in nature.

Performer further acknowledges and agrees that Producer shall have the right to use Performer's name, portrait, picture, voice, and biographical information to promote or advertise the Production and to authorize others to do the same; however, nothing shall require Producer to use Performer's name, voice, or likeness in any of the manners described in this license or to exercise any of the rights set forth herein.

Performer warrants and represents that he or she is free to enter into this license and that this agreement does not conflict with any existing contracts or agreements to which Performer is a party. Performer agrees to hold Producer and any third parties harmless from and against any and all claims, liabilities, losses, or damages that may arise from the use of Performer's voice or image in the Production. Performer understands that in proceeding with the Production, Producer will be relying on the foregoing consent, permission, and indemnity.

As complete consideration for the foregoing grant of rights, Producer agrees to pay Performer a fee of $_____.

- or -

It is agreed that the foregoing grant of rights is made for promotional consideration only, and Producer's exercise of the grant of rights shall be deemed full and complete consideration for such grant.

Figure 5.3 Sample performer release. (continued)

AGREED AND ACCEPTED:

PERFORMER:

Signature _____

Printed Name _____

Social Security # _____

Address _____

City _____

State _____ Zip _____

Date _____

FOR PRODUCER:

Signature _____

Printed Name _____

Title _____

In the event that Performer is a minor:

I acknowledge that I am the legal guardian of Performer described above. Acting as Performer's legal guardian, I consent to the terms of this license and to the granting of the rights described herein. I also consent to indemnify and to hold harmless Producer and all third parties against claims that may arise from the use of the minor's name, image, or likeness in the Production.

Signature _____

Printed Name _____

Relationship to Performer _____

Audience Releases

Some productions, particularly recordings of live presentations or performances, feature shots of audience members. Ideally, each audience member should execute a written release, such as that shown in Figure 5.3, expressly authorizing the use of his or her image in the production. When production logistics prevent this, you should post the following notice prominently at all entrances to the production location:

> This performance is being videotaped for television and other public exhibition. The production will include shots of the audience. Anyone not wishing to appear in the production is hereby advised against attending this taping. By entering the premises, you are granting permission to be included in the production for all purposes and in all media. Thank you, and enjoy the taping.

Some producers combine the posting of this notice with a short-form written release that audience members are required to sign before entering the production site. This option works well for live studio audience productions when the audience is relatively small and the producer is in control of the production venue. A short-form release should include the key elements of the release shown in Figure 5.3 (i.e., a grant of permission to record the individual's image in connection with the production and an acknowledgment that the producer will have the right to distribute the production containing the individual's image in all media in perpetuity).

Location Releases

Part of the right to privacy is the right to "zones of solitude" where individuals can reasonably expect to be left alone. Under most legal definitions of privacy, these zones include places that generally are recognized as private, particularly a person's home. Under some statutes and case law, however, privacy zones can include public places (such as offices, hotel rooms, restaurants, and parks) where there is a reasonable expectation of privacy.

If you plan to conduct a shoot in a private area, be sure to obtain a location release. Otherwise, you leave yourself open to action for trespass or invasion of privacy, even though it may be only the person's property pictured in the production. Along with protecting you from charges of illegal intrusion, location releases serve as contracts that define the terms under which you will be allowed to occupy the property and the rights you will have to use pictures and footage from the shoot.

Figure 5.4 is a model location release that you can modify to meet the needs of your production. Like performer releases, location releases should be written rather than oral. They should specify the following:

- The dates that the production company will be allowed to occupy the property, with a provision for changing the dates if weather conditions or production delays require shifts in the schedule
- The rights of the production company to bring equipment and sets onto the property
- The rights that the production company will have to use and distribute the video and sound material recorded at the location
- The consideration that the property owner will receive for allowing the location to be used for the shoot

To protect the property owner, releases sometimes also stipulate that the owner will not be liable for injuries or property damage incurred by parties to the production, particularly when those injuries or damages result from negligence by the production company. Conversely, to protect producers who are paying substantial fees for the use of a location, releases can require the property owner to guarantee that the premises will be safe and in good order.

Requiring Releases

As the preceding sections have shown, releases can help protect productions from charges of violating a person's right of publicity—the area of privacy law that raises the most immediate concerns for most media producers. Of course, obtaining this sort of blanket protection requires one key ingredient: a subject or subjects who are willing to sign the release form. When this ingredient is missing, producers should find another subject or shooting location. Proceeding without the appropriate release is simply too risky.

Figure 5.4 Sample location release.

The undersigned ("Owner") hereby grants to _____
("Producer") the permission, right, and license to photograph, film, and
videotape the premises located at _____ (the
"Premises") for a media production (the "Project") that is tentatively titled
_____.

Under the terms of this agreement, Producer is permitted to occupy and use
the Premises for the period beginning (unless weather conditions or
schedule delays results in a changed beginning date) and extending until
_____. During this period, Producer may place all
necessary sets, equipment, and facilities on the Premises.

Producer agrees to exercise reasonable care to protect the Premises from
damage and to leave the Premises used in the condition that they were
found, with reasonable wear excepted. Producer warrants that it carries
liability insurance that covers the presence of production employees and the
operation of equipment on the Premises. Producer further warrants that it
will hold the undersigned harmless from, and indemnify the undersigned
against, any injury to any persons that may occur on the Premises as a
result of Producer's activities during the production period, provided,
however, that Producer shall control the defense of any claim for which it
provides such indemnity.

Any pictures or recordings taken of the Premises, including those of
any signs that may appear on the property, under the terms of this license
will become the sole and exclusive property of Producer in perpetuity.
Producer will retain the full and irrevocable right to produce, copy,
distribute, exhibit, and transmit the pictures and recordings by means of
broadcast or cablecast, videotape, DVD, film, print, Internet, or any other
electronic or mechanical method or medium now known or hereafter
invented. Owner and Owner's successors and assigns shall have no right to
bring legal action against Producer for any use of the pictures or
recordings.

Owner represents and warrants that Owner is the sole owner of the
Premises and that Owner has the full right to grant Producer the license
and other rights granted herein. Owner further represents and warrants
that Owner will not bring, institute, or assert, or consent that others bring,
institute, or assert, any claim or action against Producer or Producer's
successors, licensees, or assigns on the ground that anything contained in
the Project or in the advertising or publicity issued in connection therewith
violates any of Owner's rights, and hereby releases, discharges, and

Figure 5.4 Sample location release. (continued)

acquits Producer and Producer's successors, licensees, or assigns from and against any and all such claims, actions, causes of actions, suits, and demands.

Owner understands that Producer is relying on Owner's consent and agreement herein contained in the preparation, production, and exhibition of the Project, and that this consent and acknowledgment is given to Producer as an inducement for Producer to proceed with the preparation, production, and exhibition of the Project. Owner agrees to indemnify and hold Producer, Producer's employees, agents, licensees, assigns, and successors harmless from and against all loss, damages, costs, and liabilities resulting from any breach by Owner of any of the terms hereof.

In the event that more than one person, firm, or corporation signs below as an owner of the Premises, the term "Owner" as used herein shall be deemed to mean all such persons, firms, or corporations, and all such parties shall be jointly and severally responsible for all of the Owner's representations, warranties, and agreements set forth herein.

As full and complete consideration for the rights granted herein, Producer agrees to pay Owner a fee of $_____ payable when Producer has completed its use of the Premises. No other fees or payments shall be due under the terms of this agreement.

Nothing in this agreement shall obligate Producer to use the Premises for filming or recording purposes or to include material shot on the Premises in the Project. Producer may at any time cancel this agreement by notifying Owner, in writing, of its intent not to use the Premises. If this cancellation occurs before Producer has occupied the Premises, no payment shall be due to Owner. If cancellation occurs after Producer has occupied the Premises, payment shall be due for each day or part thereof that the Premises were occupied.

AGREED AND ACCEPTED:

OWNER:

Signature _____

Printed Name _____

Social Security or Tax ID #_____

Figure 5.4 Sample location release. (continued)

Address _____

City _____

State _____

Date _____

FOR PRODUCER:

Signature _____

Printed Name _____

Title _____

Other Privacy Concerns

Obtaining the appropriate releases is a key step in protecting a production against invasion-of-privacy challenges. Producers may also find themselves in situations that pose other, more complex privacy concerns, however. Several of those situations and concerns are discussed next.

Privacy Laws and News Programs

Privacy presents special challenges for producers of news programs. By their nature, news programs often disclose embarrassing facts about individuals. In addition, the individuals portrayed in news productions often are unwilling to sign releases authorizing either the disclosure of those facts or the use of their names or likenesses. This is particularly true when the program deals with matters that may be the subject of a criminal investigation.

Fortunately for news producers, the courts have acknowledged that, along with the special challenges that news programmers face, they also enjoy special privileges. Specifically, the courts have recognized "newsworthiness" as a legitimate defense in lawsuits that center on the public disclosure of private facts.[4] If a producer can show that the disclosure of private facts served a legitimate news purpose, the lawsuit challenging that disclosure usually will be dismissed. This common law defense does not necessarily protect news producers who have knowingly placed a person before the public in a false light, however, or news producers who have obtained private facts by trespassing on private property or by trampling on an individual's right to solitude and seclusion. As discussed in the section on libel that appears later in this chapter, it also does not protect news producers who have deliberately or recklessly misrepresented the facts.

Furthermore, the newsworthy defense does not protect media producers who appropriate news footage for non-news uses. In other words, a producer who takes news footage of a celebrity and uses it in a music video or television commercial would not be protected against a lawsuit for illegal appropriation simply because the original footage was newsworthy. In these instances, the producer's appropriation of the celebrity's image clearly would not have served a legitimate news purpose, and the celebrity in all likelihood could bring a successful right of publicity action. The only certain defense to such an action is to obtain, in advance, the individual's consent, preferably through a written release.

The Right of Publicity

As discussed previously, one component of privacy law is the right of publicity, defined generally as the individual's right to protection against the unauthorized use of his or her name or likeness for commercial purposes. In contrast to privacy generally, which has been defined as a personal right under both statutory and common law, the right of publicity is a less well-defined property right that evolved initially through case law.

A key issue debated by the courts is whether the right of publicity dies with the individual. In other words, is it safe to appropriate the image or name of an individual who is no longer living? In one case decided by the California Supreme Court in 1979, the court ruled that the right to publicity could not be inherited or "descended," denying the heirs of actor Bela Lugosi the right to prevent Universal Pictures from marketing T-shirts and other items that depicted Lugosi in his famous Dracula role.[5] In another case, the U.S. Court of Appeals for the Sixth Circuit ruled in 1980 that, under Tennessee law, Elvis

Presley's right of publicity did not survive him, thus leaving anyone free to exploit Presley's name or likeness for commercial purposes.[6] However, because the right to exploit a deceased person's name for commercial purposes is a matter of case law in many states, subsequent court decisions may place restrictions and qualifications on this right. For example, despite the Sixth Circuit's decision applying Tennessee law in the Elvis Presley case, a Tennessee court subsequently held that the right of publicity in fact was descendible, permitting a celebrity's heirs to pursue claims based on that right.[7]

In addition to state and federal courts, some state legislatures have been active in defining the right of publicity and delineating whether that right descends to an individual's heirs. California and several other states already have enacted statutes that grant celebrities and their heirs some level of control over the celebrity's image, and the New York legislature has considered a so-called Dead Celebrities Bill that would keep a celebrity's image under family control for a specified number of years after his or her death.[8] If current trends continue, the right of publicity increasingly will become a matter of state statutory law, as more states enact legislation that codifies individuals' common law right to control the commercial exploitation of their names and likenesses.

In many states that have right of publicity statutes, the statutes include a "safe harbor" for using the celebrity's name and likeness in news and informational productions, as long as the production does not depict the celebrity as endorsing a particular product or service.[9] Such safe harbor provisions, for example, would protect a producer's use of former President Richard Nixon's name and likeness in a film about Nixon's life (such as Oliver Stone's film *Nixon*). Those statutory safe harbors would not, however, protect the producer of a television commercial in which Nixon appears to endorse a product or the manufacturer of merchandise items featuring Nixon's image, unless Nixon's heirs had authorized these uses of his name and likeness.[10]

In recent years, some celebrities have also begun to enlist the help of federal law in seeking to stop the unauthorized use of their names and likenesses in commercial contexts. Although there is no specific federal right of publicity statute, Section 43(a) of the Federal Trademark Act of 1946 (the Lanham Act) does forbid "false designations of origin and false descriptions" in the sale of goods or services, including commercial advertising and promotion.[11] As discussed in the next section, singer Tom Waits called on Section 43(a) in winning a suit against Frito-Lay, Inc., over the use of a Waits sound-alike in a commercial for snack food products. In that case, Waits was awarded damages of more than $2 million.

Keeping all of this in mind, producers should consult with a lawyer who is familiar with the latest developments in right of publicity law at the state and federal levels before appropriating anyone's image or likeness for inclusion in a production, regardless of whether the person is living or dead.

Celebrity Look-Alikes and Sound-Alikes

Some producers try to get around the right of publicity problem by using celebrity look-alikes or sound-alikes in their productions. Courts have found, however, that this often can be considered a violation of the right to publicity because it does in fact involve an appropriation of the celebrity's image. Woody Allen has prevailed in two celebrity look-alike challenges,[12] and Bette Midler has won a sound-alike case.[13] The Midler case is discussed in more detail in Chapter 6.

More recently, singer Tom Waits prevailed in a sound-alike suit against Frito-Lay, Inc. Through its ad agency, Frito-Lay had approached Waits hoping to use his distinctive voice and vocal style in a commercial for its Doritos snack chips. When Waits declined, Frito-Lay produced the commercial using a sound-alike performer. Waits sued, asserting claims under state right of publicity law and Section 43(a) of the federal Lanham Act. After Waits prevailed in the federal district court, the U.S. Court of Appeals for the Ninth Circuit affirmed the judgment on appeal, holding that a "celebrity whose endorsement of a product is implied through a distinctive attribute of the celebrity's identity has standing to sue for false endorsement under Section 43(a) of the Lanham Act."[14]

The "Changed Name" Defense

Is it safe to disclose private facts about individuals or facts that place individuals in a false light as long as you do not use their real names? This issue is particularly relevant, and particularly problematic, to producers of docudramas or other fictional works that are based on real events or real people. Until a 1980 California case, writers and producers could usually protect themselves by simply changing the names and descriptions of the real people, places, and events on which the work is based. In the case of *Bindrim v. Mitchell*, however, a California appeals court ruled that a person's privacy could still be considered invaded if the individual can prove that he or she remained "reasonably recognizable" in the work, even if names and descriptions have been changed.[15]

The Bindrim decision set a troublesome precedent for writers and media producers because it opened the courtroom doors to almost any individual who believes that he or she is the model for a character in a production. Although subsequent decisions in other states have helped to lessen the impact of *Bindrim v. Mitchell*, this remains a difficult and complex area of privacy law. As a result, producers who are planning a docudrama or other work of "faction" should consult a lawyer who is familiar with the latest precedents and other developments.[16]

The Privacy Checklist

If this discussion of privacy law has left you confused, you are not alone. With no comprehensive and preemptive federal privacy statute, much privacy law remains a bewildering blend of state statutes and case law that can leave even the most experienced lawyers perplexed.

Figure 5.5 is a privacy checklist that should help clarify some of the confusion surrounding the areas of privacy law that are most relevant to media producers. The privacy checklist works much like the fair use checklist from Chapter 4. To use it, simply answer yes or no to each question. If all of the responses come up no, you probably are protected from privacy challenges. One or more yes responses indicates a potential problem, and a call to a lawyer who is experienced with privacy law is in order. The more yes responses, the more vulnerable you are to successful privacy lawsuits.

Libel

Libel suits against the media have become big news. In one heavily publicized case, actress Carol Burnett sued a national tabloid newspaper for several sensational stories that the paper ran about her personal life. In two other widely reported cases, General Ariel Sharon sued *Time* magazine over its portrayal of his involvement in the 1982 massacres of Palestinians in Lebanese refugee camps, and General William

Figure 5.5 Privacy checklist.

1. *Have you violated someone's right of publicity by appropriating his or her name or likeness for commercial purposes without his or her permission?* This is one of the most common privacy violations committed by media producers and, as far as the courts are concerned, one of the most clear-cut. If you plan to use someone's name, voice, or likeness in a commercial production (a category that includes corporate video productions), be sure to get the person's permission in the form of a written release (see Figure 5.3) or a performer's contract. Failure to do so will leave your production open to unlawful appropriation or other invasion-of-privacy actions.

2. *Have you conducted a location shoot on private property without the property owner's permission?* Whenever you shoot on private property, be sure to obtain a written location release like the sample shown in Figure 5.4.

3. *Are you disclosing embarrassing or offensive facts about a private individual?* Private individuals have a reasonable right to protection against public disclosure of embarrassing facts about their behavior, attitudes, history, and personal preferences. This right is not shared by elected officials and other public figures, who are fair game for such disclosures—as long as you can show that the disclosures have at least some relationship to their status as public persons. If your production does disclose embarrassing facts about a private individual, you have two defenses against a legal challenge. You can try to prove that the individual consented to the disclosures (an unlikely circumstance, and one that is best substantiated through a written release), or you can try to prove that the disclosures were newsworthy. To substantiate the newsworthy defense, you will need to show that the primary purpose of the disclosures was to inform the public and that the disclosures were of legitimate public interest. In addition, unless the disclosures detail recent actions or events, you will need to show that the passage of time has not dimmed the public's interest, turning these once-public facts into private facts.

4. *Might your production place someone in a false light?* Sometimes, when facts are used creatively or haphazardly, they can place individuals in a false light. For example, imagine a situation in which a producer creates a television documentary about illegal drugs that includes hidden camera shots of actual drug transactions. One of the scenes shows a prominent businessman talking to several people who had just participated in one of the transactions. The inclusion of the scene and the tone of the

Figure 5.5 Privacy checklist. (continued)

accompanying narration imply that the businessman may also be involved with illegal drugs. As it turns out, however, the businessman was there as part of an antidrug campaign started by a church group. The businessman sues, alleging that the video documentary violated his privacy by placing him before the public in a false light. To avoid this sort of false-light lawsuit, make sure that your productions portray scenes and situations accurately, particularly when you are juxtaposing shots for creative effect in documentary-style productions.

5. Does your production include fictional material that is based on real people or events? Docudramas and other forms of "faction" raise privacy concerns that require producers to exercise extra caution. If your production falls into this category, consult a lawyer who specializes in privacy matters.

C. Westmoreland sued CBS for allegations made during a report about the deliberate distortion of enemy troop strength during the Vietnam War.[17] More recently, singer Wayne Newton sued NBC for libel in connection with a news segment that connected him to an organized crime figure.[18]

Although many of the specific issues differ, these celebrated libel cases share one key characteristic. In each case, the plaintiff charged that the defendant distorted the truth. This characteristic distinguishes libel lawsuits from most invasion-of-privacy cases, in which the plaintiff usually does not contest the truth of the information disclosed but instead challenges the defendant's right to bring the facts before the public. In general, if you are telling the truth, you are protected against a libel judgment. However, if you have disclosed private, embarrassing facts about an individual or violated someone's right of publicity, you might still be vulnerable to a lawsuit for invasion of privacy or unlawful appropriation.

Defamation, Libel, and Slander

Libel is a tort, a civil (rather than criminal) wrong for which the court provides remedy. Libel and its twin tort, slander, form the larger legal category called *defamation law*. Historically, *libel* has been applied to defamation that is written or portrayed pictorially, whereas *slander* has meant defamation that is spoken or conveyed orally. In recent years, however, the boundary between libel and slander has become blurred, particularly in cases involving the audiovisual media. *Libel* is now often used as a general term that encompasses slander, even though the two forms of defamation remain technically distinct.

Although the exact definition of libel varies from state to state, a statement about an individual is generally considered to be libelous if it is a statement of false fact, if it is knowingly and deliberately communicated to at least one other person, and if it injures the individual's reputation. When these conditions are present, the injured individual may seek damages through a libel lawsuit.

Sources of Libel Law

There is no comprehensive federal libel statute. Instead, like privacy law, libel law is a mix of common law and state statutory law. Because many libel cases involve free press and free speech issues—two rights that are protected under the First Amendment to the U.S. Constitution—many of the major rulings in this area have come from the federal courts. In particular, several key U.S. Supreme Court rulings have helped establish the boundary between speech that is protected by the First Amendment and speech that can be considered libelous. Several of these Supreme Court cases are discussed in the sections that follow.

Media producers should note that, although the federal courts have established several key precedents, individual states are free to enact their own libel legislation—as long as that legislation does not conflict with federal law or the U.S. Constitution. As a result, libel law often differs from state to state. Along with reviewing the general libel guidelines discussed here, be sure to consult with a lawyer who is familiar with libel law in the state where your business is based and in any other states where you produce or distribute materials.

Elements of Libel

How can you tell if a specific statement or scene has left your production vulnerable to a successful libel lawsuit? In most cases, five elements must be present to support a libel action: falsity, injury, publication, identification, and fault. Each of these elements is described in more detail in the sections that follow.

Falsity

To be considered libelous, a statement must be a false allegation about a living person issued as a statement of fact. If the statement in question is shown to be true, a libel lawsuit usually will be dismissed out of hand. Generally, a libel suit also will be dismissed if the defendant can show that the statement in question clearly was made in jest or as an obvious expression of personal opinion, with little chance that someone would interpret it as statement of fact.

Injury

To rise to the legal definition of libel, a defamatory statement must injure an individual's reputation or result in some other personal or economic damage. Statements that tend to satisfy this criteria include those that falsely accuse a person of professional incompetence, unethical business dealings, dishonesty, promiscuity, drunkenness, criminal behavior, or physical or psychological illnesses. If the defamatory material includes one or more of these accusations and the other preconditions for libel are present, the court usually will presume that a plaintiff's reputation was injured, even if the plaintiff cannot prove that the injury resulted in tangible economic loss.

Publication

Publication is a prerequisite for libel. In the context of libel law, publication means dissemination or distribution of the offending material to one or more third parties. Privately, you can have all the libelous thoughts or make all of the defamatory statements that you want. You can even communicate your libelous thoughts to the person who is the subject of your ill will, as long as no third party is present to witness the communication.

The logic behind the publication prerequisite is simple. Without publication, there is little risk that the offending material will injure the plaintiff's reputation or otherwise result in economic loss. And, without such injury or loss, there is no libel case.

Media producers should keep in mind that there are different degrees of publication and that publication can mean different things in different circumstances. For example, a corporate video program that contains defamatory statements about an employee could trigger a successful libel suit, even if the program was shown only to the employee's supervisor. In this case, publication exists because the program was screened by at least one third party. Also, because the third party was the defamed employee's boss, the employee probably could prove that the program injured the person's reputation and affected his or her career opportunities.

Identification

Along with proving that a production contains defamatory statements, the plaintiffs in libel cases must show that others will identify them as the targets of the statements. If the plaintiffs are actually named or shown in the production, identification exists as a matter of course. If they are not actually named or shown, plaintiffs can still establish identification if they can prove that the libelous statements clearly referred to them or that reasonable people who knew the plaintiffs would recognize them as the subjects of the statements.

Identification becomes more problematic when a member of a group sues for defamatory statements directed at the group as a whole. When this is the case, the court must determine whether the statements made about the group are likely to damage the reputations of individual members. To make this determination, the court usually focuses on two key considerations: (1) the size of the group in question and (2) the degree to which the defamatory statements single out certain members. The larger the group is and the broader the libelous statements made about the group are, the less likely it is that the court will find sufficient identification to support a libel action.

Fault

To win a libel lawsuit in many states, the plaintiff must establish fault by showing that the defendant displayed at least negligence, or lack of care, in publishing the defamatory material. When the case concerns defamatory statements directed at a public official, the plaintiff must go even further and prove "actual malice" on the part of the defendant. The actual malice requirement is discussed in more detail in the section that follows.

Public Officials, Private People, and Actual Malice

In 1964, the U.S. Supreme Court decided a case that has become a land-mark in libel law. The case, *New York Times Co. v. Sullivan*,[19] involved the appeal of a libel suit brought against *The New York Times* by L. B. Sullivan, the commissioner of public affairs in Montgomery, Alabama. Sullivan had sued *The New York Times* because of an advertisement that civil rights groups had placed in the paper in 1960. The advertisement asserted, among other things, that police and public officials in several southern cities, including Montgomery, had taken improper and unlawful actions against individuals who were participating in civil rights protests.

In filing his suit, Sullivan claimed that several of the factual asser-tions made in the ad were untrue and that, even though he was not actually named in the allegations, his reputation as a public official had been damaged. A jury in an Alabama state court agreed, awarding Sullivan a large libel judgment that was affirmed, on appeal, by the Alabama Supreme Court.

Defeated at both the trial and appellate court levels in Alabama, *The New York Times* appealed to the U.S. Supreme Court. Although it traditionally had left matters of civil libel law to the state courts, the Supreme Court recognized that the Alabama judgment raised impor-tant free press considerations under the First Amendment, and it agreed to review the case.

After extensive deliberation, the Supreme Court unanimously reversed the Alabama libel judgment, citing several reasons for its decision:

- If the original Alabama state court judgment stood, it would open the door for a new form of press censorship through civil libel suits. This in turn would make the press reluctant to cover controversial topics, fearing that such coverage might trigger libel challenges by public officials in local communities.
- Because public debate is important in a democracy, the press requires some "breathing space" in its coverage of critical issues. When the press pursues these issues vigorously, some factual errors must be both expected and tolerated.
- Once they decide to seek public positions, individuals such as L. B. Sullivan should expect less privacy and more scrutiny by the press than the general public. Also, once they secure

government positions, public officials usually can command more access to the media to reply to libelous allegations than private citizens. For these reasons, public officials should both expect and receive less libel protection than the protection that the law affords to private citizens.

Taking the last rationale one step further, the Supreme Court ruled that public officials who file libel suits against the media must prove that the statements in question were made with "actual malice." In other words, to win a libel lawsuit, a public official must prove that a libelous statement was made "with knowledge that it was false or with reckless disregard of whether it was false or not." Needless to say, because actual malice is difficult to prove, the Supreme Court's *New York Times v. Sullivan* decision has made it much more difficult for public officials to win libel judgments against the media.

Although the Supreme Court's ruling resolved the issues raised in this particular case, *New York Times v. Sullivan* also created a troublesome new problem. Now that public officials must be treated as special cases under libel law, just how do judges determine who is a public official and who is not? Does the term *public official* refer only to elected officials or does it include anyone who holds a government position? What about film stars, professional athletes, political activists, retired politicians, and other prominent people? Do these public figures qualify as public officials under the *New York Times v. Sullivan* ruling?

Gertz v. Robert Welch, Inc.

In the years since the *New York Times v. Sullivan* decision, the Supreme Court has helped answer these questions through a series of additional libel rulings. In *Gertz v. Robert Welch, Inc.,* a 1974 decision, the Supreme Court held that private citizens who are public figures for a limited purpose (in Gertz's case, an attorney who had represented the family of a black man killed by the Chicago police) do not need to prove actual malice as plaintiffs in libel suits against the media, as long as they have not deliberately sought public figure status in the context of the case at hand. The Gertz ruling did, however, require private citizens to prove some level of fault on the part of the media. In other words, it is not enough to prove that the media simply published a false and libelous statement. Instead, a private citizen suing the media for libel must also prove some degree of negligence or intent on the part of the defendant.

It is significant that the Gertz ruling left it to state courts to determine just how much fault private persons are required to prove in libel suits. As a result, under Gertz, the required level of fault can vary greatly from state to state. In some states, private citizens must prove the same level of fault or malice as public officials. In others, private citizens must prove only simple negligence on the part of the media. An attorney who specializes in libel law will know which standard applies in the states where you produce and distribute programs.

Firestone v. Time, Inc.

Within the framework established by the *New York Times* and *Gertz* decisions, the courts have continued to struggle to define the boundary between public figures and private citizens who have been involuntarily placed in the public eye. For example, the Supreme Court's 1976 ruling in *Firestone v. Time, Inc.*[20] established that people do not necessarily become public figures simply because they are involved in prominent court cases:

> While participants in some litigation may be legitimate "public figures," either generally or for the limited purpose of that litigation, the majority will more likely resemble [the] respondent [Mrs. Firestone], drawn into a public forum largely against their will in order to attempt to obtain the only redress available to them or to defend themselves against actions brought by the state or by others. There appears to be little reason why these individuals should substantially forfeit that degree of protection which the law of defamation would otherwise afford them simply by virtue of their being drawn into a courtroom.

For media producers, the message conveyed by *Firestone v. Time, Inc.* and related Supreme Court rulings is clear: Do not assume that you are immune from libel suits simply because the target of your accusations is a celebrity or some other figure who is currently in the news. In most states, only government officials or individuals who have voluntarily placed themselves at the forefront of specific public controversies must prove actual malice in libel lawsuits against the media.

Other Important Libel Cases

The interplay between libel law and free speech rights under the First Amendment has continued to occupy the attention of the U.S. Supreme Court. Decisions of particular interest to media producers include the following:

- In *Anderson v. Liberty Lobby, Inc.,*[21] a case decided in 1986, the Supreme Court reaffirmed and reinforced its *New York Times v. Sullivan* actual malice requirement, instructing lower courts to examine the plaintiff's proof in libel cases extremely closely to determine if the plaintiff stands any real chance of satisfying this and other constitutional requirements. If not, the court should grant a defense motion for summary judgment (a pretrial motion contending that, given the undisputed facts before the court, the case or some portion thereof may be decided by the judge as a matter of law).

- In *Philadelphia Newspapers, Inc. v. Hepps,*[22] also decided in 1986, the Supreme Court rejected the common law presumption of falsity in libel cases that involve both media defendants and speech dealing with issues of public concern, ruling that the burden is on the plaintiff to establish the falsity of the statements at issue in cases of this type. Under the traditional common law rule, the burden is on the defendant to prove that the allegedly defamatory statements are true.

- In the 1986 *Hustler Magazine, Inc. v. Falwell*[23] decision, the Supreme Court held that a public figure may not do an "end run" around the "actual malice" requirement by suing for intentional infliction of emotional distress rather than libel. The Court also ruled that a plaintiff may not recover when the speech at issue (in this case, an outlandish advertising parody featuring a renowned evangelist) "could not reasonably have been interpreted as stating actual facts about the public figure involved."

- In the 1990 *Milkovich v. Lorain Journal Co.*[24] decision, the Supreme Court reaffirmed the prevailing rule that "a statement of opinion relating to matters of public concern which does not contain a probably false factual connotation" should receive full protection under the First Amendment. The Court rejected, however, the argument that there should be a broader constitutional protection for opinion, leaving the door open for libel plaintiffs where a statement that the defendant contends is merely opinion "impl[ies] an assertion of objective fact."

For the most part, these and related decisions have reaffirmed and, in some contexts, extended the special protections that media defendants have enjoyed in libel cases since *New York Times v. Sullivan*. Media producers should keep in mind, however, that these protections extend furthest in cases involving statements concerning public figures and issues of public importance. When the person at issue instead is a private figure and the statements do not involve issues of public importance, most media defendants will find themselves in the same position as any other libel defendants. That is, in most states, the defendant will have the burden of proving that the statements at issue were true, and the plaintiff will not carry the heavy burden of establishing that the media defendant acted with actual malice. Moreover, media producers also should recognize that the types of special protections available to media defendants under the U.S. Constitution are not necessarily available in libel cases brought outside the United States. As discussed in Chapter 8, this issue is especially problematic for information distributed internationally over the Internet.

Other Libel Defenses

In addition to the constitutional defenses to libel established under *New York Times v. Sullivan*, media producers can benefit from other defenses available under the common law and state statutory law. For example, under the common law "official reporting" privilege, journalists are generally protected from libel liability when they report libelous statements that were made by others at a public meeting or court proceeding or in governmental reports, transcripts, or other official documents. Some jurisdictions qualify this privilege, however, by requiring that the reporter exercise sufficient care to ensure that the statements are reported fairly and accurately. Similarly, the "neutral reporting" privilege recognized in some jurisdictions protects the fair and accurate reporting of libelous statements made by third parties against a public official when those statements were not made at a public meeting or court proceeding—as long as the statements are directed to the official's public duties or an issue of public importance.[25] In addition, the common law defense of "fair comment" protects the expression of honest opinion on an issue of public importance, a defense that has been subsumed under and surpassed by the constitutional defenses available since *New York Times v. Sullivan*. Several states have enacted statutory versions of one or more of these common law privileges.

Retraction Statutes

More than 30 states have retraction statutes that can mitigate, to varying degrees, the media's exposure to large libel judgments.[26] Under the typical retraction statute, a media defendant in a libel action will be protected from punitive (but generally not actual) damages if the defendant issues a full, timely retraction of the statements at issue. Most retraction statutes specify certain criteria that the media defendant must satisfy to qualify for this protection from punitive damages. For example, the California statute[27] requires that the retraction be issued within three weeks of receiving a complaint from the offended individual or entity and that the retraction be published or displayed in "as conspicuous a manner" as the original, offending statements. In addition, like many other states with retraction statutes, California requires that plaintiffs who believe they have been libeled by the media demand a retraction to become eligible to seek punitive damages in litigation against a media defendant.

Because the specific requirements of retraction statutes differ from state to state, producers who believe they may have become exposed to a libel lawsuit should consult with an attorney to determine whether their state has a retraction statute and, if so, what the requirements of that statute are. An attorney who is experienced in libel law will also be able to determine whether a retraction is in order given the facts of a particular case and the privileges and constitutional protections otherwise available to media defendants.

Libeling Corporations and Organizations

Like individuals, a corporation can sue for libel if its reputation has been defamed by false statements. When a corporate entity is libeled, however, the right to sue for libel is not tied to the life span of individual officers or employees. As a result, corporations can, and sometimes do, pursue libel lawsuits for years. Similar rules apply when clubs, nongovernment agencies, and unincorporated organizations sue for libel.

"Trade libel" or "trade disparagement" is a special sort of libel that occurs when false and damaging statements are directed at a specific product or service sold by a company, rather than at the company itself. In filing a trade libel action, the company must prove that the defamatory statement, rather than the vagaries of the marketplace, resulted in reduced sales for the product or service. Because this can be difficult to prove, trade libel lawsuits can be very difficult to win. In addition, in trade libel cases involving media defendants, the plaintiff must satisfy the applicable constitutional requirements established in *New York Times v. Sullivan, Philadelphia Newspaper, Inc. v. Hepps,* and related cases.[28]

Unlike corporations and private organizations, government agencies cannot sue for libel. Individual employees of government agencies can sue, however, provided they can establish that the defamatory statements damaged their personal reputations.

Who Pays for Libel?

You have just been hired by a small video production company. One of your first assignments is to produce a program about toxic waste disposal violations. The program, which was written by a freelance scriptwriter and financed by a national foundation, alleges that the vice president of a waste-hauling firm approved the illegal dumping of toxic substances near a public water supply. The program is transmitted over several cable television systems that are owned by a large media corporation.

After seeing the program, the vice president of the waste-hauling firm is furious. Alleging that the accusations made in the production are untrue, he decides to sue for libel. But who does he sue? You? Your company? The writer? The foundation that financed the production? The cable systems that transmitted it? The corporation that owns the systems?

In theory the answer is "all of the above" because all of the parties involved in the production and publication of libelous material can be held responsible. The exception to this rule in some instances is parties that can show they were simply distributors or retransmitters of the material, with no knowledge of or editorial control over its contents.

In actual practice, however, many plaintiffs, in consultation with their lawyers, will pick one or two targets for the suit. Depending on their purpose in filing the suit, the plaintiffs will pick either the party with the deepest pockets (the individual or group that can afford to pay the largest judgment) or the party that they would most like to teach a lesson.

Contractual Liability Provisions

If you are about to sign a contract to write, produce, distribute, or display a media production, be sure to check the contract for libel liability language. To protect themselves from liability in libel suits, many companies include clauses in their contracts that require the second party to the agreement (the party that will produce or provide materials under the terms of the contract) to assume responsibility for any libelous statements contained in the materials. The libel liability language is usually part of the representations and warranties and indemnification sections of the contract.

Review this language carefully, and make sure you can buy into it before signing the contract. If you have any questions about what you are signing or about potentially libelous statements contained in your materials, contact a lawyer who is familiar with libel law.

Libel Insurance

As the threat of libel suits has increased, many media production and distribution groups have begun to carry libel insurance, often as part of an errors and omissions or media professional liability policy. Although most such policies require substantial deductibles, they do help protect media companies and their employees from the sting of large libel judgments (as well as from the often equally onerous sting of legal fees). In some cases, the policies can be extended to insure writers and producers who have contracted to provide materials for the company. If you are about to sign such a contract, check to see if the company carries insurance that could cover your work. If you can be covered, make sure that a clause to that effect is included in your contract with the company.

Protecting and Defending Against a Charge of Libel: The Libel Checklist

The best protection against libel is to tell the truth. Start by checking the facts conveyed in your production, particularly those facts that form the basis of potentially libelous statements. As mentioned earlier, statements that bear special checking include those that accuse individuals or groups of professional incompetence, unprofessional behavior, unethical business dealings, dishonesty, promiscuity, drunkenness, laziness, criminal behavior, or physical or psychological illnesses. If your production contains these sorts of accusations or implications, ask yourself if they are essential to the program. If they are not, cut them. If they are and you decide to keep them, make sure that the statements are true. If you have substantial doubts about the accuracy of the statements, assume that they are false and edit them from the program (or, at a minimum, make it clear that they are offered as opinion, not fact).

What if you are not in a position to remove potentially libelous material from a program? For example, what if you are a distributor who has negotiated for a program that contains problematic statements, but the producer insists that you take it as is or forget the deal? Or, what if you are a producer who has already released a program, only to discover that the book on which the program is based is the subject of a libel suit? Under circumstances like these, how can you know just how vulnerable you may be to a successful libel challenge?

Start by reviewing the libel checklist shown in Figure 5.6. If that review reveals that you are at risk, consult a lawyer. With multimillion-dollar libel judgments making headlines, it does not make sense to take chances.

Production Insurance and Completion Bonds

With production costs rising rapidly, most major film and television producers are choosing to protect their investments through the purchase of production insurance. Typically, the premiums for a comprehensive policy run from 3 to 5 percent of the total production budget, with the exact cost determined by the risk factors (e.g., extensive location work, hazardous stunts) present in the project, the amount of the policy deductibles, and the limits of the insurance company's liability.

A comprehensive production insurance policy usually includes the following types of coverage:

- Cast insurance, which protects the company against any extra production costs caused by the death, injury, or illness of a performer or director

Figure 5.6 Libel liability checklist.

This checklist is designed to help producers gauge the degree to which accusatory statements made in a media production carry the risk of being found libelous in a court of law. Before reviewing the checklist items, ask yourself one key question: Are the statements true? If the accusatory statements in question are true, and if you can prove that they are true, you should prevail in a libel lawsuit; however, you may still face the burden and cost of defending against a libel challenge in court. In addition, even if the statements are true, you may still be vulnerable to an invasion-of-privacy suit. The only sure way to avoid these unpleasantries is to remove the problematic material from the production.

If the statements may not be true, if they imply a condition or fact that may not be true, or if you cannot prove that they are true, the safest step is to edit the statements from the production. When this is not an option, review the questions that follow, answering yes or no to each one. If you answer no to all of the questions, you and your production definitely are at risk. If one or more of the answers is yes, you are protected, to some degree, from being found liable for libel. To determine the exact degree of that protection, consult a lawyer who is familiar with libel law in the state or states where the program was produced and distributed.

1. *Were the statements clearly offered as matters of opinion, rather than as declarations of fact?* The First Amendment protects your rights to offer statements of opinion, no matter how inaccurate or potentially injurious, as long as it is clear that you are offering an opinion. In other words, there is a big difference between saying "I find Mr. Smith to be extremely irritating" and "Mr. Smith cheats his customers." In the first case, you clearly are offering the statement as a matter of personal opinion, so the First Amendment protects you from a libel judgment (unless, as the Supreme Court has held, there is an implied factual basis for the opinion that is found to be untrue). In the second case, you are offering the statement as a matter of fact, so you had better be able to prove it. Do not assume, however, that you are shielded from a libel lawsuit simply because you preface a defamatory statement with "It is alleged . . ." or some similar qualifier. Although qualifying a statement in this way may provide some protection, it is by no means a complete libel defense. To a lesser degree, you also are protected if the remarks were clearly made in jest, with no danger that a listener or viewer would mistake them for statements of fact.

2. *Were the statements made about the job performance of a public official?* Unlike private citizens, public officials must prove "actual malice"

Figure 5.6 Libel liability checklist. (continued)

(defined as knowing that the statements are false or offering the statements with "reckless disregard for the truth") on the part of the media to win libel judgments. Although this makes it much more difficult for public officials to win libel cases, it does not make them fair game for any accusations that you care to toss their way. If you feel compelled to attack a public official, make sure that the attack focuses on the official's performance in office, rather than on his or her private or professional life outside of public service. Of course, to be fully protected from a libel judgment, you should make sure that the accusations are also based in fact and that you are not guilty of actual malice toward the official.

3. *Were the statements the result of mistakes made during the production of a news program?* The courts tend to be somewhat more forgiving when the defamatory statements result from honest mistakes made during the production of news programs, particularly the production of regularly scheduled newscasts. Recognizing the pressures involved in preparing newscasts and acknowledging the important role that newscasts play in keeping the public informed of breaking news stories, the courts tend to expect less-detailed fact checking on the part of reporters and other employees who broadcast breaking news stories under pressing deadlines.

4. *Were the statements a fair reporting of direct quotes taken from public proceedings, records, or transcripts?* Under a common law concept called the "official reporting" privilege, a news program is protected, to some measure, if libelous statements contained in the program are direct quotations from public proceedings (e.g., trials, government hearings, legislative sessions) or public records (e.g., trial transcripts, government reports). To be fully privileged, however, the statements must have been made by a public official or someone who is speaking at a public proceeding and the statements must be reported accurately, fully, and fairly.

5. *Were the statements attributed to a normally reliable source?* Although attribution is not a complete defense, it can provide some protection against a libel challenge, particularly when it is used with one or more of the other defenses described in this checklist.

6. *Did the subject of the statements consent to publication?* Consent is a complete libel defense. If the subjects of the statements were generous enough to consent to publication, and if you can prove that consent, you are protected from a libel judgment if a subject subsequently changes

Figure 5.6 Libel liability checklist. (continued)

his or her mind. As always, the best proof of consent is a signed, written release.

7. If the production is a fictional work based on actual events, have you changed the names and descriptions of the people and places involved in the actual events? As discussed in this chapter, changing the identities of people and places to protect the innocent—or even the guilty—no longer guarantees that a production is fully protected from libel challenges, but it can help. The more aspects that are changed (e.g., name, age, physical description, dates), the greater the protection.

8. Do the statements fall within the provisions of a state retraction statute? As discussed in this chapter, some states have retraction statutes that provide some degree of protection from large damage awards if a media entity promptly retracts libelous statements. A lawyer who is experienced in libel law will know whether your state has such a statute and whether you might benefit from its protections.

- Bad weather insurance, which reimburses the production company for extra costs incurred if a shooting day must be canceled because of inclement weather
- Equipment insurance, which covers damages to equipment leased or owned by the production company
- Wardrobe, props, and set insurance, which pays for fixing or replacing items damaged during production
- Animal mortality insurance, which insures the company against the death of any animal featured in the production that is listed on the policy
- Videotape and negative film insurance, which reimburses the production company for damaged or lost videotape stock or negative film, recorded videotape, or exposed film and recorded soundtracks
- Aircraft and watercraft liability insurance, which protects the company against claims related to the use of planes, helicopters, and boats in a production

- Property damage liability insurance, which covers the cost of repairing or replacing property belonging to others that is damaged or destroyed during production
- Comprehensive general liability and auto liability insurance, which shield the production company from claims for property damage and bodily injury as a result of accidents during production

Comprehensive liability insurance is particularly important on productions that involve location work. When you are shooting on location, all sorts of accidents and mishaps can, and seemingly always do, happen. With the proper liability coverage, your production is protected from the many claims for personal injury and property damage that can result from even simple accidents. In addition (and as discussed earlier in the chapter), many states and municipalities require proof of liability insurance when you file for a shooting permit.

In some states, you may also be required to carry workers' compensation insurance for production employees. In addition, some union and guild agreements specify that you must provide additional types of insurance for their members, including flight accident policies that cover travel to and from production locations. For more information about guild agreements, see Chapter 7. Many comprehensive production policies also provide for some level of errors and omissions coverage. For more information about errors and omissions insurance, see Chapter 4.

Along with the conventional categories of protection just described, large production projects (e.g., feature films, television miniseries) are often covered by a separate type of insurance, called *completion bonds*. Sold by insurers known as *completion guarantors*, completion bonds shield the financial backers of a production from the effects of budget overruns, delays, and other problems that can cripple the potential profitability of a film or television project. In return for providing this protection, the completion guarantor receives a substantial fee and the authority to exercise substantial control over key aspects of the production, including the right to approve casting selections. Most guarantors also reserve the right to take control of a faltering production, although this option is usually exercised only as a last resort after all other attempts at intervention have failed. For more information about completion bonds, contact a reputable completion guarantor. You will find the names of guarantors listed in the film and video producer's guides that are published in New York, Los Angeles, and other major production centers.

Summary

- *What are shooting permits?* Shooting or location permits are temporary licenses that authorize production companies to conduct location shoots in public areas, including public parks, buildings, streets, and highways. The permits are usually issued by state or municipal film liaison offices, often in conjunction with the government agencies that are responsible for the locations and facilities where the shoot will take place.
- *What other permits and licenses must media producers obtain?* Depending on the type of project and the area where the production will take place, producers may need to obtain several additional permits beyond the basic forms issued by state or municipal authorities. Those additional permits may include federal consent forms for shooting on property owned by the U.S. government; county permits for shooting on county-owned roads or facilities; work permits and releases for employing minors and other special categories of workers; pyrotechnic or fire department permits to cover any special effects that involve explosions, smoke, or open flames; and authorizations from local animal regulation bureaus for any animals that will be used in the production.
- *What are the penalties for shooting without the proper permits?* If you are caught shooting without the proper permits, you will usually be forced to suspend production until you obtain the necessary clearances, a delay that can prove extremely costly as talent, crew members, and rented equipment stand idle. You also may be subject to substantial fines and, for some severe violations, criminal penalties.
- *What is privacy law?* Privacy law is the body of common and statutory law that protects an individual's right to be left alone. In the United States, the legal right to be left alone includes the right to protection against intrusion on your solitude and private affairs, the appropriation of your name or likeness for commercial purposes (often called the *right of publicity*), disclosures that place you before the public in a false light, and the

public disclosure of embarrassing facts about your private life.

- *What are the sources of privacy law?* In the United States, privacy law is a mix of state and federal case law, state statutes directed at specific kinds of privacy violations, and a growing number of federal statutes aimed at preventing the misuse of government records and electronic surveillance. At this time, however, there is no comprehensive federal privacy law.

- *How can you protect a production against invasion-of-privacy lawsuits?* The best protection against invasion-of-privacy challenges is to secure a signed, written performer release from each person whose voice or likeness appears in the production. If the production will include location segments shot on private property, you should also secure written location releases from the property owners.

- *What is libel?* Libel occurs when a false and injurious statement is made about an individual, group, or corporation. Although the exact guidelines vary from state to state, a statement about an individual generally is considered to be libelous if it is false, knowingly and deliberately communicated to at least one other person, and injures the individual's reputation. When these conditions are present, the injured individual may seek damages through a libel lawsuit.

- *What is the difference between libel and slander?* Libel and slander form the larger legal category called *defamation law*. Historically, *libel* has been applied to defamation that is written or portrayed pictorially, whereas *slander* has meant defamation that is spoken or conveyed orally. In recent years, however, the boundary between libel and slander has become blurred, particularly in cases involving the audiovisual media.

- *What are the sources of libel law?* There is no comprehensive federal libel law. Instead, like privacy law, libel law is a mix of common law and state statutory law. Because many libel cases involve free press and free speech issues, many of the major judicial rulings in this area have come from the federal courts, particularly the U.S. Supreme Court. Individual states are free to enact their own libel legislation, as long as that legislation does not conflict with federal law or the U.S. Constitution.

- *How can you protect a production against libel lawsuits?* The best protection against libel actions is to tell the truth. Check all facts presented in your production, particularly those facts that form the basis of potentially libelous statements, such as those that accuse individuals or groups of professional incompetence, unprofessional behavior, unethical business dealings, dishonesty, promiscuity, drunkenness, laziness, criminal behavior, or physical or psychological illnesses. Ask yourself if such statements are essential to the program. If they are not, eliminate them. If they are necessary, make sure that the statements are true. If you have made libelous allegations as part of a news program, the courts recognize several additional defenses. In particular, the courts require public officials who are filing libel lawsuits to prove "actual malice" on the part of the news media.

- *What is production insurance?* Production insurance is a special type of insurance coverage that protects a company against many of the accidents, mishaps, and acts of nature that can cause problems during a media production. A comprehensive policy provides protection against extra production costs caused by the death, injury, or illness of a performer or director; the cancellation of shooting because of inclement weather; damages to equipment, wardrobes, props, and sets leased or owned by the production company; the death of an animal featured in the production; damaged or lost videotape stock or negative film, recorded videotape, or exposed film, and recorded soundtracks; and claims related to the use of planes, helicopters, and boats employed in the production. Production insurance policies should also include comprehensive general liability and auto liability coverage, which shield the production company from claims for property damage and bodily injury that result from accidents during production.

- *What is a completion bond?* Large production projects (e.g., feature films, television miniseries) are often covered by a separate type of insurance, called *completion bonds*. Sold by insurers known as *completion guarantors*, completion bonds shield the financial backers of a production from the effects of budget overruns, delays, and other production problems. In return for providing this protection, the completion guarantor receives a substantial fee and contingent authority to exercise substantial control over key aspects of the production.

Notes

1. In some localities, there is no film and video office at the state or local level. When this is the case, direct your initial inquiries to the mayor's office or police department in the community where you plan to conduct the shoot.

2. Samuel D. Warren and Louis D. Brandeis, "The Right to Privacy," 4 HARVARD LAW REVIEW 193 (December 15, 1890).

3. As discussed later in this chapter, false light is related to but distinct from libel. Libel involves untruthful assertions that damage an individual's reputation. False light involves the revelation of private information about an individual that, although it may not diminish the individual's reputation (an essential element of a libel action), places the individual in a false or embarrassing light before the public. For example, an unauthorized biography of baseball pitcher Warren Spahn included material depicting him as a war hero, which he was not. Even though these statements, if anything, would have enhanced rather than injured Spahn's reputation, Spahn was able to bring a successful "false light" action claiming that the statements had caused him emotional distress. See *Messner Inc. v. Spahn*, 393 U.S. 1046 (1947).

4. An early case defining the "newsworthy" defense is *Sidis v. F. R. Publishing Corporation*, 113 F.2d 806 (2nd Cir. 1940).

5. See *Lugosi v. Universal Pictures*, 25 Cal. 3d 813, 603 P.2d 425 (1979). The holding in this case was effectively overturned with the passage of California's right of publicity statute, which currently states that the right of publicity survives for 70 years following an individual's death.

6. See *Memphis Development Foundation v. Factors Etc., Inc.*, 616 F.2d 956, (6th Cir. 1980), *cert. denied*, 449 U.S. 953 (1980).

7. See *Commerce Union Bank v. Coors*, 7 Med.L.Rptr. 2593 (Tenn. Chanc. Ct. 1981).

8. New York's current right of publicity statute protects living individuals from unauthorized appropriation of their images for commercial purposes but does not grant a deceased celebrity's heirs the right to prevent such unauthorized appropriation. See NEW YORK CIVIL RIGHTS LAW, §§ 50–51. In addition to California, the following states have right of publicity statutes that expressly grant a deceased celebrity's heirs the right to control commercial use of the celebrity's image: Florida, Indiana, Kentucky, Nevada,

Oklahoma, Tennessee, and Texas. In several other states, including Connecticut, Georgia, New Jersey, and Utah, a postmortem right of publicity is well established under common law.

9. California's right of publicity statute is CALIFORNIA CIVIL CODE § 3344. A sister statute, CALIFORNIA CIVIL CODE § 3344.1 (formerly § 990), effectively overrules the Lugosi decision discussed earlier by applying the right of publicity to deceased celebrities, allowing a celebrity's heirs to control the commercial use of their names, likenesses, and so on for 70 years following the celebrity's death. Section 3344 includes a "safe harbor" for use of the celebrity's name and likeness in news and informational programs. The "safe harbor" provision of Section 3344.1 is even more broad, stating that the section does not apply to uses of a deceased personality's name, voice, likeness, and so on in "a play, book, magazine, newspaper, musical composition, audiovisual work, [or], radio or television program, . . . if it is fictional or nonfictional entertainment, or a dramatic, literary, or musical work."

10. This example assumes that, under the applicable right of publicity statute, Nixon's heirs have the right to control commercial use of his image. This would be the case under the law of California, where Nixon was domiciled at the time of his death.

11. 15 U.S.C.§ 1125 (Lanham Act § 43) (1997).

12. See *Allen v. National Video, Inc.*, 610 F. Supp. 612 (S.D.N.Y 1985); *Allen v. Men's World Outlet, Inc.*, 679 F. Supp. 360 (S.D.N.Y 1988).

13. See *Midler v. Ford Motor Co.*, 849 F.2d 460 (9th Cir. 1988).

14. *Waits v. Frito-Lay, Inc.*, 978 F.2d 1093, 1098 (9th Cir. 1992), *cert. denied*, 113 S.Ct. 1047 (1993). In another celebrated case of celebrity "identity misappropriation," famed television letter turner Vanna White sued Samsung Electronics over a commercial for its products featuring a robot wearing a blond wig in front of a Wheel of Fortune game board. See *White v. Samsung Electronics America, Inc.*, 971 F.2d 1395 (9th Cir. 1992).

15. *Bindrim v. Mitchell*, 92 Cal. App. 2d 61, 155 Cal. Rptr. 29 (1979).

16. To help head off this sort of privacy lawsuit, many productions include a disclaimer declaring that "the events and characters depicted in this program are fictitious. Any similarity to actual persons, living or dead, or to actual entities or events is purely coincidental." Although this disclaimer may help deter casual lawsuits, it is unlikely to dissuade serious plaintiffs from pressing their cases. Furthermore, attaching a disclaimer to a production will not provide a blanket defense if the case reaches court. You

will still need to defend yourself against the plaintiff's claim that, contrary to what the disclaimer states, the production does depict a real person.

17. See *Westmoreland v. CBS, Inc.*, 596 F. Supp. 1170 (S.D.N.Y. 1984).

18. See *Newton v. National Broadcasting Co.*, 930 F.2d 662 (9th Cir. 1990), *cert. denied*, 502 U.S. 866 (1991).

19. *New York Times Co. v. Sullivan*, 376 U.S. 254 (1964).

20. *Firestone v. Time, Inc.*, 424 U.S. 448 (1976).

21. *Anderson v. Liberty Lobby, Inc.*, 477 U.S. 242 (1986).

22. *Philadelphia Newspapers, Inc. v. Hepps*, 475 U.S. 767 (1986).

23. *Hustler Magazine, Inc. v. Falwell*, 485 U.S. 46 (1986).

24. *Milkovich v. Lorain Journal Co.*, 497 U.S. 1 (1990).

25. The "neutral reporting" privilege was first set forth in detail in *Edwards v. National Audubon Society*, 556 F.2d 113 (2nd Cir. 1977), *cert. denied*, 434 U.S. 1002 (1977). But see *McCall v. Courier-Journal & Louisville Times Co.*, 623 S.W.2d 882 (Ky. 1981), *cert. denied*, 456 U.S. 975 (1982) (declining to recognize the neutral reporting privilege in Kentucky).

26. The states that have some form of retraction statute are Alabama, Arizona, California, Connecticut, Florida, Georgia, Idaho, Indiana, Iowa, Kentucky, Maine, Massachusetts, Michigan, Minnesota, Mississippi, Montana, Nebraska, Nevada, New Jersey, North Carolina, North Dakota, Ohio, Oklahoma, Oregon, South Dakota, Tennessee, Texas, Utah, Virginia, Washington, West Virginia, Wisconsin, and Wyoming.

27. The California retraction statute is CALIFORNIA CIVIL CODE § 48a.

28. See *Bose Corp. v. Consumers Union*, 466 U.S. 485 (1984). In this case, the Supreme Court ruled that plaintiff Bose Corp. had not satisfied the *New York Times v. Sullivan* "actual malice" requirement in challenging statements made by the defendant in reviewing Bose's stereo equipment.

6

Adding Music: Special Concerns Surrounding the Use of Music in Media Productions

The right music can bring a great deal of emotion and impact to a media production. That is why the Nike Corporation was willing to pay a great deal for the right to use the Beatles' song "Revolution" in its 1987 television commercials introducing a "revolutionary" line of sport shoes. Unfortunately, music can also introduce a whole host of hidden legal concerns. That is why Nike and its advertising agency soon found themselves caught up in a dispute contesting their right to use the Beatles' recording of "Revolution," even though they thought they had purchased all of the necessary rights to the song.

Nike was not naive. The company knew that it needed to secure the proper permissions to use "Revolution," and it assumed that it had done just that. Specifically, Nike paid for and received permission from Capitol Records, Inc., and EMI Records, Ltd., the two companies that controlled the worldwide release of Beatles records. But Nike did not secure permission from Apple Records, Inc., the music company that represented some of the Beatles' interests. Alleging that the Nike ad "wrongfully traded on the good will and popularity of the Beatles," Apple Records filed a civil suit in New York seeking $15 million in damages.

The Music Permissions Process

Nike's problem points out just how complex music rights can be, particularly when you plan to use a popular recording in a media production. At its most basic level, the permissions process for music is the same as the process for film clips, photographs, and other non-music materials discussed in Chapter 4. You first contact the individual or group that controls the rights to the materials. Then you negotiate an agreement that specifies the rights that you will receive to use the materials and the compensation that the copyright owner will receive for granting those rights.

With recordings of musical works, however, this fairly straightforward process can become complicated quickly. First, usually at least two parties control the rights to the recording: the music publisher or songwriter that owns the copyright to the song and the record company that distributes the sound recording. Second, as Nike discovered, many more parties may claim some sort of rights in the work: the independent production company that originally brought the song to the record company, the musicians who performed on the sound recording, and so forth. Finally, assuming that you can contact the correct parties and negotiate for the right to use the work, you should know that two distinct types of rights may be involved: synchronization rights and performance rights. To know which of these rights you need, you must know how you will use the song in your production and how the finished production will be displayed or distributed.

The sections that follow attempt to sort out these and many other issues and definitions related to the use of music in media production projects. Much of the discussion assumes that you are familiar with the fundamentals of copyright law introduced in Chapter 4.

Musical Works and the Copyright Law

In most respects, the copyright law treats music the same as any other work that is eligible for copyright protection. Like the copyrightable materials discussed in Chapter 4, music properties are protected by copyright as soon as they are created in fixed form and the term of copyright currently runs for the life of an individual copyright owner plus 70 years. In addition, the registration, infringement, work-made-for-hire, and fair use provisions discussed in Chapter 4 all apply to music properties.

But music also receives some special treatment under U.S. copyright law. For example, the law provides for several categories of musical rights: mechanical rights, synchronization rights, and performance rights. The copyright law also provides protection for several types and categories of music properties: songs or compositions, sound recordings, and phonorecords. In addition, music is one of the few categories of intellectual property to which a compulsory license provision applies under U.S. law. Each of these special terms, definitions, and provisions is discussed in more detail in the sections that follow.

Musical Works

Under the U.S. copyright law, a song is not a song, it is a musical work. As defined in the current copyright law, a *musical work* consists of the music—the particular combination of notes that defines the composition as an original work—and the lyrics (if there are lyrics). A rock-and-roll song, a symphony, an opera, and any other musical composition that can be performed or recorded are all musical works. It is important to note that a musical work exists as a separate, copyrightable entity that is distinct from sound recordings, copies, and phonorecords of the work. Think of a musical work as the notes and words that would appear on sheet music for the composition.

Sound Recordings

When musicians perform the notes and words of a musical work and the performance is recorded, the result is a sound recording. Like the musical work itself, each sound recording is a distinct, copyrightable property. In other words, each time a musical work is recorded, a new, copyrighted sound recording is created. For example, Norman Whitfield and Barrett Strong wrote "I Heard It through the Grapevine," a popular music classic that has been recorded by many performers, including Marvin Gaye, Gladys Knight and the Pips, and Creedence Clearwater Revival. The song "I Heard It through the Grapevine" exists as a distinct musical work, the copyright for which was initially owned by Whitfield and Strong. In addition, each time "Grapevine" is recorded, a new sound recording is created as a separate, copyrightable work that is distinct from all other recordings of the work (e.g., Marvin Gaye's recording of "Grapevine" is a distinct, copyrightable work, Gladys Knight's recording is a distinct work, and so on). Of course, because the song "Grapevine" is a copyrighted musical work, Marvin Gaye, Gladys Knight, and all others who record the song are required to compensate Whitfield and Strong (or, more likely, the musical publisher or other entity that currently owns the copyright) for their use of this musical work.

Copies and Phonorecords

Once you understand the distinction between musical works and sound recordings, you should become familiar with two more terms that are important in the music rights world: copy and phonorecord. A *copy* is sheet music that shows the notes and words that constitute the composition or some other physical manifestation of a musical work that allows it to be perceived visually.

A *phonorecord* is the physical object (e.g., phonograph record, audiocassette, CD, DVD, computer disk) that contains the fixed sounds of a sound recording. To create phonorecords, you first create a sound recording of the musical work. Then you copy the sound recording to audiocassettes, CDs, or some other distribution medium. Each physical copy that you create from the sound recording is a phonorecord. Note, however, that a phonorecord is not a copy of the musical work or sound recording in the copyright definition of that term because you cannot actually see the notes and words that form the musical work or the audio signals that make up the sound recording by simply looking at the phonorecord.

Role of Music Publishers and Record Companies

In the music industry, particularly the popular music industry, very few composers and performers act as independent agents. Instead, most are affiliated with one or more music publishers and record companies that own part or complete interest in their songs and sound recordings. Remember, under copyright law, a song and a sound recording are different, distinct works. As a result, the individual who wrote the song does not necessarily have an ownership stake in sound recordings of the song, and the performers and record companies who created the sound recordings do not necessarily have any ownership interest in the song.

Here is how the process typically works. Once a song is created, and before it is recorded, the composer or songwriting team usually assigns the song to a music publisher. Under the standard publishing arrangement, the publisher receives the entire or a portion of copyright to the song, and in return, the composer receives a guaranteed percentage of the income generated by the publisher's efforts to promote and sell the song. Typically, the composer will receive about 50 to 75 percent of the publisher's income from the song, after the publisher has deducted 10 to 20 percent of the gross revenue as an administration fee.

In years past, music publishers generated the bulk of their revenue by convincing popular performers to record or "cover" songs. Additional income came from licensing songs for use in movie and television soundtracks. Like many aspects of the music industry, however, publishing practices have become more complex in recent years, particularly as more performers have written and recorded their own songs and as more songwriters and record companies have formed their own music publishing ventures. Today, a typical song might be published by the songwriter/performer's own music publishing company. The songwriter/performer then records the song as a work-made-for-hire for a record company, which pays the performer's publishing company for the rights to create a sound recording of the song.

Note that, under this fairly standard setup, the songwriter/performer owns neither the song nor the sound recording of the song. The copyright for the song is owned by the music publishing company (which may, in fact, be partly or wholly owned by the songwriter/performer), and the copyright for the sound recording is owned by the record company. As mentioned before, the contract between the songwriter/performer and the publishing company requires the publisher to pay the songwriter a percentage of its income from licensing rights to the song. In addition, a separate contract with the record company requires the record label to pay the performer a percentage of its income from selling copies of the sound recording. The performer also receives a percentage of any income that the record company generates by licensing the sound recording for use in film or television soundtracks. Finally, the music publisher and songwriter share the performing rights royalties generated by public performance (primarily through radio airplay) of the sound recording.

The contractual relationships among songwriters, performers, publishers, and record labels can become very complicated, particularly when third and fourth parties are involved. For example, a rock group might have a contract with an independent producer to record a song that one member of the group wrote several years earlier and sold to a music publisher. Once the independent producer has secured the rights to the song from the music publisher and the group has made a sound recording, the producer will try to sell distribution rights to the sound recording to a major record label.

It is usually not necessary for media producers to know the full copyright history of a song they are interested in including in a production. In most cases, it is enough to know who currently controls the rights to the song and who controls the rights to the sound recording.

Implications for Media Producers

What difference do all of these definitions and distinctions make to producers who are simply interested in adding a little music to a production? Consider the fictional case of Paula Hernandez and Howard Allen, two producers who are developing a motivational video called "Together Today, Together Tomorrow" for a Fortune 500 corporation. As a musical theme for the production, Hernandez and Allen plan to use "Made for Each Other," a popular song written by Jerry Miles and published by Miles Ahead Music, Inc. The hit version of the song was recorded by a group called Sure Thing for Dynamic Records, Inc.

The producers, Hernandez and Allen, have two basic options: (1) they can secure the rights to use the musical work (the song itself) and the Sure Thing sound recording of the work, or (2) they can secure the rights to just the musical work and arrange for other musicians to perform the version that will be used in their production. In both cases, Hernandez and Allen must obtain the rights to the musical work from Miles Ahead Music, Inc. In the first case, they must also secure from Dynamic Records the rights to use the sound recording of the song by Sure Thing.

Which is the right choice for Hernandez and Allen? That depends on their priorities. If the production budget and schedule are their main concerns, they must determine which option will cost the least time and money: securing the rights to the Sure Thing recording of "Made for Each Other" from Dynamic Records or buying the rights to the song from Miles Ahead Music and paying to have their own version recorded. Of course, Hernandez and Allen must also consider how their choice will affect the quality and impact of their production. Is it critical to have the Sure Thing version of the song, or will a remake suffice?

In actual practice, it is usually easier and cheaper to secure permission from a music publisher to create your own version of a song than it is to receive permission from the record company to use the original recording. The reason for this is simple: Music publishers make money by selling the types of rights you are requesting, whereas record companies make money by selling records. Unless you can convince the company that your use of the recording will boost record sales, the company will probably be reluctant to grant your request. Also, in some cases, the contract between the recording artist and the record company prohibits the company from licensing the sound recording for commercial applications without the artist's permission. Of course, the right amount of money may convince even the most reluctant artists to allow their recordings to be used commercially. In 1995, Mick Jagger and Keith Richards, who had historically declined requests to use Rolling Stones' recordings in television commercials, had a change of heart when Microsoft reportedly offered several million dollars to use their recording of "Start Me Up" in commercials introducing its Windows 95 system software.

If you plan to record your own version of a popular song, it may be possible to purchase a prerecorded instrumental track, or "music bed," over which you add your own version of the vocal track. If you do this, you will still need to secure all of the rights and permissions previously described. In addition, you should obtain a written agreement with the company that provides the instrumental track. The agreement should spell out the terms under which the company will provide the instrumental track and the exact extent of your right to use it.

Record companies can be particularly tough on corporate video producers who are thinking of adding a popular sound recording to an in-house production, as there is little chance that this type of non-broadcast use will result in a significant increase in record sales. When record companies do grant permission for corporate use of a popular recording, the price is usually high—from several thousand dollars for a license that permits one-time use of the recording (in other words, permission to use the recording in a production that will be shown once) to $10,000 and up for a license that permits longer-term use. Of course, you will also need to pay the music publisher for the right to use the song contained in the sound recording. Fortunately, these fees are usually a bit more reasonable, typically running from 25 to 35 percent of the charge that record companies would assess for granting rights to the sound recording.

In some circumstances, a producer may need to seek other types of permissions from a music publisher or recording company, including the right to alter the lyrics to fit the needs of a particular production or to use an existing sound-alike recording of the work. This is often true in the production of television commercials and corporate sales presentations, where the producer wants to modify the lyrics of a popular song to promote a particular product. For a more complete discussion of these options, see the music rights checklist that appears later as Figure 6.3.

Types of Rights

Before you begin negotiating for the right to add a song or sound recording to a production, you need to know which types of rights you require. For media producers, the two most important kinds of rights are synchronization and performance rights. You should also be familiar with master recording rights, compulsory mechanical licenses, and a few other terms that can come up during licensing discussions.

Synchronization Rights, Master Recording Licenses, and Performance Rights

If you are licensing music materials for use in a production, you will usually require both synchronization and performance rights to the material. Synchronization rights allow you to link the song to the video track of your production. Performance rights allow you to show the completed production that contains the song to an audience. In addition, if you are seeking to use an original sound recording in a production, you will need to acquire master recording rights.

Securing Synchronization and Master Recording Rights

How do you go about securing synchronization rights to a musical work? As discussed in the preceding section, you must first determine whether you are seeking rights to the musical work or song alone or to both the song and a specific recording of it. If you are seeking rights to the song alone (in other words, if you plan to record your own version of the song), you will need to obtain permission from the music publisher in the form of a synchronization ("synch") license. If you are seeking the rights to a specific recording of the song, you will need permission from both the music publisher (for rights to the song) and the record company (for rights to the sound recording). The permission from the record company should be in the form of a master recording license that grants you the right to use the recording in your production. The music publisher and record company should be listed on the jacket, label, or liner notes of the cassette or CD that contains the sound recording. If the record company owns or otherwise controls the necessary rights to both the sound recording and the underlying song, it may be possible to acquire both synchronization and master recording rights through a single synchronization and master recording license executed by the record company. This type of a combined license should include a representation and warranty by the record company that it has the right to license all of the relevant rights to both the sound recording and the underlying song.

Figure 6.1 is a sample synch license granting the nonexclusive right to use a single musical work in a single nonbroadcast video program for a specified term. Although it is generally preferable to obtain rights to the musical work that are as broad as possible (e.g., not limited to nonbroadcast use, not restricted to a specified term), the individual or entity that controls the synchronization rights may not be willing to grant such a broad license, or it may require substantial added compensation for granting such expansive rights. As a result, producers should start by determining what rights they realistically need and what they realistically can afford to pay for those rights. For example, if you are producing an industrial video program or television commercial that has a likely shelf life of two or three years, it does not make sense to pay for synchronization rights in perpetuity. On the other hand, if you are producing a situation comedy for network television that you hope will survive in syndication in perpetuity, it may be necessary to negotiate and pay for perpetual rights for any songs that you use in particular episodes.

In Figure 6.1, the producer of a nonbroadcast video program is obtaining synchronization rights for an initial term of three years for a payment of $1,500, with an option to obtain the rights for an additional three-year term for an additional $1,500. This sort of option works well for many producers because it gives them the right but no obligation to continue distributing the production containing the musical work beyond the initial term for a fixed additional payment without having to renegotiate the synch license.

Note that the sample synch license in Figure 6.1 expressly excludes public performance rights in the song, which the producer in this instance must obtain, if applicable, from the appropriate performance rights society (discussed later in this chapter). Note, also, that

Figure 6.1 Sample Synchronization license.

Agreement dated as April 21, 2003 ("Effective Date"), by and between Major Music, Inc., a California corporation with offices at 16500 La Cienega Boulevard, Los Angeles, California 90066 ("Publisher"), and Insight Video, Inc., a New York corporation with offices at 1470 Davis Avenue, White Plains, New York 10605 ("Licensee"), with respect to the musical composition titled "Top of the World" (the "Work") and Licensee's nonbroadcast video production currently titled "Going for Gold" (the "Production").

1. LICENSE GRANTED. Publisher hereby grants Licensee a nonexclusive license to record and fix the Work in timed relation to the visual images contained in the Production and to display and distribute the Production containing the Work throughout the world. The foregoing grant of rights includes the right to distribute the Production containing the Work on videocassettes and videodiscs (including digital videodiscs or "DVD"), but expressly excludes: (i) the right to perform publicly the Work within the Production (such public performance rights, if required by Licensee, to be obtained and/or cleared separately by Licensee); (ii) the right to transmit the Work within the Production on commercial broadcast, cable, pay-per-view, or direct-to-home satellite television; and (iii) the right to distribute phonorecords, compact discs, and/or audiocassettes containing the Work. All other rights in the Work not expressly granted herein are reserved by Publisher. The rights granted in this paragraph 1 are hereafter referred to as "the License."

2. TERM. The Term of the License shall commence upon the "Effective Date" and terminate upon the third anniversary of that date unless renewed as provided herein. Upon expiration of the Term, all rights granted herein shall revert to Publisher.

3. PAYMENT. As full and complete consideration for the License granted herein, Licensor will pay Publisher $1,500.00 (One Thousand Five Hundred Dollars). Licensor shall have the right to renew the Term once for three additional years upon written notice to Publisher accompanied by an additional payment of $1,500.00 (One Thousand Five Hundred Dollars), provided that such notice and payment is received by Publisher at least 30 days prior to expiration of the Term.

4. NO ALTERATIONS. The License does not include the right to alter the lyric or in any other way change the fundamental character of the Work. Any such alterations or changes must be approved in advance in writing by Publisher.

Figure 6.1 Sample Synchronization license. (continued)

5. REPRESENTATION, WARRANTIES, AND INDEMNIFICATION. Publisher represents and warrants that it has the full right and authority to enter into this Agreement and to grant the License. Publisher agrees to indemnify and to hold Licensee harmless from any and all claims, damages, costs, and expenses (including court expenses and reasonable attorney fees) arising from any breach of the foregoing representation and warranty. Licensee shall promptly notify Publisher of any claim or action involving or implicating the foregoing indemnification, and Publisher shall have the option at its own expense to control or participate in the defense of any such claim or action. Licensee may not settle any such claim or action without the consent of Publisher, which consent may not be unreasonably withheld.

6. MISCELLANEOUS. This Agreement sets forth the entire agreement between Publisher and Licensee concerning the subject matter hereof and supersedes any prior understandings, communications, or agreements with respect to that subject matter. This Agreement may be modified or amended only in a writing signed by both parties. The License and rights granted hereunder are not assignable by Licensee without the advance written permission of Publisher, such permission not to be unreasonably withheld. This Agreement will be subject to and construed in accordance with the laws of the State of California applicable to agreements executed and intended to be fully performed within that state, and without regard to that state's choice of law provisions. Any dispute or controversy arising from this Agreement shall be adjudicated in courts of competent jurisdiction in the County of Los Angeles, California, and the parties hereby agree to submit to the jurisdiction of such courts. This Agreement may be executed by original or facsimile signature and in counterparts, each of which will be deemed an original, but all of which together shall constitute one and the same instrument.

IN WITNESS WHEREOF, the parties hereto have executed this Agreement as of the day and date first set forth above.

PUBLISHER   LICENSEE

_____   _____

By:_____   By:_____

Its:_____   Its:_____

the sample synch license includes the right to distribute the production containing the song on videocassette and DVDs. Historically, this "mechanical" right to distribute physical media containing the song would be secured through a separate mechanical license. Because most programs produced today are eventually distributed on videocassette or DVD, however, it is appropriate and advisable to obtain this right as part of the synch license.

Producers should be aware that many music publishers and agencies that represent music publishers insist on using their own form agreements when licensing synchronization rights in a song. Although the publisher may be hesitant to make major modifications to the rights granted and warranties made in its form agreement, such agreements are never completely cast in stone, and it is reasonable and possible to obtain changes to meet the needs of your particular production. Before executing a form synch agreement, be sure that the agreement grants the specific rights you need to use the song in your production in all relevant distribution channels and that the publisher or agency represents and warrants that it has the authority to grant those rights. This is particularly important if you are producing a nonbroadcast or other limited-distribution program, and the form license is designed to be used in connection with programs intended for broadcast or cable distribution.

When you are ready to negotiate rights to a song or sound recording, you may want to consider working with an agency that specializes in obtaining music rights and permissions for media producers. For more information, see the section "Working with Rights and Permissions Agencies" that appears later in this chapter.

Securing Public Performance Rights

A license granting performance rights is necessary whenever a production containing a musical work will be performed publicly. Not surprisingly, a public performance includes transmission of the production containing the musical work over broadcast, cable television, or direct broadcast satellite channels. Public performance also includes, however, displaying a production in such nonbroadcast venues as business conferences, the lobbies of office buildings, or on the jumbo television screens used in sports arenas and convention centers. As a result, producers of nonbroadcast video productions that will be displayed to the public in these or other ways must secure performance rights for any musical works contained in their production.

Under the U.S. copyright law, performance rights have historically attached only to musical works or compositions, and not to sound recordings containing performances of those musical works. As discussed in Chapter 8, this changed when Congress passed the Digital Performance Right in Sound Recordings Act of 1995,[1] which established a limited performance right to sound recordings that are transmitted over the Internet and other online, interactive services. Unless your production will be transmitted over such a service, however, you do not need to secure performance rights for any sound recording included in the production. Of course, as explained earlier in this chapter, if you do plan to use a sound recording in your production, you will need to obtain a master recording license from the record company that controls the rights to the recording.

If your production will be shown exclusively on broadcast television or a cable television network, you usually do not need to worry about licensing performance rights. These rights have probably already been secured for you, courtesy of the blanket licensing arrangement that the major performance rights societies, discussed later, have negotiated with broadcast and cable television networks and individual television stations and cable system operators. Although this blanket license has been challenged in the courts over the years (it is an all-or-nothing arrangement that requires licensees to pay a fee to cover all music licensed by the organization or receive no rights at all), the major television networks and most U.S. television stations still hold such licenses. As a result, producers of broadcast or cable television programs usually need only secure synchronization rights for the copyrighted songs they use in their productions.[2] However, synch licenses for broadcast or cable programs sometimes require the licensee to acknowledge and agree that it will be responsible for obtaining the required performance rights from the performance right society or other entity that controls these rights.

The two dominant performance rights societies in the United States are Broadcast Music Incorporated (BMI) and the American Society of Composers, Authors and Publishers (ASCAP).[3] ASCAP has been around longer, but BMI is currently the larger of the two groups.

ASCAP and BMI devote much of their efforts to negotiating with television broadcasters, radio broadcasters, and cable networks over the blanket performing rights licensing agreements just discussed and managing the collection and disbursement of the royalty fees that result from these blanket licenses. ASCAP and BMI can also grant public performance licenses for the musical works they represent to producers of programs intended for nonbroadcast (e.g., industrial, public arena) distribution.

Significantly, ASCAP and BMI are not set up or empowered to provide any rights other than public performance rights for the musical compositions they represent. To secure other types of rights to the musical work (e.g., synchronization rights), you must contact the music publisher directly. It is also important to note that BMI, ASCAP, and other performing rights societies currently represent composers and music publishers in their negotiations, not record companies. As a result, performance rights societies are able to license the rights to songs but not to sound recordings (although, as discussed previously, performance rights to sound recordings are currently required only in limited circumstances).

How do you know which performance rights society represents a particular author, composer, or music publisher for a particular song? Check the sheet music or the jacket of the cassette or CD. If the performing rights society is not listed there, try calling or writing ASCAP or BMI or visiting their websites. They will be able to tell you if they represent the songwriter or music publisher in question. Contact information for the major performing rights organizations is listed in Appendix B. If neither ASCAP nor BMI represents the musical work, you will need to obtain performance rights directly from the music publisher or individual that controls performance rights in the work.

Compulsory Mechanical Licenses

Imagine this scenario: Several years ago, you wrote and retained the copyright to a catchy pop song. Then you granted a popular recording group and its record label permission to create and distribute phonorecords of the song in return for a royalty on each copy sold. The recording was released, it became a big hit, and everyone made money.

Now another performer wants to record and release phonorecords of the song. You have never liked the performer, and you are concerned that the resulting sound recording might damage your song's growing reputation as a pop music classic. Is there any legal way for you to stop the performer from recording the song and selling copies?

Surprisingly, the answer to that question is no, as long as the performer is willing to fulfill the requirements of the compulsory mechanical license provision of U.S. copyright law. Under that provision, anyone can obtain a license to create and distribute phonorecords of a published musical work. To secure the license, the performer or group simply must fulfill the following requirements:

- Notify the copyright owner of its intent to use the song.
- Agree to pay the royalty rate specified in the Copyright Act.
- Agree not to change the fundamental character of the work.

Although the compulsory mechanical licensing provision does allow the performer some latitude in arranging and interpreting the song to create a distinct sound recording, any substantive changes to the lyrics or basic melody must be approved by the copyright owner through a separate agreement.

The method for computing the royalty rate for compulsory mechanical licenses is defined in Section 115 of the U.S. Copyright Act, and the rate is periodically adjusted upward to reflect changes in the consumer price index. Many performers try to obtain a rate lower than the statutory rate through a voluntary license with the copyright owner, however. To facilitate this process, most owners of musical works arrange for the Harry Fox Agency, Inc.,[4] to serve as their representative in negotiating mechanical use royalties. The Harry Fox Agency also acts as a payment processing center for its clients, collecting and distributing fees for mechanical licenses.

Media producers should note that mechanical rights and the compulsory mechanical licensing provision applies only when you are creating and distributing phonorecords or other physical copies of a musical work or a production containing a musical work. As discussed earlier, producers who are planning to add a copyrighted song to a media production must secure synchronization and, in many cases, performance rights directly from the copyright owner or the appropriate performing rights society. In addition, the compulsory mechanical license applies only to songs, not to sound recordings. The right to use a sound recording in a production and the consideration for that right must be negotiated with the record company or other entity that controls the rights in the sound recording.

Working with Rights and Permissions Agencies

Rather than seeking and securing music permissions themselves, some producers prefer to use agencies that specialize in obtaining clearances for music and other copyrighted works. The producer provides the agency with the name of the song or sound recording and, for a fee, the agency will determine who owns or controls the copyright and how much it will cost to obtain the rights you require. Most agencies will also counsel clients about the options available if the rights to the original song or sound recording are either unavailable or prohibitively expensive. For producers of nonbroadcast programs, those options include making your own original recording and buying the right to use a sound-alike recording.

Should you use an agency to secure music rights and permissions, or should you do it yourself? Because agencies specialize in this line of work and will do all of the legwork for you, going with an agency will usually save you considerable time and trouble. In addition, because they are experienced in this area of media law, an agency can help make sure that you obtain all of the music rights and permissions required for the type of project you are producing. A good agency can also provide you with form agreements that clearly define the rights you are obtaining in language that will stand up in a court of law.

Of course, all of these benefits must be weighed against the cost of doing business with an agency. In fact, for most media producers, the choice comes down to a simple cost/benefits equation. If the benefits that the agency will provide are worth the fee that it will charge, go with the agency. If not, do it yourself.

If you do decide to go with an agency, be sure to establish, up front and in writing, what services the agency will provide and how the final bill will be tabulated (flat rate or hourly fee). In addition, be sure to check on the agency's reputation before agreeing to a business arrangement. Call colleagues in the industry who might have used the agency in the past, and ask the agency for references. Appendix B lists several rights agencies that should be willing to provide you with references and descriptions of their services.

Using Music Libraries

Much of the discussion of music clearances has focused on the complex permissions process necessary when you plan to feature a copyrighted song or sound recording in a production. But what if you are simply interested in adding a bit of background music or some sound effects to a production? To fill this need, many producers use the services of one or more music libraries.

Choosing a Music Library Service

Music libraries specialize in providing copyright-clear music and sound effects to producers of radio, film, multimedia, broadcast and cable television, and corporate and educational video productions. Although most libraries offer a wide range of recordings, some specialize in selected areas (e.g., classical themes, advertising jingles, sound effects, rock-and-roll selections). Most libraries also offer their material in a range of formats: digital audiotapes, compact discs, and digital audio files. A list of several major U.S. music libraries appears in Appendix B.

How do you decide which of the many competing music library services is right for you? Start by determining which libraries offer the music or sound effects materials that match your needs. Call or write several library services and request their catalogs. Many music libraries will also provide a sample of their collections on tape or CD or in digital audio file format.

Fee Options

Once you have discovered which libraries fit your musical needs, you are ready to determine which one can best meet your financial needs. This is where the process becomes a bit more complicated. Most libraries offer at least three fee options:

1. A needle-drop fee that requires you to pay a specified amount each time you use a library selection in a production
2. A bulk rate that provides reduced fees for high-volume use of single or multiple selections
3. A yearly blanket rate or license that permits unlimited use of the library's material for a single annual fee

A few music libraries also offer a buyout option. Under this arrangement, you make one large payment up front, and the library is yours to use forever. There are no needle-drop fees, and there is no annual license payment.

Many music libraries add an extra layer of complexity to their pricing structures by charging different fees for different uses of their material. For example, producers of broadcast projects typically are required to pay more for an annual license than are producers of non-broadcast programs. In addition, needle-drop fees can vary with the length of the production. The longer your production, the higher the fee. Some music libraries also charge higher needle-drop rates when their material is used in television and radio commercials.

Annual licenses and buyout arrangements are most appropriate for large production houses with hefty appetites for the sort of stock material that music libraries provide. For smaller production companies with more limited needs, a needle-drop fee arrangement usually makes more sense. If you do go with an annual license, make sure that the deal requires the music library to provide you with any new material that it adds to its catalog during the term of the license. In all cases, be sure the music library represents and warrants, in writing, that its materials are free from any copyright or other constraints that could restrict your right to use the materials.

Music Made-for-Hire (Commissioning Original Music)

Are you unable to locate stock music material that meets your needs or obtain the permission you need to use an existing sound recording? Do you need a unique theme or musical motif for an important production? If any of these situations sounds familiar, you may be a candidate for commissioning original music.

Contrary to what some producers assume, you do not have to be working on a big-budget television or feature film project to consider commissioning original music. In fact, many producers of corporate and other nonbroadcast projects regularly contract with outside sources to obtain original songs and background music. While the heads of big-budget productions can usually afford to hire big-name composers and performers, however, producers of more modest projects must usually draw on the services of lesser-known talent.

Full-Service Production Music Facilities

If you cannot afford big-name talent, how do you go about creating original music for a production? One option is to use a full-service production music facility. A true full-service facility can take your assignment from first concept through final mixing and laying down the music track on your master, providing music composition, orchestration, and production services along the way. For the names of music composing and production companies in your area, look under "Music Arrangers and Composers" in the Yellow Pages or "Music Scoring and Production" in the various directories and production guides published for the video and film industries. As always, be sure to ask for references and samples of the company's work.

Music Production Contracts

Whenever you commission original music, the deal should be covered by a contract similar to the sample shown in Figure 6.2. The contract should start by spelling out the exact services that the individual or company will provide. Will the company be responsible for both composing and producing the music? How about for performing the final mix and playback? The contract must also specify who will own the rights to the music created under the agreement. Whenever possible, music for video productions should be created as a work-made-for-hire with you or your company, as the producer, possessing full ownership of and reuse rights to the materials. Try to avoid alternative arrangements in which the composer or music production house retains rights to the materials because such arrangements can restrict your options to distribute the production in which the materials are used.

The sample contract in Figure 6.2 also includes several other provisions that should be part of any music production agreement:

- A consideration clause that spells out how much you will pay for the materials produced under the agreement and when you will pay it
- A schedule that describes key stages of the project and when deliverables are due
- Warranty and indemnity clauses that require the contractor to state that it has the right to enter into the agreement and full title to the materials it will deliver

In addition, if the project will involve musicians who are members of the American Federation of Musicians (AFM), the contract may have

Figure 6.2 Sample music production contract.

January 16, 2002

Ms. Rachel Wright
Wright Sounds, Inc.
1775 Irving Boulevard
Suite 22-B
Dallas, TX 75212

Dear Rachel:

This letter, when signed by you in the space provided below, will constitute an agreement between Wright Sounds, Inc. ("WSI"), a Texas corporation with offices at 1775 Irving Boulevard, Dallas, TX 75212, and Industrial Media, Inc. (the "Producer"), a Texas corporation with offices at 740 Cortland Avenue, Fort Worth, TX 76109.

The Producer hereby engages you to provide sound effects and original music (the "Materials") for a fifteen-minute industrial videotape production (the "Production") that the Producer is preparing on behalf of its client, International Semiconductors, Inc. (the "Client").

I. DESCRIPTION OF SERVICES AND MATERIALS

Under the terms of this Agreement, WSI agrees to provide the following materials and services:

A. **Original Theme Music.** WSI will write, arrange, and produce original music to be used as an opening and closing theme in the Production. The full length of the theme will be 60 seconds. In addition, 5- to 10-second clips from the theme will be used to accompany four scenes indicated in the script and storyboards for the Production. The script and storyboards will be provided to WSI upon execution of this Agreement.

B. **Library Music and Sound Effects.** The script and storyboards for the Production indicate approximately 10 locations that call for library music and/or sound effects (sfx). WSI will select the music and effects in consultation with the Producer.

C. **Mixing and Layback.** WSI will mix and layback the voice tracks that the Producer provides plus the music and sound effects

Figure 6.2 Sample music production contract. (continued)

that WSI creates or supplies. Producer will provide WSI with the master and two copies of the conformed show with visible time code in a format to be specified by Producer. WSI will supervise and pay for the stripping of the track(s) off the master, their layout and mixing, and the layback of the mixed tracks onto the master.

II. CONSIDERATION

As full and complete consideration for providing the services and materials described below, the Producer will pay WSI a flat sum of $15,000, with $5,000 of this total to be paid within 15 days of the execution of this Agreement and $10,000 to be paid upon delivery and acceptance of the master with completed audio.

III. SCHEDULE

The schedule below indicates key dates in the development and delivery of the Materials. WSI agrees to conform to these dates and to notify Producer promptly of any anticipated delays.

1. February 6, 2002   Producer will provide WSI with a rough cut of the Production.

2. February 15, 2002   WSI will meet with Producer and Client to present rough concepts for the original theme music. Once Producer and Client have selected and approved a concept, WSI should schedule and complete recording of the original theme music.

3. February 22, 2002   Producer will provide WSI with the master and two copies of the conformed show. Upon receipt of these materials, WSI will begin to lay out the music and sfx tracks.

4. March 1, 2002   WSI will meet with Producer and Client to present and preview the tracks and/or proposals of sfx that WSI has for sweetening. Upon approval of the tracks and/or proposals, WSI will schedule a mix session and subsequent layback of mixed master onto the master. This work must be completed in time to permit final delivery of master tape on March 8, 2002.

5. March 8, 2002   WSI will deliver completed master to Producer.

Figure 6.2 Sample music production contract. (continued)

IV. OWNERSHIP OF MATERIALS

WSI expressly agrees that the Materials will be created for inclusion in an audiovisual work as a work-made-for-hire for Client, as that term is defined in the U.S. Copyright Act of 1976. All rights, title (including copyright), ownership, and interest in the Materials will reside with the Client. If and to the extent that the Materials are ever deemed not to be a work-made-for-hire, then WSI hereby agrees that this Agreement shall constitute an assignment to the Client of all right, title, and interest in and to the Materials. In addition, WSI agrees that the Materials are not to be reproduced or used by WSI in any fashion without the Producer's and the Client's express, written permission. Without limiting the foregoing, if Client chooses to use all or part of the Materials in other productions, no reuse fees will be due to WSI. WSI agrees to provide and/or execute any further documents necessary for the Client or its designees to perfect or register ownership of the Materials.

V. WARRANTIES

WSI represents and warrants that it has the full right and authority to enter into and fully perform the terms of this Agreement; that the Materials shall be wholly original to WSI and shall not be copied in whole or in part from any other work; that the Materials shall not infringe upon or violate the right of privacy or publicity of, constitute libel against or infringe upon the copyright, trademark, trade name, property right, or any other right of any person, firm, or other entity; that all original Materials prepared under this Agreement and any music or sound effects Materials purchased from other sources and provided under this Agreement shall, when delivered, be free and clear of any lien or claim by any party including, without limitation, any claim by any union, guild, or performing rights society for any payments hereunder, including any reuse fees for the Materials; and that WSI will obtain all of the rights, permissions, and licenses that may be required to enable Producer and Client to fully exploit the Materials.

VI. INDEMNITY

WSI shall at all times indemnify and hold harmless the Producer and the Client, their officers, directors, employees, and licensees from any and all claims, damages, liabilities, costs, and expenses, including reasonable counsel fees, arising out of the use by Producer and Client of the Materials furnished by WSI hereunder, or the exercise by Producer and Client of any rights granted to them, or any breach by WSI of any representation,

Figure 6.2 Sample music production contract. (continued)

warranty, or any other provision of this Agreement. Producer and/or Client shall promptly notify WSI of any such claims, and WSI shall have the right at its sole cost and expense to participate in the defense of any such action.

VII. MISCELLANEOUS

This Agreement constitutes the entire understanding between the parties relating to the subject matter hereof and supersedes any prior understandings or communications between the parties regarding that subject matter. This Agreement cannot be changed, amended, or terminated by the parties except by an instrument in writing duly signed by all parties. This Agreement may be freely assigned by the Producer or Client, but may not be assigned by WSI without the advance written permission of the Producer or Client. This Agreement and all matters or issues collateral thereto shall be governed by the laws of the State of Texas applicable to contracts executed and performed entirely therein. Any dispute between the parties concerning this Agreement shall be subject to the exclusive jurisdiction of courts located in Dallas, Texas, and the parties hereby agree to submit to the jurisdiction of such courts.

IN WITNESS THEREOF, the parties hereto hereby execute this Agreement as of the first date specified above.

INDUSTRIAL MEDIA, INC.

_____

By: Michael Prellinger
President

WRIGHT SOUND, INC.

_____

By: Rachel Wright
President

INTERNATIONAL SEMICONDUCTORS, INC.

By:_____
Rosemary Mueller
Executive Vice President

to address rights and residual provisions required under the AFM collective bargaining agreement. For more information on guild and union requirements, see Chapter 7.

Using Sound-Alike Performers and Recordings

Imagine that you are producing a video program for a client and the client insists that the soundtrack include a recent pop music hit titled "Ready for You." The credits on the CD containing the song reveal that "Ready for You" was written by Ginny Lewis and published by Too Loose Music, Inc. The hit version of the song was recorded by Janice Jones and released by Pacific Records, Inc.

After a few phone calls and some legal correspondence, you are able to purchase permission from the music publisher to use the song. Your earnest pleadings notwithstanding, however, Janice Jones and Pacific Records are unwilling to give you permission to use their hit recording of "Ready for You." You explain the situation to your corporate client, but the client still insists that the Janice Jones sound is what he or she wants. What's a producer to do?

In the past, you could get around this sort of problem by creating your own sound-alike recording of the song. First you would secure permission to use the song from the songwriter or music publisher. Then you would bring in performers or contract with a music production house to create a new sound recording. Usually, the idea was to end up with a recording that was as close to the original as possible. In this way, you could derive much of the benefit from using the song without having to pay for permission to use the original sound recording, assuming that this permission was even available. Many popular recording artists have always refused to grant, on artistic grounds, permission for their recordings to be used in television commercials or industrial video productions.

In 1988, however, a ruling by the U.S. Ninth Circuit Court of Appeals in San Francisco cast a legal shadow over the practice of using sound-alike recordings.[5] The ruling was a reversal of a lower court decision in a $10 million lawsuit brought by pop singer Bette Midler against the Ford Motor Company and its advertising agency, Young and Rubicam. Ford had purchased the rights to "Do You Wanna Dance," a 1958 song that it planned to use in a television commercial promoting the Mercury Sable line of cars. More specifically, Ford planned to use Bette Midler's 1973 recording of "Do You Wanna Dance" in the commercial. When Young and Rubicam approached Midler for permission, however, she refused. The agency responded by hiring one of her former backup singers and creating a new recording that mirrored Midler's version.

The Mercury Sable commercial containing the sound-alike recording hit the air in 1985. Bette Midler responded by suing Ford and Young and Rubicam, claiming that she had a property right to the voice and vocal style that were imitated in the commercial. The trial court disagreed, ruling that Midler did not have the property right that she claimed and that, accordingly, the suit should not be allowed to proceed. But the 1988 Federal Appeals Court decision reversed the lower court ruling, and the matter continued in litigation. The case was finally resolved in 1989, when a Los Angeles jury decided in Midler's favor and awarded her $400,000 in damages.

The Midler case opened the door for sound-alike challenges by other performers. For example, as discussed in Chapter 5, singer Tom Waits sued Frito-Lay, Inc., and its advertising agency over the use of a Waits sound-alike in a television commercial for Doritos snack chips.[6] As in Midler's case, the advertising agency first approached Waits about appearing in the commercial. When Waits refused, the agency turned to a sound-alike.

Waits sued Frito-Lay under several legal theories, including that the use of a sound-alike constituted a false or misleading use of his signature vocal style under Section 43a of the Lanham Act, the U.S. trademark law. Waits ultimately was awarded more than $2 million in compensatory and punitive damages.

The full fallout of the Midler and Waits cases has yet to be felt. In particular, it is not clear how widely the rulings in these cases, in which the performers involved had distinctive and recognizable vocal styles and had expressly denied permission to use their original recordings, will be applied in cases that are less clear-cut. Even so, many producers have become much more cautious in their use of sound-alike recordings and unknown performers who imitate big-name talent. One example of this new caution is the disclaimers that now appear in many commercials or promotions that feature lesser-known performers mimicking stars.

In any case, one implication of all this legal wrangling is already clear: If you plan to use a sound-alike recording in a production or to use a performer who will impersonate a star, you should be sure to consult with a lawyer who is familiar with the current status of case law in this area. Otherwise, you may become caught up in the next test case yourself.

Finally, you should not assume that you are safe from legal challenges because you create your sound-alike recording as a parody of the original. The question of whether and under what circumstances a parody of a popular song constitutes a fair use or is otherwise a protected form of creative expression has been frequently litigated in recent years, with at least one case reaching the U.S. Supreme Court.[7] These cases indicate that parodies of popular songs may be protected as a fair use under U.S. copyright law, but only if the parody survives the fair use analysis discussed in Chapter 4. That is, the court will consider the four primary fair use criteria set out in Section 107 of the Copyright Act, including the "amount and substantiality" of the original work used in the parody. An attorney who is knowledgeable in this area should be able to help you determine whether your particular parody is likely to pass the fair use test.

The Music Rights Checklist

If you are still not sure about how the rules governing music rights and permissions apply to a particular production, look over the music rights checklist in Figure 6.3. By following the instructions at the top of the checklist, you can help increase the likelihood that a particular use of music is legal and otherwise trouble free.

Summary

- *Why does music present special concerns for media producers?* With music materials, particularly sound recordings, it can be difficult for producers to determine what rights they need to the materials and who controls those rights. First, to use an existing sound recording in a production, at least three distinct rights usually come into play: synchronization rights, performance rights, and master recording rights. Second, usually at least two parties control the rights to the sound recording: the music publisher or songwriter that owns the copyright to the song and the record company that distributes the sound

Figure 6.3 Music rights checklist.

This checklist describes six different options that producers have for using existing and original music materials in a production. Start by reading all of the options listed and checking those that apply to your current situation. Then go back and review the explanation under each option you checked. The explanations describe the steps that you must take to make sure that a particular use of music is legal and trouble free. In instances that involve the use of existing music, you will usually need to secure synchronization and, sometimes, performance rights and a master recording license to the materials, all of which were defined and discussed earlier in this chapter.

Be aware that most of the checklist items assume that you will be using the music materials in an in-house, industrial production that will never be shown to the general public, transmitted on broadcast or cable television, or displayed to an audience that has been charged an admission fee. If this is not the case (e.g., if you are producing a program for cable television or a feature film), additional restrictions may apply. Also, in all cases, keep in mind that nothing obligates copyright owners to grant the permission you are seeking. For that reason, it is always good to have an alternative in case your first choice of music is not available.

1. *You plan to use all or part of an existing sound recording (e.g., a recording by a big-name rock group or jazz performer) in a production.* To use an original recording, you must secure permission from two sources: the music publisher or songwriter that owns the copyright in the song (the music and the lyrics) and the record company that controls the rights to the recording. The permissions should be in the form of written agreements, such as that shown in Figure 6.1, that specify the fees you will pay for the rights to the materials and the nature and extent of your rights to modify, distribute, and reuse the materials. In particular, you should make sure that you obtain all of the rights you need to distribute the production containing the recording in all applicable markets. The written agreement should also warrant that no hidden rights are attached to the song that could restrict your ability to distribute the finished product.

2. *You plan to record your own version of an existing song, using the music and lyrics exactly as written.* This option may make sense if the rights to a popular sound recording of the song are not available, or if you prefer a version of the song that is more closely tailored to your production needs. To use the original music and/or lyrics, you will need to secure and pay for permission from the music publisher or songwriter that owns the copyright to the song. That permission should be in the form of a written agreement that specifies the fees that you will pay for the rights to the song and the nature and extent of your rights to use and reuse your recording of

Figure 6.3 Music rights checklist. (continued)

the song. This usually takes the form of a synchronization license, like the one shown in Figure 6.1. In particular, you should make sure that you obtain all of the rights you need to distribute the production containing the song in all applicable markets. You will also need to secure written agreements or releases from the performers who are involved in the creation of your recording of the song.

3. *You plan to record your own version of the song with substantial changes to the lyrics or music.* This option is often exercised by producers of commercials or industrial productions who need to change the lyrics to accommodate references to a particular product or client. To do this, you will need all of the permissions described under option 2. You will also need written permission to make the changes you are planning (often obtained, again, as part of a synchronization license like that shown in Figure 6.1). As you may discover, this permission is not always easy to obtain because some songwriters refuse to allow their work to be altered for commercial purposes. If they do allow you to make changes, some songwriters and music publishers reserve the right to review and approve your recording of the modified song.

4. *You plan to use an existing sound-alike recording of an original song.* A sound-alike recording is a remake of a popular tune in which unknown performers strive to create a recording that sounds very close to the original hit version. Because you are not using the original recording, you will not need the permission of the record company that distributed the original version; however, you will still need to secure and pay for permission from the songwriter or music publisher that owns the copyright to the song (the music and lyrics). As always, that permission should be in the form of a written agreement like the sample synchronization license in Figure 6.1 that specifies the fees you will pay for the rights to the song and the nature and extent of your use and reuse rights.

You will also need a written agreement with the company that owns the sound-alike recording. That agreement should spell out the terms under which the company will provide the sound-alike recording and the exact extent of your rights to use the recording. The agreement should warrant that the work is free and clear of any hidden restrictions (including the right of performers to receive residuals) that could restrict your ability to distribute the finished production that contains the sound-alike recording.

As discussed earlier in this chapter, recent court decisions have raised concerns about the legality of creating and using sound-alike recordings that mimic the distinct vocal styles of well-known performers. Before adding

Figure 6.3 Music rights checklist. (continued)

a sound-alike recording to a production, you should consult with a lawyer who is familiar with the current status of litigation and legislation in this area.

5. *You plan to commission original music for a production.* If you plan to create original music for a production, you will need to commission the services of some or all of the following: a songwriter/composer, an arranger, a producer, performers (singers and musicians), a recording engineer, sound technicians, and a sound recording facility. Or, like many media producers, you may prefer to contract with a music production house that can provide the complete package of staff and services and manage the entire process for you. In any case, your relationship with each individual or group should be covered by a contract like the one shown in Figure 6.2.

The agreement should define the exact services and materials to be provided, delivery dates for the services and materials, and the compensation the contractor will receive for providing the services and materials by the dates specified. The agreement should also define who will own the materials produced under the contract and whether any royalties or residuals will be payable to the songwriter, performers, and others who worked on the project. With rare exceptions, music created for your productions should be created as a work-made-for-hire, with you—as the producer paying for all of this—retaining full ownership of and reuse rights to the material. Be aware, however, that agreements with musicians' guilds may require you to pay residuals, particularly if the production is intended for broadcast, cable, home video, or theatrical distribution. For more information, see Chapter 7.

6. *You plan to use music or sound effects purchased from a music library.* Music libraries specialize in providing rights-clear music and sound effects to media producers. When you purchase materials from a music library, be sure to let the library know exactly how you intend to use the materials, and make sure the library warrants, in writing, that the materials are free from any copyright constraints that could restrict your right to use them in the manner you intend. Your written agreement with the music library should also specify the terms under which the library will provide the materials, your rights to use the materials, and the fees you will be assessed for using and, if applicable, reusing the materials.

recording. In addition, many more parties may claim some sort of ownership in the work.

- *What are the sources of the laws and regulations governing music rights?* Musical works are protected by the U.S. Copyright Act of 1976 and international copyright law. The U.S. copyright law provides for several special categories of rights that apply exclusively or primarily to musical works: mechanical rights, synchronization rights, and performance rights. The copyright law also provides for several types and categories of musical works: songs or compositions, sound recordings, and phonorecords.

- *What are the key types of music rights?* For media producers, the most important types of music rights are synchronization and performance rights. Synchronization rights allow you to link a song to the video track of your production. Performance rights allow you to show the production that contains the song to an audience. In addition, master recording rights allow you to use a prerecorded sound recording as part of your production.

- *What are performance rights societies, and what role do they play in the music permissions process?* Performance rights societies, such as BMI and ASCAP, are organizations that act as performance rights licensing agents for composers, songwriters, and music publishers. The performance rights societies devote most of their energy to negotiating licensing agreements with television and radio stations, theaters, restaurants, night clubs, stadiums, and other venues that regularly play or perform music to public audiences; however, the societies may also assist in negotiating individual performance rights licenses for songs that will be used in nonbroadcast productions.

- *What are music libraries?* Music libraries are services that specialize in providing copyright-clear music and sound effects to media producers. As their name suggests, music libraries maintain collections, or libraries, of music and effects that they license for use in media productions. Most music libraries offer both blanket license (unlimited use) and needle-drop (single-use) fee arrangements.

- *What special concerns surround the use of originally commissioned music in a production?* In commissioning original music, producers must make sure that their relationship with the composer or music production facility is covered by a written contract. The contract should define the exact services that the individual or company will provide. The contract must also specify who will own the rights to the music created under the agreement. With rare exceptions, music for video productions should be created as a work-made-for-hire, with the producer possessing full ownership of and reuse rights to the materials.

Notes

1. Public L. 104-39 (1995) (amending Title 17 of the U.S. Code).

2. Some television programs are shown on cable television, direct broadcast satellite, or foreign television in addition to or instead of their run on U.S. broadcast television. When this is the case, producers may need to secure performance rights to cover these forms of distribution. Be aware, though, that many of the major cable networks have negotiated their own blanket licensing arrangements with the performing rights societies. You should consult with each licensee to determine whether you will need to secure performance rights.

3. Performance rights to songs published in Europe may be controlled by the Society of European Songwriters, Authors, and Composers (SESAC), the European equivalent of ASCAP and BMI.

4. The Harry Fox Agency is located at 711 Third Street, Eighth Floor, New York, NY 10017. The phone number is (212) 953-2384. A website with information about the Harry Fox Agency is located at www.nmpa.org/hfa.html.

5. See *Midler v. Ford Motor Co.*, 849 F.2d 460 (9th Cir. 1988).

6. *Waits v. Frito-Lay, Inc.*, 978 F.2d 1093, 1098 (9th Cir. 1992), *cert. denied*, 113 S.Ct. 1047 (1993).

7. The song parody case that reached the U.S. Supreme Court was *Campbell v. Acuff-Rose*, 114 S.Ct. 1164 (1994) (parody of the Roy Orbison song "Pretty Woman" by rap group 2 Live Crew). Other significant song parody cases include *Berlin v. E. C. Publications, Inc.*, 329 F.2d 57 (2nd Cir. 1964); *Elsmere Music, Inc. v. National Broadcasting Co.*, 62 F.2d 252 (2nd Cir. 1980); *Fisher v. Dees*, 794 F.2d 432 (9th Cir. 1986).

Working with Guilds and Unions

For media producers, working with guilds and unions often means having to work through a thick tangle of rules, restrictions, and requirements. First, you must be willing to guarantee that performers and other guild or union members receive wages that are at or above "scale," and you must also agree to contribute an additional percentage of the members' wages to the applicable guild or union's pension and health plans. Second, you must also make sure that working conditions on the production (e.g., total working time, meal and rest breaks) satisfy the stringent specifications laid out in guild and union agreements. Just as important, in the case of performers and other "above-the-line" talent, you must be willing to buy into the strict residual and reuse payment provisions that are part of many guild agreements.

With all of this in mind, why don't producers simply choose to conduct all of their projects as nonguild, nonunion productions? Many producers, particularly those in charge of corporate and other non-broadcast programs, do just that. Many other producers find, however, that they have no choice but to work with guild and union performers and technicians, particularly if one or more of the following conditions apply:

- The project requires the services of experienced, professional actors, actresses, writers, directors, or musicians (because most experienced professionals are guild or union members, especially if they work in or near one of the major production centers).

- The production is a feature film, broadcast television, or cable television project being produced in the United States (because this level of production almost always requires the use of professional performers and technicians, most of whom are union members).
- The program is a corporate production, and the corporation's agreements with unions require in-house producers to use union technical personnel.

Of course, some producers simply prefer to work with guilds and unions. In particular, some producers like the security of knowing that, as signatories to guild and union agreements, they can draw from a pool of top professional talent and are protected from strikes and other work actions during production, as long as they live up to the terms of the relevant agreements. Some producers also like the fact that, on guild and union projects, most of the ground rules are laid out before production actually begins, courtesy of the detailed specifications contained in the "basic agreements" between guilds and unions and the major television and film producers and in the "form" agreements supplied by many guilds and unions for use with individuals hired on a production. On nonguild and nonunion projects, these details must be worked out through individual agreements with each performer or crew member.[1] Although such individual arrangements can work to the advantage of producers, negotiating individual agreements can also create headaches and hassles at a time when most producers prefer to be focusing all of their energies on the creative task at hand.

This chapter discusses many of the major issues involved in working with guilds and unions on media production projects. Keep in mind, though, that a production does not necessarily have to be either union or nonunion. Instead, it is possible to run a production as a hybrid project that employs both union and nonunion personnel. For example, a production might use actors that are guild members but writers and a technical crew that are not. In addition, as discussed later in this chapter, it is possible to use both guild and nonguild performers on a particular production.

What Are the Sources of Labor Law?

In the United States, the relationships among unions, employees, and employers are governed by two major federal statutes: the National

Labor Relations Act (the Wagner Act) and the Labor Management Relations Act (the Taft-Hartley Act). Passed in 1935, the Wagner Act was the cornerstone legislation that established the rights of labor to organize and to enter collective bargaining agreements with employers. The Taft-Hartley Act, enacted over President Truman's veto in 1947, placed some limits on labor's rights and powers under the Wagner Act by making it clear that unions could not require all workers in a unionized shop to join unions and that unions could not engage in strikes or other labor stoppages to force an employer to discharge employees who declined to become union members. The National Labor Relations Board (NLRB), which was established under the Wagner Act, is responsible for administering many aspects of the federal labor statutes and ensuring fair practices on the parts of both employers and unions.

One important provision of federal labor law is that all employees have a right to join unions. In addition, employers are prevented from taking any action that constitutes a threat to legitimate union-organizing activity. Like all employers, media producers generally have the legal right to choose not to work with unions, but they can never legally prevent their employees from exercising their right to join unions and to participate in legitimate union activities.

Federal labor law also protects the right of unions to negotiate collective bargaining agreements that define wages and working conditions for their members. These agreements can be negotiated with individual employers or, as is sometimes the case, with groups of employers in the same industry. In some cases, two or more unions might band together to negotiate a comprehensive collective bargaining agreement with groups of employers. This is true in the television and film industry, where the Screen Actors Guild (SAG) and the American Federation of Television and Radio Artists (AFTRA), the two major guilds that represent television and film performers, often work together to negotiate agreements with the Alliance of Motion Picture and Television Producers (AMPTP), the group that represents many of the major production companies and studios that produce movies and television shows. As a result, the SAG and AFTRA "basic agreements" with the major film producers, television production companies, and television networks are essentially identical.

Producers should be aware that, because collective bargaining agreements can take a long time to negotiate, interim and amended agreements are often in effect. When in doubt, contact the appropriate unions to determine which versions of which contracts are most current. Addresses and phone numbers for the major guilds and unions involved in media production appear in Appendix C.

The Major Performer and Technician Guilds and Unions

Most professional film television and radio performers are members of SAG, AFTRA, or both. SAG and AFTRA represent actors, actresses, announcers, and other on-screen and on-air talent.[2] The Writers Guild of America (WGA) represents the scriptwriters who create the lines that are spoken by SAG and AFTRA members, and the Directors Guild of America (DGA) represents the directors who tell the SAG and AFTRA members when and how to say those lines.

Furthermore, several specialty guilds and unions serve specific groups of performers and other talent. These include the American Federation of Musicians, the Screen Extras Guild, and various stunt person's associations.

The major technical unions are the International Alliance of Theatrical Stage Employees (IATSE) and the National Association of Broadcast Employees and Technicians (NABET).[3] These two unions represent a wide range of technical and other off-camera production professionals, including sound technicians, editors, publicists, script supervisors, makeup and hair stylists, wardrobe coordinators, costume designers and wardrobe attendants, cartoonists, propmasters, and photographers.

Some productions may also require the services of technicians and crew members from other unions: electricians from the International Brotherhood of Electrical Workers, drivers from the International Brotherhood of Teamsters, and so on. See Appendix C for selected phone numbers and addresses.

Guild and Union Agreements

As already mentioned, most relationships between unions and guilds and producers are governed by carefully crafted collective bargaining agreements. These core agreements are usually preceded by many months of hard negotiations between the performer and technician unions, on the one hand, and the AMPT and other organizations representing employers in the film and television industries, on the other hand. When the negotiations break down or when the groups are unable to agree on the renewal of an existing contract, a strike sometimes results. This happened in 1980, for example, when an actors' strike shut down television production for 10 weeks. It happened again in 1988, when a strike by writers sent producers of network television programs scrambling for more than 20 weeks. In 2000, SAG and AFTRA struck against the producers of television commercials, halting the production of commercials for several months. In 2001, a threatened strike against film and television producers was narrowly avoided when SAG and AFTRA agreed to new contracts as the strike deadline loomed. Despite the settlement, however, the threat of a strike disrupted film and television production schedules for much of 2001.

When the negotiations succeed (as they always seem to do eventually), the result is a comprehensive contract or basic agreement that defines and delimits almost every aspect of the relationship between the union members and producers. For example, the current industrial/education contract between AFTRA (the SAG industrial/education agreement is virtually identical) and the producers of industrial and educational programs spells out the following terms:

- Minimum rates for various types and terms of work (as shown in the sample rate card in Figure 7.1)
- Supplemental wages for overtime or work on nights, weekends, or holidays
- Required pension and health contributions
- Additional payments required for supplemental distribution of the production (distribution beyond the industrial and education markets, as defined in the agreement)
- Payment periods, late payment surcharges, and tax withholding obligations
- Assorted rules specifying payments for and performers' rights and obligations during auditions and rehearsals and casting, makeup, wardrobe, and fitting calls
- Wardrobe allowances (assuming that the performer is required to provide a personal wardrobe)
- Numerous provisions governing travel and transportation (e.g., payment for travel time, flight insurance requirements, type and class of transportation, overnight location expenses)

Figure 7.1 Sample performer rate card.

The following are the minimum "scale" rates effective from February 1, 2001, through April 30, 2002, under the AFTRA National Code of Fair Practice for Non-Broadcast/Industrial/Educational Recorded Material. Guild members are free to negotiate for higher fees, but may not be paid less than these minimums. Separate rate cards exist for feature film, broadcast television, interactive, and other types of productions.

ON-CAMERA PRINCIPAL PERFORMERS	Category I*	Category II*
Day Performer (actor or stunt)	$423.00	$526.00
Half-Day Performer	$275.50	$342.00
(4 hours only, restrictions apply)		
3-Day Performer	$1,064.00	$1,312.00
Weekly Performer	$1,485.00	$1,839.00
(Studio, 5-day week)		
(Overnight location only, 6-day week)	$1,634.00	$2,023.00
Choreographed Dancer, Swimmer, Skater, etc.		
Per Day: Solo/Duo	$378.00	$471.00
Per Day: Group	$316.00	$396.00
3-Day: Solo/Duo	$905.00	$1,132.00
3-Day: Group	$760.00	$949.00
Weekly: Solo/Duo	$1,509.00	$1,886.00
Weekly: Group	$1,266.00	$1,582.00
Singers, per day		
Solo/Duo	$423.00	$526.00
Group	$255.00	$315.00
Step Out	$319.00	$394.00
Contractor: 50% additional		
Narrator/Spokesperson		
First day	$769.00	$911.00
Each additional day	$423.00	$526.00
OFF-CAMERA PRINCIPAL PERFORMERS		
Day Performer (Voiceover), First hour	$346.00	$385.00
Each additional half-hour	$101.00	$101.00
Singers, per hour		
Solo/Duo	$227.00	$255.00
Group	$151.00	$171.00
Step Out	$189.00	$214.00

Figure 7.1 Sample performer rate card. (continued)

Contractor: 50% additional

Retakes, Voiceover performers only

Entire script, first hour	$346.00	$385.00
Entire script, each additional half-hour	$101.00	$101.00
Partial Script, within 60 days, 30-minute session	$188.00	$188.00

EXTRA PERFORMERS

General Extra	$110.00	$110.00
Special-Ability Extra (Including Stand-in, Photo Double)	$121.00	$121.00
Silent Bit Extra	$206.00	$206.00

MISCELLANEOUS RATES

Section 44. Wardrobe Allowance

Principals (per costume change for each 2 days)

Evening Wear	$29.00
All Other Wardrobe	$19.00

Extras (for each change of wardrobe required)

First Change	$17.00
Each Additional Change	$6.00
Formal Attire, etc.	$28.00

Section 31. Meal Periods (Per Diem Allowance)

Breakfast	$11.00
Dinner	$29.00

Section 56. Travel

Mileage Allowance	$.345/mile

*The AFTRA agreement defines Category I programs as productions that are developed "to train, inform, promote a product or perform a public relations function" and that "are exhibited in classrooms, museums, libraries or other places where no admission is charged." Category II programs are productions "designed primarily to sell specific products and services to the consuming public" and that are supplied with the product as a premium or inducement or shown "to the consuming public (1) at locations where the products or services are sold, or (2) at public places such as coliseums, railroad stations, air or bus terminals, or shopping centers." Note that the higher Category II payments include the right to use the production in Category I contexts.

- Requirements for personal injury and property damage insurance to protect performers during the employment period
- Specifications for meal breaks and daily and weekly rest periods[4]

Of course, this partial listing does not even hint at the degree of detail present in the full text of union codes and contracts. For example, the complete AFTRA National Code of Fair Practice for Non-Broadcast/Industrial/Educational Material is nearly 100 pages long and includes such specifics as the need for clothes racks, locker rooms, and a suitable number of seats and cots for use by guild members on the set.

Keep in mind, also, that these agreements set out only minimum wage requirements and working conditions that producers must satisfy in hiring guild members. The more talented and experienced a guild performer is, the more likely it is that the performer (or, more probably, the performer's agent) will require a producer to go above and beyond the minimum to secure the performer's services on a production. In the case of big-name talent appearing in feature film or broadcast television productions, going above and beyond the minimal requirements may mean having to pay the performer a seven- or (for feature films) eight-figure salary plus a percentage of the production's profits and revenues from ancillary activities (e.g., merchandising, commercial tie-ins). It may also mean having to provide the performer with a plush dressing room, limousine service, and all sorts of other amenities on and off the set.

Finally, note that the sample contract terms listed here were taken from the agreement that governs the participation of guild performers in industrial and educational productions. Guild and union involvement in other types of productions is covered by other types of agreements, and those agreements can differ substantially from the industrial/educational contract. For example, the SAG agreement governing feature film production includes detailed specifications for payment of supplemental compensation from revenues generated through theatrical distribution of the film and from the sale of rights to cable television, home video, and other markets. These provisions are much less central to the industrial/education agreement because no residuals or additional payments are required, except in the unlikely event that the production is distributed outside the industrial or educational market.

Misconceptions about Guild and Union Agreements

As the preceding sections have suggested, the relationships between producers and guilds and unions are far from simple. Contract negotiations among the various groups can run for months or even years, and the agreements that result from those negotiations can contain more than 100 pages of very detailed rules and regulations. To make matters even more complex, the relationship among the parties is often complicated by misconceptions on the part of the producers, who are not fully familiar with the relevant union agreements. For instance, many producers assume that hiring SAG or AFTRA performers means that they must also use a union crew. In fact, nothing in the SAG and AFTRA agreements requires you to hire a union crew if you hire union performers. In particular, it is perfectly permissible for a corporate video department that uses its own in-house, nonunion staff as the crew to hire SAG or AFTRA performers for a production. Conversely, it is also permissible for a corporate video department that uses union technicians to employ performers who are not SAG or AFTRA members. Although some guild and AFTRA agreements do include language referring to other labor organizations, this language is generally limited to provisions that prevent producers from penalizing their members for refusing to cross picket lines set up by other unions that are conducting lawful, sanctioned strikes against the production company.

Many producers also mistakenly assume that, by signing an agreement with SAG or AFTRA, they will be required to hire only those performers who are already SAG and AFTRA members. In fact, under the Labor Relations Act of 1947 (the Taft-Hartley Act), unions are prevented from insisting that producers hire only union members on productions. Most guilds try to circumvent this Taft-Hartley restriction to the fullest extent possible, however, by including carefully worded "union shop" or "union security" clauses in their agreements with producers. The following language from the "union security" section of the AFTRA National Code of Fair Practice for Non-Broadcast/Industrial/Educational Recorded Material is typical:

> Until and unless the union security provisions of the Labor Relations Act of 1947, as amended, are repealed or amended so as to permit a stricter union security clause, it is agreed that during the term of this Agreement, Producer will employ and maintain in employment only such persons

covered by this Agreement who are members of AFTRA in good standing *or those who shall make application for membership on the thirtieth (30th) day following the beginning of employment hereunder . . .* , and thereafter maintain such membership in good standing as a condition of employment. As used herein, the requirement of AFTRA membership means the requirement to tender uniform AFTRA initiation fees and dues. [Emphasis added]

Under this language, then, a producer who is a signatory to the AFTRA Non-Broadcast/Industrial/Educational Recorded Material contract may hire non-AFTRA (or non-SAG) performers on a production. After a 30-day grace period, however, such performers must join AFTRA and/or pay the applicable AFTRA initiation fees and dues. Note that the performers, as a matter of law, may not be forced to join the guild as a condition of their employment by a producer who is an AFTRA signatory. But, as this language indicates, they may be required to pay applicable guild dues and fees if the production company is a guild signatory.

From the guild's perspective, such "union security" and "union shop" provisions prevent performers from having a free ride on the applicable guild agreements: obtaining the benefits of the agreement (e.g., minimum scale wages, work condition requirements, pension, and health) without having to pay dues and other member fees to the guild. Of course, from the perspective of performers who are not guild members, such security provisions effectively require them to join the guild, as they will be required to pay much of the cost of membership even if they decide not to join. Even so, some performers who find themselves in this position do decline to become full participating members of the guild for philosophical or other reasons.

Producers who are guild signatories should note that they are required to treat all performers on a production, even nonguild members, like guild members. That is, they will need to pay the nonguild performers at least minimum "scale" wages, make the pension and health contributions required under the guild agreements, and so on. Also, the union security provisions of the AFTRA and SAG industrial/educational agreements specify liquidated damages that a signatory production company must pay if it hires nonguild performers who do not comply with union security requirements. That is, signatory producers may hire performers who are not guild members and who do not apply to the guild within the required time limit, as long as the producer is willing to pay a penalty to the guild.

Finally, the SAG and AFTRA agreements provide exceptions to the hiring requirements for certain performers, including people portraying themselves (e.g., a CEO who will portray himself in an industrial video), extras who perform unscripted lines, and certain military personnel. There are qualifications to several of these exceptions, however. As a result, producers should consult the current relevant guild agreements to make sure that their specific exceptions satisfy the guild criteria.

Producers should never enter into guild and union agreements blindly. At the same time, producers should not be misled by the many myths and misconceptions that tend to exaggerate the dangers and complexities inherent in such agreements. When you are in doubt about what is actually contained in such an agreement or you need answers to any questions about specific provisions, call the relevant guild or union for a copy of the agreement. When in doubt about what those provisions may mean for you or your company, contact a lawyer who is familiar with the current agreements.

Signing Up: Becoming a SAG or AFTRA Signatory

To become a SAG or AFTRA signatory, you must request a copy of the appropriate agreement and return a signed copy to the guild or federation office. If you produce corporate or educational programs, you would sign the industrial/educational agreement discussed earlier. Separate agreements cover other categories of programming, including feature film and broadcast television production.

Most guild agreements run for several years. By becoming a signatory, you will be required to abide by the terms of the agreement until it expires. At that point, you can choose to sign the newly negotiated agreement (assuming that SAG and AFTRA have come to terms with the AMPTP) or you can decline to sign and return to nonsignatory status.[5]

All guild and union contracts contain detailed requirements governing the hiring and employment of members. Some of the more significant requirements are summarized in the sections that follow.

Hiring

As mentioned earlier in this chapter, the SAG and AFTRA agreements do not require signatory producers to hire only guild members. When you are hiring guild performers, the SAG and AFTRA agreements do, however, require you to give preference in hiring to qualified performers who live within a "preference zone" of 50 to 300 miles from the production location, with the exact extent of the preference zone for specific metropolitan areas defined in the agreement (e.g., 75 miles for Atlanta, 300 miles for Los Angeles). The SAG and AFTRA agreements also lay down ground rules for auditions and the hiring process. Performers must be properly notified of the time and place of the audition, and the audition must be conducted under the proper conditions (e.g., the performer must be provided with complete information about the role, scripts must be readily available at the time of the audition). In addition, the agreements specify what constitutes a firm engagement—or commitment of employment—from a producer.

Work Conditions

In the major guild agreements, much space is devoted to describing the rules that govern the conditions under which members may work. If the work condition requirements of the contract are not met, performers have the right to refuse to perform or to provide the services they were hired to deliver.

Some of the guild work rules are generic regulations that apply to all members, whereas others are specific to certain types of performers. For example, while the AFTRA National Code of Fair Practice for Non-Broadcast/Industrial/Educational Recorded Material includes many provisions requiring producers to provide the proper work conditions for all cast members, it also features additional requirements that are specific to dancers, singers, and other special categories of performers. Included in the rules for dancers, for example, are requirements that the "floors for choreographed dancers must be resilient, flexible, and level" and that the dance surface must be swept and mopped at least once a day with a "germ-killing solution."

If you are producing a project as a guild production, it pays to determine which of the work condition requirements contained in the relevant guild agreements, particularly those requirements related to health and safety concerns, apply to your production before rehearsal and shooting begins. Otherwise, you may find that your production is held up as performers file a protest with their guild.

Wages and Standard Performer Contracts

All guild and union agreements include a scale of minimum wages for performers (see Figure 7.1). As discussed later in this chapter, this scale applies to performers who are guild members and to nonguild performers who are hired on a production that is employing guild members. In other words, if the guild scale applies to at least one performer on a production, it must apply to all professional performers on the production.

As mentioned earlier, the minimum scale wages listed for various guild performers are just that—the minimum wages that must be paid to the performers. Individual performers can, and often do, negotiate a wage that is above minimum scale. If a producer decides that a performer's talent and experience justify a salary that is above scale, that salary should be specified in the contract between the performer and producer.

SAG and AFTRA provide standard form contracts for use in engaging scale performers that can be modified to include over-scale salaries. Figure 7.2 is a standard contract for industrial/educational productions. Modifications to the standard contract are permitted only when those changes work to the benefit of the performer (an actor cannot accept an under-scale wage, for example) and only when the producer and performer indicate, in writing, that they have approved the modifications. If the producer engages the performer through a separate, nonform contract, the guild may require that the contract contains language confirming that the producer and performer are bound by the terms of the current guild agreement except to the extent that these terms have been modified for the benefit of the performer in the separate agreement.

Payment and Reporting

Under most guild agreements, producers make pension and health payments directly to the guild on behalf of the guild member. In some cases, the producer may also submit checks for guild members' wages directly to the guild, which then takes care of delivering the checks to their individual members.

Most guilds require producers to submit copies of employment contracts to the guild office. In addition, producers are required to file various other forms and reports with guild offices. First, a production

Figure 7.2 Sample Screen Actors Guild standard employment contract.

The Artist Cannot Waive Any Portion of the Union Contract Without Prior Consent of Screen Actors Guild, Inc.
SCREEN ACTORS GUILD
STANDARD EMPLOYMENT CONTRACT
INDUSTRIAL/EDUCATIONAL FILM or VIDEOTAPE PROGRAMS

This Agreement made this _____ day of _____, 19 _____
between _____, Producer, and _____, Performer.

1. **SERVICES** — Producer engages Performer and Performer agrees to perform services in a program tentatively entitled _____
_____ to portray the role of _____ to be produced on behalf of _____ (client).

2. **CATEGORY** — Indicate the initial, primary use of the program.

   ☐ Category I (Industrial/Educational)
   ☐ Category II (Point of Purchase, includes Category I)

3. **NUMBER OF CLIENTS** — Indicate number of clients for which program will be used.

   ☐ Single Client
   ☐ Multiple Clients

4. **TERM** — Performer's employment shall be for the continuous period commencing _____, 19 _____ and continuing until completion of photography and recordation of said role. EXCEPTION (for Day Performers only) - Performer may be dismissed and recalled without payment for intervening period provided Performer is given a firm recall date at time of engagement. If applicable, Performer's firm recall date is _____, 19 _____.

5. **COMPENSATION** — Producer employs Performer as: ___ On-Camera ___ Off-Camera ___ On-Camera Narrator/Spokesperson

   ☐ Day Performer
   ☐ 3-Day Performer
   ☐ Weekly Performer

   ☐ 1/2-Day Performer (restricted terms)
   ☐ Dancer, Solo/Duo
   ☐ Dancer, Group

   ☐ Singer, Solo/Duo
   ☐ Singer, Group
   ☐ Singer, Step Out

   ☐ General Extra Player
   ☐ Special Ability Extra Player
   ☐ Silent Bit Extra Player

   on-camera $_____ per ☐ DAY ☐ 3-DAY ☐ WEEK
   at the salary of
   off-camera $_____ for first hour, $_____ for each additional half-hour

   Producer must mail payment not later than thirty (30) calendar day(s) after employment.

6. **OVERTIME** — All overtime rates MUST be computed on Performer's full contractual rate, up to permitted ceilings (NO CREDITING). Straight time rate is 1/8th of Day Performer's Rate, 1/24 of 3-Day Performer's Rate, 1/40th of Weekly Performer's Rate.
   Time-and-one-half rate - payable per hour (1.5 x straight time rate) **Doubletime rate** - payable per hour (2 x straight time rate) See Section 32 of the Basic Contract for details of Weekly and 3-Day Performer for time and one-half and doubletime rates per hour.

7. **WEEKLY CONVERSION RATE** — See Section 29 of the Basic Contract for details (Day Performers or 3-Day Performers Only). The Performer's weekly conversion rate is $_____ per week.

8. **PAYMENT ADDRESS** — Performer's payment shall be sent to or c/o _____

9. **ADDITIONAL COMPENSATION FOR SUPPLEMENTAL USE** — Producer may acquire the following supplemental use rights by the payment of the indicated amounts. (Check appropriate items below.) See Section 7 of Basic Contract for details of payment.

	Within 90 Days (Total Applic. Salary)	Beyond 90 Days (Total Applic. Salary)
☐ A. Basic Cable Television, 3 years	15% *	65% *
☐ B. Non-Network Television, Unlimited Runs	75%	125%
☐ C. Theatrical Exhibition, Unlimited Runs	100%	150%
☐ D. Foreign Television, Unlimited Runs outside U.S. & Canada	25%	75%
☐ E. Integration and/or Customization	100%	100%
☐ F. Sale and/or Rental To Industry	15%	25%
☐ G. "Package" rights to A, B, C, D, E & F above	200%	Not Available
☐ H. Category II (point-of-purchase use of Category I program only)	50%	100%
☐ I. Program for Government Service only.	40%	Not Available
Non-network television, theatrical and foreign television rights		* % of total actual salary

   J. Network Television (available only by prior negotiation with and approval of Screen Actors Guild)
      ☐ PERFORMER does not consent to the use of his/her services made hereunder for Network Television.
   K. Pay Cable Television (available only by prior negotiation with and approval of Screen Actors Guild)
      ☐ PERFORMER does not consent to the use of his/her services made hereunder for Pay Cable Television.

10. **SALE AND/OR RENTAL OF PROGRAMS TO THE GENERAL PUBLIC** — Producer may acquire sale/rental rights for an additional 200% of scale for the number of days worked.

11. **WARDROBE** — If PRINCIPAL PERFORMER furnishes own wardrobe, the following fees shall apply for each two-day period or portion thereof: Ordinary Wardrobe $_____ ($18.00 minimum); Evening or Formal Wardrobe $_____ ($28.00 minimum) For Extra Players' wardrobe fees, please see Basic Contract.

12. **SPECIAL PROVISIONS** —

13. **GENERAL** — All terms and conditions of the current Producer-Screen Actors Guild Industrial and Educational Contract (Basic Contract) shall be applicable to such employment.

Producer _____
by _____
    signature
    Name and Title
Address _____

Performer _____
    signature - (if minor, parent's or guardian's signature)
Soc. Sec. _____
Address _____

NOTE: PERFORMER MUST COMPLETE W-4 FORM ATTACHED.

report must be submitted in connection with any production employing guild members. This report must specify the following:

- The name of the principal production company and the name of the sponsor, if any, that is paying for the project
- The names of the performers employed on the production
- The type of program that actually is being produced (e.g., industrial videotape, feature film, television commercial)
- The total rehearsal and recording time
- Various other pieces of information that allow the guild to track the project

Some guilds and unions also require a separate report for recording payments to their health and retirement funds. Under the current agreements with the major guilds, health and retirement payments are usually approximately 13 percent of the performer's earnings on the production, exclusive of certain expenses and allowances.

Individual performers may be required to file their own reports with their guild offices as well. These reports include information similar to that contained in the production report submitted by the producer. Responsibility for filing this report resides solely with the performer, with the producer obligated only to initial the completed form.

Filing production reports and forms on time is more than simply a matter of keeping on top of your paperwork. Under the various guild and union agreements, failure to file the required reports within the specified deadlines can be considered a breach of contract that may, if not cured promptly, ultimately trigger work stoppages, fines, or both. In most cases, the guild or union supplies standard forms for any required reports.

Assumption Agreements

Following completion of production, producers often transfer ownership rights in the finished production to third parties as part of a distribution deal or similar arrangement. When the production at issue was produced as a guild production (so that there are or may be ongoing payment obligations to guild members), such a transfer of rights is subject to the guild's approval of the financial responsibility of the transferee. Most guilds also require that the agreement under which the producer assigns rights to a third party includes an

Figure 7.3 Screen Actors Guild assumption provision.

_____ (name of transferee) hereby agrees with (name of producer) that all programs covered by this agreement are subject to the Producers-Screen Actors Guild 2002–2005 Industrial and Educational Contract. The said transferee hereby agrees expressly for the benefit of Screen Actors Guild and its members affected thereby to make all payments of fees as provided in said Contract and all Social Security, withholding, unemployment insurance and disability insurance payments, and all appropriate contributions to the Screen Actors Guild-Producers Pension and Health Plans required under the provisions of said Contract with respect to any and all such payments and to comply with the provisions of said Contract with respect to the use of such program and required records and reports. It is expressly understood and agreed that the rights of transferee to use such program shall be subject to and conditioned upon the prompt payment to performers involved of all compensation as provided in said Contract and the Guild, on behalf of the performers involved, shall be entitled to injunctive relief in the event such payments are not made.

assumption provision, such as that shown in Figure 7.3. The guilds insist on these protective measures to ensure that any distributor or other entity that assumes a producer's obligations to guild members is both financially capable of and contractually required to fulfill those obligations.

Reuse Fees and Residuals

Reuse or supplemental market fees are supplementary, usually one-time payments made to guild members when the work they contributed to a production is used again in a different production or when a program produced for one market is released in another market (e.g., a program produced for network television is released to basic cable). Residuals are supplemental payments made to guild members each time a production is rebroadcast or otherwise displayed to the public. For example, the agreement between AFTRA and the producers of network television programs requires actors to be paid a residual each time that a program is "re-run on the network," with the residual payment calculated as a sliding percentage of the actor's initial fixed compensation for appearing in the program.

   Depending on the type of production, this can be tricky territory. Reuse and residual issues have become much more complex in recent years, particularly as new technologies have opened up new avenues for distributing programming and as guilds have pressed for additional compensation for supplemental uses of materials. In fact, the debate over residual and supplemental use payments on programs sold through secondary channels such as home video has been at the core of several of the more serious disputes between SAG and AFTRA and film and television producers in recent years.

Reuse Fees and Residuals for Industrial and Educational Productions

Reuse and residual issues are relatively straightforward on industrial and educational programs produced for nonbroadcast distribution. Under the current AFTRA and SAG industrial/educational contracts, industrial and educational programs are divided into Category I and Category II productions. Category I productions are programs developed "to train, inform, promote a product or perform a public relations function" and that are exhibited to select groups in "classrooms, museums, libraries or other places where no admission is charged." Category II productions include point-of-purchase displays and other programs designed to "sell specific products or services to the consuming public" and that are shown at sites "where the products or services are sold . . . , or at public places such as coliseums, railroad stations, air/bus terminals or shopping centers," or that are provided free of charge to customers as an incentive to purchase a product (e.g., a workout video provided free with the purchase of fitness equipment). Because Category II programs are designed to be displayed to the general public, the minimum scale wage for performers appearing in these productions is higher than the scale for Category I performers. For example, as shown in Figure 7.1, the AFTRA scale in 2002 was $423 per day for principal on-camera performers in Category I productions, compared to $526 for principal on-camera performers in Category II productions. This fee paid to AFTRA members covers unlimited sale and use of the production containing the member's performance, so long as the production is used within the category under which it was originally produced (i.e., there are no residual or royalty payments based on the number of times a Category I production is shown to a training group or the number of videocassette copies of a Category II production distributed to promote a product).

Changing Categories and Other Supplemental Uses

What happens if your industrial or educational production is a big hit and you have an opportunity to distribute it beyond the category for which it was originally produced? Assume, for example, that you were hiring an AFTRA actor in 2002 to appear in a training program that will be used to introduce a new product at your company's annual sales meeting, a Category I production. You hire the actor as a principal performer for a single day, and you pay him the current Category I scale wage of $423. But the production goes over so well at the sales meeting that the marketing division decides to use it as a point-of-purchase display, a Category II application. Under the terms of the AFTRA contract, obtaining Category II rights to the actor's performance will cost you an additional 50 percent of his original salary (if you are within 90 days of the date that principal photography for the production was completed) or an additional 100 percent (if you are beyond the 90-day grace period).

What if, by some odd chance, you need basic cable television rights, too? The right to run the production on basic cable for three years will cost you an additional reuse fee of 15 percent (within 90 days) or 65 percent (beyond 90 days) of the performer's salary. The AFTRA contract also lists fee structures for theatrical exhibition, non-network broadcast television use in the United States and Canada, foreign television display, sale or rental to industry, pay cable distribution, and various other forms of supplemental distribution. The contract does not, however, list fees for network television use or for the sale or rental of videotapes or DVDs to the general public. These forms of distribution are covered by separate AFTRA agreements, and they require prior negotiation with and approval of the guild. Most probably, the agreement negotiated with AFTRA for network television broadcast or videotape sale of the program would require you to pay an additional fee plus residuals to the performer.[6]

Feature Film and Broadcast Television Residuals

If you produce feature films, broadcast television programs, or television commercials, residuals are a prominent part of the production landscape. As already mentioned, however, this portion of the land-scape has been radically reshaped by the growth of new distribution channels for films and television programs. As a result of these devel-opments, residual requirements have become complex in recent years—too complex to be covered adequately in the space available here. For example, the contract between a popular actor or actress and the producer of a feature film might call for the performer to receive a certain percentage of the film's revenue from theatrical release, a dif-ferent percentage of the revenue from home video sales, and still another percentage of the money made from the network television release of the film. The contract might also call for residuals on cable television sales, sales to the broadcast syndication market, revenue from international distribution, and so on.

The current SAG and AFTRA agreements specify the residual requirements for performers appearing in theatrical films, broadcast television programs, and other relevant types of productions. Usually, residual fees are figured into the cost of distributing and exhibiting a program, rather than into the cost of production. Even though that is the case, however, any producer who is involved in commercial film or television projects should make it a point to keep current on the residual requirements contained in the latest guild agreements, partic-ularly if the producer has an equity position in the project. The best way to keep current is to request and review copies of the relevant agreements.

Working with Guild Members When You Are Not a Signatory

Imagine yourself in the following scenario: You are an independent producer who is creating an industrial video program that will be distributed to the managers of a major corporation. Although your company is not a signatory to any guild agreements, the actress you have in mind for the key role is a member of AFTRA. You really want to hire this actress for the role. How do you go about hiring her?

Of course, one option is to have your company become a signa-tory to the current AFTRA agreement governing nonbroadcast, indus-trial, and educational productions. You rule that option out, though, because it would obligate you to conduct this and all subsequent pro-ductions as AFTRA projects for the term of that agreement.

A second option would be to pay the actress on the sly with the understanding that she would not report the job to AFTRA and that she would not receive a production credit under her own name. But this arrangement would put the actress in an awkward position, and she could be disciplined by AFTRA if her subterfuge is discovered. Besides, the actress might not agree to the arrangement, and you prefer doing everything aboveboard, anyway. This combination of concerns rules out option number two.

This leaves you with two choices: (1) you can arrange for a guild payroll services contract with a third party, or (2) you can sign a one-production letter of agreement with AFTRA. Both options are discussed next. Be aware, however, that, although both options have been available under the AFTRA Non-Broadcast/Industrial/Educational Recorded Material agreement, that is not the case under all AFTRA and SAG contracts. For example, the one-production letter of agreement option is currently available under the AFTRA interactive agreement discussed in Chapter 8, but the payroll services option is not. Moreover, which of these options are available in which contexts can change with shifts in guild policy and the expiration and renegotiation of the various guild agreements. If you are considering either of these options, be sure to contact the relevant guild to determine if that option is available under the agreement that applies to your current production.

Guild Payroll Services Contracts

The first option, arranging for a guild payroll services or pay master contract, is most appropriate for companies that are unable or unwilling to take on the accounting, paperwork, and other reporting obligations involved in hiring and paying guild performers or in situations where the one-production letter of agreement option is not available. Here is how it works: As a producer who is not an AFTRA signatory, you contract with a payroll services company that is a signatory to serve as the intermediary between you and AFTRA. For a fee, the payroll services company becomes the employer of record for the AFTRA performers who will work on the production. Typically, the payroll services company pays the performers and takes care of all the recordkeeping and reporting required by AFTRA, including payments and reports related to pension and health requirements. As the producer, however, you will be responsible for fulfilling the hiring and work conditions requirements of the applicable AFTRA agreement.

One-Production Letter of Agreement

The second option, signing a one-production letter of agreement, is usually preferred by companies that have the resources to handle the guild accounting and reporting requirements. This group includes large production houses that are not guild signatories and corporate video departments whose parent companies can provide the necessary payroll and bookkeeping functions. By entering into a one-production letter of agreement, you become, in essence, a guild signatory for the term of this production. Your obligations as a signatory apply only to this production, however, and not to other projects that you may be producing at the same time or subsequently. Once you have fulfilled your obligations under the agreement, your status as a guild signatory ends. To arrange for a one-production letter of agreement, call the nearest guild office and request a copy of the contract. There is no fee for this agreement. The guilds sometimes place limits on the number of one-production agreements they allow with any one producer or production company, however.

Under the one-production agreement option, as under the payroll services option, you will be required to follow all applicable guild requirements in the hiring and employment of guild members. In other words, you will be taking on all of the obligations of a guild signatory with respect to guild members hired for the production but without incurring the obligation of conducting your subsequent productions as guild projects.

Beyond AFTRA and SAG

Much of this chapter has focused on the ins and outs of working with AFTRA and SAG, the two major performers' unions involved in television production. As a producer, you may also have occasion to work with other unions and guilds, particularly those that cover directors, writers, musicians, and technicians. In many respects, the agreements that define the rules for working with these unions and guilds follow the same structure as the SAG and AFTRA agreements. They all specify minimum scale wages and working conditions for union members, and they all provide for penalties in the event that the producer fails to comply with the terms of agreements.

The Writers Guild of America and the Directors Guild of America

The Writers Guild of America (WGA) is the guild for the writers who develop scripts for television and film productions. The Directors Guild of America (DGA) is the guild for directors and assistant directors. Like AFTRA and SAG, both the WGA and the DGA have negotiated collective bargaining agreements with film and television producers.

Along with standard language contained in the AFTRA and SAG agreements, the WGA and DGA agreements also contain provisions that are specific to the needs of their members. For example, the WGA agreement details minimum fees for the various types of writing tasks that its members might be asked to take on: treatments, plot outlines, stories, screenplays and teleplays, rewrites, and the like. The DGA agreement is just as detailed in defining the different jobs covered by that basic agreement and the minimum fees associated with each: director, unit production manager, first assistant director, key second assistant director, second assistant director, additional second assistant director, and the like.

Producers who are considering hiring DGA or WGA members should contact the guild to obtain the current agreements covering the type of production involved. Addresses and phone numbers for the DGA and WGA appear in Appendix C.

American Federation of Musicians

The American Federation of Musicians (AFM) represents musicians who perform on live and recorded television productions. This includes musicians who play on televised variety and awards shows, as well as those who play on the music tracks recorded for use on network, cable, and nonbroadcast television programs. Like the SAG and AFTRA agreements, the AFM agreements specify minimum scale, residual, and supplemental use payments that apply when AFM members work on various types of productions. In addition, the AFM agreements include rules governing work hours and conditions comparable to the work rules contained in the SAG and AFTRA agreements.

The International Alliance of Theatrical Stage Employees

Of all the guild and union agreements, those with the International Alliance of Theatrical Stage Employees (IATSE) can be the most complex for media producers, if only because there are so many of them. Dealing with the IATSE means dealing with one or more local shops, each of which represents a different category of technical employee and each of which is usually covered by its own agreement. Although there are basic East Coast and West Coast contracts that provide some standards, each local agreement may specify distinct working hours, wage scales, and certain other conditions of employment.

One provision that is part of many IATSE agreements is the "minimum crew" clause that specifies how many union members must be hired under given production circumstances. For example, the agreement with IATSE Local 644, the cinematographers' local for the eastern United States, specifies that the minimum camera crew on a filmed production that is part of a network television series must consist of a first cameraman, an operative cameraman, first and second assistant cameramen, and a still cameraman.

Although all of the different contracts and agreements can make for considerable confusion, a few phone calls to the relevant guild or union, listed in Appendix C, can usually get you most of the answers you need to determine what your options are—and whether working with or without the guild or union is in your best interest. If talking to the guild or union does not help, talk to an attorney who is familiar with the current agreements and who has your best interest at heart.

Summary

- *What are the major advantages and disadvantages of working with guilds and unions?* The major advantages of working with guilds and unions include being able to choose from a pool of professional performers and technicians (because most experienced professionals are guild or union members, particularly those who work near major production centers) and being protected from strikes or other work stoppages as long as you live up to the terms of the guild and union agreements. Some producers also like that, on guild and union projects, most of the ground rules are laid out before production actually begins, courtesy of the very detailed specifications contained in guild and union agreements.

The major disadvantages of working with guilds and unions include having to pay performers and technicians at or above scale and having to make sure that work conditions on the production satisfy the stringent guild and union specifications. In some cases, those specifications may require you to pay residuals and supplemental use fees to performers and to hire extra technicians to meet minimum crew requirements.

- *What are the sources of labor law?* In the United States, there are two major federal labor statutes: the National Labor Relations Act (the Wagner Act) and the Labor Management Relations Act (the Taft-Hartley Act). The National Labor Relations Board (NLRB) is responsible for administering aspects of both statutes and ensuring fair practice on the parts of both employers and unions.

  One important provision of federal labor law is that all employees have a right to join unions. Federal law also protects the right of unions to negotiate collective bargaining agreements with employers. In addition, employers are prevented from taking any action that constitutes a threat to legitimate union-organizing activity.

- *What are the major performer and technician unions?* In the United States, the major performer unions are the Screen Actors Guild (SAG) and the American Federation of Television and Radio Artists (AFTRA). Other unions that represent creative production personnel include the Directors Guild of America (DGA), the Writers Guild of America (WGA), the American Federation of Musicians (AFM), and the Screen Extras Guild (SEG).

  The major technical unions are the International Alliance of Theatrical Stage Employees (IATSE) and the National Association of Broadcast Employees and Technicians (NABET). Other technical or service unions include the International

Brotherhood of Electrical Workers (IBEW), the International Brotherhood of Painters and Allied Trades (IBPAT), and the International Brotherhood of Teamsters (IBT).

- *If you conduct a production as a guild project, must all the performers on the production be guild members?* The SAG and AFTRA agreements do not and *may not* (under U.S. labor law) require you to use only performers who are guild members at the time of hiring. The "union security" provisions of the SAG and AFTRA agreements do require, however, that any nonguild performers hired on a production, after a grace period, must either join the guild or submit the dues and fees required of a member. The SAG and AFTRA agreements also require signatory producers to give "preference of employment" to experienced performers who live within defined geographic proximity to the production location.
- *If you hire guild performers, will you be required to hire a union crew?* Nothing in the SAG and AFTRA agreements requires you to hire a union crew if you hire guild performers. In particular, it is permissible for a corporate video department that uses its own in-house, nonunion staff as crew to hire SAG or AFTRA performers.
- *Can a producer who is not a guild signatory hire SAG and AFTRA performers for a production?* It is permissible, under certain limited circumstances, for a producer who is not a guild signatory to hire guild performers. For example, producers of industrial or educational programs who are not signatories may be able to hire SAG and AFTRA performers by signing a one-production letter of agreement with the union or, in some circumstances, by entering into a payroll services contract with qualified companies. In either case, the producer will be required to take on all of the obligations of a guild signatory—but only for this particular production.
- *What happens if you violate the terms of an applicable guild or union agreement on a guild or union production?* If you violate the terms of a guild agreement, your production may be subject to fines, work stoppages, or both. Work stoppages usually occur only when the violation constitutes a clear health or safety hazard to union members working at the production site or when the violation is part of an ongoing pattern of problems with a particular producer.

Notes

1. Guild agreements spell out the minimum payment obligations and work condition requirements for guild members. As discussed later in this chapter, however, experienced performers and other talent can and often do negotiate compensation and perquisites that are well above guild minimums.

2. In many areas, SAG and AFTRA have negotiated "twin" agreements with the Alliance of Motion Picture and Television Producers. For example, the AFTRA National Code of Fair Practice for Non-Broadcast/Industrial/Educational Recorded Material and the SAG Industrial/Educational Contract are essentially the same agreement. Generally, SAG represents performers involved in filmed projects (e.g., feature films, television movies of the week, and other filmed television programs) and AFTRA represents performers involved in television programs recorded on videotape or broadcast "live." As this edition of *Media Law for Producers* was going to press, SAG and AFTRA voted down a controversial proposal that would have merge the two guilds to create the Alliance of International Media Artists. The vote was extremely close, however, and proponents of the merger planned to continue their campaign to combine the two guilds.

3. As a result of a 1990 merger, many NABET members involved in remote and nonbroadcast productions joined IATSE.

4. The guild and union rules governing working hours and rest periods have come under scrutiny in recent years following several traffic accidents and other incidents involving guild and union members who had been working exhausting hours. Some guilds and unions are now pushing for more severe limits on the number of hours their members may be required to work during 24-hour and multiday periods.

5. You do not necessarily need to be a guild signatory to employ guild performers. For more information, see the section titled "Working with Guild Members When You Are Not a Guild Signatory" that appears in this chapter.

6. The AFTRA agreement also sets fees for the use or integration of a guild member's performance in subsequent productions.

8

Going Multimedia: Legal Issues Related to Interactive Productions

Many television and video producers are becoming involved, by choice or necessity, with two increasingly popular forms of interactive or multimedia productions: Internet-based websites and multimedia CD-ROMs or DVD-ROMs. Today, it seems that every company with more than five employees (and some with fewer) maintains an Internet website for promotional, marketing, or sales purposes. In addition, many corporate video facilities that historically have distributed training and marketing programs on videotape are now being asked to create interactive CD-ROM or DVD-ROM versions of those programs for use by employees or customers at individual workstations. In some companies, the need to create entertaining and engaging materials in these new, computer-based formats has resulted in forced marriages between corporate video departments (resident experts in creating effective audiovisual materials) and corporate data processing or network departments (resident experts in the computing skills necessary to ensure that the resulting productions actually run on the various computer and networking technologies over which they will be distributed).

This chapter discusses several of the more significant legal issues raised by these two programming platforms. In most respects, the same fundamental legal guidelines that govern conventional media productions apply to these newer interactive productions. For example, like producers of corporate video productions, individuals who develop Internet websites must enter into contracts with third parties that will be preparing or providing materials for the site, obtain the appropriate releases from individuals who will be depicted on the site, and review the site for potentially defamatory statements. But the fact that the production is a website that can be accessed by individuals around the world may raise issues that are not implicated by a video program that is intended to be distributed and displayed domestically. For instance, statements that would not be found libelous in the United States under the protections afforded by the First Amendment might by held to be libelous if downloaded from the website by individuals residing in Great Britain and many other countries, where the absence of comparable constitutional protections has permitted the development of libel laws that are much less media friendly.

The remainder of this chapter focuses on these and other legal distinctions that come into play in developing CD-ROMs or DVD-ROMs and Internet websites. The discussion that follows assumes you are familiar with the basic principles of media law introduced in the previous chapters. Except where indicated on the pages that follow, those same principles apply to the development and distribution of CD-ROMs or DVD-ROMs and websites.

Developing Multimedia CD-ROMs

The typical CD-ROM combines motion sequences, still images, audio, and text into an interactive presentation that is orchestrated and controlled by underlying computer code. This section discusses how you can make sure that your legal bases are covered when putting together a production of this type. The same guidelines apply to the development of interactive DVD-ROMs, an increasingly viable and popular distribution format.

CD-ROM Development Agreement

CD-ROM development is still a relatively specialized enterprise that requires expertise in both the video and graphic skills necessary to create an engaging experience for users and the computer programming skills necessary to ensure that the experience flows smoothly. Because video and television producers often lack this combination of expertise in-house, many CD-ROMs are created with the assistance of outside development facilities.

If you use an outside development facility to produce a CD-ROM or DVD-ROM, your relationship with that party should be defined in a contract like the sample agreement shown in Figure 8.1. Similar in scope to the sample production agreement in Chapter 3, this sample CD-ROM development agreement spells out the responsibilities of the third-party developer, when the developer will deliver various components and versions of the CD-ROM, who will own the finished production, and when and how much the developer will be paid for its work. In addition, like the production agreement, the CD-ROM development agreement includes, as an exhibit, a work-made-for-hire agreement to be executed by any individuals (other than the developer's employees) who will provide services or materials in connection with the CD-ROM.

Because CD-ROMs are more technically complex than conventional video productions, the CD-ROM development agreement includes several definitions, provisions, and conditions that were not necessary in the sample production agreement introduced in Chapter 3. For example, paragraph 5 requires the developer to provide technical support documentation to the contracting company, so the company will be in a position to respond when a user complains that the CD-ROM will not operate properly on a particular computer configuration. In addition, because CD-ROM developers often use authoring tools and software routines licensed from third parties, paragraph 6.3 of the CD-ROM agreement requires the developer to provide the company with proof that it has the right to use these authoring tools and to include those routines in the CD-ROM developed under the agreement. The CD-ROM agreement also assumes, in the definitions and milestone delivery schedule, that the developer will need both the opportunity and time to perform technical testing and debugging on alpha and beta versions of the CD-ROM.

Several other distinctions between the CD-ROM development agreement in Figure 8.1 and the production agreement from Chapter 3 are worth noting. First, although both projects are being completed on a work-made-for-hire basis, the consideration in the production agreement includes both a series of fixed payments and contingent compensation in the form of a royalty on sales greater than 1,000 units, whereas the consideration in the CD-ROM agreement is composed solely of a series of fixed payments with no contingent compensation. This difference derives more from the nature of the projects being produced than any inherent distinction between video productions and

Figure 8.1 Sample CD-ROM development agreement.

This Agreement (the "Agreement") is made as of this 20th day of December 2002, by and between VoiceTech Industries, Inc., a Missouri corporation, having a principal place of business located at 7000 Walnut Street, Kansas City, Missouri 64106 ("Company"), and Inter-Act, Inc., a Texas corporation, having a principal place of business located at 204 East 7th Street, Austin, Texas 78701 ("Developer"), with respect to an interactive software project (defined in Exhibit A and referred to herein as the "Project"). Company and Developer hereby agree as follows:

1. **Certain Definitions.**
"Alpha Version" shall mean a version of the Project wherein all coding, scenes, navigation paths, and production tasks are 90 percent complete, all remaining production tasks are fully identified, but neither extensive testing nor debugging has been performed.

"Beta Version" shall mean a completed and functioning version of the Project that Developer will test through limited distribution to potential users of the Project identified by the Company, bug tracking, and acceptance testing.

"Company Properties" shall mean all works that are the subject matter of Intellectual Property Rights owned, controlled, or licensed by Company and that Company approves for use or inclusion in the Project as provided in Section 6.4 hereunder, including but not limited to any and all sound recordings, audiovisual works, musical compositions, text, lyrics, photographs, graphics, animation, software, and literary material.

"Developer Properties" shall mean all works that Developer makes available for inclusion in or use in connection with the Project, including but not limited to Developer's and third-party development and authoring tools, and that are the subject of Intellectual Property Rights (i) owned or controlled by Developer or (ii) licensed by third parties to Developer ("Third-Party Materials").

"Gold Master" shall mean a complete, fully functional, final version of the Project that is completely debugged and tested, contains no Nonconformities, and is ready for mastering, duplication, and distribution to the general public without any further modifications or testing.

"Intellectual Property Rights" shall mean any and all rights existing from time to time under patent law, copyright law, trademark law, trade secret law, unfair competition law, moral rights law, publicity rights law, privacy rights law, and any and all other similar proprietary rights and any renewals, extensions, and restorations thereof, now or hereafter in force and effect in the United States and throughout the universe.

Figure 8.1 Sample CD-ROM development agreement. (continued)

"Nonconformity" shall mean (i) any failure of the Project to meet the Performance Standards; (ii) any failure of the Project to interface properly with operating system software or hardware for any platform on which the Project is released; (iii) the inability of the Project to perform any intended feature or function consistently and without interruption; (iv) any misspelled or incorrect text in the Project; and/or (v) any other error or defect that has an adverse impact upon the use, performance, operability, or marketability of the Project as reasonably determined by Company; provided, however, that media defects resulting solely from the duplication and/or manufacture of copies of the Project shall not constitute Nonconformities.

"Performance Standards" means the functions, features, purposes, specifications, and other standards for the Project that are described in this Agreement and/or the Project Specification attached hereto as Exhibit A.

"Project" shall mean the compilation of the results and proceeds of Developer's services pursuant to this Agreement, Developer Properties (if any), and Artist/Company Properties in a computer program to be released initially as a CD-ROM, including but not limited to any and all packaging, artwork, manuals, and other items included with the computer program for distribution to the general public.

"Source Code" shall mean all of the source code of the Project and includes (i) programming code written for the Project in commonly used computer programming languages and (ii) programming scripts and macros written in the scripting languages of any third-party development or authoring tools.

"Third-Party Documentation" shall mean the following written documentation satisfactory to Company as required pursuant to Section 6.3: (i) a schedule listing any and all Third-Party Materials included in or used in connection with the Project, (ii) the documentation evidencing Developer's rights with respect to any and all Third-Party Materials, and (iii) the "work-made-for-hire" agreements.

"Work" shall have the meaning set forth in Section 6.1.

2. **Development Agreement.**
2.1 **Development Services; Delivery.** Developer shall (i) devote its best efforts to the design and development of the Project in accordance with the Performance Standards; (ii) complete and deliver each Milestone Event, along with an up-to-date copy of the Source Code, if any, and any and all relevant Third-Party Documentation, on or before the corresponding Milestone Completion Date in accordance with Exhibit B; and (iii) promptly notify Company of any circumstance that could delay the Project.

Figure 8.1 Sample CD-ROM development agreement. (continued)

2.2 **Approvals & Acceptance.** Company may approve or disapprove the Milestone Events and any element of the Project in its sole discretion. Company shall accept or reject each Milestone Event in writing, including a description of any Nonconformities or other reasons for rejection, within fifteen (15) business days following delivery of such Milestone Event. Developer shall use its best efforts to correct immediately any problems specified by Company, but in no event more than fifteen (15) business days following receipt by Developer of the rejection. Subject to Company's other rights provided in this Agreement, including the rights provided in Section 8.1, the acceptance procedures pursuant to this Section 2.2 shall be repeated until the Milestone Event is accepted by Company.

3. **Payments.** As full and complete compensation for the services, products, and rights provided to Company hereunder, Company shall pay to Developer the amount of Thirty-Five Thousand Dollars ($35,000.00) pursuant to the Milestone Delivery Schedule.

4. **Credits and Notices.** Provided that Developer has fulfilled its obligations hereunder, Developer shall be entitled to place a "Developed By" credit in an introductory credits screen in the Project. This screen shall be subject to the approval of, and all other credits and Intellectual Property Rights notices shall be inserted as directed by, Company in its sole discretion.

5. **Technical Support Documentation and Consultation.** Developer shall provide complete technical support documentation to Company and shall provide ongoing reasonable consultation to Company to the extent that Company is unable to solve technical problems with the Project, including but not limited to any Developer Properties. Developer shall promptly remedy any Nonconformities identified by the Company.

6. **Rights and Licenses.**
6.1 **Ownership of Rights.** Any and all results and proceeds of Developer's services pursuant to this Agreement, including but not limited to the Milestone Events and the Source Code (the "Work") and the Project, are specially ordered by Company and each shall constitute a "work-made-for-hire" for Company under all relevant copyright laws. If, for any reason, pursuant to any relevant copyright laws, any elements of the Work, the Project, or any derivative works thereof are deemed not to be a work-made-for-hire, Developer agrees that this Agreement constitutes an irrevocable, perpetual assignment to Company and its successors and assigns of any and all of Developer's right, title, and interest therein under any such relevant copyright laws, including but not limited to any and all worldwide copyrights and renewals, extensions, and restorations thereof,

Figure 8.1 Sample CD-ROM development agreement. (continued)

including but not limited to the exclusive, worldwide, irrevocable, perpetual right to perform, display, reproduce, distribute, prepare derivative works, use, advertise, promote, market, sell, manufacture, exhibit, and/or otherwise exploit the Work, the Project, any and all derivative works thereof, and any and all elements of any of the foregoing, in any and all media and manners throughout the universe, whether now known or hereafter devised. Furthermore, Developer hereby transfers, conveys, and assigns to Company and its successors and assigns all other Intellectual Property Rights in and to all elements of the Work, the Project, any derivative works thereof throughout the world, and in any language. Developer hereby waives any so-called droit moral rights, moral rights of authors, and all other similar rights however denominated throughout the world.

6.2 **Further Documentation.** Developer shall, at Company's request, execute, acknowledge, deliver, and/or record such assignments, documents, or other instruments that Company may deem necessary to evidence, establish, enforce, or defend its rights under this Agreement. Developer hereby grants Company the right, as its attorney-in-fact, to execute, acknowledge, deliver, and record in the U.S. Copyright Office or elsewhere any and all such documents that Developer fails to execute, acknowledge, deliver, and record.

6.3 **License by Developer; Third-Party Documentation.** Developer grants to Company a nonexclusive, irrevocable, perpetual, worldwide right and license to the Developer Properties (including but not limited to the Third-Party Materials) to perform, display, reproduce, distribute, prepare derivative works, use, advertise, promote, market, sell, manufacture, exhibit, and otherwise exploit the Developer Properties in connection with the Project and any derivative works thereof, in any and all media and manners throughout the universe, whether now known or hereafter devised. Developer shall not include any Third-Party Materials in the Project without (i) the prior written consent of Company and (ii) documentation satisfactory to Company evidencing Developer's rights with respect to such Third-Party Materials, including the right to sublicense such rights to Company for use in connection with the Project. Developer shall also provide a schedule satisfactory to Company listing any and all Third-Party Materials included in or used in connection with the Project. All Third-Party Materials shall be without cost to Company other than the compensation provided in Section 3 above. Developer shall not engage the services of any third party in connection with the Project or any part thereof unless, prior to commencing such services, such third party executes a "work-made-for-hire" agreement substantially in the form of Exhibit C attached hereto.

Figure 8.1 Sample CD-ROM development agreement. (continued)

6.4 **Use of Company Properties.** Developer shall not use any Company Property unless Developer has received prior written approval from Company. In addition, Developer shall comply with the terms and conditions of any clearances and licenses of Company Properties of which it is informed by Company. Company hereby grants to Developer a limited, nonexclusive, nontransferable license to use the Company Properties for the term of this Agreement solely for the purpose of developing the Project pursuant to this Agreement. Developer shall have no right to sublicense or assign the Company Properties to any person or entity, and Company retains all rights not expressly conveyed to Developer hereunder.

7. **Representations and Warranties; Indemnification.**
7.1 **Limitation.** The warranties in this Section 7 are the only warranties made with respect to the project and constitute a limited warranty. Company and Developer expressly disclaim any and all other warranties, express or implied, including but not limited to implied warranties of merchantability and fitness for a particular purpose. Except as may be required pursuant to Section 7.4 hereunder, neither Company nor Developer shall be liable to the other or to any third party for any consequential, special, indirect, or incidental damages, including but not limited to lost profits or other economic loss (whether arising from breach of contract or tort), even if apprised of the likelihood of such damages.

7.2 **Developer's Representations and Warranties.** Developer represents and warrants that (a) the Work shall be of high quality in all respects, shall contain no Nonconformities, and shall meet the Performance Standards; (b) Developer owns, controls, or has all necessary rights, including but not limited to all necessary Intellectual Property Rights, to the Developer Properties, including but not limited to the Third-Party Materials; (c) the Work shall be wholly original with Developer and shall not be copied or adapted in whole or in part from any other work or materials (except for materials in the public domain or Company Properties); and (d) neither the Developer Properties, the Work, nor the use thereof shall infringe on or violate any Intellectual Property Rights or any other right of any other person.

7.3 **Company's Representations and Warranties.** Company represents and warrants that (a) Company owns, controls, or has all necessary rights to the Company Properties, including but not limited to all necessary Intellectual Property Rights; and (b) neither the Company Properties nor the use thereof infringes on or violates any Intellectual Property Rights or any other right of any other person.

Figure 8.1 Sample CD-ROM development agreement. (continued)

7.4 **Indemnification.** Each party (the "Indemnifying Party") shall indemnify and hold the other party (the "Indemnified Party") harmless from and against all claims, demands, damages, liabilities, losses, costs, or deficiencies of any nature (including but not limited to reasonable attorneys' fees) arising out of a breach or any claim of a breach of the warranties, representations, and covenants of the Indemnifying Party. The Indemnified Party shall not settle any such claim without the Indemnifying Party's prior written consent, which may not be unreasonably withheld.

8. **Termination; Remedies.**

8.1 **Termination.** Developer may terminate this Agreement if any material breach of this Agreement by Company continues for fifteen (15) business days after notice from Developer. Company may terminate this Agreement (i) without cause by giving at least thirty (30) days' written notice specifying termination pursuant to this Section 8.1(i); (ii) if any material breach of this Agreement by Developer continues for fifteen (15) business days after notice from Company; (iii) if any Milestone Event is either not delivered within fifteen (15) days, or approved by Company within sixty (60) days, after the relevant Milestone Completion Date; (iv) if Developer becomes insolvent or makes an assignment for the benefit of its creditors; (v) if proceedings relating to Developer are commenced under any bankruptcy, insolvency, or debtor's relief law, and are not vacated within sixty (60) days; or (vi) if Developer is liquidated or dissolved.

8.2 **Effect of Termination.** If this Agreement is terminated, in addition to any other remedies Company or Developer may have, (i) Developer shall deliver immediately to Company all Work then completed or in progress; (ii) Developer shall cease all exploitation of the Company Properties and shall return immediately to Company all materials given to Developer by Company; (iii) Developer shall have no further obligation to continue development and Company shall have no further obligation to make any Milestone Payments, provided that if Company terminated this Agreement pursuant to Section 8.1 (i) or if Developer terminated this Agreement pursuant to Section 8.1, Company shall pay Developer the Milestone Payments for Milestone Events approved prior to termination, if any, and a reasonable percentage of the one (1) next Milestone Payment based on the amount of work completed on the related Milestone Event; (iv) the provisions of Sections 6.1, 6.2, and 6.3, including but not limited to the rights and licenses of the Company thereunder, shall continue, provided that if Company terminated this Agreement pursuant to Section 8.1(i), the license to Company pursuant to Section 6.3 shall terminate; and (v) the provisions of Sections 7, 8, and 9 shall continue to control.

Figure 8.1 Sample CD-ROM development agreement. (continued)

8.3 **Equitable Relief.** Developer acknowledges that, in the event of its threatened or actual breach of the material provisions of this Agreement, damages alone will be an inadequate remedy, that such breach will cause Company great, immediate, and irreparable injury and damage, and that Company shall therefore be entitled to injunctive and other equitable relief in addition to, and not in lieu of, any remedies Company may have at law or under this Agreement. Any rights and remedies Developer may have against Company or Company's successors or assigns will be limited to the right to recover damages, if any, in an action at law. Developer hereby waives any right or remedy in equity, including but not limited to any right to rescind or terminate Company's rights to the Work or to seek injunctive relief of any kind.

9. **Miscellaneous Provisions.**

9.1 **Assignment.** Developer may not assign any rights or delegate any obligations hereunder without the prior written consent of Company. Company may assign this Agreement and its rights hereunder to any person or entity and will be relieved of all its obligations to Developer to the extent that these obligations are assumed in writing by any such assignee.

9.2 **Confidentiality.** Each party agrees not to disclose the confidential and proprietary information of the other party received in the performance of this Agreement unless such information is made publicly available or was known prior to disclosure, or unless required to do so by law or pursuant to an administrative proceeding.

9.3 **Governing Law; Jurisdiction.** This Agreement will be subject to and construed in accordance with the laws of the State of Missouri applicable to agreements made and to be wholly performed therein. The parties hereby submit exclusively to the personal jurisdiction of the federal and state courts located in Kansas City, Missouri, U.S.A., and agree that each such court is a convenient forum for and has proper venue over the resolution of all disputes or claims arising out of this Agreement. Each party hereby waives all rights it has or which may hereafter arise to contest such exclusive jurisdiction or venue. Any prevailing party shall be awarded any reasonable attorneys fees and costs required to enforce its rights under this Agreement.

9.4 **Independent Contractors.** Each party is an independent contractor, and this Agreement shall not be construed as creating a joint venture, partnership, agency, or employment relationship between the parties hereto nor shall either party have the right, power, or authority to create any obligation or duty, express or implied, on behalf of the other.

Figure 8.1 Sample CD-ROM development agreement. (continued)

9.5 **Notices.** All notices or other communications that shall or may be given pursuant to this Agreement shall be in writing, in English, shall be sent by certified or registered mail with postage prepaid, return receipt requested; by facsimile, telex, or cable communication; by overnight commercial carrier with verification of receipt by signature; or by hand delivery. Such communications shall be deemed given and received upon dispatch, if sent by facsimile, overnight carrier, telex, or cable communication; or upon delivery if hand delivered; or within five (5) days of mailing, if sent by certified or registered mail, and shall be addressed to the parties as first set forth above or to such other addresses as the parties may designate in writing from time to time. No objection may be made to the manner of delivery of any notice actually received in writing by an authorized agent of a party.

9.6 **Entire Agreement; Modification; Waiver.** This Agreement, including all exhibits, is the final and exclusive expression of the parties' agreement and understanding and supersedes all prior and contemporaneous contracts, representations, and understandings, whether written or oral, express or implied, between the parties concerning the subject matter hereof. None of the terms or conditions hereof may be modified or waived, and this Agreement may not be amended, except in a writing signed by both parties. Company may make changes to the Performance Standards in writing in its sole discretion, and the Milestone Completion Dates or the Milestone Payments will be amended to reflect any changed impact on Developer of any substantial changes. This Agreement may be executed by facsimile or original signature and in any number of counterparts.

IN WITNESS WHEREOF, and intending to be legally bound hereby, the parties have caused this Agreement to be duly executed by their authorized representatives as of the date hereof.

VOICETECH INDUSTRIES, INC.   INTER-ACT, INC.

By: _____   By: _____

Its: _____   Its: _____

Date: _____   Date: _____

Figure 8.1 Sample CD-ROM development agreement. (continued)

EXHIBIT A
PROJECT SPECIFICATION

Description
The Project will be an interactive CD-ROM that introduces and trains customers and sales staff in using the Company's voice-recognition products. The Project will be similar in scope and structure to the Company's other sales/training CD-ROMs (copies of which have been provided to Developer) and will include graphics, motion video, audio, and text. Company personnel will participate in initial production meetings to assist Developer in creating storyboards and a schematic layout for the Project.

Technical Specifications

Minimum System Requirements: The Project will operate on systems running under Windows 3.1 or higher and having the following minimum requirements: 66 MHz processor; 16 megabytes RAM; 2X CD-ROM. Graphics: Screen graphics must be 640 × 480 resolution (14-inch monitors) or less. Minimum resolution: 8-bit, 256 colors. All text (other than text fields) must be bitmapped.

Video: Any video compression algorithm used other than QuickTime for Windows, AVI, or DVI must be approved by Company. Digitized video should not exceed the following rates unless a faster rate is approved by the Company:

- Single speed requires 95 k per second including sound.
- Double speed requires 175 k to 185 k per second including sound.
- Triple speed requires 245 k to 275 k per second including sound.
- Quad speed requires 370 k to 400 k per second including sound.

Sound: All music should be at least 16-bit and in stereo where applicable.

EXHIBIT B
MILESTONE DELIVERY SCHEDULE

Milestone Event	Completion Date	Payment
Acceptance of Storyboard and Schematic	1/13/03	$7,500
Acceptance of Prototype	2/17/03	$5,000
Acceptance of Alpha Version	3/17/03	$5,000
Acceptance of Beta Version	4/14/03	$5,000
Acceptance of Gold Master	5/19/03	$12,500

Figure 8.1 Sample CD-ROM development agreement. (continued)

EXHIBIT C
WORK-MADE-FOR-HIRE-AGREEMENT

This Agreement ("Agreement") is made and entered into as of _____ 20 ____ by and between [NAME OF THIRD-PARTY CONTRACTOR] ("you") and Voicetech Industries, Inc. ("Company"), with respect to your engagement by and under the supervision of Inter-Act, Inc. ("Developer"), to render services in connection with the development of a corporate training CD-ROM and any projects related thereto and/or derivative thereof (the "Project"). In consideration of the terms and conditions set forth below, Company and you agree as follows:

1. You will provide the following services and/or products in connection with the Project: [DESCRIBE SERVICES AND PRODUCTS.] Any and all results, products, and proceeds of your services in connection with the Project, including but not limited to any and all of the foregoing, are hereinafter referred to as "the Work." The Work shall be provided by you in accordance with the instructions of Developer, shall be subject to the approval of Company and Developer exercisable in their sole discretion, and shall not contain any obscene materials.

2. As full compensation for your services, the Work and any and all rights granted or assigned to Company by you under this Agreement, Company will pay you [AMOUNT TO BE PAID] as follows: [SCHEDULE OF PAYMENTS.] You acknowledge that payment to you by Company or by Developer on Company's behalf pursuant to this Paragraph 2 will constitute full and complete satisfaction of any and all payment obligations under this Agreement.

3. You acknowledge and agree that the Work is being specially ordered by Company and shall constitute a "work-made-for-hire" for Company under all relevant copyright laws. If, for any reason, pursuant to any relevant copyright laws, the Work or any element thereof shall ever be deemed not to be a work-made-for-hire for Company, you agree that this Agreement constitutes an irrevocable, perpetual assignment to Company and its successors and assigns of any and all of your right, title, and interest in and to the Work under any such relevant copyright laws, including but not limited to any and all worldwide copyrights and renewals, extensions, and restorations thereof. You hereby further transfer, convey, and assign to Company and its successors and assigns all other intellectual property rights in and to all elements of the Work, throughout the world, and in any language, including but not limited to any and all patent rights, rights of inventors, and trademark rights. You hereby waive any so-called droit moral rights, moral rights of authors, and all other similar rights, however

Figure 8.1 Sample CD-ROM development agreement. (continued)

denominated throughout the world. You will, upon Company's request, execute, acknowledge, deliver, and/or record such additional documents as Company may deem necessary to evidence and effectuate Company's rights hereunder. You hereby grant Company the right, as your attorney-in-fact, to execute, acknowledge, deliver, and record in the U.S. Copyright Office or elsewhere any and all such documents that you fail to execute, acknowledge, deliver, and record. Company will have the right to use, at its option and in its sole discretion, your name, likeness, and biographical information to promote and advertise the Project or any other use of the Work. You acknowledge that Company will not be obligated to exercise any of the rights granted to Company herein or make any use of the Work.

4. You represent and warrant that (a) you have the full power and authority to enter into and to fulfill the terms of this Agreement and to grant the rights described herein; (b) you have not entered and will not enter into any agreements or activities that will or might interfere or conflict with the terms hereof; (c) the Work is and will be wholly original with you and not copied in whole or in part from any other work except materials in the public domain or supplied to you by Company; and (d) to the best of your knowledge, neither the Work nor the use thereof infringes on or violates any right of privacy or publicity of, or constitutes a libel, slander, or any unfair competition against, or infringes on or violates the copyright, trademark rights, or other intellectual property rights of any person or entity.

5. In the event of an actual or alleged breach of this Agreement, or under any other circumstances whatsoever, any rights and remedies you may have against Company or its successors or assigns will be limited to the right to recover damages, if any, in an action at law. You hereby waive any right or remedy in equity, including but not limited to any right to rescind or terminate Company's rights hereunder or to seek injunctive relief of any kind.

6. Any information about the Project disclosed to you by Developer and/or Company during the course of the performance of this Agreement is confidential information that is proprietary to Company. You agree to maintain in strict confidence all such proprietary and confidential information, except only to the extent that such information is made publicly available or was known to you prior to any disclosure.

7. You may not assign this Agreement or your rights hereunder, or delegate your obligations hereunder in whole or in part. Company may assign this Agreement or any or all of its rights hereunder to any person or

Figure 8.1 Sample CD-ROM development agreement. (continued)

entity and will be relieved of all its obligations to you hereunder to the extent that such obligations are assumed in writing by any such assignee.

8. Each party is an independent contractor, and this Agreement will not be construed as creating a joint venture, partnership, or agency relationship between the parties hereto nor will either party have the right, power, or authority to create any obligation or duty, express or implied, on behalf of the other.

9. This Agreement will be subject to and construed in accordance with the laws of the State of Missouri applicable to agreements made and to be wholly performed therein, and is intended by the parties to be the final, complete, and exclusive expression of their agreement and understanding and supersedes all prior and contemporaneous contracts, representations, and understandings (written or oral) between the parties concerning the subject matter hereof. This Agreement may not be changed or modified except by a writing signed by both parties.

Please indicate your acceptance of and agreement to the foregoing terms and conditions by signing in the space provided below.

AGREED AND ACCEPTED:

_____

[CONTRACTOR'S SIGNATURE]

Name: _____

Date: _____

VOICETECH INDUSTRIES, INC.   INTER-ACT, INC.

By: _____   By: _____

Its: _____   Its: _____

Date: _____   Date: _____

CD-ROMs. The video program covered by the production agreement will be sold to the general public (so that a royalty based on sales makes sense), whereas the CD-ROM being produced under the agreement in Figure 8.1 is intended for internal distribution (so that such a royalty arrangement has no real relevance). Even when copies of the completed production will be sold to the public, however, it is not uncommon for a work-made-for-hire project to be done entirely on a flat-fee basis with no royalty or other contingent compensation paid to the production company.

Finally, the CD-ROM agreement includes several references to source code. In conventional linear video production, "what you see is what you've got." That is, you can detect any problems in the completed production simply by screening the production, and you can correct problems if necessary by adjusting, removing, or adding material through editing. Such "post-postproduction" is more difficult with interactive CD-ROM productions, however, because problems can remain hidden along the various pathways that users travel based on their interactions with the production, and because correcting problems that do appear often requires modifying the underlying computer code that determines those pathways. Usually, these modifications must be made by a computer programmer who has access to the source code: the human-readable version of the underlying computer code.[1] As a result, it is important that the source code is included when an outside contractor delivers a completed CD-ROM production. Some CD-ROM development agreements, including Figure 8.1, also require that a current copy of the source code be provided with the production at each stage of delivery, so that it will be possible for another contractor to complete the CD-ROM if the original contractor does not prove up to the task.

Clips, Copyright, and CD-ROMs

Chapter 4 established two fundamental principles of copyright law that all media producers should keep in mind: (1) always assume that materials that *can be* protected by copyright (e.g., literary properties, film or video materials, photographs, music) *are* protected by copyright,[2] and (2) never assume that you can use copyrighted materials in a media production without obtaining the copyright owner's permission, even when you intend to use only brief excerpts.

These principles are particularly relevant to CD-ROM production because many CD-ROMs are essentially collections of clips that are accessed through the technology's indexing, search, and linking capabilities. For example, Microsoft, Compton's, Collier's, and several other companies have published CD-ROM encyclopedias in which users enter search words to call up articles that combine original text and graphics with preexisting photographs, motion video sequences, music and other audio,[3] and so on. Some such preexisting materials, such as documents and photographs dating from the 19th century, are in the public domain and therefore free of any copyright constraints. Unless you can determine with certainty that a clip containing copyrightable subject matter is in the public domain (or unless you can be certain that your use of the material would pass the "fair use" test introduced in Chapter 4), however, the only safe course is to seek and obtain permission from the copyright owner before including the clip in your CD-ROM production. If you are unable to obtain this permission, do not use the clip.

Guild Issues

In CD-ROM production, guild issues typically arise in two contexts: (1) you want to use a clip from a film or television show in the CD-ROM and one or more performers featured in the clips are guild members; or (2) you are producing original film or video footage for the CD-ROM and you want to use a guild member (e.g., a voiceover performer who is an AFTRA member, a writer who is a WGA member) in that footage. As discussed in Chapter 7, the rules governing uses of guild members and their prior performances in conventional film and video productions are detailed in the basic agreements between the guilds and the producers of various types of productions. Not all guilds have basic agreements that cover the production of CD-ROMs and other types of interactive materials, however, and those interactive agreements that do exist sometimes are interim or side letter agreements put in place as stopgap measures. As a result, the rules governing guild involvement in interactive productions are not always clear, and the guilds often change the rules in response to new technological and industry developments. With this in mind, producers should always contact the relevant guilds to obtain the latest incarnations of their interactive agreements before deciding to use a guild performer or clips containing guild performances in a CD-ROM.

Using Clips Containing Guild Performances

Almost all television programs and feature films were produced under one or more guild agreements. As a result, using clips from these films or programs in a CD-ROM triggers permission and reuse payment obligations under the applicable guild agreements. For example, the current SAG and AFTRA interactive agreements require that, to include a clip in an interactive production, you must obtain the consent of any SAG or AFTRA member featured in the clip and pay the member the current guild "minimum day player rate."[4] Of course, these obligations actually belong to the company that produced the original film or television program because that company (and not you) is a signatory to the guild agreements under which the film or program was produced. For example, if you want to use a clip from the movie *Independence Day* in a CD-ROM, you will need to approach Twentieth Century Fox (the company that financed and distributed the film) for permission to use the clip. If it decides to grant permission, Twentieth Century Fox (as the guild signatory under whose auspices the film was produced) would be responsible for obtaining the consents of and paying the applicable reuse fee to those guild members whose work is featured in the clip. As a practical matter, however, Twentieth Century Fox might require you to take on these obligations as a condition of its granting permission to use the clip in your CD-ROM. In fact, unless you can establish that your use of the clips will have significant promotional value, some film and television producers routinely deny this permission based on their determination that the relatively small amount they are paid for clips is outweighed by the risk of guild sanctions if the proper permissions and payment procedures are not followed.

It is important to realize that the guild permissions and payment requirements just described are distinct from copyright permissions and payment requirements. For example, as owner of the copyright in *Independence Day*, Twentieth Century Fox is free to grant or deny permission for you to include clips from that film in CD-ROMs or other works. If Fox denies you that permission but you proceed to use the clips anyway, you will be liable for copyright infringement (unless you could show that your use of the clips constitutes a "fair use," as discussed in Chapter 4). If Fox grants you the permission, your use of the clips will not subject you to a copyright infringement claim, but you or (more probably) Fox could still find yourself in trouble with the guilds if you have not obtained the consent of and paid the guild members whose work is featured in the clips. Conversely, obtaining the consent of and paying guild members directly does not free you from the separate obligation to obtain permission to use the clips from Fox, the copyright owner.

Using Guild Members in Producing Original Footage

Not surprisingly, the major guilds (i.e., SAG, AFTRA, WGA, and DGA) all have rules governing the circumstances under which their members may be employed in the production of CD-ROMs and other interactive materials. Under the SAG and AFTRA interactive agreements, production companies that are guild signatories may hire only performers who are guild members or nonmembers who (as discussed in Chapter 7) agree to become guild members within 30 days of hiring. The SAG and AFTRA agreements also specify minimum scale wages for guild performers employed on interactive productions. Figure 8.2 is the AFTRA Performer Contract used when a producer hires an AFTRA performer for an interactive production.

The employment of directors who are DGA members on interactive productions, such as CD-ROMs and DVD-ROMs, is governed by the guild's Interactive Side Letter. Employment of DGA directors on productions intended for exploitation on Internet websites is governed by the guild's Internet Pictures Side Letter. These side letter agreements reference the DGA's basic agreement and incorporate many, but not all, of the terms of the basic agreement.

The WGA currently has a single-page Interactive Program Contract. Signing this agreement allows producers to hire WGA members on a "one-production-only" basis. That is, producers who use the Interactive Program Contract do not have to become signatories to the WGA basic agreement, with the ongoing obligation to use WGA member writers for the duration of that agreement. The Interactive Program Contract does not set minimum compensation levels that must be paid to WGA members employed on an interactive production. Producers must agree, however, to make the standard contributions to the WGA pension plan and health funds (contributions that currently total 12.5 percent of the gross compensation paid to the writer).

Figure 8.2 AFTRA Performer Contract for interactive productions.

PERFORMER CONTRACT
FOR INTERACTIVE MEDIA

Company: Performer:
                                             (c/o):

Title:

       ("Program")

Date Employment Starts _____   Telephone No. (   ) _____

Role(s)_____   Social Security No.: _____

Type of Employment (check one): Principal ___ Voice-Over/(4 hour day) ___ Number of Voices ___ Stunt ___

Solo/Duo Dancer ___ Group Dancer 3-8 ___ Group Dancer 9 or more ___ Solo/ Duo Singer ___ Group Singer 3-8 ___

Group Singer 9 or more ___ Sound Effects ___ Contractor ___ Extra ___

Form of Employment: Day Player ___ 3-Day ___ Weekly ____

Daily Rate $_____   3 Day Rate $_____

Weekly Rate $_____   Off-Camera Hourly Rate (Singers Only)$_____

Are Payments Being Made Now For: Remote Delivery_____ Integration _____ (Initials if required)

Additional Terms and Conditions Attached: Yes____   No ____

Special Provisions (if any):

Wardrobe supplied by Performer: Yes ____ No ____

If so, number of outfits _____ @ $ _____

(formal) _____ @ $ _____

THIS AGREEMENT covers the employment of the above-named Performer by, _____ in the Interactive
Program(s) and at the rate of compensation set forth above and is subject to and shall include, for the benefit of the Performer and the
Producer, all of the applicable provisions and conditions contained or provided for in the AFTRA Interactive Agreement of 1994, as the
same may be amended, between AFTRA and Producer. Producer shall have all the rights in and to the results and proceeds of the
Performer's services rendered hereunder, to the maximum extent provided in the AFTRA Interactive Agreement.

ACCEPTED AND AGREED:

_____   _____
Company   Performer
                                 Initial if Additional Terms and Conditions
                                 Agreed To_____

NOTICE TO PERFORMERS: RETAIN A COPY OF THIS CONTRACT FOR YOUR PERMANENT RECORDS

Figure 8.2 AFTRA Performer Contract for interactive productions. (continued)

ADDITIONAL TERMS AND CONDITIONS

I. The provisions of the relevant American Federation of Television and Radio Performer's agreement ("AFTRA Agreement") between Company and AFTRA are incorporated into this contract and if any provision hereof violates the AFTRA Agreement, the latter shall control.

II. SERVICES: Performer shall perform all services in accordance with Producer's instructions and directions in all matters including those involving artistic taste and judgment, and Performer shall be available and shall render services at such times and in such places as Producer may designate. Producer shall not be obligated to use Performer's services or any results or proceeds thereof, nor shall Producer be obligated to produce, complete the production of, release, distribute, exhibit, advertise or exploit the Program or any part thereof. Nothing in this paragraph alters or releases Producer's obligations to Performer with reference to compensation. Producer shall be entitled to the maximum work period provided by the AFTRA Agreement with respect to the services provided hereunder. Any services beyond such time shall be compensated at the rate specified on the first page to which this Rider is attached. If no rate is specified, the compensation for overtime shall be the applicable AFTRA scale.

III. DEFINITIONS: "*Interactive Media*" is: any media on which digitized product operates and through which the user may interact with such product including but not limited to personal computers, games, machines, arcade games, all CD-interactive machines and any and all analogous, similar or dissimilar microprocessor-based units and the electronic formats/platforms which may be utilized in connection therewith. "*Remote Delivery*" is any system under which digitized product may be accessed for use from a location that is remote from the central processing unit on which the product is principally used or stored, such as an on-line service, a delivery service over cable television lines, telephone lines, microwave signals, radio waves, satellite, wireless cable or any other service or method now known or hereinafter invented for the delivery or transmission of such digitized product enabling interactive use. "*Integration*": is the use of an excerpt of a performer's performance that was rendered under the terms of this Agreement, in any other Interactive program for which the performer is not engaged to perform but such other program(s) is produced by the same employer as originally employed the performer. Any other reuse of the performer's performance shall be considered "reuse" hereunder. "Integration" does not mean or include: (i) the repetition of segments of any single Interactive Program that may appear to be many different programs due to the way viewers choose or recall various segments and manipulate the program; (ii) the re-configuration or re-formulation of the material produced hereunder for a single program for the computer software code to adapt the Interactive Program to different Platforms; (iii) the use of material for Interactive Media in Linear Programs. "*Program*": A program refers to the final version of a fully-edited product for presentation to the viewer or user. "*Interactive Program*" is the final version of a fully-edited product presented on Interactive Media, notwithstanding any variations which may occur between Platforms. "Program" does not refer to the computer software code utilized in the digitization process, any type of electronic technology, patents, trademarks or any of the intellectual property rights of Producer. "*Platform(s)*": Platform refers to microprocessor-based hardware including but not limited to CD-ROM, CD-I and 3DO machines that utilize the appropriate compatible formats such as cartridges and discs, or other formats hereinafter invented which memorialize Interactive Programs for viewer use. "*Linear Programs*": Programs which do not possess interactive qualities are "*Linear*" in nature, and mean those programs which are: (i) produced and memorialized by means of videotape or film photography or any other processes now known or hereafter invented through which photographic images or other visual representations (whether live-action or animated) are used alone, or in conjunction with audio effects, and create life-like images of the characters therein, and (ii) exhibited or transmitted to the viewer by television (UHF or VHF over-the-air broadcast, cable, satellite, or any other means or methods which may be known or hereafter invented for television reception) and/or video cassettes, video discs or any other devices used in conjunction with corresponding hardware to cause a presentation to be exhibited visually on the screen of a television receiver or any comparable device; and/or film projection in motion picture theaters. "*Reuse*": means the incorporation of material produced for Interactive Media in a Linear Program and the incorporation of material produced for Interactive program(s) under this Agreement in another program that is not covered under "Integration".

IV. TRAILERS/PROMOTIONS: Producer shall have the right to make trailers including "teasers" (a short trailer) for the purpose of advertising and promoting the Interactive Program. The use of a performer's services in any such trailer or "teaser" shall not require the payment of additional compensation if the recordation of such trailer occurs during the performer's employment in connection with the applicable Interactive Program. Otherwise, applicable scale shall be the minimum compensation for services in connection with such trailers.

No use of a performer's services in a trailer as herein defined shall be used in connectiion with an endorsement of any service or product other than the Interactive Program(s) for which the performer was employed to render services. References to the hardware, platforms or Remote Delivery systems upon which the Interactive Program operates or references to other Interactive Programs shall not be deemed an endorsement of a service or product in violation of this Section 16 B. if the Interactive Program is clearly identified by its title in such promotion to the consumer.

All advertising, publicity and promotional information relating to the program including but not limited to Performer's role therein, shall be solely issued and controlled by Producer. Performer shall not have the right to issue or authorize any advertising, publicity, or promotional information (including but not limited to press releases) or to refer to the program in any publicity issued by Performer without the prior approval of Producer in writing.

VI. SCREEN CREDIT: No casual or inadvertent failure by Producer to comply with the provisions of any credit obligations shall constitute a breach of this Agreement. Performer's rights and remedies in the event of a failure or omission by Producer to provide Performer the screen credit on the Program indicated herein shall be limited to Performer's rights, if any, to recover damages at law, but in no event shall Performer be entitled by reason of any such breach to terminate this Agreement or to enjoin or restrain the distribution or exhibition of the Program.

VII. RESULTS AND PROCEEDS: Producer shall have the right to record Performer's voice and performance, and to exploit the same in connection with the Program in all Interactive Media and otherwise in accordance with the terms of AFTRA and this Agreement by any present or future method of recordation which may be devised or invented. Producer shall own all results and proceeds of Performer's services hereunder, including the copyrights thereof, and shall have all other rights of ownership, subject only to the provisions of the AFTRA Agreement requiring the payment of additional compensation for Remote Delivery and Integration and/or separate bargaining use for Linear Media and other reuse not covered in the Agreement. The Performer hereby consents to and grants Producer the exclusive right in and in connection with the Program and its advertising and promotion of the Program to use and license others to use Performer's name and likeness within the payment of additional compensation therefor in trailers and any and all promotional uses within the specifications of the AFTRA Agreement. Producer may exercise its such rights for trade, or for any other lawful or authorized purposes desired by Producer.

This Agreement may not be assigned by Performer. Producer may assign this Agreement to any other person or entity, provided that such entity assumes all of the executory obligations of Producer hereunder in compliance with the rules and regulations of AFTRA.

Producing Websites for the Internet

The rapid growth of the Internet and World Wide Web has sparked the equally rapid development of a new legal field known as Internet law or Web law. Although the terms *Internet* and *World Wide Web* are often used interchangeably, they are technically distinct. The Internet is a global computer network originally developed as a research and communications system for university and government groups.[5] The World Wide Web (or Web) is a graphical interface developed to make it easier to locate and move between documents and other resources on the Internet. The development of the World Wide Web took the Internet from its roots as a relatively obscure tool used primarily by academics and government employees to the widespread, multifunctional international phenomenon that it has become today.

A website is an entertainment or information service that resides at a location on the Internet. Individuals typically access a website from their computers by (1) connecting to the Internet through a telecommunications link offered by an Internet access service provider and (2) entering the address of the website (e.g., www.ibm.com) through a software tool called a *browser* (e.g., Netscape's Navigator or Microsoft's Internet Explorer). Following these steps will typically connect you to the website's home page, from which you can link to any other pages containing services or materials offered in connection with the site.[6] The sections that follow explore several of the more common legal concerns that arise when a company develops and operates a website for marketing, communications, or sales purposes.

Website Development and Service Agreement

As with CD-ROM development, many companies lack the expertise and experience to develop websites entirely in-house. In addition, because websites must be based and maintained on computers that are connected to the Internet through the proper technical configuration and software protocols, many companies lack the necessary technology and technical staff to establish and operate sites. Faced with these conditions and concerns, many companies have no choice but to hire outside contractors to develop and maintain their websites. As always, any such relationship with a third party should be governed by a comprehensive written agreement like the sample shown in Figure 8.3.

Figure 8.3 Sample website development and maintenance agreement.

This Agreement (the "Agreement") is made as of this 13th day of June 2002, by and between Trushoes, Inc. ("Company"), and WonderWeb, Inc. ("Developer"), with respect to the development and maintenance of one or more computer programs that will function as a World Wide Web site that promotes the Company's products (the "Website").

Company and Developer hereby agree as follows:

I.   SERVICES.

A. **Development Services; Delivery.** Developer will devote its best efforts to the design and development of the Website in accordance with the specifications set forth in this Agreement, including but not limited to the specifications set forth in the proposal dated May 9, 2002, submitted to Company by Developer (the "Proposal"). Company may make changes to the specifications set forth in the Proposal in its sole discretion upon written notice to Developer. No later than sixty (60) days after the execution of this Agreement by Company, Developer will (i) deliver the Website to Company by making available for Company's review and approval a fully functional, completely tested and debugged version of the Website, and (ii) deliver to Company all Source Code for the Website and all relevant Third-Party Documentation (as defined in Section III.D.). "Source Code" means all of the source code for the Website and includes (i) programming code written for the Website in commonly used computer programming languages, including but not limited to programming code unique to the Website that facilitates the operation of the Website on Developer's servers; and (ii) programming scripts and macros written in the scripting languages of any third-party development or authoring tools. Company will have the right to approve or disapprove any and all elements of the Website in its sole discretion. Developer will promptly notify Company of any circumstance that could delay the development of the Website, including delays by Company in providing any necessary materials or changes by Company to the specifications set forth in this Agreement and/or the Proposal. During the term of the Agreement, Developer will provide updates, modifications, and enhancements to the Website as requested by Company as soon as practicable. Developer acknowledges that for business, legal, or other reasons, Company may require the Website to be modified on short notice, and Developer will use best efforts to make such modifications as soon as possible.

B. **Website Maintenance Services.** Company grants and Developer accepts a limited, revocable, nonexclusive, nontransferable license for the term of this Agreement to carry the Website on its servers and make the Website accessible to the World Wide Web. Developer shall use its best

Figure 8.3 Sample website development and maintenance agreement. (continued)

efforts to make the Website accessible on a continuous, unlimited basis, twenty-four (24) hours per day. Developer acknowledges that the Website will be heavily used by end-users and that on an hourly basis there will be a substantial number of end-users seeking access to the Website. Developer will provide equipment and systems sufficient to handle heavy usage of the Website. Developer's equipment and systems will be secure and will provide sufficient capacity and redundancy to keep "downtime" to a minimum. Developer will provide for hyperlinks to and from other Web sites identified by Company, and agrees to cooperate with Company and any third parties operating such other Web sites to facilitate a transparent, seamless, and error-free connection between any two Web sites. Developer will provide usage tracking capability and will make usage information available to Company on a monthly basis and upon request. Developer acknowledges that Company will own any and all such usage information and any and all customer information collected through the Website (including but not limited to names, addresses, telephone numbers, and e-mail addresses), and Developer will not distribute or make any use of such usage information or customer information without Company's prior written consent. Developer will not modify the Website and/or exercise any editorial control over the Website without Company's prior written approval. Company will have the right to discontinue access to the Website temporarily or permanently at any time in its Company's sole discretion. In the event that Company notifies Developer in writing that it wishes to discontinue access to the Website, Developer will discontinue access to the Website as soon as possible, but in no event more than twenty-four (24) hours after Company's notice.

C. **Term of Maintenance Services.** Commencing on the date that (i) the operation of the Website on the World Wide Web has been reviewed and approved by Company and (ii) Developer has made the Website accessible to end users of the World Wide Web ("Start Date"), Developer shall carry and maintain the Website on its server(s) on a monthly basis, continuing from month to month unless Company notifies Developer otherwise pursuant to Section V.A.

D. **Technical Support.** For no compensation other than that provided in this Agreement, Developer will promptly remedy any Nonconformities in the Website and will provide technical support and ongoing reasonable consultation to Company with respect to the Website. "Nonconformity" means (i) any failure of the Website to meet the specifications set forth in the Proposal; (ii) the inability of the Website to perform any intended feature or function consistently and without interruption; and/or (iii) any

Figure 8.3 Sample website development and maintenance agreement. (continued)

other error or defect that has an adverse impact upon the use or performance of the Website as reasonably determined by Company.

II.   PAYMENTS.

As full and complete compensation for the services, products, and rights provided by Developer to Company hereunder, Company will pay Developer as follows:

   (a) For the design and development of the Website:
       Ten Thousand Dollars ($10,000.00) within fifteen (15) business days of the execution of this Agreement.
       Fifteen Thousand Dollars ($15,000.00) within fifteen (15) business days after the later of the Start Date or the date Company has received the Source Code and any and all relevant Third-Party Documentation (as defined in Section III.C.)

   (b) For the maintenance of the Website on Developer's server(s): One Thousand Dollars ($1,000.00) per month, payable within fifteen (15) business days after the Start Date and the anniversary thereof for each subsequent month.

III. RIGHTS; LICENSES.

A. **Work-Made-for-Hire; Ownership of Rights.** Developers agrees that any and all results and proceeds of Developer's performance and services pursuant to this Agreement, including but not limited to the Source Code (collectively, the "Work"), are specially ordered by Company and constitute a "work-made-for-hire" for Company under all relevant copyright laws. If, for any reason, pursuant to any relevant copyright laws, any elements of the Work or any derivative works thereof are deemed not to be a work-made-for-hire, Developer agrees that this Agreement constitutes an irrevocable, perpetual assignment to Company and its successors and assigns of any and all of Developer's right, title, and interest therein under any such relevant copyright laws, including but not limited to any and all worldwide copyrights and renewals, extensions, and restorations thereof. Furthermore, Developer hereby transfers, conveys, and assigns to Company and its successors and assigns all other intellectual property rights in and to all elements of the Work, the Website, and any derivative works thereof throughout the world, and in any language, including but not limited to any and all rights existing under patent law, trademark law, trade secret law, unfair competition law, moral rights law, publicity rights law, privacy rights law, and any and all other similar proprietary rights, now or hereafter in

Figure 8.3 Sample website development and maintenance agreement. (continued)

force and effect in the United States and throughout the universe. Developer hereby waives any so-called droit moral rights, moral rights of authors, and all other similar rights, however denominated throughout the world.

B. **Further Documentation.** Developer will, at Company's request, execute, acknowledge, deliver, and/or record such assignments, documents, or other instruments that Company may deem necessary to evidence, establish, enforce, or defend its rights under this Agreement. Developer hereby grants Company the right, as its attorney-in-fact, to execute, acknowledge, deliver, and record in the U.S. Copyright Office or elsewhere any and all such documents that Developer fails to execute, acknowledge, deliver, and record.

C. **License by Developer; Third-Party Documentation.**
"Developer Properties" as used herein means all preexisting works that Developer makes available for inclusion in or use in connection with the Website, including but not limited to Developer's and third-party development and authoring tools, and that are the subject of intellectual property rights owned or controlled by (i) Developer or (ii) any third party ("Third-Party Materials"). Developer grants to Company a nonexclusive, irrevocable, perpetual, worldwide right and license to the Developer Properties (including but not limited to the Third-Party Materials) including the right to perform, display, reproduce, distribute, prepare derivative works, use, advertise, promote, market, sell, manufacture, exhibit, and otherwise exploit the Developer Properties in connection with the Website and any derivative works thereof, in any and all media and manners throughout the universe, whether now known or hereafter devised. Developer will not include any Third-Party Materials in the Website without (i) the prior written consent of Company, and (ii) documentation satisfactory to Company evidencing Developer's rights with respect to such Third-Party Materials, including the right to sublicense such rights to Company for use in connection with the Website. Developer will also provide a schedule satisfactory to Company listing any and all Third-Party Materials included in or used in connection with the Website. All Third-Party Materials will be without cost to Company other than the compensation provided in Section II. Developer will not engage the services of any third party to create the Work or any part thereof unless prior to commencing such services such third party executes a "work-made-for-hire" agreement substantially in the form of Exhibit Attached hereto. "Third-Party Documentation" as used herein means the following written documentation satisfactory to Company as required pursuant to this Section III.C.: (i) a schedule listing any and all Third-Party Materials included in or used in connection with the Website,

Figure 8.3 Sample website development and maintenance agreement. (continued)

(ii) the documentation evidencing Developer's rights with respect to any and all Third-Party Materials, and (iii) any "work-made-for-hire" agreements.

D. **Use of Company Properties.** Company hereby grants to Developer a limited, nonexclusive, nontransferable license to use the Company Properties for the term of this Agreement solely for the purpose of developing the Website pursuant to this Agreement. "Company Properties" means all works that are the subject matter of intellectual property rights owned, controlled, or licensed by Company and that Company approves for use or inclusion in the Website as provided in this Section III.D., including but not limited to any and all concepts, ideas, text, names, titles, graphics, photographs, sound recordings, audiovisual works, musical compositions, software, and literary material. Developer will comply with the terms and conditions of any clearances and licenses of Company Properties of which Developer is informed by Company. Company retains all rights not expressly conveyed to Developer hereunder. Without limiting the foregoing, Developer will not create any hyperlinks to the Website from any other Web site without Company's prior written consent.

IV.   REPRESENTATIONS AND WARRANTIES; INDEMNIFICATION.

A. **Limitation.** The warranties in this Section IV are the only warranties made with respect to the Website and constitute a limited warranty. Company and Developer expressly disclaim any and all other warranties, express or implied, including but not limited to implied warranties of merchantability and fitness for a particular purpose. Except as may be required pursuant to Section IV.D. hereunder, neither Company nor Developer will be liable to each other or to any third party for any consequential, special, punitive, or incidental damages, including but not limited to lost profits or other economic loss (whether arising from breach of contract or tort), even if apprised of the likelihood of such damages.

B. **Developer's Representations and Warranties.** Developer represents and warrants that (a) the Work will be of high quality in all respects, will contain no Nonconformities, and will meet the specifications set forth in this Agreement and the Proposal attached hereto; (b) Developer's equipment and systems will be secure and will have sufficient capacity to handle heavy usage of the Website; (c) Developer owns, controls, or has all necessary rights to the Developer Properties (including but not limited to the Third-Party Materials); (d) neither the Developer Properties, the Work, nor the use thereof will infringe on or violate any

Figure 8.3 Sample website development and maintenance agreement. (continued)

right of any person or entity; and (e) the Work will not contain any obscene materials.

C. **Company's Representations and Warranties.** Company represents and warrants that (a) Company owns, controls, or has all necessary rights to the Company Properties; and (b) neither the Company Properties nor the use thereof infringes on or violates any right of any person or entity.

D. **Indemnification.** Each party (the "Indemnifying Party") will indemnify and hold the other party (the "Indemnified Party") harmless from and against all claims, demands, damages, liabilities, losses, costs, or deficiencies of any nature (including but not limited to reasonable attorneys' fees) arising out of a breach or any claim of a breach of the warranties, representations, and covenants of the Indemnifying Party. The Indemnified Party will not settle any such claim without the Indemnifying Party's prior written consent, which may not be unreasonably withheld.

V.   TERMINATION; REMEDIES.

A. **Termination.** Developer may terminate this Agreement if any material breach of this Agreement by Company continues for fifteen (15) business days after written notice from Developer. Prior to the Start Date, Company may terminate this Agreement if any material breach of this Agreement by Developer continues for fifteen (15) business days after written notice from Company. On and after the Start Date, Company shall have the right to discontinue the Website and terminate this Agreement at any time by giving twenty-four (24) hours' written notice to Developer. In the event that Company terminates this Agreement after the Start Date and Developer is not in material breach of this Agreement, Company will pay Developer the monthly fee for the full month in which notice is given.

B. **Effect of Termination.** If this Agreement is terminated, in addition to any other remedies Company or Developer may have, (i) Developer will deliver immediately to Company all Work then completed or in progress; (ii) Developer will immediately discontinue access to the Website and remove the Website from its servers; (iii) Developer will cease all exploitation of the Company Properties and will return immediately to Company all materials given to Developer by Company; (iv) the provisions of Sections III.A., III.B., and III.C., including but not limited to the rights and licenses of Company thereunder, will continue; and (v) the provisions of Sections IV, V, and VI will continue to control.

Figure 8.3 Sample website development and maintenance agreement. (continued)

C. **Equitable Relief.** Developer acknowledges that, in the event of its threatened or actual breach of the material provisions of this Agreement, damages alone will be an inadequate remedy, that such breach will cause Company great, immediate, and irreparable injury and damage, and that Company will therefore be entitled to injunctive and other equitable relief in addition to, and not in lieu of, any remedies Company may have at law or under this Agreement. Any rights and remedies Developer may have against Company or Company's successors or assigns will be limited to the right to recover damages, if any, in an action at law. Developer hereby waives any right or remedy in equity, including but not limited to any right to rescind or terminate Company's rights to the Work or to seek injunctive relief of any kind.

VI. GENERAL PROVISIONS.

A. **Assignment.** Developer may not assign any rights or delegate any obligations hereunder without the prior written consent of Company. Company may assign this Agreement and its rights hereunder to any person or entity and will be relieved of all its obligations to Developer to the extent that these obligations are assumed in writing by any such assignee.

B. **Confidentiality.** Each party agrees not to disclose the confidential and proprietary information of the other party received in the performance of this Agreement unless such information is made publicly available or was known prior to disclosure or unless required to do so by law or pursuant to an administrative proceeding.

C. **Governing Law.** This Agreement will be subject to and construed in accordance with the laws of the State of Florida applicable to agreements made and to be wholly performed therein. The parties hereby agree to submit any disputes or claims arising under this Agreement to the exclusive jurisdiction of courts located in Miami, Florida.

D. **Independent Contractors.** Each party is an independent contractor, and this Agreement will not be construed as creating a joint venture, partnership, agency, or employment relationship between the parties hereto, nor will either party have the right, power, or authority to create any obligation or duty, express or implied, on behalf of the other.

E. **Notices.** All notices or other communications that shall or may be given pursuant to this Agreement, shall be in writing, in English, shall be sent by certified or registered mail with postage prepaid, return receipt

Figure 8.3 Sample website development and maintenance agreement. (continued)

requested; by facsimile, telex, or cable communication; or by hand delivery. Such communications shall be deemed given and received upon dispatch, if sent by facsimile or telex; or upon delivery, if hand delivered; or within three (3) days of mailing, if sent by certified or registered mail. No objection may be made to the manner of delivery of any notice actually received in writing by an authorized agent of a party.

F. **Entire Agreement; Modification; Waiver.** In the event of any inconsistency between the provisions of this Agreement and the provisions of the Proposal, the provisions of this Agreement shall control. This Agreement including its exhibits is the final and exclusive expression of the parties' agreement and understanding and supersedes all prior and contemporaneous contracts, representations and understandings, whether written or oral, express or implied, between the parties concerning the subject matter hereof. None of the terms or conditions hereof may be modified or waived, and this Agreement may not be amended, except in a writing signed by both parties. This Agreement may be executed by original or facsimile signature and in any number of counterparts.

IN WITNESS WHEREOF, and intending to be legally bound hereby, the parties have caused this Agreement to be duly executed by their authorized representatives as of the date hereof.

TRUSHOES, INC.   WONDERWEB, INC.

By: _____   By: _____

Its: _____   Its: _____

Date: _____   Date: _____

Figure 8.3 Sample website development and maintenance agreement. (continued)

EXHIBIT A
WORK-MADE-FOR-HIRE AGREEMENT

This Agreement ("Agreement") is made and entered into as of _____ 20 ____ by and between [NAME OF THIRD-PARTY CONTRACTOR] ("you") and Trushoes, Inc. ("Company") with respect to your engagement by and under the supervision of WonderWeb, Inc. ("Developer"), to render services in connection with Company's World Wide Web site and any projects related thereto and/or derivative thereof (the "Project"). In consideration of the terms and conditions set forth below, Company and you agree as follows:

1. You will provide the following services and/or products in connection with the Project: [DESCRIBE SERVICES AND PRODUCTS.] Any and all results, products, and proceeds of your services in connection with the Project, including but not limited to any and all of the foregoing, are hereinafter referred to as "the Work." The Work shall be provided by you in accordance with the instructions of Developer, shall be subject to the approval of Company and Developer exercisable in their sole discretion, and shall not contain any obscene materials.

2. As full compensation for your services, the Work and any and all rights granted or assigned to Company by you under this Agreement, Company will pay you [AMOUNT TO BE PAID] as follows: [SCHEDULE OF PAYMENTS] You acknowledge that payment to you by Company or by Developer on Company's behalf pursuant to this Paragraph 2 will constitute full and complete satisfaction of any and all payment obligations under this Agreement.

3. You acknowledge and agree that the Work is being specially ordered by Company and shall constitute a "work-made-for-hire" for Company under all relevant copyright laws. If, for any reason, pursuant to any relevant copyright laws, the Work or any element thereof shall ever be deemed not to be a work-made-for-hire for Company, you agree that this Agreement constitutes an irrevocable, perpetual assignment to Company and its successors and assigns of any and all of your right, title, and interest in and to the Work under any such relevant copyright laws, including but not limited to any and all worldwide copyrights and renewals, extensions, and restorations thereof. You hereby further transfer, convey, and assign to Company and its successors and assigns all other intellectual property rights in and to all elements of the Work, throughout the world, and in any language, including but not limited to any and all patent rights, rights of inventors and trademark rights. You hereby waive any so-called droit moral

Figure 8.3 Sample website development and maintenance agreement. (continued)

rights, moral rights of authors, and all other similar rights, however denominated throughout the world. You will, upon Company's request, execute, acknowledge, deliver, and/or record such additional documents as Company may deem necessary to evidence and effectuate Company's rights hereunder. You hereby grant Company the right, as your attorney-in-fact, to execute, acknowledge, deliver, and record in the U.S. Copyright Office or elsewhere any and all such documents that you fail to execute, acknowledge, deliver, and record. Company will have the right to use, at its option and in its sole discretion, your name, likeness, and biographical information to promote and advertise the Project or any other use of the Work. You acknowledge that Company will not be obligated to exercise any of the rights granted to Company herein or make any use of the Work.

4. You represent and warrant that (a) you have the full power and authority to enter into and to fulfill the terms of this Agreement and to grant the rights described herein; (b) you have not entered and will not enter into any agreements or activities that will or might interfere or conflict with the terms hereof; (c) the Work is and will be wholly original with you and not copied in whole or in part from any other work except materials in the public domain or supplied to you by Company; and (d) to the best of your knowledge, neither the Work nor the use thereof infringes on or violates any right of privacy or publicity of, or constitutes a libel, slander, or any unfair competition against, or infringes on or violates the copyright, trademark rights, or other intellectual property rights of any person or entity.

5. In the event of an actual or alleged breach of this Agreement, or under any other circumstances whatsoever, any rights and remedies you may have against Company or its successors or assigns will be limited to the right to recover damages, if any, in an action at law. You hereby waive any right or remedy in equity, including but not limited to any right to rescind or terminate Company's rights hereunder or to seek injunctive relief of any kind.

6. Any information about the Project disclosed to you by Developer and/or Company during the course of the performance of this Agreement is confidential information that is proprietary to Company. You agree to maintain in strict confidence all such proprietary and confidential information, except only to the extent that such information is made publicly available or was known to you prior to any disclosure.

Figure 8.3 Sample website development and maintenance agreement. (continued)

7. You may not assign this Agreement or your rights hereunder, or delegate your obligations hereunder in whole or in part. Company may assign this Agreement or any or all of its rights hereunder to any person or entity and will be relieved of all its obligations to you hereunder to the extent that such obligations are assumed in writing by any such assignee.

8. Each party is an independent contractor, and this Agreement will not be construed as creating a joint venture, partnership, or agency relationship between the parties hereto nor will either party have the right, power, or authority to create any obligation or duty, express or implied, on behalf of the other.

9. This Agreement will be subject to and construed in accordance with the laws of the State of Florida applicable to agreements made and to be wholly performed therein, and is intended by the parties to be the final, complete, and exclusive expression of their agreement and understanding and supersedes all prior and contemporaneous contracts, representations, and understandings (written or oral) between the parties concerning the subject matter hereof. This Agreement may not be changed or modified except by a writing signed by both parties.

Please indicate your acceptance of and agreement to the foregoing terms and conditions by signing in the space provided below.

AGREED AND ACCEPTED:

_____

[CONTRACTOR'S NAME]

Date: _____

TRUSHOES, INC.   WONDERWEB, INC.

By: _____   By: _____

Its: _____   Its: _____

Date: _____   Date: _____

Figure 8.3 is a sample website development and maintenance agreement under which a manufacturer of athletic shoes has hired a third party to build and service a website to promote the manufacturer's products. This agreement is similar in many respects to the sample CD-ROM development agreement in Figure 8.1. For example, both agreements require that the developer deliver source code for the completed project, provide the contracting company with a license to use any "Developer Properties" (e.g., software authoring tools) incorporated into the project, and enter into work-made-for-hire agreements with any nonemployees hired on the project. Both agreements also include the usual ownership, representation and warranty, and indemnification provisions. One major difference between the two agreements, however, is that the website agreement requires the developer both to develop the site and to continue to carry and maintain the site on its computer servers, whereas the CD-ROM agreement is a pure development agreement under which the developer has no ongoing responsibilities (other than to correct any identified nonconformities) following final delivery of the project. The website developer's ongoing maintenance and support responsibilities are set forth in paragraphs I.B. and I.C. of the agreement.

Libel and Other Liability Issues on the Internet

Chapter 5 explained the basics of libel law as applied to conventional media productions. Those same basics apply to websites, with a few extra complexities. As suggested in the introduction to this chapter, one added complexity comes from the ability of websites to be accessed by individuals throughout the world. As a result, posting material on a website may constitute, in the view of some courts in some jurisdictions, a publication with the intent to distribute the material in any country where the website may be accessed. This in turn may subject an individual or company that posts potentially defamatory material to lawsuits in countries that have much broader libel laws than does the United States and much less protection for media defendants.

As of this writing, it is not yet clear how the laws that govern the jurisdiction of foreign courts and the application of foreign libel law will apply in such cases. With this in mind, producers of websites that may carry potentially libelous material (a category that includes any website that provides coverage of or commentary on current events, public figures, and celebrities) should consult with and have their sites reviewed by lawyers who are familiar with the current state of the law in this area. Producers of such sites should also consider posting a disclaimer like the one contained in Figure 8.4.

A related question is whether website operators and other online service providers may be held liable for the content of material that is placed on their websites by third parties. Some websites offer bulletin boards, discussion groups, forums, or chat rooms that permit the posting or exchange of material by site users. Although it may not seem fair to hold a website operator responsible for such postings, at least one court has held that an online service operator may be held liable for libelous statements made by a third party without the operator's knowledge. In that case, *Stratton Oakmont, Inc. v. Prodigy Services Company*,[7] a pivotal issue was whether Prodigy, the online service operator, retained editorial control over the site and removed material that it found inappropriate. The court determined that Prodigy had exercised this control, and that Prodigy therefore could be held liable as a "publisher" of the libelous statements. If Prodigy had acted, instead, as a mere "distributor or repository" that did not retain the right to edit or delete the statements, it could not have been held liable for the statements in a libel action.

Although the law in this area remains in a state of flux and development, the message of the Prodigy case is clear: If a website operator "polices" material posted by third parties on its site, the operator may be held liable for the content of those statements in libel, invasion of privacy, and other actions sparked by the statements.[8] Accordingly, website operators should tell visitors to their sites either that they do not police the content provided by third parties (preferably by displaying a disclaimer like that in Figure 8.4) or that they *do* police this material and will delete statements that appear libelous or are otherwise offensive. In the latter case, the website operator should follow through by regularly reviewing all such material and deleting items that are potentially libelous or that might otherwise subject the operator to legal action (including items that might violate the obscenity restrictions discussed next).

Transmitting Obscene or Indecent Material on the Internet

Chapter 9 discusses the legal restrictions on the transmission of indecent and obscene material over broadcast channels. The Internet has

Figure 8.4 General website legal information/disclaimer statement (to be posted prominently on the website).

IMPORTANT LEGAL INFORMATION: READ BEFORE YOU PROCEED!

Your use of this site is subject to important legal conditions and restrictions. If you are unable to accept and abide by one or more of the following conditions and restrictions, you should exit this site. By choosing to continue, you will be indicating your acceptance of and will be bound by all of these conditions and restrictions.

1. NO ASSURANCES OF PRIVACY. Some locations and features in this site give you the option of providing information or comments. You should assume that any such material that you provide is available for the world to see. Do not provide information or comments that you wish to remain private. The operator of this site accepts no liability for any use of information or comments by third parties.

2. COPYRIGHT AND TRADEMARK RESTRICTIONS ON USE OF SITE MATERIALS. Unless otherwise indicated, the entire contents of this site are copyrighted. You may download one copy of any page or portion of the site for your personal, noncommercial use. Any further downloading, copying, modification, distribution, or other use of any copyrighted material from this site without the site operator's express permission is not permitted and may leave you liable for copyright infringement. All trademarks, service marks, and logos used in this site are the property of the site operator or used with the permission of the owner. Your use of this site does not grant you any license or permission to use those trademarks, service marks, or logos.

3. WARNING AND DISCLAIMER IN CONNECTION WITH FORUMS, CHAT ROOMS, BULLETIN BOARDS, AND DISCUSSION GROUPS. The site operator does not control and accepts no responsibility for the contents of the forums, chat rooms, bulletin boards, discussion groups, or other areas on this site that allow input from the public. Those who choose to use these areas are instructed to refrain from posting offensive, obscene, or illegal material, including profanity, pornography, libelous or otherwise defamatory statements, inflammatory statements, or any material that may violate any criminal or civil statute. However, the site operator cannot guarantee that everyone will abide by this instruction. Consequently, you enter these areas at your own risk, and you should not enter if you may find such material objectionable, distressing, or otherwise harmful. Although the site operator does not regularly police material posted by the public, the operator reserves the right to remove any material that it determines, in its sole judgment, may be offensive, illegal, or otherwise

Figure 8.4 General website legal information/disclaimer statement (to be posted prominently on the website). (continued)

inappropriate. The site operator further reserves the right to deny or restrict access to this site to those who post such material. The site operator will cooperate with any law enforcement authority or court that, within the scope of its authority and jurisdiction, requests information regarding such postings.

4. OWNERSHIP OF MATERIAL THAT YOU SUBMIT. Any material or ideas submitted to this site becomes the property of the site operator and its related companies and may be used by them without restriction and with no compensation to the submitter. As a result, you should not submit ideas or material if you wish to retain ownership or control the distribution of such ideas or material.

5. NO ASSURANCES OF ACCURACY. The site operator tries to provide only accurate information on this site. However, the operator makes no representations, assurances, or promises with respect to the accuracy of the information that it provides. Any reliance on or use of the information provided by the operator on this site is at your own risk.

6. GENERAL DISCLAIMER OF LIABILITY; NO WARRANTIES. The site operator is not liable for any direct, indirect, incidental, consequential, punitive, or other damages arising from your access to or use of this site. Without limiting the foregoing, this site and all of its contents are provided to you "as is" without warranty of any kind, either express or implied, including but not limited to the implied warranties of merchantability, fitness for a particular purpose, or noninfringement to the fullest extent permissible under applicable law.

7. JURISDICTION. This site is operated and controlled from offices within the State of California, United States of America. Your use of this site is governed by the laws of the United States of America and the State of California. The operator makes no representation that the materials contained in the site are appropriate for use in other jurisdictions. Those electing to access this site from other jurisdictions are responsible for complying with local laws, to the extent that such laws apply. By using this site, you hereby agree that any dispute arising from or based upon your access to or use of this site will be subject to the exclusive jurisdiction of courts in Los Angeles, California, USA.

been subject to its own restrictions in this area, primarily in response to concerns that sexually explicit material on the Internet was too easily accessible to minors. Reacting to these concerns, Congress passed the Communications Decency Act of 1996 (CDA).[9] The CDA provides criminal penalties for any individual or entity that transmits indecent or obscene material by means of a "telecommunications device," knowing the recipient of such communications is younger than 18 years of age, or that uses an interactive computer service to display in a manner available to a person younger than 18 years of age any comment, request, suggestion, proposal, image, or other communication that, in context, depicts or describes, in terms patently offensive as measured by contemporary community standards, sexual or excretory activities or organs.[10]

In June 1996, a panel of federal judges in Pennsylvania upheld the grant of a preliminary injunction preventing the enforcement of the CDA provisions aimed at "indecent" materials.[11] The panel determined the law as applied to indecent content was overly broad; that is, enforcement of these provisions was likely to unduly restrict transmission of speech that is protected under the First Amendment. In June 1997, this ruling was upheld by the U.S. Supreme Court.[12] As a result, the providers and transmitters of sexually oriented content on the Internet may now be prosecuted under the CDA only if their materials satisfy the legal definition of obscenity.[13]

The problem for those who may be involved with such transmissions is that, while the Internet is inherently interstate and international, the legal definition of *obscenity* in the United States employs local "community standards," with the relevant community standard for federal prosecution being that in which the trial takes place.[14] Thus, given that information transmitted on the Internet may be received from any location in the United States, a party that posts or transmits sexually explicit material on the Internet risks prosecution under the CDA if the material would be considered obscene under the standards of any U.S. community. This fact may have a chilling effect on the transmission of sexually oriented materials over the Internet, in that information providers will be required to tailor their materials to meet the obscenity standard of the most conservative U.S. communities.[15] Various solutions have been proposed to address this concern, including the adoption of an Internet or cyberspace-specific standard of obscenity or a return to the older national standard.[16] Until such time, however, companies and individuals engaged in the transmission of sexually oriented material on the Internet should be aware that they risk criminal prosecution if their materials would be considered obscene under the standards of any U.S. community in which they can be received.[17]

Children's Online Privacy Protection Act

In response to concerns that children were especially vulnerable to privacy abuses on the Internet, Congress passed the Children's Online Privacy Protection Act (COPPA).[18] Enacted in 1998, this important legislation imposes a series of obligations and restrictions on operators of websites directed to children younger than age 13 that collect personal information online. Significantly, operators of general-audience websites that are not specifically directed at children but that have actual knowledge that they are collecting personal information from children younger than age 13 are also subject to COPPA.

Operators of websites covered by COPPA must (1) provide notice of their information collection practices; (2) obtain "verifiable parental consent" before collecting personal information from children (subject to several important exceptions); (3) provide parents with access to information collected from their children; and (4) maintain the confidentiality, security, and integrity of the information they collect. Finally, operators of covered websites may not condition a child's participation in a game, contest, or other online activity on the child's disclosing more personal information than is reasonably necessary to participate in the activity.

The Federal Trade Commission (FTC) is responsible for enforcing COPPA, with violations of the COPPA requirements being treated as unfair or deceptive practices under the Federal Trade Commission Act. The best way for media producers to stay informed about the current FTC rules implementing COPPA is to visit the commission's website at www.ftc.gov. Also, producers of online sites that are not intended for children younger than age 13 may want to make this clear through a notice on the site's home page and a statement within the site's legal information and disclaimer statement.

Obtaining Domain Names

If you want to operate a website on the Internet, you will need to register a domain name for the site. For example, IBM has registered www.ibm.com as the domain name for its site, and MTV has registered www.mtv.com for its site. The "www." prefix of every domain name identifies this as a location on the World Wide Web. The ".com" extension, also known as a top-level domain or TLD, indicates that this is a commercial site. Other extensions include ".edu" for sites operated by educational institutions, ".org" for sites operated by nonprofit organizations, and ".gov" for sites operated by government agencies.[18]

During the initial development of the World Wide Web, domain names were exclusively issued by a registration service operated by Network Solutions, Inc. (NSI), under a contract with the National Science Foundation.[19] Currently, however, domain names are issued by dozens of registration services worldwide. To ensure that the registration process goes smoothly, however, it is best to use a registration service accredited by the Internet Corporation for Assigned Names and Numbers (ICANN). A list of ICANN accredited registration services is available at www.internic.net.

A potential roadblock to the domain name registration process appears when a company finds that its name and trademarks are already registered as domain names by unrelated parties. In the early years of domain name registration, companies such as Coca-Cola and McDonald's were dismayed to discover that their key trademarks and trade names (e.g., www.coke.com, www.mcdonalds.com) were already registered as domain names by speculators with no connection to their companies. In several cases, the affected companies found it necessary to bring infringement suits or similar legal actions to force the speculators to relinquish the domain names.

One issue that arose in these cases is whether the use of a company's name or mark as a domain name by speculators is in fact a "trademark use" sufficient to support a claim of trademark infringement.[20] Most courts have concluded that domain names may be used in a trademark sense, so that trademark owners can bring infringement and related actions against parties that use trademarks as domain names without the trademark owner's permission.[21]

In 1999, ICANN adopted a Uniform Domain Name Dispute Resolution Policy (UDNDRP) intended both to deter disputes between trademark owners and domain name registrants and to address such disputes if they do arise. The UDNDRP first requires parties that are registering a domain name through an accredited registrar to represent and warrant that (1) all statements made in the registration agreement are complete and accurate; (2) the registration of the domain name will not, to the applicant's knowledge, infringe on the rights of any third party; (3) the applicant is not registering the domain name for an unlawful purpose; and (4) the applicant will not knowingly use the domain name in violation of applicable laws and regulations. The UDNDRP further requires all applicants to agree to submit to a "mandatory administrative proceeding" conducted by an approved "administrative dispute resolution services provider" in that event that, once the application process is complete and the domain name has been issued, a third-party complainant alleges that (1) the domain name is identical or confusingly similar to a trademark in which the complainant has rights; (2) the applicant has no rights or legitimate interests in the domain name; and (3) the domain name has been registered and is being used in bad faith. The complete text of the UDNDRP is available at ICANN's website, www.icann.org.

If you are developing a website for a company, first check to see if the company has registered one or more domain names. If it has, the company may direct you to use one of these as the domain name for the site that you are developing or to incorporate your website materials as part of an existing company site. If not, ask the company if it wants you to complete the domain name registration process on its behalf (keeping in mind, however, that you will be required to make certain representations and warranties on behalf of the company as part of the process). Because domain name registration has become intertwined with trademark registration and protection, you should also consult an attorney who is familiar with the company's trademark policies and procedures.

Public Performance Rights for Music

Chapter 6 explained public performance rights to musical works and the roles that the two major performance rights societies, ASCAP and BMI, play in licensing these rights. Transmission of a musical composition over the Internet constitutes a public performance of that composition. As a result, individuals and companies that operate websites that play or otherwise incorporate copyrighted musical compositions must license public performance rights to those compositions. The procedure for obtaining performance licenses is discussed in Chapter 6. Both ASCAP and BMI have license agreements that cover Internet performance of musical compositions.

Congress complicated the issue of public performance rights on the Internet by passing the Digital Performance Right in Sound Recordings Act of 1995 (the 1995 Act).[22] As explained in Chapter 6, performance rights historically had attached only to musical works (the song itself) and not to sound recordings comprising a recorded performance of the song. That changed with the 1995 Act, which established a limited performance right in sound recordings that are transmitted digitally over the Internet and other interactive, online services.

The 1995 Act seems to be directed primarily at "music-on-demand" and similar online services, and it is not yet clear how the new performance right established by the act applies to the use of sound recordings as soundtracks or background music on websites. To be safe, website developers should secure performance rights from the record company or other entity that owns the rights in the sound recording as part of the master recording license required whenever a sound recording is used as part of an audiovisual production. For more information about sound recordings and master recording licenses, see Chapter 6.

Guild Issues

As discussed earlier in this chapter, most of the major guilds have interactive agreements or side letters that govern use of guild performers and clips from guild productions in developing CD-ROMs. These same agreements and side letters also apply to the development of websites. For example, if you want to include clips from a SAG film on a website, you will need to adhere to the permissions and minimum payment requirements of the SAG interactive agreement. Similarly, if you want to use an AFTRA member to provide voiceover narration in connection with a website, you will need to satisfy the minimum scale wage and working conditions requirements of the AFTRA interactive agreement.

Unfortunately, the guild interactive agreements and side letters do not always anticipate all of the issues that can arise in using guild performers or clips from guild productions on websites. For example, under the AFTRA interactive agreement, paying scale wages or above to an AFTRA member "buys" a producer the right to use the member's performance in a single CD-ROM or other interactive product. If you want to reuse the performance in other productions or contexts, you will need to pay the member supplemental use fees. But the current AFTRA interactive agreement does not state what usage rights a producer receives when the production is a website that may be accessed by individual users thousands or even millions of times over the site's effective lifetime. Does the producer receive the right to use the performance on the website in perpetuity, or does the right terminate at some point?

When questions like this come up, as they always seem to do, your only recourse is to contact the relevant guild for an answer. Always ask the guild to provide its response in writing, so you have a record to retain as part of your production files. In the example just provided, AFTRA has stated on at least one occasion that the payment of guild scale or above and compliance with other guild requirements covers the right to use a member's performance on a website for one year. If this remains the rule, any use of the performance beyond one year would require paying the AFTRA member an additional fee.

Other Internet Issues

The Internet has sparked many additional legal concerns and controversies, too many to cover in any depth in a book on media production law. For example, many companies take orders for, rather than simply advertise and promote, products over the Internet. In addition, for products such as computer software that can be transmitted digitally, some companies ship orders directly to customers over the Internet. It is not yet clear, however, how the Uniform Commercial Code (UCC), the Statute of Frauds, and other laws that historically have regulated business contracts and the sale of goods apply to these transactions via the Internet.[23] As a result, there is added legal uncertainty and risk for both buyers and sellers doing business over the Internet.

One popular type of online contract is the so-called clickwrap agreement. In this type of contract, visitors to a website are asked to click on an "I agree" (or similarly phrased) button to indicate their assent to an online "terms of use" agreement (like the disclaimer shown in Figure 8.4) or to an agreement governing the purchase of goods or downloading of materials from the site. The validity of clickwrap agreements has been challenged in several cases, usually on the grounds that clicking on an "I agree" button does not constitute a sufficient indication of acceptance to form a binding contract. Increasingly, courts seem willing to conclude that clickwrap agreements are binding, as long as the individual is required to take an affirmative step, such as clicking on a button to indicate acceptance (rather than, for example, indicating acceptance by simply continuing to use the website, as called for in some website "terms of use" agreements).[24] As a result, website operators should require this sort of affirmative step whenever individuals are being asked to assent to the terms of any online agreement. Of course, website operators should also make sure that their online agreements contain the other essential elements of an enforceable agreement discussed in Chapter 2.

On another legal front, some members of Congress have become concerned that website operators may use data obtained online in ways that violate the privacy of consumers. This concern is based on the fact that many companies have begun to employ their websites as tools for collecting detailed information on potential customers for their products. For example, an automobile manufacturer might ask visitors to its website questions concerning their preferences in cars. The manufacturer might also ask visitors to provide their phone numbers, ages, mailing addresses, e-mail addresses, and other personal data that are of potential use in marketing and promotional campaigns. It is also possible for website operators to track who is visiting their site and to obtain certain other information without the visitors' knowledge.

As discussed earlier in this chapter, Congress enacted the Children's Online Privacy Protection Act (COPPA) to address existing and potential abuses of information collected from children by website operators. The House of Representatives has also considered legislation that would require businesses to notify all website visitors and obtain their consent before selling or reusing data collected online. In addition to its obligation to implement COPPA, the FTC has also gotten involved in the online privacy debate by seeking comments and recommendations on whether and to what extent the government should regulate the collection and dissemination of personal data on the Internet. With all of this legislative and regulatory activity, any company that collects information on the Internet should be sure to have its practices and procedures reviewed by an attorney who is familiar with the current status of the law in this area. This goes double for companies that obtain personal data through their websites by having visitors complete contest registration forms because contests and sweepstakes have become a heavily regulated area. The FTC's website at www.ftc.gov lists many of the current rules and regulations in this area.

Still another legal controversy on the Internet centers on the practice of "framing" the contents of one website within another site. Framing occurs when one website allows users to access the content of other websites, displaying that content within the first site surrounded by a border or frame containing advertising and other information provided by the operator of the first site. In February 1997, the *Washington Post* and several other news organizations (including CNN, Times Mirror, and Reuters) filed a suit against Total News, a website that serves as a gateway to the websites operated by these and other news vendors but that provides little content of its own. The plaintiff news organizations alleged that Total News's display and framing of their website content constituted, among other things, trademark and copyright infringement.[25] This case was watched closely by other practitioners of framing on the Internet, as well as by those concerned that the strict application of traditional intellectual property law to the Internet will restrict the growth and viability of this new medium. Under a settlement agreement reached in June 1997, Total News may continue to provide links to websites operated by news organizations to frame the content of their sites with advertising or other material generated by Total News.

Summary

- *What legal issues are unique to CD-ROM and website development?*
  In most respects, the same fundamental principles of media law that apply to conventional audiovisual productions also apply to the development of interactive CD-ROMs and websites. Producers of CD-ROMs and websites also need to be aware, however, of several concerns that are specific to these new programming platforms. This is particularly true for websites because the Internet raises important new concerns in areas such as libel liability, obscenity, and privacy that have become the focus of legislative and judicial activity around the globe. Both CD-ROM and website development add new twists to old issues, such as the use of existing film and video materials, music licensing, and the hiring of performers who are guild members.

- *What additional considerations must producers address when entering into production contracts with third parties to develop CD-ROMs or websites?* In addition to the standard production contract provisions discussed in Chapter 3, agreements for CD-ROM and website development should require the outside contractor to (1) meet milestone delivery dates that permit testing of the project at different stages of development; (2) license the hiring company for the right to use any developer properties and third-party materials (e.g., proprietary graphics or fonts, third-party software tools) incorporated into the project; (3) deliver final source code for the finished project; and (4) correct any nonconformities in the project as delivered and provide ongoing technical support. In addition, for website development and service contracts, the agreement should specify the terms under which the contractor will provide continuing service and maintenance for the site.

- *What rules govern the hiring of guild performers for and use of guild clips in interactive productions?* Most guilds have developed interactive agreements or interactive side letters that set forth the terms under which their members may participate in the development of CD-ROMs and websites. These same documents specify the permissions and payment process that producers must follow to use clips from guild productions in interactive projects. Producers are advised to contact the relevant guilds to obtain the most recent editions of their interactive agreements.

- *What libel liability issues result from posting statements on websites?* Websites may potentially be accessed by individuals throughout the world. As a result, posting potentially libelous statements on a website may constitute, for libel purposes, a publication of the statements in any country where the website may be accessed. This, in turn, may subject an individual or company that posts such statements to lawsuits in countries that have much broader libel laws than the United States and much less protection for media defendants.

- *To what extent can website operators be held liable for material posted on their sites by third parties?* The current state of the law in this area is uncertain. At least one court has held that a website operator that exercises editorial control over locations (e.g., bulletin boards, discussion groups) where third parties can post material on a website may be held liable as a "publisher" of this material. Producers who plan to open their sites to such third-party postings should consult with an attorney who is familiar with the latest developments in this aspect of Internet law.

- *What laws govern the transmission of indecent and obscene material on the Internet?* In the United States, Congress has enacted the Communications Decency Act of 1996 (CDA), a law aimed at restricting the transmission of indecent and obscene material on the Internet. In 1997, the U.S. Supreme Court upheld a lower court order striking down the provisions of the CDA aimed at indecent content. As a result, website operators and others who transmit sexually explicit content on the Internet may now be prosecuted under the CDA only if that content satisfies the legal definition of obscenity. The problem remains, however, that the legal definition of *obscenity* in the United States employs local "community standards." Given that Internet transmissions may be received anywhere in the United States, a party that posts or transmits sexually explicit material on the Internet may be prosecuted under the CDA if the material would be considered obscene under the standards of any U.S. community.

- *What organizations issue domain names for websites?* Domain names (e.g., www.ibm.com, www.mtv.com) were initially issued exclusively by the InterNic service operated by Network Solutions, Inc. (NSI), under a contract with the National Science Foundation. Currently, however, domain names may be issued by dozens of registration services worldwide (although it is advisable to use an accredited registration service, a list of which is available at www.internic.net). Domain names are issued on a first-come, first-served basis. Applicants are required to submit a registration fee and to demonstrate that they have the technical capacity required to operate a site under that name. Applicants must also represent that the requested domain name will not interfere with the rights of any third party and that the domain name is not being registered for any unlawful purpose. In addition, applicants must agree to be bound by the terms of the Uniform Domain Name Dispute Resolution Policy (UDNDRP), instituted in 1999.

- *What rights must be obtained to use music on the Internet?* As explained in Chapter 6 in connection with conventional productions, producers must obtain a synchronization license to use an existing musical work (the song itself) and a master recording license to use an existing sound recording of that work in connection with audiovisual productions, including websites. In addition, because transmission over the Internet constitutes a public performance, producers must obtain public performance rights for any musical works featured in a website. Congress complicated the issue of public performance rights on the Internet by passing the Digital Performance Right in Sound Recordings Act of 1995, which established, for the first time under U.S. copyright law, a limited performance right in sound recordings (in addition to the existing performance right in musical works) transmitted over the Internet and other online services. It is not yet clear how the new performance right established by this legislation applies to the use of sound recordings as background or soundtrack music on websites. To be safe, website producers should secure performance rights as part of the master recording license obtained from the record company that controls the rights in the sound recording.

Notes

1. "Source code" contrasts with "object code," which is the machine-readable version of a computer program that is contained on CD-ROMs or other computer discs distributed for general use.

2. The one exception to this rule is materials that are in the public domain. As discussed in Chapter 4, however, it is not always easy to determine when copyrightable materials have fallen into the public domain.

3. For the reasons discussed in Chapter 6, using music clips in a CD-ROM presents special copyright concerns. For example, if you want to use a clip from a popular performer's recording of a popular song, you will require, at a minimum, a license from the party that owns the copyright in the sound recording (typically the record company) and a license from the party that owns the copyright in the composition (song) itself (typically a music publisher).

4. In addition to SAG and AFTRA, the Directors Guild of America and Writers Guild of America require payments for the use of clips from productions involving their members, with the rates for clip

use set in the current guild guidelines. The American Federation of Musicians also requires payment for clips featuring its members, but there are no set rates, and each payment is individually negotiated.

5. The Internet was born in 1969 as ARPANet (Advanced Research Project Agency Network), a computer communications network used by the U.S. Defense Department, defense contractors, and universities involved in defense-related research. For an overview of the history and organization of the Internet, see *ACLU v. Reno*, 929 F. Supp. 824 (E.D. Pa. 1996).

6. For those unfamiliar with the basic structure of websites, it may be helpful to think of each website as a stack of documents or pages, with the top document being the website's home page. The home page usually serves as a cover and table of contents for the other pages that make up the site. Each page has its own unique address or uniform resource locator (URL). The pages are connected to each other by hyperlinks, which are graphics or highlighted text into which the URL for another page has been embedded. By using the computer's mouse to click on a hyperlink, you connect or link to that other page (which may be located either in the current website or another site). For example, many newspapers operate websites in which the home page looks like the front page of the print version of the paper, complete with headlines and photographs. By clicking on a headline or photograph, you link to the page that contains the complete story for that headline or photograph. From that page, you can link back to the home (front) page or to pages containing related stories.

7. *Stratton Oakmont, Inc. v. Prodigy Services Company*, 23 Media L. Rep. 1794, 1995 WL 323710 (N.Y. Sup. Ct.). This decision was a ruling on the plaintiff's motion for partial summary judgment. The case ultimately settled in October 1997.

8. The Telecommunications Act of 1996, Pub. L. No. 104–104, 100 Stat. 56, does include provisions that appear to limit the liability of website operators for certain statements made by third parties. The website operator may still be held liable, however, if it knew or had reason to know that potentially libelous statements were posted on its site.

9. The Communications Decency Act was included as Title V of the Telecommunications Act of 1996, Pub. L. No. 104–104, Feb. 8, 1996, which amends Title 47 of the U.S. Code.

10. Telecommunications Act of 1996, Pub. L. No. 104–104, §§ 502, 110 Stat. 56, 133–34 (amending 47 U.S.C. §223).

11. *ACLU v. Reno*, 929 F. Supp. 824 (E.D. Pa. 1996).

12. *Reno v. ACLU*, 117 S.Ct. 2329 (1997).

13. In addition to prosecution under the CDA, parties that transmit obscene material on the Internet may be fined or imprisoned under 18 U.S.C. § 1465, which criminalizes the interstate transportation of obscene material for sale or distribution. See *U.S. v. Thomas*, 74 F.3d 701 (6th Cir. 1996). Moreover, under the CDA and other federal statutes, Internet information providers may be held criminally liable for transmitting child pornography. See 18 U.S.C. § 2252(a)(1)(A).

14. See *Miller v. California*, 413 U.S. 15, 25–34 (1973).

15. See, for example, Debra D. Burke, "Cybersmut and the First Amendment: A Call for a New Obscenity Standard," 9 HARV. J. L. & TECH. 87 (Winter 1996); Cass R. Sunstein, "The First Amendment in Cyberspace," 104 YALE L. J. 1757 (May 1995); Dennis W. Chiu, "Obscenity on the Internet: Local Community Standards for Obscenity Are Unworkable on the Information Superhighway," 36 SANTA CLARA L. REV. 185 (1995); Robert F. Goldman, "Note: Put Another Log on the Fire, There's a Chill on the Internet: The Effect of Applying Current Anti-Obscenity Laws to Online Communications," 29 GA. L. REV. 1075 (Summer 1995).

16. See *Jacobelli v. Ohio*, 378 U.S. 184 (1964).

17. Because materials transmitted on the Internet may be received worldwide, an information provider, in theory, may be held liable under the obscenity laws of any nation, assuming that nation could satisfy jurisdictional and venue requirements.

18. Children's Online Privacy Protection Act, 15 U.S.C. §6501 *et. seq.* (1998).

19. InterNic can be reached on the Internet at www.internic.net.

20. For more information about how trademarks are established and registered, see Chapter 9.

21. See *Panavision Int'l LP v. Toeppen*, 945 F. Supp. 1296 (C.D. Cal. 1996). See also *Planned Parent Fed'n. v. Bucci*, 1997 U.S. Dist. Lexis 338 (S.D.N.Y 1997); *Digital Equip. Corp. v. Alta Vista Tech., Inc.*, 960 F. Supp. 456 (D. Mass. 1997); *Cardservice Int'l, Inc. v. McGee*, 950 F. Supp. 737 (E.D. Va. 1997); *Comp Examiner Agency, Inc. v. Juris, Inc.*, 1996 U.S. Dist. Lexis 20259 (C.D. Cal. 1996).

22. Public Law 104–39 (1995) (amending Title 17 of the United States Code).

23. See Geanne Rosenberg, "Legal Uncertainty Clouds Status of Contracts on Internet," NEW YORK TIMES (July 7, 1997), p. C3.

24. See *I. Lan Systems, Inc. v. Netscout Service Level Corp.*, 2002 Lexis 209 (D. Mass. 2002); *Register.com, Inc. v. Verio, Inc.*, 126 F. Supp. 2d 238 (S.D.N.Y. 2000). Contrast these two cases, which confirmed the enforceability of clickwrap agreements that required users to indicate acceptance through an affirming action, with *Specht v. Netscape Communications Corp.*, 150 F. Supp. 2d 585 (S.D.N.Y. 2001), in which the court denied to enforce an online contract that did not require an express affirming action by the user.

25. *Washington Post Co. v. Total News, Inc.*, No. 97 Civ. 1190 (S.D.N.Y., filed Feb. 20, 1997). See also *Hard Rock Cafe Int'l (USA) v. Morton*, 1999 U.S. Dist. Lexis 13760 (S.D.N.Y. 1999); *Futuredontics Inc. v. Applied Anagramics Inc.*, 1997 U.S. Dist. Lexis 22249 (C.D. Cal. 1997), *aff'd* 1998 U.S. App. Lexis 17012 (9th Cir 1998).

9

Wrapping It Up: Protecting Your Finished Production

All of the creative work is complete, and you are in the process of wrapping up your production. Along with making sure that the program really is ready to display or distribute, you should do a final check to make sure that you have left no administrative or financial loose ends. As part of the wrap-up process, you should also take the time to give the production one last legal review.

At this point, if you have been following the guidelines presented in the preceding chapters, your production should be in solid shape. First, as discussed in Chapters 2 and 3, you should have obtained signed contracts covering your relationships with performers, writers, crew members, and other production personnel. In addition, your production's legal portfolio should include the following:

- Records of any footage, clips, text, or still images acquired from outside sources and signed agreements confirming your rights to use these materials (Chapter 4)
- All city, county, state, and federal permits and licenses issued during the production (Chapter 5)
- Signed releases from all persons depicted in the program (Chapter 5)
- All location releases obtained from private property owners (Chapter 5)
- Any insurance policies purchased for the production (Chapter 5)
- All necessary agreements and records covering your use of copyrighted music materials (Chapter 6)

- Copies of any forms or records related to your use of guild or union performers or technicians (Chapter 7)

As discussed in Chapter 5, you should also check your production for any potentially libelous statements and for any depictions that might violate someone's right of privacy or publicity. If you spot any questionable material, consult a lawyer who is familiar with these areas of media law. If you have obtained an errors and omissions insurance policy for the production, the policy may require, as a condition of coverage, that a lawyer review the final production for such potentially problematic material.

As you are wrapping up a production, it is also time to think about registering your newly created property with the U.S. Copyright Office. In addition, for certain types of productions, you may want to look into registering the title of the program as a trademark with the U.S. Patent and Trademark Office. If you will be making arrangements with a third party to distribute copies of the program, you will also need to consider how to protect your rights through a distribution agreement. Finally, if your production will be broadcast, you should be aware of several federal regulations affecting the content of programs broadcast on U.S. television stations.

Copyright registration, trademarks, broadcast regulations, and distribution agreements are discussed in detail later in this chapter. First, though, you should think about how to store and protect all of those production records and legal documents that you have been collecting.

Keeping Your Records Straight

Now that you have carefully collected all necessary production records and legal documents, what should you do with them? Like all important papers, your production records and documents should be stored in a secure location. It also makes sense to make a duplicate set of your records and to store them in a separate location. In addition, if an attorney was involved in preparing any contracts or other legal documents, the law office should retain copies. Your attorney should do this as a matter of course, but it never hurts to confirm that the law office has kept copies.

The best place to store your copies of records and legal documents is in a fireproof safe or file cabinet. Store the documents from individual productions in separate folders or sets of folders. In other words, do not mix the records from more than one production. Because questions usually come up on a production-by-production basis (e.g., "What was our arrangement with the scriptwriter on that United Foods project?"), storing the records from each production separately makes it much easier to find the documents you will need to answer questions when they do come up. Also, try to keep legal records and documents separate from other production paperwork (e.g., treatments, scripts, lighting designs). This will help limit the number of times people must rummage through the legal file—and reduce the risk that key legal documents will be misplaced in the process. As a general rule, try to limit access to these production files to as few people as possible.

If, like most producers, you use a personal computer to create contracts and other production documents, a few additional precautions apply. First, if you store your document files on a hard disk drive, be sure to back up all of your files on floppy disks, recordable CD or DVD media, or a tape backup system. As anyone who has experienced a hard disk failure can attest, backing up your files is one safety step that is definitely worth the time and effort. Second, be sure to store all of the document files for a particular production on a floppy disk, CD or DVD, or tape that is labeled with the name of the production. Then place this disk or tape in the folder that contains the printed versions of the documents. If you will be storing a second document folder at a separate location, make a backup copy of the floppy disk, CD or DVD, or tape for that folder, too.

Copyright Registration

Chapter 4 explained how copyright law prevents you from using other people's creative properties without their permission. Now that you have completed a creative property of your own, you will want to make sure that it is fully protected, too. In most cases, this means that you will want to look into registering your production with the U.S. Copyright Office, an office of the Library of Congress.

As discussed in Chapter 4, registration with the Copyright Office is not required for copyright protection. Under U.S. and international law, a work is considered copyrighted as soon as it is created, and failure to register the copyright does not diminish your exclusive rights of ownership in the work. Registration with the Copyright Office does confer several important benefits, however, including the right to sue infringers for statutory damages in addition to actual damages. Even more important, registration establishes an official record for the work, a record that you can use in court as evidence to support the validity of your copyright.

To Register or Not to Register

Before proceeding with the copyright registration process, you should determine whether registration really is necessary for the production in question. Although registration can never hurt, it may not be worth the effort for certain programs, particularly those with limited lifespans. For example, registration may not be worthwhile for a corporate video production that was developed for one-time-only display at a national sales conference or for a corporate production that is so specific to your company that it would be of limited interest or usefulness to potential infringers. As a general rule, the longer the potential lifespan of the production, the broader the planned distribution and display of copies, and the higher the reuse value of footage or segments from the program, the more important it becomes to register the production with the U.S. Copyright Office.

Even if you decide not to register a production, be sure to retain records that show when the production was created, and always make sure that a full copyright notice, including the date of publication, appears on each copy of the program that you distribute. Even though a copyright notice no longer is required as a condition of continued protection, including it will provide evidence of the date that your production was created if, down the line, you are challenged by someone who claims that your program violates the copyright of material that actually was created at a later date. A copyright notice also reminds potential infringers that your program is not in the public domain, so they are not free to distribute copies of or borrow footage from the production without your permission. In addition, a copyright notice helps deter the defense of "innocent infringement" if you do bring an infringement claim against someone that has violated your copyright. For a more detailed discussion of copyright notices, see Chapter 4.[1]

Before You Register: Determining Ownership

You have decided that you do want to register your production with the Copyright Office. Before proceeding with the registration process (and before placing a copyright notice on the work), you must determine who actually owns the production. The registration application must be filed by the individual or group that owns the copyright or that owner's authorized agent.

Typically, the copyright on a media production is not owned by an individual but rather by the company that created it or the client who commissioned it. If the production was created by a video or audiovisual department within a corporation, the copyright almost always is owned by the corporation. If the production was created by an independent production house under contract with a client, the client usually will hold the copyright. In other words, most media productions are created as works-made-for-hire (a concept discussed in detail in Chapter 2), with someone other than the individual producer owning the copyright as author or assignee. This is especially true for corporate and other nonbroadcast productions. The copyright ownership question becomes much more complex when you move into the world of broadcast television and feature film production, in which several individuals and groups (e.g., the production company, the studio or distributor, the scriptwriter, the novelist on whose work the production is based, or big-name performers) sometimes share ownership in various components of the work. As discussed in Chapters 2 and 3, the ownership question should always be addressed in the contracts that define the relationships among the various groups involved in the creation of a media production.

In many cases, a production also incorporates material owned by others (stock footage, music, and so on). Unless the production is purely or primarily a compilation of preexisting material or is based on another work (as would be the case with a program based on a novel or play), you do not need to list all of these works and materials separately on the copyright registration form. You should, however, indicate in Section 6 of the registration form (Figure 9.1) that the production does include some preexisting materials, and you should retain the written agreements with the copyright owners that define your rights to use those materials or underlying work.

Figure 9.1 U.S. Copyright Form PA.

Figure 9.1 U.S. Copyright Form PA. (continued)

	FORM PA
EXAMINED BY	
CHECKED BY	
☐ CORRESPONDENCE Yes	FOR COPYRIGHT OFFICE USE ONLY

DO NOT WRITE ABOVE THIS LINE. IF YOU NEED MORE SPACE, USE A SEPARATE CONTINUATION SHEET.

PREVIOUS REGISTRATION Has registration for this work, or for an earlier version of this work, already been made in the Copyright Office?
☐ Yes ☐ No If your answer is "Yes," why is another registration being sought? (Check appropriate box.) ▼ If your answer is No, do **not** check box A, B, or C.
a. ☐ This is the first published edition of a work previously registered in unpublished form.
b. ☐ This is the first application submitted by this author as copyright claimant.
c. ☐ This is a changed version of the work, as shown by space 6 on this application.
If your answer is "Yes," give: **Previous Registration Number** ▼   **Year of Registration** ▼

5

DERIVATIVE WORK OR COMPILATION Complete both space 6a and 6b for a derivative work; complete only 6b for a compilation.
Preexisting Material Identify any preexisting work or works that this work is based on or incorporates. ▼

a

6

See instructions before completing this space.

Material Added to This Work Give a brief, general statement of the material that has been added to this work and in which copyright is claimed. ▼

b

DEPOSIT ACCOUNT If the registration fee is to be charged to a Deposit Account established in the Copyright Office, give name and number of Account.
Name ▼   **Account Number** ▼

a

7

CORRESPONDENCE Give name and address to which correspondence about this application should be sent. Name/Address/Apt/City/State/ZIP ▼

b

Area code and daytime telephone number   (   )   Fax number   (   )
Email

CERTIFICATION* I, the undersigned, hereby certify that I am the
Check only one ▶
☐ author
☐ other copyright claimant
☐ owner of exclusive right(s)
☐ authorized agent of _____
Name of author or other copyright claimant, or owner of exclusive right(s) ▲
of the work identified in this application and that the statements made by me in this application are correct to the best of my knowledge.

8

Typed or printed name and date ▼ If this application gives a date of publication in space 3, do not sign and submit it before that date.
                                                          Date
Handwritten signature (X) ▼
☞   x _____

Certificate will be mailed in window envelope to this address:
Name ▼
Number/Street/Apt ▼
City/State/ZIP ▼

YOU MUST:
• Complete all necessary spaces
• Sign your application in space 8
SEND ALL 3 ELEMENTS IN THE SAME PACKAGE:
1. Application form
2. Nonrefundable filing fee in check or money order payable to *Register of Copyrights*
3. Deposit material
MAIL TO:
Library of Congress
Copyright Office
101 Independence Avenue, S.E.
Washington, D.C. 20559-6000

Fees are subject to change. For current fees, check the Copyright Office website at www.copyright.gov, write the Copyright Office, or call (202) 707-3000.

9

*17 U.S.C. § 506(e): Any person who knowingly makes a false representation of a material fact in the application for copyright registration provided for by section 409, or in any written statement filed in connection with the application, shall be fined not more than $2,500.

Rev: June 2002—20,000 Web Rev: June 2002 ♻ Printed on recycled paper

U.S. Government Printing Office: 2000-461-113/20.021

Completing Form PA

Figure 9.1 shows Form PA from the U.S. Copyright Office, the form used for registering works of the performing arts. As defined by the copyright law, the performing arts category includes motion pictures, video productions (which the registration rules generally treat the same as motion pictures), and other audiovisual works. You can also use Form PA to register, as distinct works, treatments, scripts, and musical and other component pieces that underlie a production. Registering these pieces as separate works usually makes sense only when the copyright for the components is held by someone other than the owner that will be listed for the entire work or when they will be distributed separately (as when the script for a feature film is published in text form). Otherwise, a single registration will cover the work as a whole and all of its component parts.

When you apply to register a media production with the U.S. Copyright Office, you must always complete and file Form PA. Like most copyright office forms, Form PA is available online at www. copyright.gov. Other forms used in applying for copyright registration include Form SR (for registering sound recordings) and form TX (for registering books, manuals, and computer programs). If the production is a multimedia package that includes some combination of film, video, slide, sound, and print materials, it is not necessary to use separate forms to register each type of component as a distinct work. Instead, the entire multimedia kit can be registered as a single, integral work using Form PA. This registration will cover all of the component parts.

In Section 1 of Form PA, you must specify the title of the work, any previous or alternative titles, and the nature of the work. For nature of the work, indicate the type of production that you are registering: motion picture, television program, video program (intended for distribution on videocassette), slide/tape show, or the like.[2] It is not necessary to be too descriptive here. If the work is part of a series, you must register each episode or segment separately because each is considered a distinct work for copyright purposes. It is permissible, however, to group the segments on a single PA form, as long as you list each item that is being registered. If you are registering a multimedia kit, however, you should list the types of materials that compose the kit (e.g., "multimedia kit, including videotape and accompanying text").

Section 2 of Form PA is where you designate who owns the media materials you are registering. If the entire production was created as a work-made-for-hire, as is the case with many corporate productions, the employer or client for whom the work was created should be listed as the sole author and should file the registration form. But what if the production was not created as a pure work-made-for-hire? For example, what if one or more individuals is claiming a legitimate ownership interest in the work? If this is the case, you should list each of the individuals in the blanks labeled "name of author." Section 2 of Form PA has slots for listing three authors, and you can list more on separate sheets. In addition, in the blanks labeled "nature of ownership," you should indicate what each individual contributed to the work (e.g., script, original music, animated sequences, the novel on which the script was based).

Section 3 of Form PA asks you to indicate when the work was completed and when it was first published. Although the completion and publication of media productions can occur almost simultaneously, these dates are usually different. Under U.S. copyright law, the date of completion is defined as the point at which the work first appears in fixed form. For a video production, for example, this typically would be the point at which you have completed the original tape or DVD that you will use as the master for creating copies. The date of publication is defined, in most cases, as the point at which you actually begin distributing the copies.

In the case of a production created over an extended period, it is possible to register preliminary versions of the production that are fixed at a particular point in time. Just be sure to file a separate Form PA when the production is complete and indicate, in Section 5 of the form, that previous versions of the work had been registered. Along similar lines, it is also possible to register a completed work that has not yet been published. In this instance, simply leave the "date of publication" blank.

In Section 4 of Form PA, you must designate who is claiming the copyright for the work that is being registered. The copyright claimant is either the author of the work (which, in the case of a work-made-for-hire, is the employer or client for whom the work was created) or the individual or group to whom the original author has assigned or transferred the copyright. If the copyright was transferred to an individual or group that is now claiming ownership of the work, Form PA requires you to indicate how the transfer took place. For example, if the transfer occurred through a written contract with the original owner, as is often the case with media productions, you would simply type or write "by written contract" in the space provided. If the copyright was instead assigned to the claimant, indicate "copyright assignment" here.

As already mentioned, in Section 5 of Form PA, you indicate whether the work has been registered before. If the work was registered previously, you must check the appropriate box to explain why you are seeking another registration. Legitimate candidates for re-registration include productions that were registered in unpublished form and that are now published, productions for which the copyright claimant may have changed through a transfer of ownership following the original registration, and productions that are changed versions of a previously registered work. If the latter is the case, you must explain how the work has changed in Section 6.

Section 6 of Form PA applies to productions that are derivative works or compilations. It also applies to works that were registered in one or more previous versions. When completing Section 6, you must begin by identifying the preexisting copyrighted or public domain materials on which the work is based. Then you must explain what new material you have added to justify a claim of originality and the need for a new registration. For example, if your work is a television production based on a copyrighted short story, you would begin by providing the name of the short story in item 6a. Then, in item 6b, you would explain that your production is a "dramatization for television." Similarly, if you are registering a new version of a previously registered production, you would begin by providing the name of the previous version, even if it is the same as the name for the new version. Then, in item 6b, you would explain how the version you are currently registering differs from the previous version (e.g., "revisions to more than 10 scenes," "revisions to many scenes and three new scenes added").

Sections 7, 8, and 9 ask you to supply some additional information that will help the Copyright Office process your application. Be sure to indicate the correct address to which correspondence about your application and the registration certificate should be sent. This typically will be your business address or, if you use an attorney on copyright matters, your attorney's address. If you or your company has an account with the Copyright Office and you want the copyright fee to be charged to that account, complete the deposit account item in Section 7 of the application form.

Filing for Registration

Once you have completed Form PA, you are ready to file for registration with the Copyright Office. Along with your completed Form PA, you must submit a check or money order for the designated (currently $30) processing fee (unless you have indicated on Form PA that you are charging the fee to your deposit account). You also must submit the required "deposit materials."

Under U.S. copyright law, producers of motion pictures and videotapes that are published with a copyright notice are required to send the Copyright Office both one complete copy of the film or tape and a written description of the contents. You must submit these deposit materials within three months of publication (the date at which you begin distributing copies of the work), regardless of whether you plan to register the work. Because you must make the deposit anyway, however, it makes sense to submit the required materials along with Form PA and your registration fee. If you submit the materials outside of the registration process and then decide to register the production at a later date, you will have to deposit an additional copy.

The Written Description

For most nonbroadcast productions, a brief summary of the program is sufficient as the written description required to be submitted with your registration. For major television productions, however, the description submitted for deposit should include a shooting script, continuity, or some other complete production document that provides a full accounting of the work.[3] The written description for television programs should also include the following information:

1. The title of the work. If the work is part of a series, both the continuing title and the episode title and/or number, if any, of the particular episode, installment, or segment
2. A statement of the nature and general theme of the work and the summary of its plot or contents
3. The date when the production was fixed (generally when filming or recording and editing were completed). If the production consists of an authorized video recording of a live television program made simultaneously with the

telecast, the description should make this clear and should contain information about the telecast
4. If the work has been transmitted on television, the date of the first telecast
5. The running time
6. The credits appearing on the work, if any

Of course, you are free to include other information that will help identify and distinguish your production.

Submitting a Copy of the Work

Along with the written description, you must submit a copy of the production to the Copyright Office (which, as discussed later, will then submit the copy to the Library of Congress). Under the rules for registering copyrights, there are separate requirements for depositing copies of unpublished and published works. If the work is unpublished, you have a choice. You can go the full route and deposit a description and one complete copy of the production that contains all of the visual and aural elements that you want the registration to cover. Alternately, if you are unable to provide a copy of the work, you can opt to deposit what the Copyright Office calls "identifying material." If you go with this second option, contact the Copyright Office to determine what materials will be sufficient to satisfy the deposit requirement.

If you are registering a published motion picture or videotape, or if you have published (distributed) the production and are submitting the required copy outside the registration process, you do not have a deposit option. You must submit both the written description and a complete copy that represents the best edition of the production. The Copyright Office defines the terms *complete copy* and *best edition* as follows:

- A copy is *complete* if it is clear, undamaged, and free of splices and defects that would interfere with viewing the work.[4]
- The *best edition* is defined, in descending order of preference, as follows:
  1. Film
     - Preprint material, by special arrangement

  - 35 mm positive prints
  - 16 mm positive prints
2. Videotape
   - 1-inch open reel tape
   - Betacam SP
   - D-2
   - Betacam
   - Videodisk[5]

If it is not practical to submit the deposit (e.g., a 1-inch videotape) in the same package with Form PA and the registration fee, you can send the deposit separately. If you do this, make sure that the package contains a clear request that the deposit materials be held in connection with an application for registration that is being filed under separate cover.

Exceptions to the Deposit Rule

If fulfilling the deposit requirements will present severe problems for a producer, it is possible to apply for a waiver or exception under two provisions of the regulations: the Motion Picture Agreement and the procedure of special relief.

The first option, the Motion Picture Agreement, helps if you are able and willing to submit the deposit copy but you would like to get it back. By requesting and signing the Motion Picture Agreement, you can have your deposit returned to you, at your expense, after the copyright registration is complete. The deposit is subject to recall for addition to the permanent collection of the Library of Congress for a period of two years, however, and you must agree to resubmit a copy of archival quality if the Library of Congress exercises that option. For more information about the Motion Picture Agreement, write to the Copyright Office's Motion Picture, Broadcasting, and Recorded Sound Division (MBRS) at the following address: Library of Congress, MBRS, Attn: Reference Assistant, 101 Independence Avenue S.E., Washington, D.C. 20540-4805. You can also call the MBRS at (202) 707-5604.

The second option, special relief, is worth looking into if extenuating circumstances prevent you from submitting a deposit that satisfies the complete copy and best edition standards described previously. Special relief is considered on a case-by-case basis. To be considered, write to the Chief of the Examining Division of the Copyright Office at the Library of Congress address provided. In your correspondence, indicate that you are requesting special relief and provide a detailed description of the reasons for the request. The correspondence must be signed by or on behalf of the person applying for copyright registration.

The Film Collection of the Library of Congress

Although producers tend to view the copyright deposit requirements as burdensome, they do result in one significant, and largely unrecognized, benefit for media professionals. Most of the materials obtained through the deposit requirements are placed in the Library of Congress's film and video collection. Once they are entered into the collection, the materials can be screened by individuals who are conducting research for a publishing or production project. There are some restrictions governing access to the collection, however. Works from the collection can be viewed only at the library, and reproduction or loaning of materials is not permitted without the prior written consent of the copyright owner. In addition, access to the collection must be arranged in advance.

The Certificate of Registration

You have submitted a completed, signed Form PA to the Register of Copyrights. You have also submitted the required filing fee and the required deposit materials. Now what happens? The Register of Copyrights will review and, if everything is in order, approve your application. Then the Copyright Office will send you a Certificate of Copyright Registration. Although this piece of paper may not look like much, it will prove very valuable if you ever find yourself involved in an infringement action or some other dispute over ownership of the registered materials. For this reason, the Certificate of Registration should be stored in a secure place with your other production documents.

It is important to note that, in registering materials, the Copyright Office is not certifying their authenticity or originality, only that they existed on the date specified in the Certificate of Registration and that the ownership information from Form PA has been entered in the copyright records. If a production that you have submitted for registration includes material "stolen" from other works, for example, the Register of Copyrights will not know that, and it will go ahead and issue a Certificate of Registration anyway. At a later point, however, the owners of the materials that you have stolen may come after you with proof of their own, including their own Certificate of Registration and copies of the original materials, to show that you used their work illegally. If they prove their case, the Copyright Office may also come after you for failing to disclose your use of previously copyrighted materials on the registration form, an offense that can subject you to substantial fines.

Protecting Titles through Trademarks

As you know, copyright law protects the content of your production—the sounds and images that make up the program—from unauthorized use. But what about the title of the production? For example, if you produced an executive exercise program called "The No Sweat Workout," would copyright law prevent someone else from using the same name for another production?

First the bad news: Under copyright law and the rules of the Copyright Office, names, titles, and short phrases or expressions are not subject to copyright protection. In other words, nothing in the copyright statute or the copyright office regulations would prevent other producers from stealing your terrific title. Now for the good news: Although copyright law cannot help, you may be able to protect your title by turning to another area of intellectual property law—trademark law.

What Is a Trademark?

A *trademark* is a "word, phrase, symbol, or design, or a combination of words, phrases, symbols, or designs that identifies and distinguishes the source of the goods or services of one party from those of another."[6] In other words, a trademark is a name design or logo that helps establish an identity for a product and that distinguishes the product from its competition. Examples of well-known trademarks include Xerox® (for copiers and other office equipment), Kodak® (for film and photographic equipment), Dolby® (for a noise-reduction system used in audio equipment), and Coppertone® (for suntan lotion). When the mark distinguishes a service rather than a product (e.g., AutoExpress[SM] for a fast check-out service for rental cars), it is called a service mark.

When a trademark appears in print, it is usually accompanied by the ™ or ® symbol. The ™ indicates that the mark is in the process of being registered or that the owner intends to register it. The ® indicates that federal registration has been secured and that the mark is now a registered trademark.

What Are the Sources of Trademark Law?

In the United States, trademark law is governed by a mix of common law and state and federal statutes. This contrasts significantly with copyright law, which is governed by a single federal statute: the Copyright Act of 1976. The difference derives from the U.S. Constitution, which specifically gives Congress the power to grant and govern copyrights and patents, but which includes no comparable provision for trademarks. As a result, Congress has had to approach trademarks less directly, through its constitutional power to regulate interstate commerce. This situation has limited federal jurisdiction primarily to regulating the interstate use of trademarks, a limitation that left the door open for the state courts and legislatures to play a continuing role in shaping trademark law.

The federal trademark statute is the Trademark Act of 1946, known as the Lanham Act. The Lanham Act defines the types of names that can benefit from federal trademark protection, the scope and duration of that protection, and procedures for federal registration of trademarks. In the United States, registration and other federal trademark procedures are administered by the Patent and Trademark Office (PTO) of the U.S. Department of Commerce.

On November 16, 1988, Congress passed the Trademark Law Revision Act of 1988, a comprehensive revision of the Lanham Act. One of the major changes introduced by the 1988 legislation is its provision for registering a trademark before the mark has actually been used in interstate commerce. For more information, see the section on the federal trademark registration process that appears later in this chapter.

Individual states also have their own trademark laws. In most cases, the state laws and registration procedures parallel the federal trademark provisions, with trademark status being granted on a "first-use" basis to qualified trade names. In other words, at both the federal and state levels, the first person or company that uses a product name has the right to claim the name as a trademark, as long as that name is sufficiently distinct from other existing marks. However, the PTO and the courts have been kept busy over the years trying to sort out exactly what constitutes first use and a distinct mark. Through their involvement in these and related issues, the state and federal courts have created a considerable body of case law in the areas of trademarks and unfair competition.

Trademark registration at the state level can play a significant role in establishing the first use of a product name and in protecting the titles of products and services that are distributed only within the boundaries of a particular state. Because most products, including most media productions, are distributed across state lines, however, anyone who is serious about trademarking a name or title should probably pursue federal registration. Most of the discussion that follows focuses on the federal trademark regulations and registration procedures. Information about a state's trademark laws can be obtained from the agency responsible for registering corporations (usually the Secretary of State's office) or regulating commerce within that state.

Trademarking the Titles of Creative Works

What types of names can be registered for federal trademark protection? For manufactured goods, the rules are clear and straightforward. With few exceptions, almost any name that distinguishes a company's manufactured products is eligible for federal trademark registration, as long as the product has been sold in interstate commerce or there is a bona fide intent to sell the product in interstate commerce, and as long as the PTO does not conclude that the mark is confusingly similar to an existing trademark in the same or a closely related category of products (e.g., clothing, games and toys, medical apparatus).

The trademark rules are less clear-cut when it comes to registering the titles of books, media productions, and other creative works. One intent of trademark law, as it has evolved, is to protect the names of goods and services that are likely to have a lasting lifespan in the marketplace. In other words, trademark regulations assume that the titles of products and services need to be protected because they attempt to establish and maintain an identity in a marketplace that is often crowded with competing goods and services. There also is a recognized need to protect marks that are used to label entire lines of products (e.g., Macintosh® computers, Bic® pens), so companies can have a reasonable opportunity to recover the investments they have made in developing and establishing a product line.

As products go, most creative properties are fairly ephemeral. For example, most individual books and media productions go into and out of distribution in a matter of a few years. This means that, if you went ahead and tried to register the title of a book or production as a trademark, it might well be on its way out of distribution by the time the registration was issued. This is significant because continued use of the mark in commerce is a requirement of continued trademark protection. Once you have registered a trademark, you must continue to use it or you will lose it.

Also, although a good title can help sell a creative work, the title usually is not the essential feature that distinguishes one creative product from another in the marketplace. For example, if you produced a film and called it *Casablanca*, it is unlikely that many people would buy a ticket to your film assuming that they were going to see the Humphrey Bogart original—unless you were also guilty of some serious false advertising. However, if you manufactured a washing machine and distributed it under the Maytag or Westinghouse label, you might well cause considerable confusion in the marketplace for major appliances. In other words, media productions and other individual creative properties are not like washing machines, microwave ovens, or any other type of product for which brand-name recognition often plays a major role in the purchasing decision. As a result, because there is less threat of confusion in the marketplace for media productions, there is less perceived need to protect the names of creative properties through trademark registration.[7] In addition, the PTO has long held the position that the title of an individual creative work is inherently descriptive of that work. As discussed later in this chapter, marks that are primarily descriptive of particular goods or services are usually not eligible for trademark registration.

For these and other reasons, the PTO is usually reluctant to grant federal trademark protection to the titles of individual media productions or other creative works. It generally is willing, however, to register the name of a series of media productions, books, or other intellectual properties. This means, for example, that, although you probably would not be allowed to trademark the title "No Sweat Workout" if it was attached to just one exercise video, you probably could trademark the title if it covered a series of programs that would have an extended lifespan in the marketplace (e.g., "The No Sweat Workout: Original Classic Edition," "The No Sweat Workout: Low Impact Edition," "The No Sweat Workout: No Impact Edition"). It would also be possible to protect the title by registering it in connection with its use on manufactured merchandise (a possibility if, for example, you are marketing a line of executive exercise clothing called No Sweat Sweats alongside your "No Sweat Workout" videos). The increasing importance of film- and television-related merchandising has resulted in film and television producers becoming increasingly aware and protective of the trademarks associated with their productions (e.g., *Star Wars, Star Trek*, "The Simpsons," etc.).

For most media productions, then, registering the title as a trademark really is not an option unless the production is part of a series of programs sold under the same title, or unless you also are planning to use the name on manufactured merchandise or other production-related products. Even if your title is not eligible for federal trademark registration, however, it might qualify for protection under state statutes and case law governing trademarks and unfair competitive practices. In addition, you may be able to register a particular design or logo that is used in connection with a production or title, and you might want to register the name of your production company. For more information about the criteria that determine whether it makes sense to try to register for federal trademark protection, see the section that follows.

The Federal Trademark Registration Process

You have decided that the title "No Sweat Workout" is catchy and potentially valuable enough to be worth protecting in connection with videos and merchandise, and you would like to register it as a federal trademark. How do you go about it? As a first step, you should evaluate whether trademark registration is really worth the effort. As the next step, assuming that you decide to proceed, you will need to conduct a search to determine if the name, or a similar name, is already trademarked or being used by someone else in the same or a closely related category of goods or services. Then, if you find that your title is unique, you will need to fill out and file the appropriate registration forms with the Patent and Trademark Office.

Once you file for federal trademark registration, be prepared to wait. It can take six months or more for an initial ruling from the

PTO and a year or more for the full registration process to run its course.

Step 1. Determining If Trademark Registration Is Worth the Effort

Earlier in this chapter, the section on copyright registration warned that, for some productions, copyright registration might be more trouble than it is worth. This is even more true for trademark registration. First, compared to copyright registration, the federal trademark registration process is more complicated and costly. Second, even if you complete the application process, the PTO may ultimately rule against your application. As discussed earlier, as a general rule, only titles that cover a series of productions or that are used in connection with merchandise materials (and that satisfy the other registration requirements) are eligible for trademark protection.

For these reasons, you should begin by asking if your title meets the minimum eligibility requirements for registering the title of a creative work. Does the title cover a series of programs? Is it used on merchandised materials? If neither is the case, you should probably forget about proceeding with trademark registration because your title probably is not eligible for federal trademark registration. If you feel that yours is a special case and you still would like to proceed, it would pay, at this point, to discuss matters with an attorney who specializes in trademark law. The attorney should be able to tell you if yours is a special enough case to stand a chance of being made an exception to the PTO's general rules.

Even if your title meets the minimum eligibility requirements, federal trademark registration may not necessarily be the right route for you. If you proceed with registration, you will need to take the time or spend the money to conduct a trademark search. You will also need to determine whether your title is distinct and protectable enough to withstand both the scrutiny of the PTO and challenges from other trademark holders. This determination is best made with counsel from a trademark attorney—and such counsel costs money. Finally, once you have registered the mark, you will need to make sure that you follow all of the proper procedures to guarantee that the trademark retains its protected status.

To decide whether registration is worth this effort and expense, you need to assess what the title truly is worth to you. Do you have definite plans to continue developing programs or materials that use the title? Will the programs or materials enter a market in which a brand name is important? Will you be using the title to identify Internet-based sites or services? In other words, how much do you stand to gain from trademarking the title, and what do you stand to lose if you do not register it?

As you are making this assessment, keep in mind that federal trademark registration is not the only way to protect a title. You can look into registering the mark at the state level, for example, and many states have passed unfair competition laws that will prevent others from simply stealing your mark. In fact, you do not have to register the trademark to enjoy many of the protections provided by federal trademark law. Registration with the PTO does provides several advantages, however, including the following:

- The right to sue in federal court for trademark infringement, and the right to recover profits, damages, and costs (including the possibility of recovering treble damages and attorney's fees) through an infringement action
- Prima facie evidence of the validity of the registration, the registrant's ownership of the mark, and the registrant's exclusive right to use the mark in commerce in connection with the goods or services specified in the certificate
- "Constructive" notice of a claim of ownership (which eliminates a good-faith defense for a party adopting the trademark subsequent to the date of registration)
- The right to deposit the registration with U.S. Customs to stop the importation of goods bearing an infringing mark, and a basis for filing trademark applications in foreign countries.

Because other prospective trademark users will usually check the federal trademark listings before adopting a mark, registering your title with the PTO will also put out the word that the title is already in use. Getting the word out in this way will help deter others from adopting the same or a similar mark.

If you have determined that your title is eligible for federal trademark protection, and if the benefits of registration listed here outweigh the costs, proceed to step 2. If you decide not to proceed, you may still want to consider speaking with a trademark attorney to determine what protection might be available outside the federal registration process.

Step 2. Determining the Protectability of Your Title

Your title, "No Sweat Workout," covers a series of programs, so you know that it satisfies one of the key criteria for registering the titles of creative works. You also have decided that the title is valuable enough to justify the time and expense involved in registering the title with the PTO. The next step is to determine whether the title, in its present form, is distinct enough to be protected against challengers under U.S. trademark regulations.

In evaluating protectability, prospective trademarks are usually classified in one of four categories: generic marks, descriptive marks, suggestive marks, and arbitrary or coined marks. Under trademark law, generic marks receive the least protection, arbitrary marks receive the most protection, and descriptive and suggestive marks fall in between.

Generic marks are terms such as *automobile* and *computer* that encompass entire classes of goods and services. Common sense dictates that generic marks cannot be trademarked by any one company because doing so would prevent all other companies from using the generic term in describing their products. Think, for example, of what would happen if IBM were allowed to trademark the term *computer*. Not only would companies such as Apple Computer, Inc., and Compaq Computer, Inc., be required to change their corporate names, but they would also be reduced to calling their products data processing units, automatic calculating and display devices, or something similarly awkward. If your title is a generic name or a very general term such as Management Training or The Workout, the PTO will not allow you to register it as a trademark.

Descriptive marks are names such as One Coat for house paint or Quick Stop for convenience stores that describe the product or service in some manner. If a title is purely descriptive, it is usually ineligible for trademark protection. Descriptive titles can qualify for trademark protection, however, if they acquire a secondary meaning in the minds of customers (i.e., if through use of the mark by one company in connection with particular goods or services, customers come to associate the goods sold under that mark with the company). Superglue® for a brand of adhesive is one example of a descriptive mark that acquired sufficient secondary meaning to be eligible for registration on the principal trademark register.

Suggestive marks are names that, although they may include descriptive elements, do not directly describe the product or service.

Instead, suggestive marks use language that suggests some connection between the product and a particular image or quality. Irish Spring® soap and Arid® antiperspirant are examples of suggestive trademarks. Most suggestive marks are strong candidates for trademark protection, with no requirement that the mark acquire secondary meaning in the marketplace before registration is allowed to proceed.

As you might suspect, the exact boundary between descriptive and suggestive marks is difficult to define. In fact, the question of just where this boundary lies has been the basis of a continuing series of disputes between trademark applicants, who insist that their name or title is eligible for protection because it is suggestive, and the PTO or trademark challengers, who argue that the mark cannot be protected because it is descriptive. For example, the PTO might argue that your title, "The No Sweat Workout," is purely descriptive, whereas you might argue that the title is cute, clever, and poetic enough to be protectable as a suggestive mark.

The best way to guarantee that your name is eligible for federal trademark registration protection is to invent an arbitrary or coined mark: a name that carries little or no natural connection to the goods or services that it identifies. Although arbitrary and coined marks are sometimes considered together as a single classification, they are different. An arbitrary mark is a real word that acquires new meaning when it is applied to a product or business, as when Apple was applied to a line of computers. In contrast, a coined mark is an invented word that has no meaning except when it is used in connection with a product or business, as when UNISYS® was coined as the name for the new company created by the merger of Burroughs and Sperry Rand. Because they are based on invented words or connections, there is little chance that the public would confuse one arbitrary or coined mark with another. As a result, arbitrary and coined marks are the most protectable of all trademarks.

What do these definitions and distinctions tell a media producer who is attempting to trademark a title? First, if your title falls into the generic or merely descriptive category, it is probably not worth proceeding to the next step in the trademark registration process. If the title is a suggestive or an arbitrary or coined term, however, it is probably worth proceeding. If you believe that your title might fall on the boundary between descriptive and suggestive marks, or if you believe that you have a descriptive title that has acquired or may acquire secondary meaning, consider running the title by a trademark attorney.

An attorney can tell you whether your title is likely to pass the protectability test and, if it may not, how you might modify it to make it more protectable.

Step 3. Conducting a Trademark Search

You have determined that your title is eligible for federal trademark registration and that it is protectable. The next step in the registration process is to make sure that no one else is already using your title or a title that is close enough to yours to cause confusion. To find this out, you must conduct a trademark search.

Although you can conduct a trademark search yourself, many parties prefer to hire a professional search firm to do the job or a trademark lawyer who will take care of the search for them. If you prefer to complete some preliminary research yourself, you can conduct a search online using the PTO's Trademark Electronic Search System (TESS). Available through the PTO's website (www.uspto.gov), TESS contains more than 3 million records for pending, registered, and canceled or otherwise dead trademarks. TESS is not a particularly user-friendly system, however, and inexperienced users may find it difficult to conduct truly comprehensive searches. Another, more old-fashioned research option is to check your title against those listed in *The Trademark Register of the U.S.*, a print publication that is available in many large libraries. Even though *The Trademark Register of the U.S.* is updated annually, you should also check the *Trademark Official Gazette*, a weekly publication of the PTO, to see if any potentially conflicting marks have been recorded since the last published edition of *The Trademark Register*. You may also search registered and pending trademarks at the PTO's Trademark Public Search Library located in Arlington, Virginia, or at a Patent and Trademark Depository Library (PTDL). PTDLs are located throughout the country, and there is at least one PTDL in each state. Many PTDLs are housed within public or university libraries.

This sort of preliminary research can help rule out titles that are in obvious conflict with existing marks registered with the PTO. If your research indicates that there is no conflicting mark, however, you will probably still want to proceed with a full trademark search. Conducting the search through an attorney or directly with a trademark search firm[8] is advisable because you can be reasonably sure that a professional search will cover all of the relevant records, including the following:

- The files at the PTO, which include records of pending, issued, abandoned, expired, and canceled federal trademark registrations
- The trademark registers in each state
- Trade directories and telephone books, which will turn up uses of the mark that may not be covered by federal or state registration but that may be protected by common law rights

The report that results from a trademark search is simply a list of the known names that may conflict, in some way, with your title. Significantly, the report will include no recommendation as to whether the title is safe for you to use. Although you can review the report and decide on your own, this is one point at which it almost always pays to talk to an experienced trademark attorney. An attorney will be able to examine the report for you, evaluate any conflicting titles, point out any potential problems that you might have missed, and recommend ways that you could change your title to avoid trouble.

Step 4. Filing the Trademark Registration Form

Your preparatory research is complete. You have determined that your title is eligible for federal trademark registration and that it is protectable. You have also determined, through a trademark search, that no conflicting titles appear to be in use. Does this mean that you are finally ready to register the trademark? Almost. To file the registration forms with the PTO, you will need one more item: evidence that you have either shipped your product across state lines or a sworn statement that you have a bona fide intent to do so.

Under the original Lanham Act, you could not file to register a product name as a trademark until the name had been used in interstate commerce. This meant that you had to wait until you had sold the product across state lines before you could even begin the trademark registration process, a wait that could prove scary if you had invested heavily in the production, packaging, and marketing of a new product.

The Trademark Law Revision Act of 1988 changed this by establishing a two-track trademark application system based on either "intent to use" or "actual use" of the mark. Under the new system, trademark applicants who have a bona fide intent to register a product name as a trademark can, in effect, reserve the name by filing a trademark application before the product is actually released.

How will the PTO know if your application is based on a bona fide intent to use the mark? In most cases, the PTO will simply take your word for it once you sign and file the application, which must include a declaration or other sworn statement verifying your intent to use the mark. Once the PTO approves your intent-to-use application, however, you will eventually need to show that you have gone ahead and used the mark in interstate commerce or that you still have definite plans to do so. The PTO will not actually register a mark that was filed under the intent-to-use procedure until you submit an Allegation of Use form and a specimen showing that the product bearing the name has been sold in interstate commerce.

Of course, you can still register the old, actual use way, waiting until your product has actually been shipped in interstate commerce and then applying to the PTO. In either case, you will need to file a trademark application form. The PTO recommends that you file the application form directly over the Internet using the Trademark Electronic Application System (TEAS) available at www.uspto.gov. Filing through TEAS has several advantages, including online help explaining each section of the application and a validation function that identifies missing information. If you file through TEAS, you will also receive an immediate filing receipt by e-mail that contains the assigned application serial number and a summary of the application. If you prefer not to use TEAS, you can file the traditional way using the paper form shown in Figure 9.2.

Along with the electronic or paper application form, the filing must include the following:

- A drawing of the mark
- Specimens of the mark showing actual use in connection with goods and services (assuming that you are filing based on actual use of the mark rather than an intent to use the mark)
- The filing fee indicated on the application form (currently, $325 for each class of goods/services identified in the application)

Notice that the application form requires you to indicate whether you are filing based on actual use of the mark in interstate commerce or your intent to use the mark. If you are filing an intent-to-use application, you need not provide specimens at this time. As discussed later, however, you will need to include the specimens when submitting the follow-up form required by the PTO.

Figure 9.2 U.S. Patent and Trademark Office Trademark or Service Mark Registration Form.

TRADEMARK/SERVICE MARK APPLICATION, PRINCIPAL REGISTER, WITH DECLARATION	MARK (Word(s) and/or Design)	CLASS NO. (If known)

TO THE ASSISTANT COMMISSIONER FOR TRADEMARKS:

APPLICANT'S NAME:

APPLICANT'S MAILING ADDRESS:

(Display address exactly as it should appear on registration)

APPLICANTS ENTITY TYPE: (Check on and supply requested information)

	Individual - Citizen of (Country):
	Partnership - State where organized (Country, if appropriate): _____ Names and Citizenship (Country) of General Partners: _____
	Corporation - State (Country, if appropriate) of Incorporation:
	Other (Specify Nature of Entity and Domicile):

GOODS AND/OR SERVICES:

Applicant requests registration of the trademark/service mark shown in the accompanying drawing in the United States Patent and Trademark Office on the Principal Register established by the Act of July 5, 1946 (15 U.S.C. 1051 et. seq., as amended) for the following goods/services **(SPECIFIC GOODS AND/OR SERVICES MUST BE INSERTED HERE):**

_____

BASIS FOR APPLICATION: (Check boxes which apply, but never both the first AND second boxes, and supply requested information related to each box checked)

[ ]	Applicant is using the mark in commerce on or in connection with the above identified goods/services. (15 U.S.C. 1051(a), as amended.) Three specimens showing the mark as used in commerce are submitted with this application. • Date of first use of the mark in commerce which the U.S. Congress may regulate (for example, interstate or between the U.S. and a foreign country): _____ • Specify the type of commerce: _____ (for example, interstate or between the U.S. and a specified foreign country) • Date of first use anywhere (the same as or before use in commerce date): _____ • Specify manner or mode of use of mark on or in connection with the goods/services: _____ (for example, trademark is applied to labels, service mark is used in advertisements)
[ ]	Applicant has a bona fide intention to use the mark in commerce on or in connection with the above identified goods/services. (15 U.S.C. 1051(b), as amended.) • Specify intended manner or mode of use of mark on or in connection with the goods/services: _____ (for example, trademark will be applied to labels, service mark will be used in advertisements)
[ ]	Applicant has a bona fide intention to use the mark in commerce on or in connection with the above identified goods/services, and asserts a claim of priority based upon a foreign application in accordance with 15 U.S.C. 1126(d), as amended. • Country of foreign filing _____ • Date of foreign filing: _____
[ ]	Applicant has a bona fide intention to use the mark in commerce on or in connection with the above identified goods/services and, accompanying this application, submits a certification or certified copy of a foreign registration in accordance with 15 U.S.C 1126(e), as amended. • Country of registration: _____ • Registration number: _____

NTOE: Declaration, on Reverse Side, MUST be Signed

PTO Form 1478 (REV 6/96)
OMB No. 0651-0009 (Exp. 06/30/98) There is no requirement to respond to this collection of information unless a currently valid OMB Number is displayed.

U.S. DEPARTMENT OF COMMERCE/Patent and Trademark Office

Figure 9.2 U.S. Patent and Trademark Office Trademark or Service Mark Registration Form. (continued)

DECLARATION

The undersigned being hereby warned that willful false statements and the like so made are punishable by fine or imprisonment, or both, under 18 U.S.C. 1001, and that such willful false statements may jeopardize the validity of the application or any resulting registration, declares that he/she is properly authorized to execute this application on behalf of the applicant; he/she believes the applicant to be the owner of the trademark/service mark sought to be registered, or if the application is being filed under 15 U.S.C. 1051(b), he/she believes the applicant to be entitled to use such mark in commerce; to the best of his/her knowledge and belief no other person, firm, corporation, or association has the right to use the above identified mark in commerce, either in the identical form thereof or in such near resemblance thereto as to be likely, when used on or in connection with the goods/services of such other person, to cause confusion, or to cause mistake, or to deceive; and that all statements made of his/her own knowledge are true and that all statements made on information and belief are believed to be true.

_____
DATE

_____
SIGNATURE

_____
TELEPHONE NUMBER

_____
PRINT OR TYPE NAME AND POSITION

INSTRUCTIONS AND INFORMATION FOR APPLICANT

TO RECEIVE A FILING DATE, THE APPLICATION MUST BE COMPLETED AND SIGNED BY THE APPLICANT AND SUBMITTED ALONG WITH:

1. The prescribed **FEE ($245.00)** for each class of goods/services listed in the application;
2. A **DRAWING PAGE** displaying the mark in conformance with 37 CFR 2.52;
3. If the application is based on use of the mark in commerce, **THREE (3) SPECIMENS** (evidence) of the mark as used in commerce for each class of goods/services listed in the application. All three specimens may be the same. Examples of good specimens include: (a) labels showing the mark which are placed on the goods; (b) photographs of the mark as it appears on the goods, (c) brochures or advertisements showing the mark as used in connection with the services.
4. An **APPLICATION WITH DECLARATION** (this form) - The application must be signed in order for the application to receive a filing date. Only the following persons may sign the declaration, depending on the applicant's legal entity: (a) the individual applicant; (b) an officer of the corporate applicant; (c) one general partner of a partnership applicant; (d) all joint applicants.

SEND APPLICATION FORM, DRAWING PAGE, FEE, AND SPECIMENS (IF APPROPRIATE) TO:

Assistant Commissioner for Trademarks
Box New App/Fee
2900 Crystal Drive
Arlington, VA 22202-3513

Additional information concerning the requirements for filing an application is available in a booklet entitled **Basic Facts About Registering a Trademark,** which may be obtained by writing to the above address or by calling: (703) 308-HELP.

This form is estimated to take an average of 1 hour to complete, including time required for reading and understanding instructions, gathering necessary information, recordkeeping, and actually providing the information. Any comments on this form, including the amount of time required to complete this form, should be sent to the Office of Management and Organization, U.S. Patent and Trademark Office, U.S. Department of Commerce, Washington, D.C. 20231. Do NOT send completed forms to this address.

The application form also requires that you describe the goods and services that will be sold or provided in connection with the mark and that you specify a class of goods and services. To do this, you must select from the 42 classes listed on the International Schedule of Classes of Services used by the PTO. For example, if your application is for the title of a broadcast television series, you would select class 41, which encompasses entertainment services. On the other hand, if your application is for the title of a series, such as "The No Sweat Workout," which will be distributed exclusively on videocassette and DVD, you could select class 9, which includes "apparatus for recording, transmission, or reproduction of sound or images" or class 41, which, in addition to encompassing entertainment services, also includes education, providing of training, and sporting and cultural activities. As this example shows, selecting the correct class is not always a simple matter.

The drawing of the trademark required with your application must show the mark as it is actually used in interstate commerce or as you intend it to be used. The PTO has fairly strict rules for formatting the drawing, particularly if you want to protect a specific depiction (e.g., type treatment, logo, design elements) of the trademark rather than simply the words that form the mark. Those rules are described in detail in the instructions that accompany the application form. If you are filing electronically through TEAS, the system will automatically generate a drawing for you in the proper form based on the information entered.

The PTO rules state that the specimens included with your application (or, in the case of an intent-to-use application, included with the Allegation of Use form filed later) should be actual labels, tags, containers, displays, or the like, as long as they are capable of being arranged flat and of a size not larger than 8 $\frac{1}{2}$ by 11 inches. This means that, if the mark is displayed on packaging that can be made to lie flat, you should submit the packaging as your specimen, rather than copies of actual videotapes or other bulky program materials. If packaging is not available, you should submit copies of a photograph or photocopy that shows the trademark displayed on your product. If you are filing electronically, you must attach an image of the specimen in .gif or .jpg format.

Step 5. Inside the PTO

Once you have submitted your actual use or intent-to-use application, a PTO employee will check to make sure it is complete. If it is not, it will be returned to you with a request to provide the missing information or materials. If the application is complete, it will be passed on to a trademark examining attorney, who will make what, in PTO parlance, is called an initial determination of registrability. If the examining attorney determines that a mark is not registrable based on the information in the application, the attorney will issue an office action in the form of a letter describing the deficiencies. If you receive such a letter, it is usually because the examining attorney has determined that your mark meets one of the following criteria:

- Does not function as a trademark to identify the goods or services as coming from a particular source (e.g., the matter applied for is merely ornamentation)
- Is immoral, deceptive, or scandalous
- May disparage or falsely suggest a connection with persons, institutions, beliefs, or national symbols, or bring them into contempt or disrepute
- Consists of or simulates the flag or coat of arms or other insignia of the United States, or a state or municipality, or any foreign nation
- Is the name, portrait, or signature of a particular living individual, unless he has given written consent; or is the name, signature, or portrait of a deceased President of the United States during the life of his widow, unless she has given her consent
- So resembles a mark already registered in the PTO as to be likely, when applied to the goods of the applicant, to cause confusion, or to cause mistakes, or to deceive
- Is merely descriptive or deceptively misdescriptive of the goods or services
- Is primarily geographically descriptive or deceptively misdescriptive of the goods or services of the applicant
- Is primarily merely a surname[9]

If you receive an office action refusing your application on these or other grounds, you have six months to respond with clarifications or additional information. If the examining attorney is still not convinced, you may appeal the decision denying registration to the Trademark Trial and Appeal Board, an administrative tribunal within the PTO.[10]

Once the examining attorney has approved your application or you have successfully appealed a refusal of registration, your mark will be published in the *Trademark Official Gazette*. At this point, any party that wants to challenge your registration of the mark has 30 days to do so or to indicate its intent to do so and to request an extension. If the mark is challenged and you are not able to reach an accommodation with the opposing party, the matter must be resolved in a proceeding before the Trademark Trial and Appeal Board.

If there is no opposition to your mark or you defeat the opposition before the Trademark Trial and Appeal Board, the PTO will proceed to register your trademark. Assuming that you did not get caught up in a procedure before the Trial and Appeal Board, the PTO should issue the registration approximately 12 weeks after the date that your mark was first published in the *Official Gazette*.

Keep in mind that, if you have filed an intent-to-use application, the PTO will not actually register the trademark until you submit an Allegation of Use form and proof that you have used the mark in interstate commerce. The Allegation of Use is called either an Amendment to Allege Use, if the actual use occurred before the PTO approved the mark for publication in the *Official Gazette*, or a Statement of Use, if the actual use occurred after the mark was published in the *Official Gazette* and the PTO has issued a Notice of Allowance that no opposition was filed. In either case, the form must be accompanied by the specimens described earlier and an additional $100 filing fee for each class of goods covered by your application(s).

What if you have run into delays and are having trouble proving actual use? Once the Notice of Allowance is mailed from the PTO, you will have six months to use the mark and file the Statement of Use form. If the six months expire and you still have not used the mark, you must file Form 1581, Request for Extension of Time. When you submit Form 1581, you are required to include the designated fee (currently $150 for each class of goods) and a description of your continuing efforts to move the mark into use in interstate commerce. Working in six-month increments, you can keep extending the deadline in this manner for up to three years from the point that the Notice of Allowance was issued.

The Care and Feeding of Your Trademark

When you receive your certificate of registration, file it in the same safe place as your other production documents. If you have used the services of a trademark attorney, the attorney's office should also receive a copy of the registration certificate.

A trademark registration used to be good for 20 years. The Trademark Law Revision Act of 1988 reduced this to 10 years. At the end of the 10-year term, you can file to renew the trademark for another 10 years. The renewal process can continue indefinitely, as long as the trademark owner can show that the mark is still in use.

Both the original Lanham Act and the Trademark Law Revision Act of 1988 also have a "sixth-year provision" that requires trademark holders to show actual use of the trademark during the sixth year of registration. To satisfy this requirement, you must file an affidavit affirming continued use, a specimen of the mark, and evidence affirming that the mark is still in use in connection with all of the goods and services indicated in the registration. The sixth-year provision and the reduced registration period are both designed to help weed out abandoned trademarks from the registration roles.

When you display your registered trademark in the production or on packaging or marketing materials, it should always be followed by the ® symbol. You should also include a trademark credit line or "legend" that identifies who owns the mark, as in "The No Sweat Workout is a registered trademark of Workmate Productions, Inc." This warns others of the registered status of the mark, and materials that carry these notices provide evidence for you to use in renewing the registration and establishing continued use. If registration is still pending, use the ™ symbol and say that the mark is "a trademark of Workmate Productions, Inc."

If the trademark appears more than once on a particular product, you do not have to keep repeating the ® or ™ symbol and trademark line. Instead, you can use the symbol and trademark line the first time the mark appears and the title alone after that point.

Patents

Three major types of protection are available for intellectual properties: copyright, trademarks, and patents. Of the three, copyright is of the greatest concern and interest to media producers because copyright law affects both how you use existing materials in putting your production together and how you protect the production once it is finished. That is why copyright has received the greatest amount of attention in this book. Trademarks are of lesser interest to media producers because trademark registration applies only to names and titles and because only certain types of titles can be trademarked. That is why trademark law has received less attention than copyright law in this book.

The third type of intellectual property protection, patent protection, is of the least interest and relevance to media producers because patents apply to inventions, not to media productions or other creative properties. In addition, to be eligible for patent protection, the invention must usually be either a process (e.g., a new method for manufacturing paper), design machine, or manufactured item. In other words, you can forget about patents unless you have a sideline as an inventor of, say, video equipment or new editing processes.

Even if you are an inventor, you may want to think twice before attempting to patent your latest breakthrough. Patent registration is a lengthy, costly, and often unsuccessful process. Because a patent awards a monopoly to an inventor for a 20-year period,[11] the PTO does not simply hand out patents to everyone who applies. Instead, the burden is on you to prove that your invention falls into one of the categories of products or processes that is eligible for patent protection and that it meets the PTO's strict criteria for "novelty" and "lack of obviousness."

Although it is possible to complete the rigorous patent registration procedure yourself, most applicants work with an attorney throughout the process. Because the process can take two years or more with no guarantee of success, patent applicants can end up with a large legal bill and nothing to show for it. With this in mind, many independent inventors choose to forego applying for a patent and choose, instead, to rely on some combination of copyright, trademark, trade secret, and unfair competition law to protect their creations.

Broadcast Law

If you produce programs intended for broadcast distribution, you should be familiar with several provisions of broadcast law that affect program content. Those provisions include the Fairness Doctrine and Personal Attack Rule, the Equal Time Provision, and the rules affecting sponsor identification and the broadcast of obscene or indecent material.

Sources of Broadcast Law

In the United States, the fundamental source of broadcast law is the Communications Act of 1934, the legislation that established the Federal Communications Commission (FCC) and the system for allocating and regulating radio and television stations that the FCC administers. Under that system, the FCC grants a broadcaster a license to use a specific channel assignment for a defined period. During the license period, the broadcaster is responsible for any program material transmitted on its station. At the end of the period, the broadcaster can renew its license, provided that it can show that the station has operated in the public interest by adhering to the rules established by the Communications Act of 1934 and extended and enforced through subsequent FCC rulings.

Because broadcast channels are valuable commodities, television station owners stand to lose a great deal if their licenses are not renewed. For that reason, most are extremely careful about the programming they carry. Keep in mind that, if a television station decides to buy and broadcast a program that in some way violates broadcast regulations, the station owner rather than the producer of the program is at risk. The FCC can regulate program producers only indirectly, through its power to influence station owners and the type of programs they tend to purchase.

Do state and local governments play a role in regulating television stations? Not really. Because broadcast signals carry across state lines, broadcast regulation is almost exclusively a federal matter, a manifestation of Congress's constitutional authority to regulate interstate commerce. State and local governments can and often do assume an active role in regulating cable television, however. Because cable systems do not use the public airwaves to transmit signals across state lines, and because most cable systems are franchised locally, the federal government has only a more limited ability to regulate cable system operators. Many state and local governments have stepped in to fill this void, passing regulations or writing local franchise contracts that require cable operators to provide services such as government and public access channels free of charge and to seek government approval for rate increases.

The Fairness Doctrine

Evolution of the Fairness Doctrine

Since its inception in 1934, the FCC has issued several rulings aimed at ensuring that broadcasters cover issues of public importance in a fair, balanced manner. Over the years, these rulings and various restatements of the commission's position have come to be known as the Fairness Doctrine. As discussed here, the FCC's current position is that active enforcement of the Fairness Doctrine is no longer in the public interest. The doctrine has been the subject of considerable controversy over the years, however, and some members of Congress continue to push for its revival. As a result, producers of television programs that may be broadcast should at least be aware of what the Fairness Doctrine is and how it can affect what types of programs television stations are willing to broadcast.

The Fairness Doctrine, as it evolved, established a twofold responsibility for television broadcasters. First, each television station was required to devote a reasonable portion of its air time to covering controversial issues that are important to the community the station serves. Second, the coverage was required to be balanced, presenting different sides of an issue rather than simply a single point of view. This did not mean that the station must give exactly equal air time to every viewpoint on every issue that it covered or that advocates of each opposing position automatically received free air time. It did mean, however, that the station must be able to show the FCC that, overall, it had covered controversial issues of local importance and that it had done so in a fair manner.

How might the Fairness Doctrine have affected you as a video producer? Assume, for example, that you were a producer in the video department of an industrial company that is one of the major employers in a community but that is also the target of protests by environmentalists who oppose the manner in which the company disposes of its waste products. In conjunction with the public relations department, you put together a 10-minute video about a new manufacturing process that, when fully implemented at the plant, promises to create 500 new jobs and cut the amount of waste product the plant produces. You then approached a local television station about using the video as part of a weekly program that covers business developments in the area. The producer of that program likes what you have done but, after consulting with the station's lawyers, decides to decline your offer because airing the video could open the station up to a fairness complaint from (and the obligation to provide response time to) environmental groups who feel that your company is not going far enough in cleaning up its disposal problems.

Included within the Fairness Doctrine regulatory umbrella is a provision called the Personal Attack Rule. This rule states that when, during coverage of controversial issues, an attack is made on the character, integrity, or personal qualities of an identified individual or group, the station must both notify the individual or group and provide the opportunity to respond. Significantly, this rule does not apply when the person being attacked is a public official or when the attack is made while the station is covering or reporting on a bona fide news event.

Decline of the Fairness Doctrine

It is important to note that, despite some apparent supporting language in a 1959 amendment to the Communications Act of 1934, the Fairness Doctrine was never formally codified as part of U.S. statutory law.[12] As a result, the manner in which the doctrine was interpreted and enforced varied over the years, depending on the mood of the FCC and the status of case law in this area. Broadcasters historically have been very vocal opponents of the doctrine, claiming that it violated their constitutional rights under the First Amendment and that it actually works to discourage television stations from covering controversial issues. This was the cornerstone of the broadcast industry's position in *Red Lion Broadcasting Co., Inc. v. FCC,*[13] the 1969 U.S. Supreme Court case in which the industry challenged the FCC's enforcement of the Fairness Doctrine as unconstitutional. The Supreme Court sided with the FCC, ruling that the Fairness Doctrine did not violate the First Amendment in view of the scarcity of broadcast frequencies, the government's role in allocating those frequencies, and the legitimate claims of those unable without governmental assistance to gain those frequencies for the expression of their views.

Bolstered by the *Red Lion* decision, the FCC actively enforced the Fairness Doctrine throughout the 1970s. With the onset of the 1980s and the push toward deregulation promoted by the Reagan administration, however, the FCC began backing off enforcing the doctrine. This shift in attitude was formalized in 1985, when the commission issued a report concluding that the Fairness Doctrine no longer was warranted given the increased competition to broadcasters from cable television, home satellite distribution systems, and other new technologies that, in the commission's view, were bringing a "multiplicity of voices" to the television marketplace.[14] In 1989, a federal appeals court upheld the FCC's right not to enforce the doctrine, concluding that the commission was empowered to determine whether enforcement was in the public interest.[15] The Supreme Court declined to review this decision.

The FCC's shift in attitude toward the Fairness Doctrine was met with much resistance by some members of Congress, many of whom are sensitive to fairness concerns in the coverage of public issues that so often are also highly political issues. But, despite several efforts to resurrect the Fairness Doctrine, it currently remains dormant. The question of whether broadcasters should be required to provide fair coverage of important issues as part of their public interest obligations remains, however, a hot topic in Washington. As a result, producers should stay attuned to efforts to reinstate some form of the Fairness Doctrine.[16]

The Equal Time Rule

If you have ever produced promotional materials for candidates running for public office, you are probably already familiar with the Equal Time Rule. Unlike the Fairness Doctrine, which never became a formal part of U.S. statutory law, the Equal Time Rule has its own section in the Communications Act of 1934. Section 315(a) of the Communications Act states that

> If any licensee shall permit any person who is a legally qualified candidate for any public office to use a broadcasting station, he shall afford equal opportunities to all other such candidates for that office in the use of such broadcasting station.[17]

In addition to this equal time provision, Section 312(a)(7) of the Communications Act states that the FCC may revoke a broadcast license if the licensee fails to provide "reasonable access to or to permit purchase of reasonable amounts of time"[18] by legally qualified candidates in federal elections. Although this statutory provision applies, on its face, only to candidates for federal elective office (unlike Section 315, which applies to candidates for all public offices), the FCC has stated separately that broadcasters also have an obligation to provide some access to air time for nonfederal candidates.

The equal time requirements do not mean that station owners must give away air time to candidates, only that they must make equivalent air time available to all candidates for the same office on equivalent terms. For example, if a station offers one candidate for sewer commissioner (remember, the Equal Time Rule applies to any legitimate candidate for any elected office) a 30-second slot in prime time for $5,000, it must make 30-second slots in prime time available to all other candidates for sewer commissioner for $5,000. In this sense, the Equal Time Rule is really the "Equal Time at Equal Cost Rule."

If your production will feature a performer who happens to be running for public office, be careful. The Equal Time Rule applies not just to political commercials but also to any recognizable appearance by a candidate in any type of program or context. That is why President Gerald Ford's role in a television campaign for the United Way created equal time concerns, as did the airing of Ronald Reagan's movies during his election campaigns. And that is why using an actor who is running for, say, county dog catcher in a commercial intended for local broadcast during the election period could also cause problems.

Sponsor Identification

A consumer electronics company has hired your company to produce a program about the future of home entertainment systems. The company gives you a big budget and creative control of the production. It does request, however, that you feature its products in the program.

You deliver the program, and the sponsoring company loves it. The company shows the production to its employees and distributors, and they love it, too. Excited by the response, the company decides to offer copies free of charge to any television station that wants to air the program, either in its entirety or in excerpts. Several stations indicate they do intend to broadcast the program.

Is there a problem here? No, not as long as the stations that broadcast the production identify the program as sponsored material. Under Section 317 of the Communications Act, broadcast licensees are required to tell viewers when a program is commercial in nature and to identify the sponsor.[19] The rules are particularly stringent for commercial spots that are designed to advocate a particular position while disguising the sponsor's identity. For example, when a pharmaceutical company creates a series of infomercials that advocate a particular approach to treating high blood pressure—an approach that happens to involve a drug the company manufactures—the stations airing the ads better be sure that the pharmaceutical company is identified as the sponsor. Otherwise, the stations may be subject to FCC sanctions, and the pharmaceutical company may find that it is the subject of an investigation by the FTC.

Moreover, in addition to these broadcaster responsibilities set forth in Section 317 of the Communications Act, Section 508 details similar disclosure requirements for individuals that produce or provide such programs for broadcast. Section 508 is aimed primarily at deterring "plugola," the practice of paying producers to embed product placements and references in a production without disclosing that fact. For television producers, the operative language from Section 508(b) is as follows:

> [A]ny person who, in connection with the production or preparation of any program or program matter which is intended for broadcasting over any [television] station, accepts or agrees to accept, or pays or agrees to pay, any money, services or other valuable consideration for the inclusion of any matter as part of such program or program matter, shall, in advance of such broadcast, disclose the fact of such acceptance or payment to the payee's employer, or to the person for whom such program or program matter is being produced, or to the licensee of such station over which such program is broadcast.[20]

A parallel provision, Section 508(c), places similar constraints on parties that provide (e.g., sell or license, rather than produce) programming to broadcasters. The penalties for violating either provision can be severe: a fine of up to $10,000, a jail term of up to one year, or both. With this in mind, many television networks and production companies that hire third parties to produce programs for broadcast require those parties to represent and warrant that they are familiar with and that they have not and will not violate these provisions of federal communications law.

Indecent and Obscene Content

If your productions tend toward the risqué, do not plan on seeing them aired on broadcast television in the United States. This is particularly true if the programs include language that could be considered indecent or obscene. Section 505 of the Communications Act of 1934 gives the FCC the power to act against broadcasters who air programs containing profane or obscene words, language, or images. In addition, transmitting obscene material may subject broadcasters to criminal penalties.

Of course, the standards that define what is obscene or indecent have changed over the years, and broadcast television today often seems more risqué than it was even a few years ago. Still, broadcasters tend to be sensitive about this issue, particularly because they must be concerned about the reactions of local parent, church, and community groups. In addition, the FCC has indicated that it will be willing to take action against material that it considers indecent, especially when that material is broadcast during family viewing hours.[21]

These same rules do not apply to cable television networks (including basic cable, pay cable, or pay-per-view services) or local cable operators because they generally are not considered broadcasters. Cable system operators must be sensitive to the standards of the community in which they are franchised, however, and many cable systems provide lock-out boxes that parents can use to prevent—or at least try to prevent—minors from viewing adult programming. Cable networks may also be subject to penalties for transmitting material that is deemed obscene (not simply indecent) under U.S. law. Finally, as discussed in Chapter 8, a separate federal statute is aimed specifically at preventing the transmission of obscene material to children over the Internet.

Distribution Agreements

Chapters 2 and 3 discussed how contracts can help you define relationships with the performers, crew members, and subcontractors who will help you produce a program. Now that you have completed production, you may be thinking of entering into an arrangement with a distributor or video publisher who will sell the finished program. This section discusses how contracts can help make sure that you cut the right distribution deal.

If you are a producer working within a corporate video department, you may never need to worry about distribution contracts. Once you finish a program, it will simply be displayed or distributed internally according to the plan that was worked out as part of the original production arrangement. This also holds true for independent production companies who produce programs as works-made-for-hire for corporations; however, as the home and business video markets have flourished, many corporate video departments have begun to look to outside distribution of productions as a way to build their operating budgets and perhaps even to turn a profit for the company. Similarly, many independent production companies have begun either to retain the copyright to their corporate video productions or to look for production deals that permit them to profit from sales to supplemental markets. In these cases, both corporate and independent producers would do well to become wise in the ways of distribution license agreements.

The Components of a Distribution Agreement

A distribution license agreement should include the three main components that make up all contracts: the offer, consideration, and acceptance. Of course, as discussed in Chapter 2, the boundaries between these different components often become blurred in the actual contract, and most contracts include several additional provisions, conditions, and guarantees.

A distribution contract should begin by establishing in clear, unambiguous terms just what you are offering the distributor (*distributor* is used here as a generic term that encompasses both distributors and publishers of video programming) to distribute and what rights the distributor will have in the materials. What sort of program is this? Will you retain the copyright in the work (almost always the preferable option for the producer), or are you transferring all or a portion of the copyright to the distributor?

In a distribution license, it is especially important to establish the term and scope of the deal. How long will the distributor retain the rights to sell the program and in which markets? Is this an exclusive agreement, or will you have the right to enter into similar contracts with other distributors? In the sample contract shown in Figure 9.3, most of this is spelled out in the Grant of Rights section.

Figure 9.3 Sample video distribution agreement.

License Agreement (the "Agreement") dated as of August 4, 2003, by and between WorkMate Productions, Inc. ("Grantor"), a Connecticut corporation with offices at 253 Myrtle Road, Stamford, CT 06905, and Davis Video, Inc. ("Distributor"), a New York corporation with offices at 1630 Broadway, New York, NY 10019, with respect to the video program "The No Sweat Workout."

1. **Definitions.** As used herein, the following terms shall have the following definitions:

   (a) The "Term" shall mean the period from January 1, 2004, through December 31, 2006.
   (b) The "Territory" shall mean the United States, including its possessions and territories, Canada, the United Kingdom, and Australia.
   (c) The "Program" shall mean "The No Sweat Workout," a 30-minute exercise video program or copies of that video program made pursuant to rights granted under this Agreement.
   (d) "Royalty" shall mean the consideration more fully described in Section 6(b).
   (e) "Master Tape" shall mean a complete version of the final, edited Program in a format to be agreed upon by Grantor and Distributor and to be delivered to the Distributor for use as a duplicating master.

2. **Grant of Rights.**

   (a) Grantor hereby grants to the Distributor the exclusive right during the Term to duplicate videocassette and DVD copies of the Program from the Master Tape and to sell, rent, or otherwise distribute the copies throughout the Territory. The foregoing grant of rights includes all rights necessary to distribute copies of the Program on videocassette or DVD, including the right to use the name of the Program and the voice and likeness of any party who rendered services in connection with the Program in the packaging, advertising, promotion, and publicizing of the Program. Grantor further grants Distributor the right to sublicense the foregoing rights, subject to Grantor's reasonable approval rights over any such sublicense.
   (b) All rights not specifically granted herein to the Distributor shall be reserved to the Grantor. Such reserved rights shall include all merchandising rights to the Program and the right to transmit the Program via broadcast, cable, satellite, and Internet channels or networks and to grant others the right to do the same.

Figure 9.3 Sample video distribution agreement. (continued)

3. **Delivery of Master Tape.** Grantor agrees to deliver the Master Tape to the Distributor on or before December 15, 2003.

4. **Copyright and Trademark Rights.** Copyright in the Program and ownership of any and all trademarks associated with the Program shall be retained by the Grantor. Grantor shall be responsible for placing appropriate copyright and trademark notices on the Master Tape. Distributor agrees to reproduce such copyright and trademark notices on all copies of the Program and related packaging.

5. **Modifications to Program.** Distributor agrees that it shall not edit or otherwise modify the Program without Grantor's prior written consent. Grantor may withhold that consent in its sole discretion.

6. **Consideration:** Advance Against Royalties and Royalty Payments.

   (a) In consideration of the foregoing grant of rights, Distributor agrees to pay the Grantor an advance against royalties of Twenty Thousand Dollars ($20,000) payable as follows: Ten Thousand Dollars ($10,000) upon execution of this Agreement and Ten Thousand Dollars ($10,000) upon Grantor's compliance with Section 3. This advance against royalties will be applied against royalties payable to the Grantor under this Agreement. In no event, however, will the advance against royalties be repayable in whole or in part, regardless of royalties due under this Agreement.

   (b) Distributor further agrees to pay Grantor a Royalty of ten percent (10%) of net receipts from distribution of copies of the Program. "Net Receipts" shall mean the gross receipts actually received by Distributor (exclusive of sales, use, excise, and other taxes, packing, insurance, shipping, and similar charges reimbursed by customers) from the sale, rental, and licensing of the Program, less the amount of any credits or refunds for returns, taking into account any reserves previously established by Distributor as provided below.

   (c) Distributor may withhold a reasonable portion of royalties due as a reserve against returns, provided that reserve shall not exceed twenty percent (20%) of royalties otherwise due to Grantor for a particular accounting period. Any such reserve shall be liquidated no later than with the rendition of the third accounting statement following the accounting statement in which the reserve was established.

7. **Accounting and Payments.**
   (a) Distributor shall account to Grantor for royalties based on Net Receipts received by Distributor during each six-month period

Figure 9.3 Sample video distribution agreement. (continued)

ending on June 30 and December 31 of each year. Within ninety (90) days after the end of each such accounting period, Distributor shall furnish Grantor a report showing the number of copies of the Program sold or otherwise distributed, Net Receipts received from such sales distribution, and a calculation of the royalties payable for such period.

(b) At the time of each such report, Distributor shall pay Grantor the amount of royalties due, after deducting the amounts of:

(i) any unrecovered advances against royalties with respect to the Program in question

(ii) any other costs incurred by Distributor that are expressly deductible hereunder

(iii) reasonable reserves for returns in accordance with Section 6(c)

(iv) any taxes, duties, or other amounts required by law to be withheld by Distributor

(c) Grantor may designate a certified public accountant who may audit and copy Distributor's books and records concerning the sale and distribution of the Program. Said examination shall be at the Grantor's sole cost and expense (unless the examination reveals royalties due to Grantor in excess of five percent (5%) of royalties paid, in which event such cost and expense shall be borne by Distributor), conducted during normal business hours and upon reasonable notice, and may not be conducted more than once annually. The books and records for a particular accounting period may be audited only during the three (3) years following rendition of the statement for such period, at the end of which period such books and records shall be deemed final and binding upon Grantor.

8. **Replacement and Promotional Copies.** Net Receipts shall not include any receipts from copies of the Program that are distributed by Distributor to customers as replacements for defective copies. In addition, no royalties shall be credited or paid to Grantor with respect to any receipts from copies distributed for promotional purposes to the press, trade, sales representatives, or potential customers, so long as no more than 500 copies of the Program are so distributed and so long as no payments are received by Distributor for such promotional copies. If more than 500 copies of the Program are so distributed, then Grantor shall receive a royalty payment of ten percent (10%) of the latest advertised retail price for each copy in excess of 500 so distributed.

Figure 9.3 Sample video distribution agreement. (continued)

9. **Commencement of Marketing and Minimum Level of Sales.**

　(a) Distributor agrees to make a reasonable and substantial effort to commence public distribution of the Program through sales and/or licenses within three (3) months after Distributor's receipt of the Master Tape. If Distributor fails to distribute the Program within such three (3) month period, Grantor may give written notice of its intent to terminate this Agreement. If Distributor fails to commence public distribution of the Program within two (2) months after receipt of such notice, this Agreement shall terminate as set forth in Section 10 hereunder, and Grantor shall retain any payments previously received under this Agreement.

　(b) Distributor makes no representations or warranties that the Program will be successfully marketed or that any minimum level of sales or licensing will be achieved. If, however, the total of all Net Receipts for the first four (4) six-month accounting periods described in Section 7(a) do not exceed Two Hundred Thousand Dollars ($200,000), Grantor shall have the option to terminate this Agreement as set forth in Section 10 hereunder.

10. **Termination.** Upon the expiration of the Term, or upon receipt of a written termination notice as described in Sections 9(a) and 9(b), Distributor shall cease manufacturing the Program and all rights granted in this Agreement will revert to the Grantor. For a period of six (6) months thereafter, however, Distributor shall have the nonexclusive right to sell and/or rent the inventory of copies of the Program remaining as of the expiration or termination date. At the end of this period, Distributor shall at its election erase or destroy any remaining copies of the Program and, upon Grantor's request, furnish Grantor an affidavit thereof. Notwithstanding the foregoing, Distributor's "sell-off" rights hereunder shall be subject to Grantor's option to purchase all copies of the Program in Distributor's possession at the date of termination at a cost not to exceed Distributor's actual cost of manufacturing such copies.

11. **Representations and Warranties.** Grantor represents and warrants that it has the right and authority to enter into and fully perform this Agreement and grant the rights granted herein; that Grantor owns or controls or is the authorized representative of the party that owns or controls the right to distribute videocassette or DVD copies of the Program; that Grantor has not entered into or shall not enter into any agreement that would limit or impair the rights granted herein; and that the exercise of the rights granted hereunder will not

Figure 9.3 Sample video distribution agreement. (continued)

infringe on any rights (including but not limited to contract, copyright, trademark, privacy, and publicity rights) of any third party.

Distributor represents and warrants that it has the right and authority to enter into and perform this Agreement; that Distributor has not entered or shall not enter into any agreement that would affect its ability to perform fully its obligations hereunder; and that Distributor will take no action that would impair, infringe on, or challenge Grantor's rights in the Program.

12. **Indemnification.** Each of Grantor and Distributor shall at all times indemnify and hold the other harmless from any and all charges, claims, damages, costs, and expenses, including reasonable attorney's fees, incurred in connection with the breach of its representation or warranty hereunder. The indemnitee will promptly notify the indemnitor of any such claim. The indemnitor will adjust, settle, defend, or otherwise dispose of such claim at its sole cost. If the indemnitor has been so notified and is not pursuing such matter, the indemnitee may take such action on behalf of itself and/or as attorney-in-fact for the indemnitor to adjust, settle, defend, or otherwise dispose of such claim in which case the indemnitor shall, upon being billed therefor, reimburse the indemnitee in the amount thereof. Notwithstanding the foregoing, Grantor shall have the sole right and authority to initiate and pursue actions against third parties in connection with any infringement or alleged infringement of Grantor's copyright, trademark, or other intellectual property rights in the Program.

13. **Notices.** All notices, requests, consents, demands, and other communications hereunder shall be in writing delivered by hand, transmitted by facsimile, or mailed by first-class mail to the respective parties to this Agreement set forth above or to such other person or address as a party hereto shall designate to the other party hereto from time to time in writing forwarded in like manner. Any notice, request, consent, demand, or communication given in accordance with the provisions of this paragraph shall be deemed to have been given or made seven (7) days after deposit in the mail, postage prepaid, or when hand delivered, or transmitted by facsimile and verified received, provided that communications with respect to a change of address shall be deemed to be effective when actually received.

14. **Execution of Contract.** Grantor shall have a period of fifteen (15) days from receipt of this Agreement to sign and return the Agreement to the Distributor. If the signed Agreement is not returned to the Distributor within that period, Distributor shall have the option to withdraw its offer of agreement. This Agreement may be executed by

Figure 9.3 Sample video distribution agreement. (continued)

original or facsimile signature and in counterparts, each of which will be deemed an original, but that together will constitute a single instrument.

15. **Miscellaneous.** Grantor and Distributor shall execute or cause to be executed any and all documents needed to effectuate the purposes and intents of this Agreement and/or to protect Grantor's rights in the Program. This Agreement contains the entire understanding and supersedes all prior and contemporaneous understandings between the parties hereto relating to the subject matter herein, and this Agreement can be modified or amended only in a writing signed by the parties. Grantor will, upon Distributor's request, promptly furnish to Distributor copies of such agreements or other documents as Distributor may desire in connection with any provisions of this Agreement. This Agreement and all matters or issues collateral thereto shall be governed by the laws of the State of New York applicable to contracts executed and performed entirely therein. The parties hereby agree to submit any dispute concerning this Agreement to the exclusive jurisdiction of courts of competent jurisdiction located in New York, New York.

IN WITNESS WHEREOF, the parties hereto hereby execute this Agreement as of the date first specified above.

GRANTOR
WorkMate Productions, Inc.

DISTRIBUTOR
Davis Video, Inc.

By: _____

By: _____

Its: _____

Its: _____

Date: _____

Date: _____

The sections of the contract that deal with consideration should detail the compensation that you will receive for granting the distributor the privilege of selling your program. Is the deal being done on a royalty basis, or will you receive a lump sum payment? If this is a royalty deal, will there be an advance against royalties (an advance payment to the producer that is then recouped by the distributor from royalty payments due to the producer)? Will the rights granted in the contract revert back to you if the distributor either ceases selling the program or fails to meet specified minimum sales levels? How many free or reduced-price copies is the distributor allowed to provide to reviewers or for promotional purposes? Even more important, what will the royalty percentage be and how will it be calculated? Will the calculations be based on gross sales or, more typically, net receipts calculated as gross sales less specified deductions? Is there a minimum guaranteed royalty, even if the program does not sell well? How and when will royalty checks be issued? What accounting records will the distributor be required to keep, and what rights will you have to examine those records? Also, if the production involved guild performers, who will be responsible for figuring and making any required residual and supplemental market payments? As discussed in Chapter 7, this responsibility will remain with the producer unless the distributor executes an assumption agreement with the relevant guild.

Finally, toward the end of the contract, there should be language that indicates how much time both parties can take to respond to the agreement and how the parties will indicate that they have accepted the terms of the agreement.

In addition to these core provisions, the distribution agreement should include language that defines the procedures for terminating the deal, the representations and warranties that cover the arrangement, and several boilerplate contract provisions, all of which are covered in the sample agreement.

Sample Distribution Agreement

Figure 9.3 is a sample distribution agreement for the "No Sweat Workout" video. Note that this contract covers an arrangement in which the video program is already completed and the production company is placing it with a distributor. For a sample agreement in which a distributor is commissioning a company to produce a program, see the production agreement (Figure 3.5) in Chapter 3.

Note also that this is one sample contract, designed to fit one type of distribution deal. Because each publishing and distribution deal is unique, you should make sure that each of your contracts is custom fitted to the deal at hand.

Negotiating the Agreement

Like most distribution agreements, this sample was drawn up by the distributor based on its standard contract and offered to the production company as the basis for their deal. The production company then reviewed the contract, marking any sections that required clarification or negotiation. Figure 9.3 shows the finished contract after all areas of dispute have been resolved to the satisfaction of both parties.

As the producer being asked to accept an agreement offered by a distributor, you should anticipate having to negotiate and even eliminate some sections of the contract. In fact, the negotiating process should start before the contract is even drawn up, in discussions with the distributor through which you define the core components of the deal. What rights will you be granting to the distributor and for how long? How much will the distributor be paying you for the rights?

When you receive the written contract, think of it as a draft that must be reviewed, studied, and discussed. First, check to make sure that the core components of the deal, as detailed in the contract, match the understanding you had reached in your discussions with the distributor. Then, make sure that the rest of the agreement contains no other definitions or provisions that may present problems.

At this point, as a matter of policy, many producers pause to have a lawyer review the contract. A lawyer can help translate any legal language that you might not understand and locate any subtle provisions and fine print that will work to your disadvantage. If you are not adept at figuring financial details, you may also want to have an accountant or other person with financial expertise examine the consideration part of the deal. If you work within a corporate setting, company regulations may require you to have the contract reviewed and approved by the legal department.

One contract provision that distributors sometimes will try to sneak by you and that you will almost always want to reject is the "option on next work" clause. This provision gives the distributor the right of first refusal on your next production. Because this does not buy you anything (you could always give the distributor the right of first refusal at a later date if you wanted to), the advantage is all to the other party. Because experienced producers recognize this situation, distributors almost expect to have the contract returned with this clause crossed out. Do not disappoint them.

Most distributors also expect that some negotiation will occur over the basic terms of the agreement. Do not disappoint them here, either. You will not offend a distributor by asking to have a provision in the contract clarified or by requesting changes. Of course, the extent to which the distributor will be willing to comply with your requests for changes will depend on how reasonable the changes are and how highly the distributor prizes your production. But you should never be afraid to ask. You should also not be afraid to back away from a deal if the distributor insists on terms that simply will not work for you.

Reviewing the Sample Agreement

As distribution agreements go, the sample shown in Figure 9.3 is relatively simple. The major areas that tend to create problems in this sort of contract—delimiting the territory and defining the rights granted to the distributor and the royalties to be paid to the producer—are all fairly straightforward.

In Section 2.a of the agreement, WorkMate Productions, Inc. (the "Grantor"), grants Davis Video, Inc. (the "Distributor"), the right to make and distribute videocassette and DVD copies of "The No Sweat Workout" (the "Program") throughout the territory defined in Section 1.b for the term defined in Section 1.a. Given the definitions that the contract provides for Territory and Term, this means that Davis Video will have the right to sell the Program on videocassette and DVD in the United States, Canada, the United Kingdom, and Australia for the three-year period beginning January 1, 2004, and ending December 31, 2006. As described in Section 2.b, however, WorkMate Productions is retaining the merchandising rights to the Program (the right to sell "No Sweat" sweatsuits and any similar ancillary items) and the right to distribute the Program on broadcast, cable, and satellite channels—as well as any other rights that are not specifically granted to Davis Video through this agreement. As stated in Section 4, the copyright for the Program will remain with WorkMate.

Section 6 specifies the consideration that WorkMate Productions will receive in return for the rights granted to Davis Video. On signing the agreement, WorkMate will receive a nonrefundable advance against royalties of $10,000 and another $10,000 on turning over the master tape to the distributor. Over the term of the agreement, Work-Mate will also be paid a royalty of 10 percent of the net receipts from sales of copies of the Program. Of course, WorkMate will not actually see a royalty check until the $20,000 advance against royalties has been earned out. Given the royalty rate of 10 percent, this will happen when Davis Video's net receipts from sales of the work reach $200,000.

The consideration section of every distribution or publishing contract must be examined very carefully. In particular, distributors can have peculiar ways of defining net receipts and the other terms that determine just how much money you will make from the deal. The definition in this sample contract is relatively simple and fair. It gives Davis Video the right to withhold a reasonable amount as a reserve against returned copies (Section 6.c) but does not give Davis the right to deduct any of the other marketing or packaging expenses or distribution fees that some publishers and distributors try to tack onto an agreement. In addition, in some agreements, the royalty arrangements can get complex, with the royalty rate changing based on the number of copies sold and where and how they are sold. If you find that you do not fully understand these financial details, consult with an attorney or accountant who can explain them to you.

How did Davis Video and WorkMate Productions come up with $20,000 as the figure to use for the advance against royalties that will be paid to WorkMate? In most cases, the advance figure is the result of negotiations between the two parties. From its side, if Davis is like most publishers and distributors, it started by running some numbers through a not very scientific formula that figures in several factors, including what its break-even point will be on the project and how many copies it reasonably could expect to sell over the term of the agreement. Even more important, because a nonrefundable advance like this one is essentially a guarantee to WorkMate Productions, Davis Video probably tried to figure how small an advance it could get away with paying WorkMate. From the other side, WorkMate had to determine how much of an advance it needed to make the deal worthwhile and how much it could reasonably expect Davis Video to pay. The result of these calculations and negotiations is the $20,000 advance specified in the contract.

In publishing and distribution agreements based on a royalty arrangement, it is always preferable to include a way for the grantor to get the rights to the materials back in the event that the distributor or publisher does not perform as promised. As described in Section 10, the agreement between WorkMate and Davis Video can be terminated in either of two ways: (1) it can simply run its course and expire at the end of the term, or (2) WorkMate can end it if Davis fails to market the program within a reasonable time period or fails to achieve the minimum sales level specified.

Most of the other sections of the sample distribution agreement should be familiar to you from the sample contracts in Chapter 3. Like all of the sample contracts in this book, this one is meant to serve as a model that suggests the structure and scope of a typical agreement. You should not assume, however, that you can use this sample as the basis for your own contract or that you can simply pick and mix provisions from this agreement to build a contract that meets your needs. When in doubt, talk to an attorney who is familiar with your particular situation.

Summary

- *What steps should you take to protect your completed production?* The first step toward protecting your finished production is to make sure that all of your production records are stored in a secure place. Then, you should consider registering the copyright with the U.S. Copyright Office and, for some productions, the title as a trademark with the U.S. Patent and Trademark Office. If you will be making distribution arrangements with a third party, you will also need to consider how to protect your rights through a distribution contract. If your production will be broadcast, you should be aware of several federal regulations affecting the content of programs broadcast on U.S. television stations.

- *How does copyright registration help to protect your production?* Registration with the Copyright Office is not required for copyright protection. Registration with the Copyright Office does confer several important benefits, however, including the right to sue infringers for statutory damages. Even more important, registration establishes an official record for the work that the courts will accept as evidence supporting the validity of your copyright.

- *How do you register the copyright of a media production with the Copyright Office?* To register the copyright of a media production, you must complete and file a copy of Form PA, along with the designated processing fee. You must also deposit a copy and written description of the production.

- *What is a trademark?* The U.S. government defines a *trademark* as a "word, phrase, symbol, or design, or a combination of words, phrases, symbols, or designs, that identifies and distinguishes the source of the goods of one party from those of others."

- *What are the sources of U.S. trademark law?* U.S. trademark law is governed by a mix of common law and state and federal statutes. The major federal trademark statute is the Trademark Act of 1946, known as the Lanham Act. In 1988, Congress passed the Trademark Law Revision Act of 1988, the first comprehensive revision of the Lanham Act. In the United States, trademark registration and other federal trademark procedures are administered by the Patent and Trademark Office (PTO) of the U.S. Department of Commerce.

- *Can you register the title of a media production as a trademark?* Generally, you can trademark the titles of creative works only when the title covers a series of works or when the title is used in conjunction with manufactured products.

- *What are the benefits of trademark registration?* You do not have to register the trademark to enjoy several of the protections provided by federal trademark registration. Registration with the PTO does provide important advantages, however, including the right to sue in federal court for trademark infringement, prima facie evidence of the validity of the registration and the registrant's ownership of the mark, and the right to deposit the registration with U.S. Customs in order to stop the importation of goods bearing an infringing mark. Also, registering your title with the PTO will put out the word that the title is already in use. This will help deter others from adopting the same or a similar mark.

- *How do you register a trademark with the Patent and Trademark Office?* Before you try to register a title with the PTO, you must first determine if the title meets minimum eligibility requirements for registration. You should also conduct a trademark search to determine if any existing or pending registrations might conflict with your mark. To file for registration, you submit the appropriate form, a drawing of the mark, the required filing fee, and three specimens of the mark showing actual use. The specimen requirement assumes that you are filing based on actual use of the mark in interstate commerce. Under the 1988 revisions to U.S. trademark law, it is possible to file for registration before you have actually used the mark, as long as you can show that you have a bona fide intent to use the mark. The PTO encourages trademark applicants to file electronically through its Trademark Electronic Application System (TEAS).

- *What federal laws and regulations affect the content of broadcast television programming?* The federal laws and regulations affecting the content of broadcast programming include the Fairness Doctrine (although it currently is not enforced by the FCC), the equal time provision, and the rules affecting sponsor identification and the broadcast of obscene material.

- *What are the main components of a video distribution license agreement?* A video distribution license should include the three major components that make up all contracts: the offer, consideration, and acceptance. In distribution agreements, you should pay particular attention to defining the term (duration) of the agreement; the exact rights that you are assigning through the agreement; the territory in which the distributor will be able to sell the production; how royalties, if the deal involves royalties, or other consideration will be computed and paid; and who will hold the copyright to the production. It is also important to include a provision for terminating the agreement if the distributor fails to bring the production to market or to meet minimum sales levels. Conversely, it is important that the agreement not include language that gives the distributor the right of first refusal to market your next production.

Notes

1. If you place a copyright notice on your production and you publish (distribute) one or more copies to the public, you are required by law to deposit a copy with the Copyright Office. This

is true regardless of whether you plan to register the copyright. More information about the deposit requirements is included in the section titled "Filing for Registration."

2. If the soundtrack from the production will be issued as a separate sound recording, it may also be necessary to file Form SR with the Copyright Office to register the recording as a distinct work. For more information, contact the U.S. Copyright Office.

3. "Copyright Registration for Motion Pictures including Video Recordings," Circular 45 (Washington, DC: Copyright Office, Library of Congress, 1999), p. 5.

4. Ibid.

5. Ibid.

6. "Basic Facts About Trademarks" (Washington, DC: U.S. Department of Commerce, Patent and Trademark Office, 2002).

7. This is not meant to suggest that it is safe or acceptable to use *Casablanca* or any other existing and known title as the name for your production. Although doing so would probably not be considered trademark infringement, you could leave yourself open to unfair competition or "false designation of origin" challenges. In addition, if your production is a feature film, you could also run into trouble with the Motion Picture Association of America (MPAA), the industry group that gives films audience ratings (e.g., G, PG, PG-13) and that operates a title registration service. The MPAA will not give a rating to or allow its members to distribute a motion picture whose name is likely to be confused with that of a film that is already in distribution.

8. If you want to work directly with a trademark search firm, rather than through a lawyer, you can ask a lawyer to recommend a firm, you can look in the phone book under Trademark Search Services, or you can call Research on Demand at (800) 200-4095. Research on Demand provides computerized research services, including a trademark search service. Another such service is Government Liaisons Services, Inc., which can be reached at (888) 869-8930.

9. 47 U.S.C. § 508(b) (2002).

10. If your application is rejected for one of the latter three reasons and if your appeal fails, your mark may still be eligible for registration on the *Supplemental Register*. Although this designation does not carry all of the benefits of being listed on the *Primary Register*, it does provide you with some significant benefits, including the right to sue for trademark infringement in federal courts and a record of your date of first use of the mark. Also, once your

mark has been listed on the *Supplemental Register* for five years, it is presumed to have acquired the secondary meaning necessary for registration on the *Principal Register*. For more information about the distinction between the *Primary* and *Supplemental Registers*, consult a trademark attorney.

11. Under a recent revision to U.S. patent law, a patent is valid for 20 years from the date that the patent application was filed with the U.S. Patent and Trademark Office. Formerly, the patent term was 17 years from the date that the patent issued. See 35 U.S.C. § 154(a)(2) (2002).

12. The fact that the Fairness Doctrine was not codified in U.S. law was affirmed by a federal appeals court in *Telecommunications Research and Action Center v. FCC*, 801 F.3d 501 (D.C. Cir. 1986), *cert. denied*, 482 U.S. 919 (1987).

13. *Red Lion Broadcasting Co., Inc. v. FCC*, 395 U.S. 367 (1969).

14. See Inquiry into Section 73.1910 of the Commission's Rules and Regulations Concerning the General Fairness Obligations of Broadcast Licensees, 102 F.C.C. 2d 143 (1985).

15. See *Syracuse Peace Council v. FCC*, 867 F.2d 654 (D.C. Cir. 1989), *cert. denied*, 493 U.S. 1019 (1990).

16. Many members of Congress continue to press the FCC to require broadcasters to live up to their public interest obligations as licensees under the Communications Act of 1934. For example, even as the federal courts were confirming that the FCC had the right to not enforce the Fairness Doctrine, Congress was busy drafting and passing the Children's Television Act of 1990, Pub. L. No. 101–437, 104 State. 996–1000, codified at 47 U.S.C. §§ 303a, 303b, 394. This act directed the FCC to consider, in reviewing each television station's license renewal application, "the extent to which the licensee . . . has served the educational and information needs of children through the licensee's overall programming, including programming specifically designed to serve such needs." The FCC subsequently has issued rules and guidelines instructing television broadcasters on the amount and type of programming that will fulfill their public interest obligations to children under the act.

17. 47 U.S.C. § 315(a) (2002).

18. 47 U.S.C.§ 312(a)(7) (2002). This provision states in full that the FCC may revoke a broadcast station's license "for willful or repeated failure to allow reasonable access to or to permit purchase of reasonable amounts of time for the use of a broadcasting

station by a legally qualified candidate for Federal elective office on behalf of his candidacy."

19. 47 U.S.C. § 317 (2002).

20. 47 U.S.L. § 508 (b) (2002).

21. Because it raises First Amendment concerns, the extent of the FCC's authority to restrict the broadcast of indecent material has been the subject of many federal court decisions over the years. Generally, the courts have held that the FCC has the authority to place reasonable restrictions on the broadcast of indecent material, particularly when the goal of the restrictions is to prevent access to that material by children. See *FCC v. Pacifica Foundation*, 438 U.S. 726 (1978); *Action for Children's Television v. FCC*, 932 F.2d 1504 (D.C. Cir. 1991), *cert. denied*, 112 5. Ct. 1281 (1992). In contrast, the FCC has the right to ban outright broadcast of material that is determined to be obscene based on standards set by the U.S. Supreme Court because such material is not protected under the First Amendment.

Appendix A:
State and Provincial Film and Television Offices

Note: Not all states have film and television offices, and offices sometimes close or are merged with other agencies for budgetary reasons. Some states and provinces also have local film and television offices that serve specific areas. The state or provincial office listed here should be able to refer you to the appropriate local agency. You can also direct queries to the Association of Film Commissioners International, 314 North Main Street, Suite 307, Helena, MT 59601; (406) 495-8040. The Association's website address is www.afci.org.

Alabama Film Office
401 Adams Avenue
Montgomery, AL 36104
(334) 242-4195
Fax: (334) 242-2077
Website: www.alabamafilm.org

Alaska Film Program
550 W. 7th Avenue, Suite 1770
Anchorage, AK 99501
(907) 269-8114
Fax: (907) 269-8125
Website: www.alaskafilm.org

Alberta Film Commission
10155 102nd Street, 5th Floor
Edmonton, Alberta T5J 4L6
Canada
(780) 422-8584
Fax: (780) 422-8582
Website: www.albertafilm.ca

Arizona Film Commission
3800 N. Central Avenue, Building D
Phoenix, AZ 85012
(602) 280-8161
Fax: (602) 280-1384
Website:
    www.azcommerce.com/film

Arkansas Film Office
1 Capitol Mall, Room 4B-505
Little Rock, AR 72201
(501) 682-7676
Fax: (501) 682-FILM
Website: www.aedc.state.ar.us/film

British Columbia Film Commission
375 Water Street, Suite 350
Vancouver, British Columbia V6B
  5C6
Canada
(604) 660-2732
Fax: (604) 660-4790
Website:
  www.bcfilmcommission.com

California Film Commission
7080 Hollywood Boulevard, Suite
  900
Hollywood, CA 90028
(323) 860-2960
Fax: (323) 860-2972
Website: www.film.ca.gov

Colorado Film Commission
1625 Broadway, Suite 1700
Denver, CO 80202
(303) 620-4500
Fax: (303) 620-4545
Website: www.coloradofilm.org

Connecticut Film, Video, and Media
  Office
805 Brook Street, Building #4
Rocky Hill, CT 06067
(860) 571-7130
Fax: (860) 721-7088
Website: www.ctfilm.com

Delaware Film Office
99 Kings Highway
Dover, DE 19901
(302) 739-4271
Fax: (302) 739-5749
Website: www.state.de.us/dedo

Florida Governor's Office of Film
  and Entertainment
Executive Office of the Governor
The Capitol
Tallahassee, FL 32399-0001
(877) 352-3456
Fax: (850) 410-4770
Website: www.filminflorida.com

Georgia Film, Video & Music Office
285 Peachtree Center Avenue, Suite
  1000
Atlanta, GA 30303
(404) 656-3591
Fax: (404) 656-3565
Website: www.filmgeorgia.org

Hawaii Film Office
No. 1 Capitol District Building
250 South Hotel Street, 5th Floor
Honolulu, HI 96813
(808) 586-2570
Fax: (808) 586-2572
Website: www.hawaiifilmoffice.com

Idaho Film Bureau
700 W. State Street
Boise, ID 83720-0093
(208) 334-2470
Fax: (208) 334-2631
Website: www.filmidaho.com

Illinois Film Office
100 W. Randolph Street, 3rd Floor
Chicago, IL 60601
(312) 814-3600
Fax: (312) 814-8874
Website: www.filmillinois.state.il.us

Indiana Film Commission
1 N. Capitol Avenue, Suite 700
Indianapolis, IN 46204-2288
(317) 232-8829
Fax: (317) 233-6887
Website: www.filmindiana.com

Iowa Film Office
200 E. Grand Avenue
Des Moines, IA 50309
(515) 242-4726
Fax: (515) 242-4859
Website: www.state.ia.us/film

Kansas Film Commission
1000 S.W. Harrison, Suite 100
Topeka, KS 66612-1354
(785) 296-4927
Fax: (785) 296-6988
Website: www.filmkansas.com

Kentucky Film Office
2200 Capital Plaza Tower
500 Mero Street
Frankfort, KY 40601
(502) 564-3456
Fax: (502) 564-7588
Website: www.kyfilmoffice.com

Louisiana Film and Video
 Commissioin
343 Third Street, Suite 400
Baton Rouge, LA 70801
(225) 342-8150
Fax: (225) 342-5389
Website: www.lafilm.org

Maine Film Office
59 State House Station
Augusta, ME 04333-0059
(207) 624-7631
Fax: (207) 287-8070
Website: www.filminmaine.com

Manitoba Film and Sound
 Development
410-93 Lombard Avenue
Winnipeg, Manitoba, R3B 3B1
Canada
(204) 947-2040
Fax: (204) 956-5261
Website: www.mbfilmsound.mb.ca

Maryland Film Office
217 E. Redwood Street, 9th Floor
Baltimore, MD 21202
(410) 767-6340
Fax: (410) 333-0044
Website: www.marylandfilm.org

Michigan Film Office
717 W. Allegan, 5th Floor
Lansing, MI 48909
(517) 373-0638
Fax: (517) 241-2930
Website: www.michigan.gov/hal

Minnesota Film Board
401 N. Third Street, Suite 460
Minneapolis, MN 55401
(612) 332-6493
Fax: (612) 332-3735
Website: www.mnfilm.org

Mississippi Film Office
P.O. Box 849
Jackson, MS 39205
(601) 359-3297
Fax: (601) 359-5048
Website: www.mississippi.org/film

Missouri Film Commission
301 West High Street, #720
Jefferson City, MO 65102
(573) 751-9050
Fax: (573) 522-1719
Website:
  www.showmemissouri.org/film

Montana State Film Office
301 S. Park
Helena, MT 59620
(406) 841-2876
Fax: (406) 841-2877
Website: www.montanafilm.com

Nebraska Film Office
301 Centennial Mall South, 4th Floor
Lincoln, NE 68509
(402) 471-3680
Fax: (402) 471-3365
Website: www.filmnebraska.org

Nevada Film Office
555 E. Washington Avenue, Suite
  5400
Las Vegas, NV 89101
(702) 486-2711
Fax: (702) 486-2712
Website: www.nevadafilm.com

New Brunswick Film
Assumption Place
770 Main Street, 16th Floor
Moncton, New Brunswick, E1C 8R3
Canada
(506) 869-6868
Fax: (506) 869-6840
Website: www.nbfilm.com

Newfoundland & Labrador Film
  Development Corporation
189 Water Street, 2nd Floor
St. Johns, Newfoundland, A1C 1B4
Canada
(709) 738-3456
Fax: (709) 739-1680
Website: www.newfilm.nf.net

New Hampshire Film and TV Office
172 Pembroke Road
Concord, NH 03302-1856
(603) 271-2665
Fax: (603) 271-6870
Website: www.filmnh.org

New Jersey Motion Picture and TV
  Commission
153 Halsey Street
Newark, NJ 07101
(973) 648-6279
Fax: (973) 648-7350
Website: www.nj.com/njfilm

New Mexico Film Office
1100 South St. Francis Drive
Santa Fe, NM 87504-5003
(800) 545-9871
Fax: (505) 827-9799
Website: www.nmfilm.com

New York State Governor's Office
for Motion Picture and TV
  Development
633 Third Avenue, 33rd Floor
New York, NY 10017
(212) 803-2330
Fax: (212) 803-2339
Website: www.nylovesfilm.com

North Carolina Film Commission
301 N. Wilmington Street
Raleigh, NC 27699-4317
(919) 733-9900
Fax: (919) 715-0151
Website: www.ncfilm.com

North Dakota Film Commission
400 E. Boulevard Avenue, Suite 50
Bismarck, ND 58502-2057
(800) 328-2871
Fax: (701) 328-4878
Website: www.ndtourism.com

Nova Scotia Film Development
  Corporation
1724 Granville Street, 2nd Floor
Halifax, Nova Scotia B3J 1X5
Canada
(902) 424-7177
Fax: (902) 424-0617
Website: www.film.ns.ca

Ohio Film Commission
77 S. High Street, 29th Floor
Columbus, Ohio 43216-1001
(614) 466-8844
Fax: (614) 466-6744
Website: www.ohiofilm.com

Oklahoma Film Commission
15 N. Robinson, #802
Oklahoma City, OK 73102
(800) 766-3456
Fax: (405) 522-0656
Website: www.otrd.state.ok.us/
film_commission

Ontario Media Development
Corporation
175 Bloor Street East
North Tower, Suite 300
Toronto, Ontario M4W 3R8
Canada
(416) 314-6858
Fax: (416) 314-2495
Website: www.to-ontfilm.com

Oregon Film and Video Office
121 S.W. Salmon Street, Suite 1205
Portland, OR 97204
(503) 229-5832
Fax: (503) 229-6869
Website: www.oregonfilm.org

Pennsylvania Film Office
Commonwealth Keystone Building
Harrisburg, PA 17120
(717) 783-3456
Fax: (717) 787-0687
Website: www.filminpa.com

Quebec City Area Film and TV
Commission
1126 Chemin St. Louis Boulevard
802
Sillery, Quebec G1S 1E5
Canada
(418) 681-8232
Fax: (418) 681-5215
Website: www.filmquebec.com

Rhode Island Film and TV Office
1 West Exchange Street
Providence, RI 02903
(401) 222-2601
Fax: (401) 273-8270
Website: www.rifilm.com

Saskatchewan Film & Video
Development Corporation
1831 College Avenue
Regina, Saskatchewan S4P 3V7
Canada
(306) 798-9898
Fax: (306) 798-7768
Website: www.saskfilm.com

South Carolina Film Office
1201 Main Street, Suite 1750
Columbia, SC 29202
(803) 737-0490
Fax: (803) 737-3104
Website: www.scfilmoffice.com

South Dakota Film Commission
711 E. Wells Avenue
Pierre, SD 57501-3369
(605) 773-3301
Fax: (605) 773-3256
Website: www.state.sd.us

Tennessee Film, Entertainment and
Music Commission
312 8th Avenue North, 9th Floor
Nashville, TN 37243
(615) 741-3456
Fax: (615) 741-5554
Website: www.filmtennessee.com

Texas Film Commission
P.O. Box 13246
Austin, TX 78711
(512) 463-9200
Fax: (512) 463-4114
Website:
www.governor.state.tx.us/film

Utah Film Commission
American Plaza III
47 West 200 South, Suite 600
Salt Lake City, UT 84101
(801) 741-4540
Fax: (801) 741-4549
Website: www.film.utah.gov

Vermont Film Commission
10 Baldwin Street, Drawer 33
Montpelier, VT 05633-2001
(802) 828-3618
Fax: (802) 828-0607
Website: www.vermontfilm.com

Virginia Film Office
901 E. Byrd Street, 19th Floor
Richmond, VA 23219-4048
(800) 854-6233
Fax: (804) 371-8177
Website: www.film.virginia.org

Washington D.C. Office of Motion
  Picture and Television
441 4th St. NW, Suite 1170
Washington, DC 20001
(202) 727-6609
Fax: (202) 727-3246
Website: www.filmdc.com

Washington State Film Office
2001 Sixth Avenue, Suite 2600
Seattle, WA 98121
(206) 256-6146
Fax: (206) 256-6154
Website: www.filmwashington.com

Wisconsin Film Office
201 W. Washington Avenue, 2nd
  Floor
Madison, WI 53703
(800) 345-6947
Fax: (608) 266-3403
Website: www.film.state.wi.us

Wyoming Film Office
214 West 15th Street
Cheyenne, WY 82002-0240
(800) 458-6657
Fax: (307) 777-2838
Website: www.wyomingfilm.org

Yukon Film Commission
Box 2703
Whitehorse, Yukon Y1A 2C6
Canada
(867) 667-5400
Fax: (867) 393-7040
Website: www.reelyukon.com

Appendix B:
Resources for Commissioning or Licensing Music

Performance Rights Societies

American Society of Composers, Authors, and Publishers (ASCAP)
1 Lincoln Plaza
New York, NY 10023
(212) 621-6000
Fax: (212) 724-9064
or
7920 Sunset Boulevard, Suite 300
Los Angeles, CA 90046
(323) 883-1000
Fax: (323) 883-1049
Website: www.ascap.com

Broadcast Music Inc. (BMI)
320 W. 57th Street
New York, NY 10019-3790
(212) 586-2000
Fax: (212) 245-8986
or
8730 Sunset Boulevard, 3rd Floor West
Hollywood, CA 90069
(310) 659-9109
Fax: (310) 657-6947
Website: www.bmi.com

Society of European Songwriters, Authors, and Composers (SESAC)
152 W. 57th Street, 57th Floor
New York, NY 10019
(212) 586-3450
Fax: (212) 489-5699
or
501 Santa Monica Boulevard, Suite 450
Santa Monica, CA 90401-2430
Fax: (310) 393-6497
Website: www.sesac.com

Selected Rights and Permissions Services

BZ Rights and Permissions
121 West 27th Street, Suite 901
New York, NY 10001
(212) 924-3000
Fax: (212) 924-2525
Website: www.bzrights.com

Copyright Clearinghouse
405 Riverside Drive
Burbank, CA 91506
(818) 558-3480
Fax: (818) 558-3474
Website: www.musicreports.com

MPI Clearance Services
19537 Wells Drive
Tarzana, CA 91356-3826
(818) 708-9996 (phone and fax)
Website:
www.earthline.net/~rhenson

Second Line Search, Inc.
12959 Coral Tree Place
Marina Del Rey, CA 90060
(866) 473-5264
Fax: (310) 577-2939
Website: www.secondline.com

Total Clearance
P.O. Box 836
Mill Valley, CA 94942
(415) 389-1531
Fax: (415) 380-9542
Website: www.totalclearance.com

Suzy Vaughan Associates, Inc.
6848 Firmament Avenue
Van Nuys, CA 91406
(818) 988-5599
Fax: (818) 988-5577
Website: www.suzyesq.com

Selected Music Libraries and Archives

AOK PRO
173 20th Street
Union City, NJ 07087
(201) 865-5337 (phone and fax)
Website: www.clipsingles.com

Associated Production Music
6255 Sunset Boulevard, Suite 820
Los Angeles, CA 90028
(800) 543-4276
Fax: (323) 461-9102
or
240 Madison Avenue, 11th Floor
New York, NY 10016
(800) 276-6874
Fax: (212) 856-9807
Website: www.apmusic.com

Capitol/OGM Production Music
6922 Hollywood Boulevard, Suite 718
Hollywood, CA 90028
(213) 461-2701 or (800) 421-4163
Fax: (213) 461-1543

Dick Clark Media Archives
3003 W. Olive Avenue
Burbank, CA 91510
(818) 841-3003
Fax: (818) 954-8609

Creative Musical Services
13547 Ventura Boulevard, Suite 358
Sherman Oaks, CA 91423
(818) 385-1517
Fax: (818) 385-1266
Website:
www.creativemusicalsvcs.com

CSS Music
1948 Riverside Drive
Los Angeles, CA 90039
(800) 468-6874
Website: www.cssmusic.com

The Hollywood Film Music Library
9000 Sunset Boulevard, 3rd Floor
Los Angeles, CA 90069
(818) 789-2954
Fax: (818) 985-6926
Website: www.screenmusic.com

Killer Tracks/bmg Production Music
6534 Sunset Boulevard
Hollywood, CA 90028
(323) 957-4455 or (800) 454-5537
Fax: (323) 957-4470
Website: www.killertracks.com

Megatrax Production Music
7635 Fulton Avenue
North Hollywood, CA 91605
(818) 503-5240 or (888) 634-2555
Fax: (818) 503-5244
Website: www.megatrax.com

Promusic Inc.
941-A Clint Moore Road
Boca Raton, FL 33487
(561) 995-0331 or (800) 322-7879
Fax: (561) 995-8434
or
11846 Ventura Boulevard, Suite 304
Studio City, CA 91604
Website:
  www.promusic-inc.com

Soper Sound Music Library
P.O. Box 869
Ashland, OR 97520
(541) 552-0830 or (800) 227-9980
Fax: (541) 552-0832
Website: www.sopersound.com

Southern Library of Recorded Music
810 7th Avenue
New York, NY 10019-5818
(212) 265-3910
Fax: (212) 489-2465

Brad Stanfield Music
12400 Ventura Boulevard, Suite 240
Studio City, CA 91604
(818) 990-4487
Fax: (818) 379-9952

TRF Production Music Libraries
747 Chestnut Ridge Road
Chestnut Ridge, NY 10977
(845) 356-0800 or (800) 899-6874
Fax: (845) 356-0895
Website: www.trfmusic.com

The Who Did That Music Library
12211 W. Washington Boulevard
Los Angeles, CA 90066
(310) 572-4646 or (800) 400-6767
Fax: (310) 572-4647
Website:
  www.whodidthatmusic.com

Zomba Music
9000 Sunset Boulevard, Suite 300
West Hollywood, CA 90069
(310) 247-1057 or (800) 858-8880
Fax: (310) 247-8366

Appendix C:
Guilds, Unions, and Associations

This appendix provides contact information for selected national television and film guilds, unions, and associations in the United States. Many entries include information for both New York and California offices. Some unions and guilds also have local offices in other cities. For information about these local offices, contact the New York or California office listed here.

Guilds, Unions, and Alliances

Actor's Equity Association (AEA)
165 West 46th Street
New York, NY 10036
(212) 869-8530
Fax: (212) 719-9815
or
5757 Wilshire Boulevard
Los Angeles, CA 90036
(323) 634-1750
Fax: (323) 634-1777
Website: www.actorsequity.org

Alliance of Motion Picture and
  Television Producers (AMPTP)
15503 Ventura Boulevard
Encino, CA 91436
(818) 995-3600
Fax: (818) 382-1793
Website: www.ampt.org

American Federation of Musicians
  (AFM)
1501 Broadway, Suite 600
New York, NY 10036
(212) 869-1330
Fax: (212) 764-6134
or
817 North Vine Street
Hollywood, CA 90038
(323) 462-2161
Fax: (323) 461-3090
Website: www.afm.org

American Federation of Television
and Radio Artists (AFTRA)
260 Madison Avenue, 7th Floor
New York, NY 10016
(212) 532-0800
Fax: (212) 532-2242
or
5757 Wilshire Boulevard, 9th Floor
Los Angeles, CA 90036
(323) 634-8100
Fax: (323) 634-8246
Website: www.aftra.org

American Guild of Variety Artists
(AGVA)
184 Fifth Avenue
New York, NY 10010
(212) 675-1003
Fax: (212) 633-0097
or
4741 Laurel Canyon Boulevard
North Hollywood, CA 91607
(818) 508-9984
Fax: (818) 508-3029

Director's Guild of America (DGA)
110 West 57th Street, 2nd Floor
New York, NY 10019
(212) 581-0370
or
7920 Sunset Boulevard
Hollywood, CA 90046
(310) 289-2000
Fax: (310) 289-2029
Website: www.dga.org

International Alliance of Theatrical
Stage Employees (IATSE)
1430 Broadway, 20th Floor
New York, NY
(212) 730-1770
Fax: (212) 730-7809
or
10045 Riverside Drive
Toluca Lake, CA 91602
(818) 980-3499
Fax: (818) 980-3496
Website: www.iatse.lm.com

International Brotherhood of
Electrical Workers (IBEW)
225 W. 34th Street
New York, NY 10122
(212) 354-6770
Fax: (212) 819-9517
or
6255 Sunset Boulevard
Hollywood, CA 90028
(323) 851-5515
Fax: (323) 446-1793
Website: www.ibew.org

National Association of Broadcast
Employees and Technicians
(NABET)
1865 Broadway
New York, NY 10023
(212) 757-7191
Fax: (212) 247-4356
or
1918 W. Burbank Boulevard
Burbank, CA 91506
(818) 846-0490
Fax: (818) 846-2306
Website: www.nabetcwa.org

Screen Actors Guild (SAG)
360 Madison Avenue, 12th Floor
New York, NY 10017
(212) 944-1030
Fax: (212) 944-6774
or
5757 Wilshire Boulevard
Los Angeles, CA 90036
(323) 954-1600
Fax: (323) 549-6603
Website: www.sag.org

Theatrical Teamsters
1 Hollow Lane
Lake Success, NY 11042
(516) 365-3470
Fax: (516) 365-2609

Writers Guild of America (WGA)
555 West 57th Street
New York, NY 10019
(212) 767-7800
Fax: (212) 582-1909
or
7000 W. Third Street
Los Angeles, CA 90048
(323) 951-4000
Fax: (323) 782-4800
Website: www.wga.org

Professional Associations and Industry Groups

Academy of Motion Picture Arts
and Sciences
8949 Wilshire Boulevard
Beverly Hills, CA 90211
(310) 247-3000
Fax: (310) 859-9619
Website: www.oscars.org

Association of Independent
Commercial Producers (AICP)
3 West 18th Street, 5th Floor
New York, NY 10011
(212) 929-3000
Fax: (212) 929-3359
or
650 North Bronson Avenue
Suite 223B
Los Angeles, CA 90004
(323) 960-4763
Fax: (323) 960-4766
Website: www.aicp.com

Cable Television Administration and
Marketing Society, Inc. (CTAM)
201 North Union Street, Suite 440
Alexandria, VA 22324
(703) 549-4200
Fax: (703) 684-1167
Website: www.ctam.com

Casting Society of America (CSA)
2565 Broadway, Suite 185
New York, NY 10025
(212) 868-1260
Fax: (212) 868-1261
or
606 N. Larchmont Boulevard, Suite
4B
Los Angeles, CA 90004
(323) 463-1925
Fax: (323) 463-5753
Website: www.castingsociety.com

International Documentary
Association
1201 W. 5th Street, Suite M320
Los Angeles, CA 90017
(213) 534-3600
Fax: (213) 534-3610
Website: www.documentary.org

Media Communications Association
 International
1000 Executive Parkway, Suite 220
St. Louis, MO 63141
(314) 514-9995
Fax: (314) 576-7989
Website: www.mca-i.org

Motion Picture Association of
 America (MPAA)
15503 Ventura Boulevard
Encino, CA 91436
(818) 995-6600
Fax: (818) 382-1799
Website: www.mpaa.org

National Academy of Television Arts
 and Sciences
111 W. 57th Street
New York, NY 10019
(212) 586-8424
Fax: (212) 246-8129
Website: www.emmyonline.com

National Association of Broadcasters
 (NAB)
1771 N. Street N.W.
Washington, DC 20036
(202) 429-5300
Fax: (202) 429-4199
Website: www.nab.org

National Association of Television
 Program Executives (NATPE)
2425 Olympic Boulevard
Santa Monica, CA 90404
(310) 453-4440
Fax: (310) 453-5258
Website: www.natpe.org

National Cable and
 Telecommunications Association
 (NCTA)
1724 Massachusetts Avenue N.W.
Washington, DC 20036
(202) 775-3550
Fax: (202) 775-3604
Website: www.ncta.com

Glossary

Note: Words in italics are defined elsewhere in the glossary.

acceptance: The component of a *contract* in which each *party* indicates that it agrees with and consents to be bound by the terms of the contract. Also the act of agreeing to the terms of a contract.

actual damages: See *damages*.

administrative law: Laws created by government agencies through the issue and enforcement of rules, regulations, orders, and policies pursuant to the agency's authority and mandate. See also *statutory law*.

affidavit: A sworn statement of fact submitted as a document in legal proceedings.

arbitration: A means of settling a dispute in which the matter is submitted to an independent person or agency for resolution. Arbitration often is used as an alternative to *litigation*. Contracts sometimes include "arbitration clauses" requiring that any dispute concerning the contract be submitted to arbitration.

appellate (appeals) court: A court that reviews previously judged cases to determine if the case was properly presented and the law was properly applied.

breach of contract: The failure of one or more parties to abide by the terms of a contract. See also *remedy*.

case law: See *common law*.

circuit court: A court whose jurisdiction covers several districts, counties, or regions in the United States. Another term for "federal courts of appeals."

civil law: In the term's most common use in the United States, the body of law concerned with noncriminal matters. In civil cases, the dispute generally is a private matter between two parties, rather than between an accused criminal and the state. Compare to *criminal law*.

code: An indexed compilation of laws (*statutes*) arranged around specific subjects (e.g., the penal code, the motor vehicle code). An "annotated" code includes the law plus case citations and commentary.

collective bargaining agreement: An agreement between an employer and a group of employees, usually organized and represented by a union, that establishes and regulates the terms of employment. The "basic agreements" between guilds and television and film producers are collective bargaining agreements.

common law: In its most general use, law based on judicial precedents. The body of common law on a particular legal subject consists of all of the previous judgments and judicial opinions on that subject. Contrast with *statutory law*.

compensatory damages: See *damages*.

consideration: The component of a *contract* that defines what compensation will be paid or detriment incurred by each party under the terms of the contract. See also *acceptance* and *offer*.

constitutional law: In the United States, the body of law based on the articles and amendments that form the U.S. Constitution; the supreme law of the United States, as interpreted and enforced by the U.S. federal courts, particularly the U.S. Supreme Court.

contract: A legally binding agreement that creates obligations between two or more parties. See also *offer, consideration,* and *acceptance*.

copyright: The right of ownership in an item of *intellectual property*, such as a book, film, television program, or computer software. The exclusive right to reproduce and distribute such an intellectual property. In the United States and many other countries, the rights of copyright owners to control the reproduction and distribution of their works is specified by statute. Compare to *patent* and *trademark*.

copyright infringement: Unauthorized use of copyrighted material in violation of the rights of the copyright holder, an illegal act under U.S. copyright law.

criminal law: The body of laws intended to protect society. Criminal cases include cases involving allegations of burglary, robbery, murder, and other crimes that threaten the safety or well-being of society. Contrast with *civil law*.

damages: Compensation, usually monetary, awarded by a court or arbitrator to an individual or group injured by the actions of another. *Actual damages* and *compensatory damages* compensate the injured party for financial losses or other injury that it can specifically prove are the results of the actions of the wrongdoer. *Punitive damages* are extra compensation beyond actual or compensatory damages awarded to punish the wrongdoer.

defamation: Making untrue, derogatory statements that bring into disrepute the good name of or otherwise injure another. When the statements are made verbally, the defamation is *slander*. When they are made in writing or in any recorded medium (e.g., videotape, film, or audiotape), the defamation is *libel*.

defendant: In *civil law* proceedings, the person who is responding to the complaint brought by the *plaintiff*. In *criminal law* proceedings, the person who has been accused of the crime.

diversity jurisdiction: The authority of federal courts to hear cases and disputes between citizens of different states or between a U.S. citizen and a foreigner.

Equal Time Provision: The statutory provision established in Section 315(a) of the Communications Act of 1934 that requires U.S. broadcasters who provide political candidates with advertising opportunities or other air time to do so on an equal basis for all candidates running for the same office.

express contract: A *contract* that is declared at the time that it is made. A contract in which the terms are made explicit and in which all parties are clearly aware that they are agreeing to those terms. Contrast with *implied contract*.

Fairness Doctrine: A body of rules promulgated by the Federal Communications Commission (FCC) to ensure that broadcasters cover issues of public importance in a fair, balanced manner. Under the Fairness Doctrine, each U.S. broadcast station must devote a reasonable portion of its air time to covering controversial issues of public importance, and the coverage must be fair and balanced. Over the years, the FCC has enforced the Fairness Doctrine with varying degrees of diligence, and broadcasters have challenged the constitutionality of the doctrine.

fair use: A provision of U.S. copyright law that allows individuals and groups to use certain copyrighted materials under certain circumstances without obtaining permission from or paying compensation to the copyright owner. Under Section 107 of the U.S. Copyright Act, whether a particular use is considered fair use depends, among other factors, on the purpose of the use (with fair use usually being reserved for nonprofit purposes), the nature of the copyrighted work, the amount of the work used, and the effect of the use on the market for the work.

felony: A serious crime. Usually, a crime that is punishable by imprisonment for more than one year or death. Contrast with *misdemeanor.*

guild: A union for actors, writers, directors, or certain other professionals who work in media production.

implied contract: A *contract* that is not made explicit but instead is implicit in a transaction between parties. Contrast with *express contract.*

indemnity: A contractual provision in which one party agrees to compensate another for any loss or *damages* that it causes in fulfilling or failing to fulfill its obligations under the contract. See also *warranty.*

infringement: See *copyright infringement.*

injunction: A court order directing a person to do or to refrain from doing a certain act or acts.

intellectual property: Materials such as books, inventions, paintings, films, and television programs that are products of the intellect and imagination and that can be protected as property under U.S. copyright, trademark, and patent laws. Also, the category of law that includes copyright, trademark, and patent law. See *copyright, patent,* and *trademark.*

judge-made law: See *common law.*

libel: See *defamation.*

litigant: An individual, group, or legal entity involved in a lawsuit.

litigation: A lawsuit or, more generally, any legal action or contest for which a court is the primary forum. Contrast with *arbitration.*

mechanical right: The right to reproduce and sell copies of a copyrighted musical work. See also *performance rights* and *synchronization rights.*

misdemeanor: A relatively minor crime. Usually, a crime that is punishable by a fine or, at most, brief imprisonment in a local jail or facility other than a penitentiary. Contrast with *felony.*

offer: The fundamental proposal that forms the core of any *contract.* The component of the contract in which the parties promise to do or to refrain from doing some specified act in return for some specified consideration. See also *consideration, acceptance.*

oral contract: A *contract* that is made and agreed to vocally rather than in writing. Although oral contracts are valid in many (but not all) circumstances, it is preferable to place all business contracts in writing. See also *written contract.*

party: An individual or group that plays a direct role in a legal matter or that enters into a *contract* or other legal relationship. In litigation, there are two primary parties: the *plaintiff* and the *defendant.*

patent: A government grant that gives an individual or group the right to own and control an invention or design for a specified period. A patent gives the owner, in essence, a legal monopoly over the invention. In the United States, patents are administered by the Patent and Trademark Office.

performance right: For media producers, the right that allows the public display or broadcast transmission of a recording of a copyrighted musical work that has been included in the soundtrack of a production. This assumes that *synchronization rights* to the musical work already have been secured. Performance rights in musical works usually are licensed through a performance rights society, such as the American Society of Composers, Authors, and Publishers (ASCAP) or Broadcast Music Inc. (BMI).

plaintiff: The person, group, or legal entity that initiates a lawsuit. Contrast with *defendant.*

precedent: A previously decided case that serves as an example for and guides rulings in later cases that involve the same or similar issues of law. Also, a rule of law that is established in a certain case and that carries authority in deciding subsequent cases. See also *common law*.

prima facie: Literally, "at first view." Evidence of a legal matter that can be taken at face value and that is presumed valid.

public domain: Creative properties, such as written materials or video or film footage, that are free from *copyright* protection. Public domain materials are properties that are not subject to copyright protection (such as most U.S. government publications) or for which the copyright has expired or been abandoned. Once a work falls into the public domain, it can be used freely, with no requirement that the user request permission from or compensate the creator or original copyright owner.

punitive damages: See *damages*.

regulatory law: See *administrative law*.

release: The act of giving up a right or claim, such as the *right of privacy*. Also, the written *contract* that verifies that an individual has given up a right or claim. Media producers should obtain releases from all performers and property owners whose images and property appear in a production.

remedy: In a *contract*, the section that defines the compensation that a *party* will receive or the actions that it can take if the other party breaks the terms of the agreement. Also, more generally, any compensation or redress that a court or arbitrator provides to an injured party. See also *breach of contract* and *damages*.

residuals: Supplemental payments made to *guild* members, above the initial compensation that they received for working on a production, each time the production is rebroadcast or otherwise displayed to the public. See also *reuse payments*.

reuse payments: Supplemental, usually one-time, payments made to *guild* members above the initial compensation that they received for working on a production when the material that they contributed to the production is used again in a different production or when a program produced for one market is released in another market. Payments for releasing a production in a second market (e.g., releasing a program originally produced for network television on basic cable) also are sometimes called *supplemental market payments*.

right of privacy: The legal right to be left alone, free from unwarranted publicity or interference. The right of privacy includes the right not to be portrayed in a media production unless other factors, such as the newsworthiness of an event, outweigh the right of privacy. To protect themselves from privacy challenges, media producers should obtain a *release* from each individual who is depicted in a production. See also *right of publicity*.

right of publicity: An individual's right to control and to profit from the commercial use of his or her name and likeness. A form of the *right of privacy*.

signatory: A party that has agreed to and signed a treaty or *collective bargaining agreement*.

slander: See *defamation*.

statute: A law that is enacted through legislative action. A law that is created by the U.S. Congress, a state or local legislature, or some other legislative body that is acting on constitutional authority.

statutory law: Law that is based on *statutes* rather than judicial precedents or interpretations of the constitution. Compare to *common law* and *constitutional law*.

summary judgment: A decision rendered by a judge before the case has been referred to a jury or, in many cases, before the case has been brought to trial. Summary judgment is possible when the material facts in a case are beyond reasonable dispute and all or some of the litigated issues may be resolved by the judge as a matter of law.

supplemental market payments: See *reuse payments*.

synchronization rights: In a media production, the right to add a copyrighted musical work to a production and to conform it to the video track. See also *performance right*.

term: In a *contract*, the duration of the agreement or a specific provision of the agreement. Also, a word or phrase that has a specific meaning within the context of a contract.

tort: Generally, any wrong other than a *breach of contract* in which a party claims injury by another party and for which a court can provide redress. See also *remedy*.

trademark: A word, symbol, design, or combination word and design that identifies and distinguishes the goods or services of one party from those of another. In the United States, trademarks can be registered through the Patent and Trademark Office. Compare to *copyright* and *patent*.

warranty: In a *contract*, assurances by one party with respect to the subject of the contract on which the other party to the contract may rely. For example, the party that will be delivering materials under a media production contract might warrant that it is the sole owner of the materials. Usually, the party making the warranty will indemnify the other party against any losses that occur if the warranties prove untrue. See also *indemnity*.

work-made-for-hire: A book, media production, or other copyrightable property that is owned by the employer for whom the work was made or the party that commissioned the work, rather than by the creator of the work. In most cases, U.S. copyright law confers the right of ownership on the party that creates a work. The work-made-for-hire exception to this general principle encompasses works (1) created by an employee within the scope of employment, in which case the work is owned by the employer, and (2) created under a written contract that specifies that it is a "work made for hire" and that falls within the types of works (such as a contribution to an audiovisual production) listed in Section 101 of the U.S. Copyright Act, in which case the work is owned by the party commissioning the work.

written contract: A binding agreement that is placed in writing and that the parties sign to indicate their acceptance of the terms of the agreement. Compare to *oral contract*.

Bibliography

Bernacchi, Richard L., et al. *Bernacchi on Computer Law: A Guide to the Legal and Management Aspects of Computer Technology.* Boston: Little, Brown and Company, 1995.

Bezanson, Randall P., et al. *Libel Law and the Press: Myth and Reality.* New York: The Free Press, 1987.

Black, Henry Campbell. *Black's Law Dictionary*, 5th ed., edited by Joseph R. Nolan, et al. St. Paul, MN: West Publishing, 1983.

Blumenthal, Howard J., and Oliver R. Goodenough. *This Business of Television: A Practical Guide to the TV/Video Industries for Producers, Directors, Writers, Performers, Agents, and Executives.* New York: Billboard Books, 1991.

Boorstyn, Neil. *Boorstyn on Copyright.* New York: Clark Boardman Callaghan, 1997.

Bremer, Daniel L., Monroe E. Price, and Michael L. Meyerson. *Cable Television and Other Nonbroadcast Video.* New York: Clark Boardman Callaghan, 1997.

Carter, T. Barton, Marc A. Franklin, and Jay B. Wright. *The First Amendment and the Fourth Estate: The Law of Mass Media*, 4th ed. Mineola, NY: The Foundation Press, 1988.

Chickering, Robert B., and Susan Hartman. *How to Register a Copyright and Protect Your Creative Work.* New York: Charles Scribner's and Sons, 1987.

Copyright Office, Library of Congress. *Copyright Basics* (Circular 1). Washington, DC: U.S. Government Printing Office, 2002.

———. *How to Investigate the Copyright Status of a Work* (Circular R22). Washington, DC: U.S. Government Printing Office, 2002.

Crawford, Tad. *Legal Guide for the Visual Artist*, 4th ed. New York: Allworth Press, 1999.

Crawford, Tad, and Tony Lyons. *Writer's Legal Guide*, 3rd ed. New York: Allworth Press, 2002.

Creech, Kenneth C. *Electronic Media Law and Regulation*, 2nd ed. Boston: Focal Press, 1996.

Delta, George B., and Jeffrey H. Matsura. *Law of the Internet*, 2nd ed. New York: Aspen Law and Business, 2002.

Dill, Barbara. *The Journalist's Handbook on Libel and Privacy*. New York: The Free Press, 1986.

Elias, Stephen R. *Trademark: Legal Care for Your Business & Product Name*, 5th ed. Berkeley, CA: Nolo Press, 2001.

Farber, Donald C., ed. *Entertainment Industry Contracts*. New York: Matthew Bender, 2002.

Ferris, Charles D., Frank W. Lloyd, and Thomas Casey. *Cable Television Law: A Video Communications Practice Guide*. New York: Matthew Bender, 1997.

Fishman, Steven. *The Copyright Handbook*, 6th ed. Berkeley, CA: Nolo Press, 2002.

———. *The Public Domain: How to Find Copyright-Free Writings, Music, Art & More*. Berkeley, CA: Nolo Press, 2000.

———. *Web & Software Development: A Legal Guide*, 3rd ed. Berkeley, CA: Nolo Press, 2002.

Geller, Paul Edward, ed. *International Copyright Law and Practice*. New York: Matthew Bender, 2002.

Gifis, Steven. *Law Dictionary*. Woodbury, NY: Barron's Educational Services, 1984.

Gilson, Jerome, Anne Gilson Lalonde, and Karin Green. *Trademark Protection and Practice*. New York: Matthew Bender, 2002.

Goodale, James C. *All About Cable*. New York: Law Journal Seminars Press, 1997.

Henn, Harry G. *Henn on Copyright Law*. New York: Practicing Law Institute, 1991.

Hilliard, Robert L. *The Federal Communications Commission: A Primer*. Boston: Focal Press, 1991.

Hollywood Reporter. *2002 Blu-Book Film and TV Production Directory.* Los Angeles: Hollywood Reporter, 2002.

Kane, Siegrun D. *Trademark Law: A Practitioner's Guide.* New York: Practicing Law Institute, 1987.

Kirsch, Jonathan. *Kirsch's Handbook of Publishing Law.* Los Angeles: Acrobat Books, 1995.

———. *Kirsch's Guide to the Book Contract.* Los Angeles: Acrobat Books, 1999.

Koenigsberg, I. Fred, and Katherine C. Spelman. *Understanding Basic Copyright Law 1996.* New York: Practicing Law Institute, 1996.

Kohn, Al, and Bob Kohn. *Kohn on Music Licensing,* 3rd ed. New York: Aspen Law and Business, 2002.

Lewis, Anthony. *Make No Law: The Sullivan Case and the First Amendment.* New York: Random House, 1991.

Lindey, Alexander. *Lindey on Entertainment, Publishing, and the Arts, Agreements and the Law,* 2nd ed. New York: Clark Boardman, Ltd. 1995.

Litwak, Mark. *Contracts for the Film and Television Industry,* 2nd ed. Los Angeles: Silman-James Press, 1998.

———. *Dealmaking in the Film and Television Industry: From Negotiations through Final Contracts,* 2nd ed. Los Angeles: Silman-James Press, 2002.

McCarthy, J. Thomas. *The Rights of Publicity and Privacy.* New York: Clark Boardman Callaghan, 1997.

———. *Trademarks and Unfair Competition,* 4th ed. New York: Clark Boardman Callaghan, 1997.

Miller, Arthur P., and Michael H. Davis. *Intellectual Property: Patents, Trademarks, and Copyright.* St. Paul, MN: West Publishing, 1985.

Nimmer, Melville B., and David Nimmer. *Nimmer on Copyright.* New York: Matthew Bender, 2002.

Patry, William F. *Copyright Law and Practice.* Washington, DC: Bureau of National Affairs, 1994.

Rosden, George Eric, and Peter Eric. *The Law of Advertising*, 4th ed. New York: Matthew Bender, 1989.

Rose, Lance. *Netlaw: Your Rights in the Online World.* Berkeley, CA: Osborne McGraw-Hill, 1995.

Sanford, Bruce W. *Libel and Privacy*, 2nd ed. New York: Aspen Law and Business, 1997.

Scott, Michael D. *Scott on Multimedia Law.* New York: Aspen Law and Business, 1996.

Selz, Thomas P., Melvin Simensky, and Patricia Acton. *Entertainment Law: Legal Concepts and Business Practices.* New York: Clark Boardman Callaghan, 1997.

Smolla, Rodney A. *Smolla and Nimmer on Freedom of Speech.* New York: Clark Boardman Callaghan, 2002.

Stim, Richard. *Music Law: How to Run Your Band's Business*, 2nd ed. Berkeley, CA: Nolo Press, 2002.

Swanson, James L., ed. *First Amendment Law Handbook.* St. Paul, MN: West Publishing, 2002.

Teeter, Dwight L., Don R. Leduc, and Bill Loving. *Law of Mass Communications: Freedom and Control of Print and Broadcast Media*, 10th ed. Westbury, NY: Foundation Press, 2001.

U.S. Department of Commerce, Patent and Trademark Office. *Basic Facts About Trademarks.* Washington, DC: U.S. Government Printing Office, 2002.

———. *General Information Concerning Patents.* Washington, DC: U.S. Government Printing Office, 2002.

Index

Page numbers followed by "f" denote figures